THE CHRISTIAN WRITERS
MARKET GUIDE
2017

THE CHRISTIAN WRITERS
MARKET GUIDE

2017

Your Comprehensive Resource for Getting Published

STEVE LAUBE

TABLE OF CONTENTS

FOREWORD
YOU'VE COME TO THE RIGHT PLACE

I KNOW WRITERS WHO COLLECT REJECTION SLIPS, hoard them, even paper their walls with them—believing this proves they are busy, in the game.

Here's a better idea: Avoid rejection slips like radioactive waste. I don't want even one.

And you don't need to ever read another.

Here's how: *Do your homework.* Know what your target market is looking for. Sure, occasionally you'll hear back that your idea didn't ring a bell. But that's not a rejection; that's a business transaction. You did a bit of work, solicited editors' interest, they passed. You move on.

Now, had you written an entire *article* or even whole *book* before determining their interest, you deserved that rejection.

Even if you're new to writing, save yourself fruitless work by trying to get an editor on board with you early. Even if she expresses only speculative interest (e.g., "Happy to give it a look, provided you . . ."), consider what comes after that as your marching orders.

Does she want it longer than you proposed? Shorter? In first person, rather than third? Does she have suggestions for other angles, other people to interview?

To the best of your ability, do everything she suggests. By proving yourself able to work with an editor, you're nearly forcing her to stick with you—even if your writing is light-years from where it will be someday.

By showing that you can take input and you recognize that published work is never a solo, but always a duet between writer and editor, you've given yourself the best chance at a sale.

And you've avoided rejection.

That, I assume, is why you've chosen this book. You've come to the right place. As you immerse yourself in all that's offered here, remember:

- ➥ **Writing takes skill.** When you hang out your shingle as a writer, be prepared for unintended slights. People tell me all the time that they have a book in them, if they only had the time to write. That would be like my saying I have a mansion in me, if only I had the time to build it. Writing, and building, take a lot more than time.

- **Don't think of writing as competitive.** Anyone who has succeeded was once unknown and unpublished. Rejoice with, and learn from, those ahead of you.
- **Read everything you can find on the craft.** Your goal should be to become a lifelong learner.
- **Start with *The Elements of Style*.** Few single books can make an immediate, significant improvement in a writer like Strunk and White's masterpiece, a small volume worth reading annually. For the inspirational market, two other volumes are no-brainers for your library: The one you hold in your hands and *The Christian Writer's Manual of Style*.
- **Even *sacred* writing can be edited.** Only Scripture is God-breathed. The result of your writing might very well be sacred; but if you regard your word choice sacred, as in untouchable, each word had better be divinely perfect. Or God gets a bad rap. Frankly, writers who make this claim are immediately branded amateurs. An inside joke among editors in inspirational publishing is that God is the worst literary agent ever.
- **Too few writers do their homework.** Pitch writing that make sense for your target market based on your research, and that research starts right here with this unparalleled resource.

The Christian Writers Market Guide is no cover-to-cover read. Peruse the Contents page, and zero in on your areas of specialty and interest. Then, when you're ready, start shopping your writing.

As inspirational writers, we have a duty to do justice to a worldview that may bend but will never be crushed under the weight of hopelessness. Our burden, our task, our privilege is to represent hope. That doesn't mean Pollyanna stories in which everyone lives happily ever after—at least this side of heaven.

People suffer. Innocents die. But if we believers cannot crack the door to hope, we dare not call ourselves inspirational writers.

Ours is a message of hope, of reconciliation, of forgiveness. True art will communicate that without preaching.

The path is crowded and the passage long, but the reward is worth it. Welcome to the journey.

–**Jerry B. Jenkins**
Colorado Springs, Colorado
www.JerryJenkins.com

INTRODUCTION

THERE HAS NEVER BEEN A MORE EXCITING TIME TO BE A WRITER.
Opportunities abound for great content from great authors. Traditional methods for publication have expanded due to the diversity of online opportunities. In addition, independent-publication options have made it easy to see your byline on a book, a blog post, or an online magazine.

While it may seem like the industry is shrinking, in reality it is simply changing. Thus you have to research more to find the best place for your work to shine.

One of the biggest mistakes a writer can make is to ignore the guidelines of an agent, a publisher, or an editor. Some publishers even dropped their listings in this guide due to writers failing to follow the instructions posted on their websites or in here. Editors are looking for writers who understand their periodicals or publishing houses and their unique approaches to the marketplace. This book will help you be such a writer. With a little time and effort, you can meet an editor's expectations, distinguish yourself as a professional, and sell what you write.

A few periodical publishers work only by assigning topics to a select group of writers. If you work hard, you can establish yourself and your reputation among editors and become one of those go-to writers.

When approaching agents, read the material on their websites and look at the authors they represent. Most of the large publishers will work only with agents, so having a good representative is crucial. You'll find a list of agents in this guide to help you with your search.

If you can, I recommend you attend a writers conference. It is good to meet new people and become familiar with the best teachers in the industry. Many faculty members are agents or editors looking for your work even if they work for houses that don't take unsolicited manuscripts. The chapter with conferences will help you locate one.

If this is the first time you've used this guide, read the "How to Use This Book" section. If you run into an unfamiliar term, look it up in the glossary in back and learn the terminology.

May God bless your writing journey. We are on a mission to change the world, word by word. To that end, strive for excellence and make your work compelling and insightful. Great writing is still in demand. But it must be targeted, crafted, edited, critiqued, polished, and proofread until it shines.

This edition could not have happened without the incredible work of Lin Johnson. She poured over every listing to make sure it was accurate to the best of our information. She put hours into this and has agreed to be the administrator for the online edition and future editions of the book. I would also like to acknowledge my wife Lisa. Her love, support, and encouragement have been incalculable. We make a great team!

Steve Laube
President
The Christian Writers Institute
The Steve Laube Agency
24 W. Camelback Rd. A-635
Phoenix, AZ 85013
www.christianwritersinstitute.com
www.stevelaube.com

To update a listing or to be added to the next edition or online: *admin@christianwritersmarketguide.com*

For direct sales questions, email the publisher: *admin@christianwritersinstute.com*

For books and courses on the writing craft, visit The Christian Writers Institute: *www.christianwritersinstitute.com*

HOW TO USE THIS BOOK

THE *CHRISTIAN WRITERS MARKET GUIDE 2017* IS DESIGNED to make it easier for you to sell your writing. It will serve you well if you use it as a springboard to become thoroughly familiar with the markets best suited to your style and areas of interest and expertise.

Start by getting acquainted with the setup of this guide.

Part 1 lists Christian book publishers with contact information and what they are looking for. Notice that many houses accept manuscripts only from agents or through meeting with their editors at a writers conference. If you need an agent, check the agent listings in Chapter 16.

Since independent book publishing is a viable option today, Part 2 provides resources to help you. Chapter 2 lists independent book publishers, many of which provide all the services you need as packages or à la carte services. If you decide to publish on your own, Chapters 3 and 4 list design, production, and distribution services. You'll also want to hire a professional editor, so see Chapter 19 for help in this area.

Part 3 lists periodical—magazine, newspaper, and newsletter—publishers. Chapter 5 will help you find markets by topics (e.g., marriage, church life, evangelism) and types (e.g., how-to, poetry, personal experience). Although these lists are not comprehensive, they can provide a shortcut for finding appropriate markets for your ideas.

Cross-referencing may be helpful. For example, if you have an idea for a how-to article on parenting, look at the lists in both the "how-to" and "parenting" categories. Also, don't overlook writing on the same topic for different periodicals, such as money management for a general adult magazine, a teen magazine, a women's newsletter, and a magazine for pastors. Each would require a different slant, but you would get more mileage from one idea.

If you run into words in the listings that you are not familiar with, check the glossary at the back of the book.

In Part 4, "Specialty Markets," you'll find nonbook, nonperiodical markets like daily devotionals and drama. Here you can explore types of writing you may not have thought about but that can provide a steady writing income.

As a writer, you'll need support to keep going. Part 5 provides information for various kinds of support.

One of the best ways to get published today is to meet editors at writers conferences. Check out Chapter 17 for a conference or seminar near you—or perhaps in a location you'd like to visit. Before deciding which conference to attend, check the websites for who is on faculty, what houses are represented, and what classes are offered that can help you grow your craft and writing business. You may also want to factor in the size of the conference. Don't be afraid to stretch outside your comfort zone.

For ongoing support and feedback on your manuscripts, join a writers group. Chapter 18 lists groups by state. If you can't find one near you, consider starting one or join an online group.

Since editors and agents are looking for polished manuscripts, you may want to hire a professional editor. See Chapter 19 for people who offer a variety of editorial services, including coaching.

Whether you publish your book with a royalty house or go the independent route, you'll need to do most, if not all, of the promotion. If you want to hire a specialist with contacts, check out Chapter 20, "Publicity and Marketing Services."

Entering a writing contest can boost your sales, supplement your writing income, lead to publication, and sometimes give you valuable feedback on your writing. Check out Chapter 21 for a list of contests by genre. Many of them are not Christian oriented, but you can enter manuscripts with a Christian worldview.

Once you get acquainted with this guide, start using it. After you identify potential markets for your ideas and/or manuscripts, read their writers guidelines. If those are available on the website, the URL is included. Otherwise, email or send (with a SASE) for a copy. Also study at least one sample copy of a periodical (information to obtain one is given in most listings) or the book publisher's website to see if your idea truly fits there. Never ever send a manuscript without doing this market study.

Above all, keep in mind that this guide is only a starting point for your research, and change is the one constant in the publishing industry. It is impossible for any market guide to be 100 percent accurate since editors move around, publications and publishing houses close, and new ones open. But this guide is an essential tool for getting published in the Christian market and making an impact on God's Kingdom with your words.

PART 1

BOOK PUBLISHERS

1

BOOK PUBLISHERS

Before submitting your query letter or book proposal, it's critical that you read and follow a publisher's guidelines exactly. In most cases the guidelines are available on the website and a direct link is given in the listing. If you do not have a literary agent—and even if you do—check out a publisher thoroughly before signing a contract.

1517 MEDIA (FORMERLY AUGSBURG-FORTRESS PRESS)
See listings for Fortress Press and Sparkhouse Family.

AADEON PUBLISHING COMPANY
PO Box 223, Hartford, CT 06141
www.aadeonmedia.com
> **Submissions:** Mail only. Query first. Nonfiction 140,000-200,000 words. Responds in six weeks. Only considers manuscripts that have been edited by a professional book copy editor.
> **Types and topics:** cultural and moral makeup of society in the U.S. and its impact on Christianity.
> **Guidelines:** *www.aadeonmedia.com/submissions.html*

ABINGDON PRESS
PO Box 801, Nashville, TN 37202 | 615-749-6000
www.abingdonpress.com
Mary C. Dean, editor-in-chief, *mdean@umpublishing.org* | Constance Stella, Bible, leadership, and theology, *cstella@umpublishing.org* | Dawn Woods, Christian living, *dwoods@umpublishing.org* | Paul Franklyn, academic books and church supplies, *pfranklin@umpublishing.org*
> **Denomination:** United Methodist
> **Submissions:** Email proposal with sample chapters to *submissions@ umpublishing.org*. Publishes 120 titles per year; receives 2,000 submissions annually. Less than 5% of books from first-time

authors. Accepts manuscripts through agents only for Christian living. No longer publishing fiction. Royalty begins at 7.5% on net. Average first printing 2,500-4,000. Publication within eighteen months. Preferred Bible version: Common English Bible.

Guidelines: *www.abingdonpress.com/submissions.html*

Tip: "We develop and produce materials to help more people in more places come to know and love God through Jesus Christ and to choose to serve God and neighbor."

ACTA PUBLICATIONS

4848 N. Clark St., Chicago, IL 60640 | 800-397-2282
acta@actapublications.com | *www.actapublications.com*
Greg Pierce, *gfapierce@actapublications.com*

Denomination: Catholic

Submissions: Mail only with proposal and sample chapter. Accepts unsolicited manuscripts. No electronic submissions. No advances.

Types and topics: prayer, devotions, spirituality, personal growth, social justice

Guidelines: *actapublications.com/about-us*

AMBASSADOR INTERNATIONAL

411 University Ridge, Ste. B14, Greenville, SC 29601 | 864-751-4844
864-751-4847 | *publisher@emeraldhouse.com*
www.ambassador-international.com
Sam Lowry, publisher

Submissions: Dedicated to spreading the gospel of Christ and empowering Christians through the written word. Submit proposal with three chapters through the website, via email, or via mail. Publishes fifty titles per year.; hardcover, trade paperbacks, gift books, e-books. Receives 750 submissions annually. 50% of books from first-time authors. Accepts manuscripts through agents or authors. Prefers 144+ pages. Royalty 15-20% of net, 25% for e-books; no advance. Average first printing 2,000. Publication within six to eight months. Considers simultaneous submissions. Responds within thirty days. Preferred Bible versions: KJV, NIV, ESV, NKJV, NASB.

Types and topics: theology, devotionals, biography, inspirational, children's, business, finance, topical, Bible studies; fiction for teens, new adults, and adults

Guidelines: *ambassador-international.com/get-published/submission-guidelines*

Tip: "We're most open to a book which has a clearly defined market and the author's total commitment to the project. We do well with first-time authors. We have full international coverage. Many of our titles sell globally."

AMERICAN CATHOLIC PRESS

16565 State St., South Holland, IL 60473-2025 | 708-331-5485
acp@acpress.org | www.acpress.org, www.leafletmissal.com
Father Michael Gilligan, editorial director

> **Denomination:** Catholic
>
> **Submissions:** Publishes four titles per year. Receives ten submissions annually. Query first via mail. Pays $25-100 for outright purchases only. Average first printing 3,000. Publication within one year. No simultaneous submissions. Responds in two months. Bible version: prefers NAS.
>
> **Types and topics:** only publishes material on the liturgy
>
> **Guidelines:** www.americancatholicpress.org/faq.html#faq5
>
> **Tip:** "We publish only materials on the Roman Catholic liturgy. No poetry or fiction."

AMG PUBLISHERS

6815 Shallowford Rd., Chattanooga, TN 37421 | 800-266-4977
423-894-6060 | *sales@www.amgpublishers.com | www.amgpublishers.com*
Amanda Jenkins, author liaison | Angie Byles, operations and production manager

> **Parent company:** AMG International
>
> **Submissions:** "God's Word to you is our highest calling." We are unique in that proceeds from our sales are funneled into world missions through our parent organization. Publishes one to five titles per year; trade paperbacks, gift books, e-books, POD. Receives 500 submissions annually. Query letter first. Accepts manuscripts through agents or authors. Prefers 40,000-60,000 words (128-224 pages) for Bible studies; 60,000-100,000 words (208-400 pages) for trade nonfiction. Royalty 10-20% of net; 30-40% for e-books. Average first printing 3,500. Publication within twelve to eighteen months. Prefers accepted manuscript by email. Responds in one to four months. Bible version: prefers NASB 95, NKJV, ESV, or NIV 2011.
>
> **Guidelines:** *www.amgpublishers.com/main/pdf/Prospective_Author_Guidelines.pdf*; catalog for 9 x 12 SASE with five stamps.
>
> **Types and topics:** Bible studies (highly recommended that they fit

the Following God series format), devotional, applied theology, apologetics, Bible reference, African-American, Hispanic. No longer publishes fiction. Also does Bible software, Bible CD-ROMs.

Imprints: Living Ink Books, God and Country Press

Tip: "Most open to an interactive workbook Bible study geared for small groups that effectively taps into a largely female audience. We are currently placing priority on books with strong bibliocentric focus."

ANCIENT FAITH PUBLISHING

PO Box 748, Chesterton, IN 46304 | 800-967-7377
www.ancientfaith.com/publishing
Katherine Hyde, adult acquisitions, *khyde@ancientfaith.com* | Jane Meyer, young adult and children's acquisitions, *jmeyer@ancientfaith.com*

Denomination: Orthodox Christian Archdiocese of N.A.

Submissions: Publishes only books by and for Orthodox Christians. Publishes eight to eighteen adult titles per year; two to four children's titles per year Receives 100 submissions annually. 20% of books from first-time authors. Accepts manuscripts through agents or authors. Prefers 40,000-80,000 words. Pays royalty; no or small advance. Average first printing 2,000. Email submissions only. Responds in ten months. Bible version: prefers NKJV.

Types and topics: Orthodox spirituality suitable for laypeople, prayer, worship, the church year, stories of Orthodoxy in other lands, how to live out Orthodox faith in contemporary life, young adults, picture books, middle-grade readers, fiction for all ages

Guidelines: *www.ancientfaith.com/publishing#af-resources*

Tip: "Please explore our Website before submitting and carefully follow posted guidelines. "We reserve the right not to respond to inappropriate submissions."

ANEKO PRESS

203 E. Birch St., PO Box 652, Abbotsford, WI 54405 | 715-223-3013
info@lspbooks.com | *www.anekopress.com*
Jeremiah Zeiset, acquisitions editor

Submissions: Niche is publishing ministry-related books. Publishes thirty-six titles per year; hardcover, trade paperback, mass-market paperback, e-book, and audio. Receives 100+ submissions annually. 40% first-time authors. Accepts books submitted by agents. Does print-on-demand for slower-moving titles. Submit complete manuscript. Prefers 50,000 words or 200 pages. Royalty 30% of net; no advance. Average first printing 1,000 offset or 50 POD. Publishes within six months. Responds in three weeks.

Types and topics: Nonfiction; fiction for all ages is considered, provided the main goal is to share the Gospel or to encourage Christians in their walk with the Lord

Guidelines: *anekopress.com/write-for-us*

Tip: "Have a main goal of sharing the Gospel or encouraging Christians in their walk with the Lord."

ASHBERRY LANE PUBLISHING

PO Box 665, Gaston, OR 97119 | 503-860-5069
christina@ashberrylane.com | *ashberrylane.com*
Christina Tarabochia, acquisitions editor | *Sherrie Ashcraft, co-owner*

Submissions: Submit proposal with sample chapters. Publishes six to nine titles per year; trade paperback, e-books, audio. Receives seventy submissions annually. 50% of books from first-time authors. Print-on-demand. Preferred book length: adult novel 85,000-100,000 words. Royalty 50%, paid twice a year. Publication in six to nine months. Responds in one to two months. Catalog free on request.

Types and topics: Fiction only. Publishes Heartfelt Tales of Faith—stories that point to God while touching emotions.

Guidelines: *ashberrylane.com/submissions-guidelines*

Tip: Reading a newer Ashberry Lane title will reveal what kind of writing appeals to this house.

ASPIRE PRESS

17909 Adria Maru, Carson, CA 90746 | 310-353-2100
info@aspirepress.com | *www.aspirepress.com*

Parent company: Rose Publishing

Submissions: Publishes books that are "compassionate in their approach and rich with Scripture," giving "godly insight and counsel for those personally struggling and for believers who have a heart to minister and encourage others." Need credentials in helping others. Submit manuscripts through *ChristianManuscriptSubmissions.com.*

Types and topics: Christian living, counseling

BAAL HAMON PUBLISHERS

244 Fifth Ave., Ste. T279, New York, NY 10001 | 646 233 4017
www.baalhamon.com
Temitope Oyetomi, managing and acquisitions editor,
publishers@baalhamon.com

Parent company: Joy and Truth Christian Ministry

Submissions: Publishes twenty to thirty books per year. Receives 300 proposals per year. 30% from first-time authors. Length: 40,000-60,000 words. Submit proposal with sample chapters via email. Responds in three to six weeks. Royalty 30% on net. Sometimes offers negotiable advance. Bible version: NKJV. Guidelines via email.

Types and topics: fiction (general, historical), biographies, Christian living, devotionals, general nonfiction, theology, African-American

Tip: "For nonfiction, include a cursory highlight of your book's comparative advantage over similar books."

BAKER ACADEMIC

6030 E. Fulton Rd., Ada MI 49301 | 616-676-9185
submissions@bakeracademic.com | *www.bakeracademic.com*
Jim Kinney, editorial director

Parent company: Baker Publishing Group

Submissions: Publishes fifty titles per year; hardcover, trade paperback. 10% of books from first-time authors. Accepts manuscripts through agents, submission services, or editor's personal contacts at writers conferences. Pays royalty and advance. Publication within one year.

Types and topics: religious academic books, professional books for students and church leaders

Guidelines: *bakerpublishinggroup.com/bakeracademic/contact/submitting-a-proposal*

BAKER BOOKS

6030 E. Fulton Rd., Ada, MI 49301 | 616-676-9185
www.bakerbooks.com
Rebekah Guzman, acquisitions editor, rguzman@bakerpublishinggroup.com

Parent company: Baker Publishing Group

Submissions: Publishes hardcover, trade paperbacks. No unsolicited proposals.

Types and topics: family, parenting, business, leadership, marriage, Christian living, spiritual growth, personal growth, self-help, memoir/personal narrative, biography, cultural engagement, theology, apologetics, church life, ministry resources

Guidelines: *bakerpublishinggroup.com/contact/submission-policy*

B&H PUBLISHING GROUP

1 Lifeway Plaza, MSN 188, Nashville, TN 37234 |
ManuscriptSubmission@lifeway.com | *www.bhpublishinggroup.com*

Parent company: LifeWay Christian Resources

Submissions: "Because we believe Every Word Matters, we seek to provide innovative, intentional content that is grounded in biblical truth." Query first. Publishes 90-100 titles per year; hardcover, trade paperback, e-book. Receives 3,000 submissions annually. 10% of books from first-time authors. Royalty on net; advance. Publication within eighteen months. Responds in two to three months. Bible version: prefers HCSB.

Types and topics: Christian living, leadership, reference, women, Bible study helps, church growth, college textbooks, evangelism, theology, marriage, parenting, worship, children's

Imprints: B&H Books, B&H Kids, B&H Academic, Holman Bible Publishers, Holman Reference, Broadman Church Supplies, B&H Español

Guidelines: *www.bhpublishinggroup.com/consumer-faq/#3*

Tip: "Follow guidelines when submitting. Be informed that the market in general is very crowded with the book you might want to write. Do the research before submitting."

BARBOUR PUBLISHING, INC.

1810 Barbour Dr., PO Box 719, Uhrichsville, OH 44683 | 740-922-6045
submissions@barbourbooks.com | *www.barbourbooks.com*
Annie Tipton, acquisitions editor

Submissions: Fiction proposals only through agents. Nonfiction via email. Publishes 300+ titles per year; hardcover, flexibound, trade paperbacks, mass-market paperbacks. Responds only if interested.

Types and topics: fiction, popular Bible reference, devotions, gift books, Christian classics, children's, practical Christian living

Guidelines: *www.barbourbooks.com/pages/writersguide.aspx*

BAYLOR UNIVERSITY PRESS

1 Bear Place 97363, Waco, TX 76798-7363 | 254-710-3522
www.baylorpress.com
Carey Newman, editorial director, Carey_Newman@baylor.edu | *Dr. Jordan Rowan Fannin, acquisitions editor, Jordan_Fannin@baylor.edu*

Submissions: Requires email submissions.

Types and topics: academic

Guidelines: *www.baylorpress.com/en/Publish_With_Us*

BEACON HILL PRESS

PO Box 419527, Kansas City, MO 64141
crm@nph.com | *www.nph.com*
René McFarland, submissions editor

Denomination: Nazarene

Types and topics: Christian living, spiritual growth, ministry resources
Guidelines: *www.nph.com/nphweb/html/bhol/FAQ.jsp*

BETHANY HOUSE PUBLISHERS

6030 E. Fulton Rd., Ada, MI 49301
www.bethanyhouse.com

Parent company: Baker Publishing Group
Submissions: Publishes biblically based books that encourage
evangelicals to grow in relationship with God. Publishes
approximately eighty titles per year; hardcover, trade paperback.
10% of books from first-time authors. Accepts manuscripts
through agents only. Negotiable royalty on net, negotiable
advance. Publication within eighteen months.
Types and topics: nonfiction: devotionals, Christian living, spiritual
life, relationships, prayer, women's interests, spiritual warfare;
fiction: Amish, biblical, contemporary, contemporary romance,
historical, romantic suspense, speculative, suspense
Guidelines: *bakerpublishinggroup.com/contact/submission-policy*
Tip: "We do not accept unsolicited queries or proposals."

BLINK

3900 Sparks Dr. S.E., Grand Rapids, MI 49546 | 616-698-3431
blinkyasubmissions@harpercollins.com | *www.blinkyabooks.com*
Jillian Manning, editor, jillian.manning@harpercollins.com

Parent company: Zonderkidz
Submissions: Query letter only via email, from agents only. Publishes
six to eight books per year. Receives 1,000 proposals per year.
20% of books from first-time authors. Preferred book length 60-
90,000 words. Replies in four to six weeks. Royalty depends on
the project; gives advance. Average first print run depends on the
project. Preferred Bible version: NIV.
Types and topics: YA fiction and nonfiction; clean teen fiction (PG
or PG-13 rating in terms of content); fiction: contemporary,
historical, romance, adventure, light fantasy, thriller; African-
American, Hispanic
Guidelines: none
Tip: "Please note that Blink books do not contain overt Christian
content. These books are intended to be 'clean' teen reads aimed
toward the ABA market. We seek established authors, authors
with growing social-media platforms, and/or authors with strong
literary connections. We look for novels that have bestseller or

literary award potential. We look for nonfiction by well-known individuals with a strong platform to reach readers."

BMH BOOKS

PO Box 544, Winona Lake, IN 46590 | 800-348-2756, 574-372-3098
lcgates@bmhbooks.com | www.BMHbooks.com
Liz Cutler Gates, editor, publisher

> **Denomination:** Grace Brethren
>
> **Submissons:** Shows preference to Grace Brethren authors who have important and worthwhile messages that need to be heard. Trinitarian theology, dispensational eschatology, emphasis on exegesis. Publishes three to five titles per year; hardcover, trade paperback. Receives thirty submissions annually. 50% of books from first-time authors. Query first; no unsolicited manuscripts. Requires accepted manuscripts by email. Prefers 50,000-75,000 words or 128-256 pages. Royalty 8-10% on retail; rarely pays an advance. Average first printing 2,000. Publication within one year. Prefers not to consider simultaneous submissions. Responds in three months. Bible version: prefers KJV or NIV.
>
> **Types and topics:** primarily used as texts in Bible colleges, Bible institutes, and seminaries; revives and refreshes the classics; Brethren history and doctrine
>
> **Guidelines:** *bmhbooks.com/faqs*
>
> **Tip:** "Most open to a small-group study book or text for Bible college/ Bible institute and biblically based, timeless discipleship material."

BOLD VISION BOOKS

PO Box 2011, Friendswood, TX 77549-2011 | 832-569-4282
boldvisionbooks@gmail.com | www.boldvisionbooks.com
George Porter, publisher | Karen Porter, senior editor | Gloria Penwell, acquisitions editor

> **Submissions:** We are small enough to give you personal service, and we are big enough to get your book into the marketplace. Publishes ten to fifteen titles per year; trade paperback, mass-market paperback, e-book, print-on-demand. Receives 100 submissions annually. 85% of books from first-time authors. Accepts submissions from agents or authors. Prefers 40,000 words or 280 pages. Royalty 25-50% on net; no advance. Publication within eighteen months. Responds in one to three months.
>
> **Types and topics:** Nonfiction: Compelling stories of life change and spiritual growth. Narrative nonfiction with great storytelling techniques. Well-written, compelling books on Christian living.

Looking for fresh voices and clear concepts. Adult fiction: romance and mystery with strong story and compelling characters who experience life change. Fiction for younger readers: exciting stories with relatable characters. No fantasy in chapter books. Query letter first only via email.

Also does: booklets and minibooks

Imprints: Nuts 'n Bolts (craft books for business and the arts), Optasia Books (fee-based for pastors and ministry leaders)

Guidelines: *www.boldvisionbooks.com/Page_6.html*

Tip: "Editing is the key to getting noticed. Invest in a strong professional editor before sending us your project. Show us that you have a clear, concise handle on your project, subject matter, audience, and benefit to the reader. Your best opportunity with Bold Vision is strong writing and a powerful takeaway message. To be noticed by our editors, write in crisp, tight, and authoritative language and offer answers that lead to transformation."

BONDFIRE BOOKS

7680 Goddard St., Ste. 220, Colorado Springs, CO 80920 | 719-260-7080
submissions@bondfirebooks.com | *www.bondfirebooks.com*
Debbie Christian, acquisitions editor

Parent company: Alive Literary Agency

Submissions: Bondfire Books is an e-publisher focused on kindling thought and action through Christian and inspirational content while maximizing e-book prospects for authors. Publishes more than fifty per year. Receives 5,000 proposals per year. 10% first-time authors. Accepts books submitted by agents. Proposal with two chapters. E-books only. Preferred length: 50,000 words. Royalty 50% on net; no advance. Average time for publication is two months. Responds in four to six weeks. (If you don't hear by six weeks, you can assume it is not interested.) Contemporary fiction or big nonfiction book tied to a news maker. Primarily interested in working with authors with established platforms and audiences. Not currently taking submissions, but check the website for changes.

Types and topics: memoir, fiction for teens and adults, nonfiction, tie-ins to news events; out-of-print with rights reverted, in-print works with available electronic rights

Guidelines: *www.bondfirebooks.com/submission*

Tip: "Publishers and agents are being much more selective with what they say yes to. And yet amidst increased competition, the cream always rises to the top. The great books get noticed and picked up."

BRAZOS PRESS

6030 E. Fulton Rd., Ada, MI 49301 | 616-676-9185
submissions@brazospress.com | www.brazospress.com
Henry Carrigan, acquisitions editor

> **Parent company:** Baker Publishing Group
> **Submissions:** Publishes books that creatively draw on the riches of our catholic Christian heritage to deepen our understanding of God's creation and inspire faithful reflection and engagement. Authors typically hold advanced degrees and have established publishing platforms. Hardcover, trade paperback.
> **Guidelines:** *bakerpublishinggroup.com/brazospress/contact/submitting-a-proposal*

BREATH OF FRESH AIR PRESS

PO Box 12, St. Clair, NSW, Australia 2759 | +61 412 530 765
debporter@breathoffreshairpress.com.au | www.breathoffreshairpress.com.au
Deborah Porter, acquisitions/submissions editor

> **Submissions:** Publishes three to five books per year. Receives thirty-five to forty-five proposals per year. 100% from first-time authors. Length: 60-85,000 words. Submit proposal with sample chapters via email. Responds in two to three months. Royalty 9.5-15%; $150 advance. POD only. Bible version: NIV but flexible.
> **Types and topics:** most YA and adult fiction, fresh Christian nonfiction, humor always appreciated, Christian living, marriage, inspirational, relationships, light nonfiction
> **Guidelines:** *www.breathoffreshairpress.com/for-authors*
> **Tip:** "We are looking for fresh talent and creative ideas that are not a repeat of the same old thing. Make sure you highlight the ways your manuscript is different and how it stands out from the pack."

BRIDGE LOGOS

17750 N.W. 115th Ave., Bldg. 200, Ste. 220, Alachua, FL 32615
386-462-2525 | manuscripts@bridgelogos.com | www.bridgelogos.com
Peggy Hildebrand, acquisitions editor, phildebrand@bridgelogos.com

> **Submissions:** Publishes classics, books by Spirit-filled authors, and inspirational books that appeal to the general evangelical market. Publishes forty titles per year; hardcover, trade paperback, mass-market paperback. Receives 200+ submissions annually. 30% of books from first-time authors. Accepts manuscripts through agents or authors. Email proposal with three to five chapters. Prefers 250 pages. Royalty 10% on net; rarely pays $500 advance. Average first printing

4,000-5,000. Publication within six to twelve months. Responds in six weeks Prefers accepted manuscripts by email; free catalog.

Types and topics: Bible study, biographies of notable Christians, business, finance, personal money management, Christian living, contemporary issues, devotionals/personal growth, encouragement, eschatology, evangelism, families and marriage, Messianic work, material on our nation's heritage (history and patriotism), men's issues, political issues, prayer, singles, social issues, spirit-filled topics, timely topics, unusual outreach ministries, women's issues, youth, African American, Hispanic

Imprint: Synergy

Guidelines: *www.bridgelogos.com/manuscript-submission*

Tip: "Looking for well-written, timely books that are aimed at the needs of people and that glorify God. Have a great message, a well-written manuscript, and a specific plan and willingness to market your book. Looking for previously published authors with an active ministry who are experts on their subject."

BROADSTREET PUBLISHING

8646 Eagle Creek Cir., Ste. 210, Savage, MN 55378 | 855-935-2000
www.broadstreetpublishing.com
David Sulka, editorial director

Submissions: Prefers working with agents but will work directly with authors.

Types and topics: biographies, Majestic Expressions adult coloring books, Christian living, fiction, devotionals, and Bible promise books. Publishes 150-200 titles per year.

Imprint: Belle City Gifts (women's journals, devotional journals, and planners)

CAREPOINT PUBLISHING

PO Box 870490, Stone Mountain, GA 30087 | 800-378-9584
404-625-9217 | info@carepointministry.com | carepointministry.com

Submissions: "Interested in fresh perspectives and unique angles/ approaches to common 'dis-eases' facing contemporary Christians. We are seeking grace&truth-full materials/programs that integrate timeless biblical principles with sound helping strategies to mediate the love, grace, and mercy of the Lord Jesus in a broken world." Novellas 15,000-25,000 words.

Types and topics: care-group resources about running a care ministry for people facing a specific life challenge, such as pornography/sex addition, abortion, grief, physical disability, and sex abuse; novellas

Imprints: 5 Loaves Press/Way-Out Books (novellas)
Guidelines: *www.carepointministry.com/writers.html*
Tip: "If you write to encourage the discouraged, give hope to the hopeless, joy to the joyless, and grace to us all, we want to hear from you."

CASCADIA PUBLISHING HOUSE

126 Klingerman Rd., Telford, PA 18969
editor@CascadiaPublishingHouse.com | CascadiaPublishingHouse.com
Michael A. King, publisher, editor

Submissions: Query only by mail or email.
Types and topics: creative, thought-provoking, Anabaptist-related material
Guidelines: *www.cascadiapublishinghouse.com/submit.htm*
Tip: "All Cascadia books receive rigorous evaluation and some form of peer or consultant review."

CASTLE GATE PRESS

submissions@castlegatepress.com | www.castlegatepress.com
Suzanne Hartman, editorial director

Submissions: Accepts submissions from agents or authors. Publishes POD, e-book, and sometimes audiobook. Length: 70,000-100,000 words. Royalty 50%. Email a query with one-page, single spaced synopsis and the first 50 pages, double-spaced.
Types and topics: only fiction, likes speculative fiction or at least a touch of speculative, novellas, adults, new adults, young adults
Guidelines: *www.castlegatepress.com/submissions*
Tip: "We highly recommend that you have your work reviewed by other authors before submitting. We are seeking polished manuscripts with intriguing plots, compelling characters, and an understanding of basic grammar, punctuation, and writing style."

CATHOLIC BOOK PUBLISHING CORP.

77 W. End Rd., Totowa, NJ 07572 | 973-890-2400
info@catholicbookpublishing.com | www.catholicbookpublishing.com
Anthony Buono, editor

Denomination: Catholic
Submissions: Primarily assigns books but will look at mailed queries. No simultaneous submissions or submissions from agents. Outright purchases; no royalties or advances. Responds in two to three months. Publication in twelve to fifteen months.
Imprint: Resurrection Press

Types and topics: liturgical books, Bibles, missals, prayer books; for Resurrection Press: readable nonfiction titles for popular Catholic and general Christian markets in the areas of prayer, healing and spirituality, as well as pastoral and liturgical resources,
Guidelines: *www.catholicbookpublishing.com/faq.php#manuscript*

THE CATHOLIC UNIVERSITY OF AMERICA PRESS
240 Leahy Hall, 620 Michigan Ave. N.E., Washington, DC 20064
walkert@cua.edu | cuapress.cua.edu
Trevor Lipscombe, director | Theresa Walker, managing editor
Denomination: Catholic
Submissions: Mailed proposal only.
Types and topics: history (ecclesiastical and secular), language and literature, philosophy, political theory, theology
Guidelines: *cuapress.cua.edu/resources/EditorialPolicyProcedures.cfm*

CHALICE PRESS
483 E. Lockwood Ave., Ste. 100, St. Louis, MO 63119 | 800-366-3383
submissions@chalicepress.com | chalicepress.com
Brad Lyons, publisher, blyons@chalicepress.com
Submissions: Open to receiving any publishing proposal that "aligns with our mission to publish resources inviting all people into deeper relationship with God, equipping them as disciples of Jesus Christ, and sending them into ministries as the Holy Spirit calls them. Particularly interested in publishing content by and for women, young adults (age 18 to 35), and racial/ethnic cultures for our academic, congregational leadership, and general audiences." Print, e-books, multimedia formats. Send e-query only initially.
Types and topics: academics (homiletics, biblical studies, theology, Christian education); congregational leadership (preaching, evangelism, hospitality, leadership development, discipleship/equipping ministries); general (faith and life, inspiration/devotion, Bible study/application, mission/evangelism
Guidelines: *www.chalicepress.com/AuthorGuidelines.aspx*
Tip: "Our theological tradition is evangelistic (we share with others our experience of God), inclusive (we are guests at a table where everyone is welcome) and mission-oriented (our gratitude to God compels us to serve others)."

CHARISMA HOUSE
600 Rinehart Rd., Lake Mary, FL 32746 | 407-333-0600
charismahouse@charismamedia.com | www.charismamedia.com
Submit to Acquisitions Assistant.

Submissions: To inspire and equip people to live a Spirit-led life and walk in the divine purpose for which they were called. Accepts proposals only through agents. Publishes 150 titles per year; hardcover, trade paperback. Receives 1,500 submissions annually. 65% of books from first-time authors. Reprints books. Prefers 55,000 words. Royalty on net or outright purchase; advance. Average first printing 7,500. Publication within nine months. Responds in four to eight weeks.

Topics and types: Charisma House: Charismatic/Pentecostal perspective on Christian living, work of the Holy Spirit, prophecy, prayer, Scripture, adventures in evangelism and missions, popular theology. Siloam: living in good health—body, mind, and spirit, including alternative medicine; diet and nutrition; and physical, emotional, and psychological wellness; prefers manuscripts from certified doctors, nutritionists, trainers, and other medical professionals. Frontline: contemporary political and social issues from a Christian perspective. Realms: adult Christian fiction in the supernatural, speculative genre, 80,000-120,000 words; also considers historical or biblical fiction if supernatural element is substantial. Excel: targeted toward success in the workplace and businesses. Casa Creación: books in Spanish; contact: 800-987-8432; casacreacion@charismamedia.com; www.casacreacion.com. Publicaciones Casa: same as Creation House but for people who like to copublish in Spanish; contact same as Casa Creación.

Guidelines: *charismahouse.com/index.php/submit-book-proposal*

CHICKEN SOUP FOR THE SOUL BOOKS

See listing in the periodicals section, "**Adult Markets**."

CHOSEN

6030 E. Fulton Rd., Ada, MI 49301 | 616-676-9185
jcampbell@chosenbooks.com | *bakerpublishinggroup.com/chosen*
Jane Campbell, editorial director | *Kim Bangs, nonfiction acquisitions editor,*
KBangs@bakerpublishinggroup.com

Parent company: Baker Publishing Group

Submissions: Email proposal with two chapters.

Types and topics: Charismatic, Spirit-filled–life, a few thematic narratives

Guidelines: *bakerpublishinggroup.com/chosen/contact/submitting-a-proposal*

CHRISTIAN FOCUS PUBLICATIONS

Geanies House, Fearn, Tain, Ross-shire IV20 1TW, Scotland, UK
01862 871011 | *submissions@christianfocus.com* | *christianfocus.com*
Catherine.Mackenzie, children's editor, Catherine.Mackenzie@christianfocus.com

Submissions: Submit proposal with two chapters via email or mail.

Types and topics: Christian Focus: popular works, including biographies, commentaries, basic doctrine, and Christian living. Mentor: written at a level suitable for Bible college and seminary students, pastors, and other serious readers, including commentaries, doctrinal studies, examination of current issues, and church history. Christian Heritage: classic writings from the past. Children's: Bible story books, devotionals, craft books, puzzle books, activity books, game books, material for family devotions, biography series (Trailblazers for ages 9-14, retells the stories of well-known Christians past and present; Torchbearers for ages 8-11 about real martyrs), and several fiction series.

Guidelines: adults: *www.christianfocus.com/pages/guidelines_adult/-/-* | children: *www.christianfocus.com/pages/guidelines_children/-/-*

Tip: "Read our website please. Don't send us stuff we don't publish."

CHURCHGROWTH.ORG

PO Box 510, Twin Peaks, CA | 434-525-0022
info@churchgrowth.org | *www.ChurchGrowth.org*
Bill Greig III, bill.greig@churchgrowth.org

Submissions: Provides timeless tools for Chriatian growth. "We prefer our writers to be experienced in church leadership and church growth." Query via email. Publishes two titles per year; trade paperback. Receives 20 submissions annually. 7% of books from first-time authors. No manuscripts through agents. Prefers 64-160 pages. Royalties vary, 6% on retail or outright purchase; no advance. Average first printing 100. Publication within one year. Responds in three months. Requires requested manuscript by email.

Types and topics: nonfiction on church growth; self-discovery and evaluation tools, such as surveys

Guidelines: *www.churchgrowth.org*

Tip: "Currently concentrating on own Team Ministry/Spiritual Gifts resources and updating backlist. Accept very few unsolicited submissions. Most open to ministry how-to manuals for ministry leaders—something unique with a special niche. Must be practical and different from anything else on the same subject—or must be a topic/slant few others have published. May consider evaluation tools as mentioned above. No devotionals, life testimonies, commentaries, or studies on books of the Bible."

CISTERCIAN PUBLICATIONS

dutton@ohio.edu
www.cistercianpublications.org
Marsha L. Dutton, executive editor

> **Submissions:** Prefers a proposal. All submissions must be accompanied by a summary form that's available on the website. Before submitting a manuscript, request the style sheet and instructions.
>
> **Types and topics:** studies on the Christian monastic tradition and monographs reflecting contemplative monastic spirituality
>
> **Guidelines:** www.cistercianpublications.org/Contact/manuscript

CLADACH PUBLISHING

PO Box 336144, Greeley, CO 80633 | 970-371-9530
office@cladach.com | *www.cladach.com*
Catherine Lawton, publisher, editor, cathyl@cladach.com | *Christina Slike, assistant editor*

> **Submissions:** Publishes four or five titles per year; trade paperback, ebook, and some audiobooks. 58% of books from first-time authors. Considers book proposals from authors they meet at writers conferences or when introduced through present authors or mutual acquaintances, including literary agents. Query letter first, preferably via email in the message. Prefers 180-224 pages. Royalty 7-20% on net; $100 advance. Publication within nine months. Responds within three months. Bible version: prefers NIV, NRSV.
>
> **Types and topics:** creative nonfiction, memoir, poetry, fiction (historical, frontier, contemporary; prefers stories set in Colorado), nature writings, devotional, relationships, some compilations
>
> **Guidelines: cladach.com/authors**
>
> **Tip:** "We are family owned and small enough to be entrepreneurial, to take risks on new authors and ideas. Peruse the titles and authors on our website, read our books in your interest area."

CLC PUBLICATIONS

701 Pennsylvania Ave., Fort Washington, PA 19034 | 215-542-1242
submissions@clcpublications.com | *www.clcpublications.com*
Erika Cobb, managing editor

Parent company: CLC Ministries International

Submissions: We are an evangelical publishing company that is committed to maintaining sound biblical truths, and seeks to publish works that align with this purpose and mission. The purpose of CLC is to make evangelical Christian literature available to all nations so that people may come to faith and maturity in the Lord Jesus Christ. Publishes sixteen titles per year; hardcover, trade paperbacks, e-books, POD. Receives 120 submissions annually. 50% of books from first-time authors. Prefers manuscripts through agents. Query letter/proposal only with sample chapters; complete manuscript on request. Length: prefers under 50,000 words or 200 pages. Royalty 12-16% of net, 12% for e-books; pays advances. Publication within eighteen months. Responds in three months. Requires accepted manuscripts by email. Bible version: prefers ESV.

Types and topics: Christian living, church life, church renewal, discipleship, evangelism, family life, forgiveness, healing, holiness, inspirational, leadership, marriage, missions, parenting, pastors' helps, personal growth, personal renewal, prayer, relationships, spiritual life, spiritual warfare, theology. Looking for books that approach a given topic of the Christian life—marriage, family, personal relationships, missions, evangelism, redemptive history, Christians worldwide, prayer, discipleship, etc. Not interested in fiction, self-help, poetry, or basic new believer material.

Guidelines: *www.clcpublications.com/about/prospective-authors-submissions*

Tip: Looking for books on the deeper life. "We are most open to manuscripts that bring a fresh and unique perspective to timeless subjects that are relevant to the daily life of Christians. We prefer first-time authors to have an already-established platform (from blogs, social media, connections to a large church or ministry, etc.)."

COLLEGE PRESS PUBLISHING

PO Box 1132, 2111 N. Main St., Ste. C, Joplin, MO 64801 | 800-289-3300
collpressbooks@gmail.com | *www.collegepress.com*

Denomination: Christian Churches/Churches of Christ

Submissions: Requires a query or proposal first. Responds in two to three months.

Types and topics: Bible studies, topical studies (biblically based), apologetic studies, historical biographies of Christians

Guidelines: *www.collegepress.com/pages/for-authors*

CONARI PRESS

665 Third St., Ste. 400, San Francisco, CA 94107
submissions@rwwbooks.com | www.redwheelweiser.com
Ms. Pat Bryce, acquisitions editor

> **Parent company:** Red Wheel/Weiser, LLC
> **Submissions:** Takes proposals and full manuscripts from agents and authors via email or mail. Publishes thirty titles per year. Responds in three months.
> **Types and topics:** spirituality, personal growth, parenting, women's issues
> **Guidelines:** *redwheelweiser.com/p.php?id=8*
> **Tip:** "Our mission is to publish quality books that will make a difference in people's lives—how we feel about ourselves and how we relate to one another. We value integrity, compassion, and receptivity, both in the books we publish and in the way we do business."

CONCORDIA ACADEMIC PRESS

3558 S. Jefferson St., St. Louis, MO 63118 | 800-325-3040
314-268-1000 | www.cph.org | sarah.steiner@cph.org
Sarah Steiner, production editor

> **Denomination:** Lutheran Church, Missouri Synod
> **Submissions:** Send a proposal with the Peer Review Proposal Form from the website.
> **Types and topics:** resources that support pastoral and congregational ministry; scholarly and professional books in exegetical, historical, dogmatic, and practical theology
> **Guidelines:** *www.cph.org/t-topic-proacabooks-manuscript.aspx*

CONCORDIA PUBLISHING HOUSE

3558 S. Jefferson Ave., St. Louis, MO 63118-3968 | 314-268-1080
www.cph.org
Rev. Paul T. McCain, publisher, executive director of editorial,
paul.mccain@cph.org

> **Denomination:** Lutheran Church, Missouri Synod
> **Submissions:** Send proposal and sample chapters. Publication within two years. Responds in six weeks.
> **Types and topics:** nonfiction only, no longer looking for children's books

CROSSLINK PUBLISHING

558 E. Castle Pines Pkwy., Ste. B4117, Castle Rock, CO 80108 | 888-697-4851
publisher@crosslinkpublishing.com | www.crosslinkpublishing.com
Rick Bates, managing editor

Parent company: CrossLink Ministries.

Submissions: As a small publisher, it is author focused, processes are nimble, and it prides itself on having the most transparent and participative publishing process in the industry. Publishes thirty-five titles per year in paperback. Receives 530 submissions annually. 85% of books from first-time authors. Requires manuscript submission on the website. Prefers 12,000-60,000 words. Royalty 10% of retail, 20% for e-books; no advance. Average first printing 2,000. Publication within six months. Responds within seven days.

Types and topics: adult fiction, Bible studies, devotional, inspirational, meditations, spiritual growth areas

Imprint: New Harbor Press

Guidelines: *www.crosslinkpublishing.com/submit-a-manuscript*

Tip: "We are particularly interested in providing books that help Christians succeed in their daily walk (inspirational, devotional, small groups, etc.)."

CROSSRIVER MEDIA GROUP

PO Box 187, Brewster, KS 67732 | 785-269-4730
info@crossrivermedia.com | *www.crossrivermedia.com*
Tamara Clymer, fiction editor, tamara@crossrivermedia.com | *Debra L. Butterfield, nonfiction editor, deb@crossrivermedia.com*

Submissions: Publishes four to eight titles per year; trade paperbacks, e-books, POD. Receives sixty to seventy-five submissions annually. 50% of books from first-time authors. Accepts but doesn't require submissions through agents. Length: 60,000-80,000 words. Send proposal with sample chapters via email. Replies in twelve to sixteen weeks. Royalty: 8-12%. POD. Preferred Bible version: Anything except NIV. Royalty negotiable; no advance. Publication within eighteen months. Responds within two to three months.

Types and topics: Inspirational fiction for adults (contemporary, historical, biblical, romance); Bible study, Christian living, family and marriage, inspirational, church growth, children

Imprints: CrossRiver, CrossRiver Kids

Tip: "Read our website, and follow the guidelines."

THE CROSSROAD PUBLISHING COMPANY

submissions@crossroadpublishing.com | *www.crossroadpublishing.com*

Submissions: Open to unsolicited proposals; email submissions only. Responds in six to eight weeks Accepts submissions from agents or authors. Pays royalties; no advance.

Types and topics: spirituality, Christian living, theology

Guidelines: *www.crossroadpublishing.com/crossroad/static/for-authors*

CROSSWAY

1300 Crescent St., Wheaton, IL 60187 | 630-682-4300
submissions@crossway.org | www.crossway.org
Justin Taylor, executive vice president for book publishing | Jill Carter,
editorial administrator (submit to her)

Parent company: Good News Publishers

Submissions: Publishes books that combine the truth of God's Word
with a passion to live it out, with unique and compelling Christian
content. Query letter only first, via email or mail. Publishes eighty
titles per year; hardcover, trade paperbacks, e-books. Receives
1,000 submissions annually. 2% of books from first-time authors.
Accepts manuscripts through agents or authors. Prefers at least
25,000 words. Royalty 25% on net for e-books; advance varies.
Average first printing 7,500. Publication within eighteen months.
No simultaneous submissions. Responds in six to eight weeks.
Bible version: prefers ESV.

Types and topics: contemporary issues; Christian worldview;
Christian living; academic and professional books on theology,
biblical studies, church history, preaching, and pastoral theology

Guidelines: *www.crossway.org/support/manuscript-submissions;*
free catalog

CSS PUBLISHING GROUP, INC.

5450 N. Dixie Hwy., Lima, OH 45807-9559 | 419-227-1818
editor@csspub.com | www.csspub.com
Missy Cotrell, managing editor

Submissions: Serves the needs of pastors, worship leaders, and parish
program planners in the broad Christian mainline of the American
church. Prefers query first but will also look at proposals with a
sample chapter(s) via email or mail. Publishes fifteen titles per year;
trade paperbacks, e-books, POD. Receives 500-1,000 submissions
annually. 50% of books from first-time authors. Prefers 100-
125 pages. No royalty or advance. Average first printing 1,000.
Publication within one to two years. Responds in three weeks to
three months; final decision within a year. Requires requested ms
on disk and in hard copy. Bible version: prefers NRSV.

Types and topics: lectionary-based resources for worship, preaching,
group study, drama, and use with children (but not children's
books); sermons, preaching, and worship resources for special
seasons and days of the church year and special themes or
emphasis; children's object lessons and sermons; resources for

working with youth; pastoral aids, such as materials to assist in counseling; easy-to-perform dramas and pageants for all age groups, primarily for Advent/Christmas/Epiphany and Lent/Easter (no full-length plays), parish-tested materials for use in education, youth ministry, stewardship, and church growth; a few general titles

Guidelines: *store.csspub.com/page.php?Custom%20Pages=10*

Imprints: Fairway Press (see separate listing in "Independent Book Publishers"), B.O.D. (Books On Demand), FaithWalk Publishing (see separate listing)

Tip: "We're looking for authors who will help with the marketing of their books."

DAWN PUBLICATIONS

12402 Bitney Springs Rd., Nevada City, CA 95959 | 530-274-7775
submission@dawnpub.com | *www.dawnpub.com*
Carol Malnor, acquisitions editor

Submissions: Dedicated to inspiring in children a sense of appreciation for all of life on earth through creative nonfiction. Publishes six titles per year; hardcover, trade paperbacks. Receives 2,500 submissions annually. 35% of titles are by new authors. Accepts manuscripts through agents or authors. Submit complete manuscript by mail or email. Royalty on net; pays an advance. Publication within one to two years. Responds in six months.

Types and topics: picture books, some chapter books for middle grade

Guidelines: *www.dawnpub.com/submission-guidelines*

Tip: "Most open to creative nonfiction. We look for nature awareness and appreciation titles that promote a relationship with the natural world and specific habitats, usually through inspiring treatment and nonfiction."

DAVID C. COOK

4050 Lee Vance View, Colorado Springs, CO 80918 | 719-536-0100
www.davidccook.com

Submissions: Not accepting unsolicited proposals or manuscripts at this time. However, will consider proposals from agents and invitations extended at writers conferences.

DESERT BREEZE PUBLISHING

submissions@desertbreezepublishing.com | *www.desertbreezepublishing.com*
Gail Delaney, editor

Submissions: Novellas 25,000-35,000 (prefers 30,000); super books (more than 100,000 words). Prefers 55,000-80,000 words. Will consider series. No simultaneous submissions. Releases six to twelve titles per month.

Types and topics: Romance fiction in a variety of subgenres, women's fiction with or without romance, variety of YA and new-adult fiction

Guidelines: *www.desertbreezepublishing.com/submissions*

Tip: "We are actively seeking inspirational and Christian novels with a bit more real world flair. It's not always easy being a Christian, and we would like to see novels that express that."

DISCOVERY HOUSE PUBLISHERS

PO Box 3566, Grand Rapids, MI 49501 | 800-653-8333, 616-942-9218
dhptc@rbc.org | *www.dhp.org*
Andrew Rogers, acquisitions editor

Parent company: Our Daily Bread Ministries

Submissions: Publishes nonfiction books that feed the soul with the word of God. Publishes fourteen titles per year; hardcover, trade paperbacks, e-books. Receives 300 submissions annually. 10% of books from first-time authors. Accepts manuscripts through agents or authors. Send proposal with sample chapters via email or mail; if by email, put "Attn: Ms Review Editor" in the subject line. Royalty 10-15% on net; no advance. Publication within twelve to eighteen months. Responds in four to six weeks.

Types and topics: devotional, Bible study and Bible reference materials, spiritual growth, personal growth, contemporary issues from a Christian viewpoint, memoirs, children's

Guidelines: *dhp.org/writers-guidelines* (FAQ#6); free catalog

DOUBLEDAY RELIGIOUS PUBLISHING

See Image Books.

DOULOS RESOURCES

195 Mack Edwards Dr., Oakland, TN 38060 | 901-201-4612
info@doulosresources.org | *www.doulosresources.org*

Submissions: Requires an email or e-query first to *submissions@doulosresources.org*; no attachments. Responds in four to eight weeks. Publishes four to six titles annually. Publication twelve to eighteen months.

Types and topics: practical theology, leadership resources, curricula, and resources for dissemination among congregations.

Imprint: Kalos Press (literary fiction, memoir, biography, devotional, Christian reflection, nonfiction essays)

Guidelines: *www.doulosresources.org/about/about/submissions.html*

Tip: "We publish works that are theologically consistent with the Westminster Confession of Faith; other traditions and theological trajectories will be considered accordingly. We are not interested in submissions with a polemical tone or an aggressive/antagonistic ethos; axes should be ground elsewhere. Follow our submission guidelines closely."

DOVE CHRISTIAN PUBLISHERS

PO Box 611, Bladensburg, MD 20710 | 240-342-3293
publishing@dovechristianpublishers.com | *www.dovechristianpublishers.com*

Submissions: Submit proposal by email only; no complete manuscripts. Responds in three to four weeks. Royalties 30% retail for sales through its website, 15% retail otherwise.

Types and topics: relationships, children's, devotionals, Christian living/self-help, Bible studies, ministry, church life, fiction (crime/detective, drama, fantasy, historical fiction, humor, mystery, picture books, realistic fiction, science fiction, short stories, suspense, thriller, adventure, children's)

Guidelines: *www.dovechristianpublishers.com/publish-with-us*

Tip: Review our website guidelines thoroughly.

EARTHEN VESSEL PUBLISHING

9 Sunny Oaks Dr., San Raphael, CA 94903 | 415-302-1199
kentphilpott@comcast.net | *www.earthenvesseljournal.com*
Kent and Katie Philpott, editors

Denomination: American Baptist and Southern Baptist (dually aligned)

Submissions: Publishes four titles per year; trade paperback, e-books, POD. Receives 30 submissions annually. 50% of books from first-time authors. Accepts manuscripts through agents or authors. Send proposal with sample chapters via email or mail. Prefers 100-300 pages. Royalty 50% of retail price, 50% for e-books; no advance. Average first printing, publication time, and response time vary. Guidelines by email.

Types and topics: nonfiction, fiction, children, teens, new adults, and adults; edgy topics that appeal to youngish non-Christians

Imprint: Siloam Springs Press

Tip: "Well-written and edited work is best. Not able to do major rewriting or editing. Lean toward, but not exclusively, Reformed thought. Our goal is to present the gospel to unbelievers and the Scriptures to believers."

EERDMANS BOOKS FOR YOUNG READERS

2140 Oak Industrial Dr. N.E., Grand Rapids, MI 49505 | 800-253-7521
616-459-4591 | youngreaders@eerdmans.com, info@eerdmans.co
www.eerdmans.com/youngreaders
Kathleen Merz, managing editor

Parent company: Wm. B. Eerdmans Publishing Co.

Submissions: Strives to publish books that are honest, wise, and hopeful—books that will stand the test of time. Submit by mail to Acquisitions Editor. For children and teens, send a proposal with three chapters for book length or complete manuscript for picture books. Publishes twelve to eighteen titles per year; hardcover, trade paperbacks, e-books. Receives 2,000-3,000 submissions annually. 10% of books from first-time authors. Accepts manuscripts through agents or authors. Length: picture books, 1,000 words; middle-grade books, 15,000 words; young adult, 35,000 words. Royalty 5-7% on retail, 7-9% on net; advance varies. Average first printing varies. Publication within one year for novels, two to three years for picture books. Responds in three to four months if interested.

Types and topics: picture books, middle reader, and young adult fiction and nonfiction; looking for stories that celebrate diversity, stories of historical significance, and stories that relate to contemporary social issues

Guidelines: *www.eerdmans.com/Pages/Item/2237/EBYR-Guidelines.aspx*

Tip: "We are always looking for well-written picture books and novels for young readers. Make sure that your submission is a unique, well-crafted story, and take a look at our current list of titles to get a sense of whether yours would be a good fit for us."

WM. B. EERDMANS PUBLISHING CO.

2140 Oak Industrial Dr. N.E., Grand Rapids, MI 49505 | 800-253-7521
616-459-4591 | info@eerdmans.com | www.eerdmans.com
James Earnest, editor-in-chief

Submissions: Publishes 120-130 titles per year; hardcover, trade paperbacks. Accepts manuscripts through agents or authors. Email proposal only. Royalty; some advances. Responds in six weeks.

Topics and types: adult nonfiction, textbooks, reference, biblical studies, theology, religious history and biography, ethics, spirituality, Christian living, ministry, social issues, contemporary cultural issues

Imprint: Eerdmans Books for Young Readers (see separate listing)
Guidelines: *www.eerdmans.com/Pages/About/Submission-Guidelines.aspx*
Tip: "Review submission guidelines carefully and check recent
catalogs for suitability. Target readerships range from academic
to semipopular. We are publishing a growing number of books in
Christian life, spirituality, and ministry."

eLECTIO PUBLISHING

4206 S. Mentor Ave., Springfield, MO 65804 | 972-987-0015
info@electiopublishing.com | www.electiopublishing.com
Acquisitions Editor, submissions@electiopublishing.com

Submissions: Publishes 60-100 titles per year. Receives 1,000+ per
year. 70-80% from first-time authors. Length: 25,000-100,000
words. Submit via email only. Responds in three months. Royalty
20%; no advance. Average first print run varies, depending on title.
Types and topics: Christian living, fiction (historical, romance,
mystery), Bible studies, memoirs, YA, African-American, Hispanic
Guidelines: *www.electiopublishing.com/index.php/abtelectio/sub-guide*
Tip: "Please read carefully the submissions guidelines listed on website."

ELK LAKE PUBLISHING, INC.

35 Dogwood Dr., Plymouth, MA 02360-3166 | 508-746-1734
ElkLakePublishingInc.com
Deb Haggerty, editor-in-chief, Deb@ElkLakePublishingInc.com

Submissions: Publishes twenty to thirty titles per year; receives sixty
per year. 80% from first-time authors. Length: 300 pages or fewer.
Send proposal with sample chapters via email; prefers submissions
from agents. Replies in two weeks. Royalty: 40% range. POD.
Preferred Bible version: NKJV or ESV.
Types and topics: fiction (romance, contemporary, speculative,
historical) and nonfiction, devotionals, children's, middle-grade, YA
Guidelines: *www.elklakepublishinginc.com/proposal-guidelines*
Tip: "Be concise, be edited well, be unusual."

ELLECHOR PUBLISHING HOUSE, LLC

Beaverton, OR 97006 | 559-744-3553
contactus@ellechorpublishing.com | www.ellechorpublishinghouse.com
Veronika Walker, managing editor | Sharon Jenkins, acquisitions editor

Submissions: Publishes fifteen titles per year. Receives 250
submissions annually. 90% of books from first-time authors.
Submit complete manuscript through the form on the website.
Responds in three to four weeks. Prefers no simultaneous

submissions. Accepts submissions through agents. Publishes trade paperbacks and e-books. Prefers 65,000 words or 280 pages. Royalty 10-30% on net, 30-50% for e-books; no advance. Average first printing 1,200. Publication within one year. Prefers KJV.

Types and topics: preschool, young adult, and adults; fiction; practical Christian living, questions and issues of contemporary Christian youth, women's concerns, singles

Guidelines: *www.ellechorpublishinghouse.com/faqs.cfm#how-to-submit*

EMPOWERED PUBLICATIONS, INC.

529 County Road 31, Millry, AL 36558 | 251-754-9335
www.empoweredpublications.com
Bridgett Henson, acquisitions editor, bridgett@empoweredpublications.com

Denomination: Conservative Pentecostal (Assemblies of God, Church of God, Independent Pentecostals)

Submissions: Publishes thirty-six titles per year; receives 500 per year. 80% from first-time authors. Length: 35,000 for nonfiction, 65,000- 80,000 for fiction. Send proposal with full manuscript via email. Replies in two weeks. Royalty: 8-30%. POD. Preferred Bible version: KJV. Guidelines on website.

Types and topics: Christian living, theology, biographies, pneumatology

Tip: "We prefer to publish ministers with an established platform."

ENCLAVE PUBLISHING

24 W. Camelback Rd. A-635, Phoenix, AZ 85013 | 602-336-8910
acquisitions@enclavepublishing.com | *www.enclavepublishing.com*
Steve Laube, publisher and acquisitions editor

Parent company: Gilead Publishing

Submissions: Enclave is the premier publisher of Christian fantasy and science fiction. Publishes twelve titles per year; trade paperbacks, e-books. Receives 500 submissions annually. 20-30% of books from first-time authors. Publishes for the adult reader but will consider YA; no middle grade. Submit proposal via the website form. Prefers 80,000 to 100,000 words. Royalties paid quarterly. Publication within nine to twelve months. Reports within forty-five days.

Types and topics: only speculative fiction (sci-fi, fantasy, supernatural)

Guidelines: *www.enclavepublishing.com/guidelines*

Tip: "Enclave is very author-friendly. From a personal connection to the publisher, Steve Laube, to contracts that are favorable to the author, we are a fellowship of Christians who write fiction."

EVERGREEN PRESS

5601-D Nevius Rd., Mobile, AL 36619 | 251-861-2525
www.evergreenpress.com
Brian Banashak and Kathy Banashak, editors-in-chief,
brian@evergreenpress.com

Parent company: Genesis Communications

Submissions: Publishes books that empower people for breakthrough living by being practical, biblical, and engaging. Publishes thirty titles per year. Receives 250 submissions annually. 40% of books from first-time authors. Accepts manuscripts through agents or authors. Submit proposal, query, or full manuscript with the Author and Book Submission Form on the website. Prefers 96-160 pages. Royalty on net; no advance. Average first printing 4,000. Publication within six months. Requires requested manuscript on CD or by email. Responds in four to six weeks.

Types and topics: Christian living, family and parenting, personal growth, business and finances, humor and pets, children's picture books, youth books, devotional and prayer, health and fitness, and recovery. Fiction: allegories, historical, fantasy and science fiction, mysteries, romance, and youth. Also does booklets.

Imprints: Gazelle Press, Axiom Press (POD for short runs), RevPress

Guidelines: *evergreenpress.com/for-authors*

Tip: "Most open to books with a specific market (targeted, not general) that the author is qualified to write for and that is relevant to today's believers and seekers. Author must also be open to editorial direction."

FAITH ALIVE CHRISTIAN RESOURCES

1700 28th St. S.E., Grand Rapids, MI 49508-1407 | 800-333-8300
616-224-0728 | Info@FaithAliveResources.org | www.faithaliveresources.org
Ruth Vanderhart, managing editor, rvanderhart@crcna.org

Denomination: Christian Reformed

Submissions: Submit via mail or email. Responds in one month.

Types and topics: educational curricula for children, teens, and adults; Bible studies; church leadership and training materials.

FAITHWALK PUBLISHING

5450 N. Dixie Hwy., Lima, OH 45807 | 419-227-1818
submissions@faithwalkpublishing.com | faithwalkpublishing.com

Submissions: Send a short email initially with sample as an attachment, or use the online submission form. Responds only if interested. Publishes print, ebooks, and audio.

Types and topics: Christian living, romance, mystery/thriller, children's
Guidelines: *faithwalkpublishing.com/submissions*

FAITHWORDS

10 Cadillac Dr., Ste. 220, Brentwood, TN 37027 | 615-221-0996
www.faithwords.com

Parent company: Hachette Book Group USA
Submissions: Through agents only.
Types and topics: devotionals, fiction, Christian living, spiritual
growth
Tip: "Many of our authors are pastors and Bible teachers."

FATHER'S PRESS

590 N.W. 1921 St. Rd., Kingsville, MO 64061-9312 | 816-566-0654
mike@fatherspress.com | *www.fatherspress.com*
Mike Smitley, editor

Submissions: Accepts manuscripts only through authors; no agents.
Send proposal. Responds in four weeks. Bible versions: KJV, ESV.
Types and topics: fiction (contemporary or historical), historical
nonfiction, reference, children's books, biblical studies, theology,
ethics, literature, religious history, regional history, cookbooks,
self-help, Christian counseling
Guidelines: *fatherspress.com/?page_id=2380*
Tip: "Father's Press is a rapidly-growing, full-service publishing
company dedicated to publishing well-written works by dynamic,
energetic new authors who are frustrated with the endless barriers
that have historically locked talented authors out of the writing
profession."

FIRST STEPS PUBLISHING

PO Box 571, Gleneden Beach, OR 97388 | 541-961-7641
www.FirstStepsPublishing.com
Suzanne Parrott, owner, publisher, sparrott@firststepspublishing.com

Submissions: Publishes four or five titles per year; receives ten
proposals per year. 99% of our books are from first time authors.
Length: children's, 700 words minimum; fiction and nonfiction,
30,000-150,000 words; sometimes shorter or longer, depending
on the topic. Email proposal with sample pages only through the
online form at www.firststepspublishing.com/get-published/
submissions. Responds in seven to fifteen days. Royalty: 15-50%,
higher for special cases; no advance. Most books are POD, but
traditional print runs average 500-1,000 to start. Preferred Bible

version: ASV, NKJV. Also designs promotional materials and table displays and helps authors with social-media promotion.

Types and topics: fiction: fantasy, historical, humor, contemporary, mystery; memoir, biography, self-help, family, faith, struggle, war, adoption, sibling rivalry, bullying; educational learning tools

Imprints: White Parrot Press (Pre-K-6th grade), West Wind Press (middle grade-young adult)

Guidelines: *www.firststepspublishing.com/get-published*

Tip: "Being authors ourselves, we've been on both sides of the fence. With more than thirty-five years of experience, we know the quality and service you want and deserve from a publisher. As your publisher, we are seeking undiscovered authors whose work is exciting and fresh and who have the potential to grow to success. With First Steps Publishing, you will never be just another 'writer.' We believe in working side-by-side with each of our authors, helping you build a solid foundation to your writing career."

FOCUS ON THE FAMILY

8605 Explorer Dr., Colorado Springs, CO 80995 | 719-531-5181
www.focusonthefamily.com

Submissions: Accepts manuscripts only via established literary agents or manuscript services. Only specific types of books are being considered.

Types and topics: family advice topics, including resources about specific elements of marriage and parenting, encouragement for women, and topics for seniors

Guidelines: *family.custhelp.com/app/answers/detail/a_id/4501/related/1*

FORGET ME NOT ROMANCES

PO Box 8047, Surprise, AZ 85374 | 623-910-4279
www.forgetmenotromances.com
Cynthia Hickey, editor, cynthiahickey@outlook.com

Parent company: Winged Publications

Submissions: Publishes twenty-five titles per year; receives 50 per year. 10% from first-time authors. Length: 45,000-80,000 words. Send proposal with sample chapters via email. Replies in two weeks. Royalty: 60%; sometimes gives advance. Publishes POD. Bible version: NIV.

Types and topics: only fiction: historical romance, contemporary romance, romantic suspense, cozy mystery; clean, wholesome stories

Guidelines: *forgetmenotromances.com/for-authors/submissions*

Tip: "Have a good grasp of the craft; but, most importantly, tell a good story."

FORTRESS PRESS

PO Box 1209, Minneapolis, MN 55440-1209
www.fortresspress.com

>   **Denomination:** Evangelical Lutheran Church in America
>   **Parent company:** 1517 Media
>   **Submissions:** Submit via the online form.
>   **Types and topics:** scholarly works in biblical studies, theology, and Christian history
>   **Guidelines:** *fortresspress.com/submissions*

FORWARD MOVEMENT

412 Sycamore St., Cincinnati, OH 45202-4110 | 800-543-1813
editorial@forwardmovement.org | *www.forwardmovement.org*

>   **Denomination:** Episcopal Church
>   **Submissions:** Focuses on discipleship. Submit through email. Responds in four to six weeks. Publishes print, e-books, PDF downloads, and smartphone applications.
>   **Types and topics:** prayer, spiritual practices, stewardship, church traditions, emerging trends, Bible study
>   **Guidelines:** *www.forwardmovement.org/Pages/About/Writers_Guidelines.aspx*

FOUR CRAFTSMEN PUBLISHING

PO Box U, Lakeside, AZ 85929-0585 | 928-367-2076
info@fourcraftsmen.com | *www.fourcraftsmen.com*
Martin Jackson, publisher | *Cecelia Jackson, chief editor*

>   **Submissions:** Publishes three books per year; receives three to five. 100% from first-time authors. Length: 40,000-80,000 words. Submit proposal with sample chapters or full manuscript via email or mail. Responds in two to three weeks. Royalty range: 10-60%; no advance. Average first print run: 25. Preferred Bible versions: NASV, NKJV, NIV.
>   **Types and topics:** testimonies, teachings, Christian living, finances, testimonies, adventures in closed nations, healing, spiritual war
>   **Guidelines:** via email
>   **Tip:** "Submit 3-5 chapters with outline; encourage active walking with/by the Holy Spirit; write with active verbs; reveal yourself and Jesus, not other commentators or writers."

FRANCISCAN MEDIA

28 W. Liberty St., Cincinnati, OH 45202 | 800-488-0488
513-241-5615 | info@franciscanmedia.org | www.FranciscanMedia.org
Mark Lombard, director, acquisitions, MLombard@FranciscanMedia.org

Denomination: Catholic

Submissions: Seeks manuscripts that inform and inspire adult Catholics, other Christians, and all who are seeking to better understand and live their faith. Goal is to help people "Live in love. Grow in faith." Publishes twenty to thirty books per year. Submit proposal by email or mail. Responds in one to three months. Royalty 10-14% on net; advance, $1,000-3,000. Prefers 25,000-50,000 words or 100-250 pages. Average first printing 4,000. Prefers NRSV. No simultaneous submissions.

Topics and types: Christian living, spiritual growth, fiction

Guidelines: *www.franciscanmedia.org/writers-guide*

FRIENDS UNITED PRESS

101 Quaker Hill Dr., Richmond, IN 47374 | 765-962-7573
friendspress@fum.org | friendsunitedmeeting.org

Denomination: Quaker

Submissions: Submit proposal with two or three chapters by mail or email; responds in three to six months. Publishes two to five books per year. Royalty 7.5%; no advance.

Types and topics: Quaker/Friends history, theology, biography, spirituality, peace, and justice

Guidelines: *shop.fum.org/category_s/38.htm*

GILEAD PUBLISHING

Grand Rapids, MI and Wheaton, IL
www.gileadpublishing.com
Susan Brower, vice president of editorial

Submissions: Submissions from agents only or meeting an editor at a writers conference.

Types and topics: fiction only: contemporary, romance, historical, science fiction/fantasy, mystery/suspense

GRACE ACRES PRESS

PO Box 22, Larkspur, CO 80118 | 303-681-9995
www.GraceAcresPress.com
Anne R. Fenske, editor, Anne@graceacrespress.com

Submissions: Publishes six books per year; receives 50. 90% from first-time authors. Preferred book length: 150-350 pages. Submit proposal with sample chapters via email or mail. Responds in one month. Royalty range: 10-15%; no advance. Average first print run: 1,500. Preferred Bible versions: NKJV, NASB, NIV.

Types and topics: biography, memoir, Bible study, missions, dispensational theology

Guidelines: PDF download from website

Tip: "Bring a substantial audience."

GRACE PUBLISHING

PO Box 1233, Broken Arrow, OK 74013-1233 | 918-346-7960
editorial@grace-publishing.com | *www.grace-publishing.com*
Terri Kalfas, publisher

Submissions: Queries or proposals with three consecutive chapters via email. Publishes five to ten titles per year; trade paperbacks, e-books, POD. Receives 250 submissions per year. 50% first-time authors. Accepts submissions directly from authors. Preferred book length: 40,000 words, 160 pages. Royalty 12-15% on net, 25% on e-books; no advance. Outright purchase varies. First run varies. Publication within one year. Responds in four months. Preferred Bible version: NIV. Also does booklets, mini books, and pamphlets.

Types and topics: Bible studies, devotionals, fiction, Christian living, leader's resources, children/homeschooling

Guidelines: grace-publishing.com/manuscript-submission

Tip: "Well written with a unique approach. Our intent is to make Christian authors and their works easily accessible to the Christian body around the world in every form of media possible; to develop and distribute—with integrity and excellence—biblically-based resources that challenge, encourage, teach, equip, and entertain Christians young and old in their personal journeys."

GROUP PUBLISHING, INC.

1515 Cascade Ave., Loveland, CO 80538 | 800-447-1070, 970-669-3836
PuorgBus@group.com | *www.group.com*

Submissions: To equip churches to help children, youth, and adults grow in their relationship with Jesus. Submit proposal with sample chapters via email or mail. Publishes more than thirty titles per year; trade paperbacks, e-books. Receives 200+ submissions annually. 50% of books from first-time authors. Accepts manuscripts directly from authors. Prefers 128-250 pages. Outright purchases of $250-3,000 or royalty of 8-10% of net; advance of $3,000. Average first printing 5,000. Publication within twelve to eighteen months. Responds in three months. Prefers NLT.

Topics and types: Practical ministry tools and resource books for chldren's, youth and young adult, adult and pastoral, and women's ministries with an emphasis on active learning. See complete list in the guidelines.

Guidelines: *www.group.com/customer-support/submissions*

Tip: "Most open to a practical resource that will help church leaders change lives; innovative, active/interactive learning. Tell our readers something they don't already know, in a way that they've not seen before."

GUARDIAN ANGEL PUBLISHING, INC.

12430 Tesson Ferry Rd. #186, St. Louis, MO 63128 | 314-276-8482
editorial_staff@guardianangelpublishing.com
www.guardianangelpublishing.com
Lynda S. Burch, publisher

Submissions: Goal is to inspire children to learn and grow and develop character skills to instill a Christian and healthy attitude of learning, caring, and sharing. Publishes sixty to seventy-five titles per year; trade paperbacks, some hardcover, e-books, POD. Receives 600-800 submissions annually. 15% of books from first-time authors. Prefers 500-5,000 words. Royalty 30-50%; no advance. Average first printing 50-100. Publication within twenty-four to thirty-six months. No simultaneous submissions. Responds in a month. Send manuscripts by email only. Submissions are open only July 1 to August 31.

Types and topics: all kinds of books for kids ages 0-12, nonfiction and fiction

Imprints: Wings of Faith, Angel to Angel, Angelic Harmony, Littlest Angels, Academic Wings, Guardian Angel Animals & Pets, Spanish Editions, Guardian Angel Health & Hygiene

Guidelines: *www.guardianangelpublishing.com/submissions.htm*

Tip: "**Most** open to books that teach children to read and love books, to learn or grow from books, and are educational."

GUIDEPOSTS BOOKS

110 William St., Ste. 901, New York, NY 10038 | 212-251-8100
bookeditors@guideposts.org | *www.guideposts.org*
Jon Woodhams, fiction editor | *Tarice L. S. Gray, nonfiction editor*

Submissions: Extremely limited acquisitions. Accepts manuscripts through agents only. Publishes twenty to thirty titles per year.

Types and topics: inspirational memoir, Christian living; contemporary women's fiction focusing on faith, family, and friendships

HANNIBAL BOOKS

313 S. 11th Street, Ste. A, Garland, TX 75040 | 800-747-0738
louismoore@hannibalbooks.com | www.hannibalbooks.com
Louis Moore, publisher

> **Submissions:** Not currently accepting new submissions, but check the website for changes in this situation.
>
> **Types and topics:** missions, marriage and family, critical issues, Bible-study curriculum

HARBOURLIGHT BOOKS

PO Box 1738, Aztec, NM 87410
inquiry@harbourlightbooks.com | www.pelicanbookgroup.com
Nicola Martinez, editor-in-chief

> **Parent company:** Pelican Book Group
>
> **Submissions:** Novels 25,000-80,000 words. Interested in series ideas. Publishes limited-edition hardback, trade paperbacks, and e-books. Royalty 40% on download, 7% on print. Pays nominal advance. Accepts unagented submissions. Responds to queries in one month, full manuscript in three months. Email submissions through the website form.
>
> **Types and topics:** fiction: action-adventure, mystery (cozy or other), suspense, crime drama, police procedural, family saga, westerns, women's fiction
>
> **Guidelines:** *pelicanbookgroup.com/ec/index.php?main_page=page&id=55&zenid=06f25d411f1d61bfa008693b5b246c4*

HARPERCOLLINS CHRISTIAN PUBLISHING

See Thomas Nelson and Zondervan.

HARPERLEGEND

353 Sacramento St. #500, San Francisco, CA 94111-3653
415-477-4400 | www.harperlegend.com

> **Parent company:** HarperOne
>
> **Submissions:** Must submit using the online form. Works directly with authors. Preferred length: 50-60,000 words. If no response after three months, assume your manuscript has been rejected; you will not receive notice of this. E-books only; may do print later. Royalties: 25-50%.
>
> **Types and topics:** Fiction only. "If you have a novel (or a trilogy or a series) that communicates wisdom, insight, transformation and/or personal growth, bring them on. We want fresh voices,

great characters, compelling storylines, and original ideas and approaches. These novels may have many different stripes and flavors including Christian, ... as long it is transformational."

HARPERONE

353 Sacramento St. #500, San Francisco, CA 94111-3653
415-477-4400 | harperone.hc.com
Julia Pastore, executive editor, Julie.pastore@harpercollins.com

> **Parent company:** HarperCollins Publishing
> **Submissions:** Requires manuscripts through agents only. Publishes seventy-five titles per year; hardcover, trade paperbacks. Receives 10,000 submissions annually. 5% of books from first-time authors. Prefers 160-256 pages. Royalty 7.5-15% on retail; advance $20,000-100,000. Average first printing 10,000. Publication within eighteen months. Responds in three months.
> **Types and topics:** religion, spirituality

HARRISON HOUSE PUBLISHERS

Box 35035, Tulsa, OK 74153 | 800-888-4126, 918-523-5400
www.harrisonhouse.com
Julie Werner, acquisitions, juliew@harrisonhouse.com

> **Denomination:** Charismatic
> **Submissions:** Not currently accepting any proposals or manuscripts, but check the webstie for changes in this situation.
> **Types and topics:** children, fiction, Christian living, devotionals, family, finances, health and healing, Holy Spirit, men's and women's issues, ministry resources, prayer, restoration and recover, youth
> **Guidelines:** *www.harrisonhouse.com/client/client_pages/publishing.cfm*

HARVEST HOUSE PUBLISHERS

990 Owen Loop N., Eugene, OR 97402
harvesthousepublishers.com

> **Submissions:** Requires submissions through agents.
> **Types and topics:** self-help (relationships, family, Christian living), Bible resources (Bible studies, topical studies), and full-color gift and children's books; no longer accepts fiction.
> **Guidelines:** *www.harvesthousepublishers.com/about/manuscript-submissions*

HENDRICKSEN PUBLISHERS

137 Summit St., PO Box 3473, Peabody, MA 01961
www.hendrickson.com
Rick Brown, publisher, rbrown@hendrickson.com

Submissions: Works only through agents or direct contact at various conferences editors attend throughout the year (most notably, the AAR/SBL annual meeting).

Types and topics: academic, Bible studies, marriage and parenting resources, new media and the arts, biblical studies and reference works for both pastors and thoughtful laypersons, devotionals, classic fiction, Christian classics, and prolife resources.

Guidelines: *www.hendrickson.com/content/getting-published*

HOPE PUBLISHING HOUSE

PO Box 60008, Pasadena, CA 91106 | 626-792-6123
hopepublishinghouse@gmail.com | www.hope-pub.com
Faith A. Sand, publisher

Parent company: Southern California Ecumenical Council

Submissions: Produces thinking books that challenge the faith community to be serious about their pilgrimage of faith. Publishes six titles per year. Query only first. Receives forty submissions annually. 30% of books from first-time authors. No manuscripts through agents. Prefers 200 pages. Royalty 10% on net; no advance. Average first printing 3,000. Publication within six months. No simultaneous submissions. Accepts manuscripts by email. Responds in three months. Prefers NRSV.

Types and topics: Christian living, church life, biography, young readers

Tip: "Most open to a well-written manuscript, with correct grammar, that is provocative, original, challenging, and informative."

HOWARD BOOKS

216 Centerview Dr., Ste. 303, Brentwood, TN 37027-3226 | 615-873-2080
simonandschusterpublishing.com/howard-books
Philis Boultinghouse, senior editor, nonfiction, Philis.Boultinghouse@
simonandschuster.com | Beth Adams, fiction acquisitions, beth.adams@
simonandschuster.com | Jonathan Merkh, Jonathan.Merkh@simonand-
schuster.com

Parent company: Simon & Schuster

Submissions: Does not accept, review, or return unsolicited manuscripts, except through agents.

Types and topics: inspirational memoir, Christian living, self-help, fiction with authors who have established track records or platforms, growing list of African-American authors

IMAGE BOOKS

1745 Broadway, New York, NY 10019 | 212-782-9000
imagebooks@randomhouse.com

crownpublishing.com/imprint/image-catholic-books
Gary Jansen, director
> **Parent company:** Crown Publishing Group, which is part of Penguin
> Random House
> **Denomination:** Catholic
> **Submissions:** Takes submissions only from agents.

INTERVARSITY PRESS

PO Box 1400, Downers Grove, IL 60515-1426 | 630-734-4000
email@ivpress.com | *www.ivpress.com*
Cindy Bunch, editorial director
> **Parent company:** InterVarsity Christian Fellowship
> **Submissions:** Publishes 110-120 titles per year; hardcover, trade
> paperbacks, e-books. Receives 1,300 submissions annually. 15%
> of books from first-time authors. Accepts manuscripts through
> agents or if you have had direct contact with an editor. Prefers
> 50,000 words or 200 pages. Negotiable royalty on retail or outright
> purchase; negotiable advance. Average first printing 5,000.
> Publication within one year. Prefers NIV, NRSV. Accepts email
> submissions after acceptance.
> **Types and topics:** IVP books are characterized by a thoughtful,
> biblical approach to the Christian life that transforms the hearts,
> souls, and minds of readers in the university, church, and the
> world, on topics ranging from spiritual disciplines to apologetics,
> to current issues, to theology. Especially looking for ethnic writers
> (African-American, Hispanic, Asian-American).
> **Imprints:** IVP Academic, Dan Reid, editor; IVP Books, Al Hsu,
> editor; IVP Connect (Bible studies and small-group resources);
> Formatio (spiritual formation); IVP Cresendo (women's books);
> IVP Praxis (ministry)
> **Guidelines:** *www.ivpress.com/submissions/guidelines.php*
> **Tip:** "Most open to books written by pastors (though not collections
> of sermons) or other church staff, by professors, by leaders in
> Christian organizations. Authors need to bring resources for
> publicizing and selling their own books, such as a website, an
> organization they are part of that will promote their books,
> speaking engagements, well-known people they know personally
> who will endorse and promote their book, writing articles for
> national publication, etc."

JOURNEY FICTION

3342 Cape Cod Dr., Las Vegas, NV 89122 | 702-570-3433
www.journeyfiction.com
Jennifer L. Farey, acquisitions, contact@journeyfiction.com

Submissions: Publishes ten to twenty books per year. 50% from first-time authors. Length: 50,000-90,000 words. Send proposal with sample chapters or full manuscript via email. Prefers series. Responds in two weeks. Royalty range: 50-60% of net sales; no advance. Publishes POD. Preferred Bible version: NKJV.

Types and topics: fiction only: romance, suspense, mystery, historical, women's fiction, speculative

Guidelines: *www.journeyfiction.com/for-authors*

Tip: "We want to introduce readers to stories which are so compelling they don't want them to end. Because of that, we're especially interested in series of three or more books."

JOURNEYFORTH/BJU PRESS

1700 Wade Hampton Blvd., Greenville, SC 29614 | 864-370-1800, ext. 4350
journeyforth@bju | *www.bjupress.com, www.journeyforth.com*
Nancy Lohr, acquisitions editor

Parent company: Bob Jones University

Submissions: Publishes eight to twelve titles per year; trade paperbacks. Receives 300 submissions annually. 10% of books from first-time authors. Accepts manuscripts directly from authors. Royalty. Average first printing varies. Publication within twelve to eighteen months. Submit proposal with three to five chapters (five for fiction) by email or mail; no multiple submissions. Responds in three to four months.

Types and topics: youth fiction and biographies that reflect a biblical worldview, Bible studies (topical and/or exegetical) and Christian living for teens and adults that encourage thoughtful interaction with Scripture and stress practical application of spiritual truth, Christian ministry, family, apologetics for laymen

Guidelines: *www.bjupress.com/books/freelance.php*; free catalog on request with SASE

Tip: "Please do not submit picture books, poetry, speculative fiction, teen romance, adult fiction, or memoir. Make sure your manuscript is well-written with a creative or unique approach to your topic. Take a look at our website to see whether your book would complement ours."

JUDSON PRESS

PO Box 851, Valley Forge, PA 19482-0851 | 800-458-3766
acquisitions@judsonpress.com | *www.judsonpress.com*
Rebecca Irwin-Diehl, editor, Rebecca.Irwin-Diehl@abhms.org

Parent company: American Baptist Churches USA/American Baptist Home Mission Societies

Submissions: Is theologically moderate, historically Baptist, and in ministry to empower, enrich, and equip disciples of Jesus and leaders in Christ's church. Publishes ten to twelve titles per year; hardcover, trade paperbacks. Receives 800 submissions annually. 25% of books from first-time authors. Submit query or proposal with two chapters. Accepts manuscripts directly by authors. Prefers 100-200 pages or 30,000-75,000 words. Royalty 10-15% on net; some work-for-hire agreements or outright purchases. Occasional advance of $300. Average first printing 3,000. Publication within eighteen months. Requires accepted submissions by email. Responds in four to six months. Prefers NRSV or CEB.

Types and topics: practical resources for the church and leaders: pastoral and sermon helps, ministry resources, Christian education and discipleship studies, seasonal program resources; multicultural books: church resources, sermons and preaching helps, inspirational and Christian living; Baptist history and identity, especially for theologically moderate Baptists; books for African-Americans, North American Asians, and Hispanics

Guidelines: *www.judsonpress.com/contact_us_manuscript_submissions.cfm*

Tip: "Most open to practical books that are unique and compelling, for a clearly defined niche audience. Theologically and socially we are a moderate publisher. And we like to see a detailed marketing plan from an author committed to partnering with us."

KENDALL NEFF PUBLISHING

PO Box 22, Talladega, AL 35160 | 256-368-1559
publr@KendallNeff.com | *www.KendallNeff.com*
Dr. Tana N. Thompson, publisher

Submissions: Publishes fewer than ten titles per year; hardcover and trade paperbacks.

Types and topics: projects that are spiritual, secular, or educational in nature, ranging from print books to digital downloads of audio, video, or text media, including children's picture books, devotionals, self-help works, and children's activity pages

Tip: "We are especially looking for products (stories, gift, and specialty products) to add to a new platform at LU.us. Send inquiries to publisher for product ideas."

KREGEL PUBLICATIONS

2450 Oak Industrial Dr. N.E., Grand Rapids, MI 49505 | 616-451-4775
kregelbooks@kregel.com | *www.kregel.com*

Submissions: Evangelical/conservative company. Does not accept unsolicited proposals or manuscripts for review. Submit only through agents or manuscript-review services. Does joint publishing with Parker Press, an imprint for African-American ministry leaders.

Types and topics: biblical studies, biography, Bible reference, children's, Christian living, church/ministry, fiction (YA, historical, romance), marriage and family, theology

Guidelines: *www.kregel.com/contact-us/submissions-policy*

LANGMARC PUBLISHING

PO Box 90488, Austin, TX 78709-0488 | 512-394-0989
langmarc@booksails.com | *www.langmarc.com*
Lois Qualben, publisher

Denomination: Lutheran

Submissions: Focuses on spiritual growth of readers. Publishes three to five titles per year; hardcover, trade paperbacks. Receives 230 submissions annually. 60% of books from first-time authors. Accepts manuscripts directly from authors. Submit proposal with three chapters. Prefers 150-300 pages. Royalty 10-14% on net; no advance. Average first printing varies. Publication usually within eighteen months. Responds in three months. Requires requested manuscript on CD. Prefers NIV.

Types and topics: Christian living, devotionals for teens and adults, Bible studies, humor

Tip: "Most open to inspirational books."

LEAFWOOD PUBLISHERS

ACU, PO Box 29138, Abilene, TX 79699
manuscriptsubmissions@groupmail.acu.edu | *www.leafwoodpublishers.com*

Parent company: Abilene Christian University

Submissions: Works directly with authors. Email proposal.

Types and topics: Christian living, women's issues, spiritual disciplines, and leadership. We do not accept manuscript submissions for poetry, children's books, or fiction.

Guidelines: *store.acupressbooks.com/pages/author-resources*

LEGACY PRESS

See RoseKidz Books.

LEXHAM PRESS

1313 Commercial St., Bellingham, WA 98225
editor@lexampress.com | *www.lexampress.com*
Dr. Brannon Ellis, publisher, brannon.ellis@faithlife.com

Parent company: FaithLife Corporation, makers of Logos Bible Software

Submissions: Publishes print, e-books, and innovative resources for Logos Bible Software. Will work directly with authors. Email proposal and one or two sample chapters.

Types and topics: evangelical scholarly and pastoral works in the areas of biblical studies (including Bible reference and original language resources); biblical, historical, and systematic theology; and ministry resources

Guidelines: *www.lexhampress.com/manuscript-submission*

LIGHTHOUSE PUBLISHING OF THE CAROLINAS

2333 Barton Oaks Dr., Raleigh, NC 27614
lighthousepublishingcarolinas@gmail.com |
lighthousepublishingofthecarolinas.com, heritagebeaconfiction.com,
fireflysouthernfiction.com, blingromance.com, brimstonefiction.com,
candlelightfiction.com, guidinglightfiction.com, sonrisedevotionals.com,
straightstreetbooks.com
Eddie Jones, founder/CEO, See websites for imprint editors

Submissions: Publishes more than forty titles per year; POD paperbacks, e-books. Receives 300+ submissions annually. 40% of books from first-time authors. Prefers/accepts submissions through agents or writers whom editors meet at conferences. Query first via email. Length varies; with POD, the fewer words the better. Monthly royalty about 40% of net for print, e-books, and audiobooks; no advance (subject to change). Publication within one year. Reports within three months. We take chances on debut authors and established authors who understand that the book publishing industry is changing fast. We care less about pedigree and more about story, message, and an author's ability to market the book online. If you can accept that your book might never see the inside of a bookstore but may sell thousands online through Amazon, then Lighthouse might be a good fit for you.

Types and topics: nonfiction, fiction, devotionals

Guidelines: *lighthousepublishingofthecarolinas.com/submissions*

Imprints: Bling! Romance, Heritage Beacon Fiction, Firefly Southern Fiction, Brimstone Fiction, Candlelight Romance, Guiding Light Women's Fiction, SonRise Devotionals, Straight Street Books

Tip: "You've heard the question: 'How do I make an editor sit up and beg for my manuscript?' Know who your main character is, what she wants, and how she will be transformed. Hint: the character who changes the most during the story is your lead character. Be prepared to answer the question: 'How would you like your reader to feel at the end of the story and what do you want readers to learn?' See imprint submission guidelines for more tips on what our editors want."

LIGHTHOUSE TRAILS PUBLISHING, LLC

PO Box 908, Eureka, MT 59917 | 406-889-3610
david@lighthousetrails.com | *www.lighthousetrails.com*
David Dombrowski, acquisitions editor

Submissions: Publishes four titles per year. Receives fifty to seventy-five submissions annually. 30% of books from first-time authors. Accepts manuscripts directly from authors. Prefers 160-300 pages. Royalty 12-17% of net, 20% of retail. Publication within nine to twelve months. Email (as attachment) a proposal with two sample chapters, or mail it on a CD. Responds in two months. Prefers KJV.

Types and topics: Publishes books that bring clarity and light to areas of spiritual darkness or deception. Always interested in stories of Christians who have risen above incredible and unusual challenges and even their own failures to illustrate God's amazing grace and strength to overcome. Well-written submissions about or by missionaries. Fiction for all ages: "We are looking for a fiction book or fiction series that would include elements from our nonfiction books exposing the emerging church and mystical/New Age spirituality; Bible prophecy/eschatological."

Guidelines: *www.lighthousetrails.com/content/11-submit-manuscript*

Tip: "Any book we consider will not only challenge the more scholarly reader, but also be able to reach those who may have less experience and comprehension. Our books will include human interest and personal experience scenarios as a means of getting the point across. Read a couple of our books to better understand the style of writing we are looking for. Also check our research website for an in-depth look at who we are (*www.lighthousetrailsresearch.com*). We also have a doctrinal statement on our website that helps to define us."

LITTLE LAMB BOOKS

PO Box 1302, Euless, TX 76039
subs@littlelambbooks.com ; | *www.littlelambbooks.com*
Rachel LaMonica Pellegrino, managing editor

Submissions: Length: middle grade for ages 8-12, 30,000-60,000 words; young adult for ages 13-18, 50,000-80,000 words. Email query only. Responds in five to eight weeks.

Types and topics: contemporary Christian/inspirational, comedy/humorous, mystery and suspense, action and adventure, science fiction and fantasy, middle grade, young adult.

Guidelines: download from the website

Tip: "We are looking for stories and characters that will enrich the lives of our readers, encourage boys and girls in their faith, and inspire young minds to think positively about themselves and the ways they can impact the world around them."

LION HUDSON

Wilkinson House, Jordan Hill Rd., Oxford OX2 8DR, UK
SubmissionstoLionBooksMonarchLionFiction@LionHudson.com
www.lionhudson.com
Becki Bradshaw, Lion Books, BeckiB@lionhudson.com | Simon Cox, Monarch Books, simonc@lionhudson.com | Jessica Tinker, Lion fiction, jessicat@lionhudson.com

Submissions: Publishes internationally; distributed in the U.S. by Kregel Publications. Email or mail a proposal and sample chapters or manuscript; mail only for children's books. If no response in three months, consider it a rejection.

Types and topics: Lion Books, Lion Children's Books, Lion Fiction: accessible books that reflect a Christian worldview to a general audience. Candle Books, Monarch Books: support Christian families, individuals and communities in their devotional and spiritual lives.

Guidelines: *www.lionhudson.com/page/contact*

LITURGICAL PRESS

2950 St. John's Rd., PO Box 7500, Collegeville, MN 56321-7500
submissions@litpress.org | www.litpress.org

Denomination: Catholic

Submissions: Email or mail proposal, using the downloadable Project Summary Form and Author Biography Form from the website.

Types and topics: biography, vocation, commentaries, chidren's, church, discipleship, liturgy, marriage and family, prayer, preaching, Bible reference books, theology, spriituality

Guidelines: *www.litpress.org/Authors/submit_manuscript*

LOVE INSPIRED

195 Broadway, 24th floor, New York, NY 10007 | 212-207-7900
www.harlequin.com

Tina James, executive editor, Tina_James@harlequin.ca | Melissa Endlich, senior editor, Melissa_Endlich@harlequin.ca | Emily Rodmell, editor, Emily_Rodmell@harlequin.ca

Parent company: Harlequin Enterprises

Submissions: Inspirational romances that feature characters facing the many challenges of life and live in today's world. Publishes 192 titles per year; mass-market paperbacks. Receives 500-1,000 submissions annually. 15% of books from first-time authors. Accepts manuscripts directly from authors. Royalty on retail; competitive advance. Publication within one to two years. Email either the first three chapters and up to a five-page synopsis or the full manuscript and synopsis. Responds in three months. Prefers KJV.

Types and topics: Love Inspired: contemporary romance, 55,000 words. Love Inspired Historical: historical romance, 70,000 words. Love Inspired Suspense: contemporary romantic suspense, 55,000 words.

Guidelines: *harlequin.submittable.com/submit*

LOVE2READLOVE2WRITE PUBLISHING, LLC
(L2L2 PUBLISHING)

PO Box 103, Camby, IN 46113 | 317-550-9755
www.love2readlove2writepublishing.com
Michele Israel Harper, acquisitions editor,
editor@love2readlove2writepublishing.com

Submissions: Publishes four to six titles per year POD; receives thirty to fifty proposals. 90% from first-time authors. Length: 60,000-120,000. Email proposal with full manuscript. Replies in six to eight weeks. Royalty: 50% of net. Advance: $50, will increase as we grow. Preferred Bible version: NKJV.

Types and topics: Christian or clean speculative fiction only; YA fantasy, paranormal, supernatural, dystopian, science fiction. Also will do coloring books and journals in the near future.

Guidelines: *www.love2readlove2writepublishing.com/submissions*

Tip: "Be professional, be succinct, and know your audience."

LOYOLA PRESS

3441 N. Ashland Ave., Chicago, IL 60657 | 773-281-1818
800-621-1008 | editorial@loyolapress.com | www.loyolapress.com
Joseph Durepos, acquisitions editor, durepos@loyolapress.com

Denomination: Catholic

Submissions: Publishes twenty titles per year; hardcover, trade paperbacks. Receives 500 submissions annually. Accepts manuscripts directly from authors. Email proposal with sample chapters. Prefers 25,000-75,000 words or 150-300 pages. Standard royalty; reasonable advance. Average first printing 7,500-10,000. Considers first-time authors without agents. Responds in three months. Prefers NRSV (Catholic Edition).

Types and topics: books that help people experience God in their lives more directly, that introduce the dynamics of the Spiritual Exercises and the Ignatian process of discernment and decision-making, and that open up Scripture as a way of encountering Jesus and books that introduce and explain Catholic tradition and the richness of our faith

Guidelines: *www.loyolapress.com/general/submissions*

Tip: "Looking for books and authors that help make Catholic faith relevant and offer practical tools for the well-lived spiritual life."

MANTLE ROCK PUBLISHING COMPANY

2879 Palma Rd., Benton, KY 42025 | 270-493-1560
mantlerockpublishing@gmail.com | *mantlerockpublishing.com*
Jerry and Katherine Cretsinger, publishers

Submissions: Novellas, 15,000-69,000 words; novels, 65,000-80,000 words; historical novels, 6,000-110,000 words. Email proposal with three sample chapters; put "proposal" in subject line.

Types and topics: historical and contemporary novels and novellas of most genres except sci-fi. No children's chapter books at this time. Accepting historical romance, historical romantic suspense, contemporary romance, contemporary romantic suspense

Guidelines: mantlerockpublishing.com/submissions-and-guidelines

Tip: "We prefer manuscripts that have been edited before sending to us. A well-edited manuscript will receive our attention quicker."

MASTER BOOKS

PO Box 726, Green Forest, AR 72638 | 800-999-3777
www.nlpg.com/submissions | *www.masterbooks.com*

Parent company: New Leaf Publishing Group

Submissions: See New Leaf Press.

Types and topics: young-earth creation material for all ages, including apologetics, homeschool resources, science and the Bible, reference titles, and children's literature

Guidelines: *www.nlpg.com/submissions*

MATERIAL MEDIA, LLC

5150 Broadway #466, San Antonio, TX 71209 | 210-508-5553
www.MaterialMedia.com
ELizabeth Cauthorn, owner, ELizabeth@MaterialMedia.com

> **Submissions:** Publishes five books per year. 50% from first-time authors. Not accepting manuscripts at this time, but check the website for changes in this situation. Responds in two months. Royalty range: 10%; no advance. Average first print run: 2,000. Also does audiobooks.
>
> **Types and topics:** prayer, contemporary fiction, historical fiction, meditation, memoir
>
> **Imprint:** New Beginnings
>
> **Guidelines:** via email
>
> **Tip:** We have a significant online presence.

MOODY PUBLISHERS

820 N. LaSalle Blvd., Chicago, IL 60610
www.moodypublishers.com

> **Parent company:** Moody Bible Institute
>
> **Submissions:** Moody Publishers exists to resource the church's work of discipling all people. Publishes fifty to sixty titles per year; hardcover, trade paperbacks, mass-market paperbacks, and e-books. Receives 3,000 submissions annually; 20% of books from first-time authors. Does not accept unsolicited manuscripts in any category; must be submitted by a literary agent, an author who has published with Moody, a Moody Bible Institute employee, or a personal contact at a writers conference. Royalty paid on net; advances begin at $500. Publication within one year. Responds in one to two months. Bible version: prefers NASB, ESV, NKJV. Query by mail, sent to Acquisitions Coordinator. Responds in one to two months.
>
> **Guidelines:** *www.moodypublishers.com/about/contact*
>
> **Types and topics:** spiritual growth, family/relationships, church leaders, women, Bible studies, next-generation resources, finance
>
> **Tip:** "Most open to books that (1) have a great idea at the core, (2) are executed well, and (3) can demonstrate an audience clamoring for the content."

MOUNTAIN BROOK INK

26 Moore Rd., White Salmon, WA 98672 | 509-493-3953
submissions@mountainbrookink.com | *www.mountainbrookink.com*
Miralee Ferrell, head of acquisitions

Submissions: Publishes ten to twelve titles per year POD; receives thirty-five to forty. 50% from first-time authors. Length: 60,000-90,000 words preferred. Email query if a first-time author, full proposal with three chapters from agents and multipublished, traditionally published authors. Replies in thirty to forty-five days. Royalty: 45-50%; advance: $25 per title. Preferred Bible versions: KJV or NKJV.

Types and topics: women's fiction; YA; contemporary or historical romance; historical nonromance; suspense; mystery, including cozies; and speculative fiction, including spiritual warfare, fantasy, sci-fi, and paranormal romance.

Guidelines: *mountainbrookink.com/submission-guidelines*

Tip: "Read our guidelines and send a clean, properly formatted, well-written, and well-edited submission. We're not looking for perfect, but we do expect you to follow the rules. Three-book series (sequels, not a true series—each can stand alone but all tied together) will have a stronger chance than a single title. You don't have to have a strong platform, but you do need to be willing to develop a strong connection with readers."

MULTNOMAH BOOKS

10807 New Allegiance Dr. #500, Colorado Springs, CO 80921
719-590-4999 | info@waterbrookmultnomah.com
www.waterbrookmultnomah.com
Laura Barker, editorial director

Parent company: Crown Publishing Group, a division of Penguin Random House

Submissions: Publishes sixty titles per year; hardcover, trade paperbacks, e-books. Royalty on net; advance. Currently not accepting unsolicited manuscripts, proposals, or queries. Queries will be accepted through literary agents and at writers conferences at which a Multnomah representative is present.

Types and topics: Multnomah Books: Christian living, discipleship and spiritual growth, Bible study, apologetics, popular theology, devotional, evangelism, pastoral helps, leadership, children's. Multnomah Fiction: Well-crafted fiction that uses truth to change lives.

Guidelines: *waterbrookmultnomah.com/submissions*

MY HEALTHY CHURCH

1445 N. Boonville Ave., Springfield, MO 65802 | 800-641-4310
417-831-8000 | newproducts@myhealthychurch.com

www.myhealthychurch.com
Julie Horner, senior director of publishing and marketing

> **Denomination:** Assemblies of God
>
> **Submissions:** We do not accept unsolicited manuscripts unless represented by a professional literary agent. For a listing of the unsolicited manuscripts we are accepting, please visit the website. Responds in two to three months.
>
> **Types and topics:** church resources for kids, youth, and adults; small group studies
>
> **Guidelines:** *myhealthychurch.com/store/startcat.cfm?cat=tWRITGUID*
>
> **Tip:** "The content of all our books and resources must be compatible with the beliefs and purposes of the Assemblies of God."

NAVPRESS

3820 N. 30th St., Colorado Springs, CO 80904
editorial.submissions@navpress.com | www.navpress.com
Caitlyn Carlson, acquisitions editor, caitlyn.carlson@navpress.com |
David Zimmerman, acquisitions editor, david.zimmerman@navpress.com

> **Parent company:** The Navigators; has a publishing alliance with Tyndale House
>
> **Submissions:** To advance the calling of The Navigators by bringing biblically rooted, culturally relevant, and highly practical products to people who want to know and love Christ more deeply. Only accepts manuscripts submitted by professional literary agents, NavPress authors, authors known to them from other publishers, or other people in the publishing industry. Publishes forty-five titles per year, hardcover, trade paperbacks, e-books. Royalties; advance. Publication in twelve to eighteen months. Responds in six to twelve weeks.
>
> **Types and topics:** Bible study guides, nonfiction, YA fiction
>
> **Guidelines:** *www.navpress.com/faq*

NEW GROWTH PRESS

PO Box 4485, Greensboro, NC 27404 | 336-378-7775
www.newgrowthpress.com
John Walt, director of acquisitions, jwalt@newgrowthpress.com

> **Submissions:** Publishes gospel-centered and Bible-based materials that empower individuals, families, and churches to grow in their love for God, their love for others, and their ability to bring healing and hope to the world. Will work directly with authors and agents.
>
> **Types and topics:** small-group resources, family, parenting, counseling

issues, sexual identity issues, missions, renewal, fiction, illustrated children's books, minibooks (short, 24-page booklets that address one specific felt need)

NEW HOPE PUBLISHERS

PO Box 12065, Birmingham, AL 35202-2065 | 205-991-8100
newhopeproposals@wmu.org | *www.newhopepublishers.com*

> **Parent company:** WMU, Southern Baptists
> **Submissions:** Publishes twenty-four to twenty-eight titles per year; hardcover, trade paperbacks. Email proposal with two sample chapters for nonfiction, complete manuscript for fiction. Responds in four months.
> **Types and topics:** Christian living, Bible studies, missional fiction, devotional, leadership, evangelism, prayer, missions, culture, personal growth, students, marriage, parenting, inspirational
> **Imprints:** Fiction (contemporary issues), New Hope Impact (missional community, social, personal-commitment, church-growth, and leadership issues), New Hope Arise (inspiring women, changing lives), New Hope Grow (Bible-study and teaching resources)
> **Guidelines:** *www.newhopepublishers.com/proposals*

NEW LEAF PRESS

PO Box 726, Green Forest AR 72638-0726 | 870-438-5288
submissions@newleafpress.net | *www.nlpg.com/imprint/new-leaf-press*
Craig Froman, acquisitions editor

> **Parent company:** New Leaf Publishing Group
> **Submissions:** Publishes thirty to thirty-five titles per year; hardcover, trade paperbacks, occasionally high-end gift titles, e-books. Receives 1,000 submissions annually. 10% of books from first-time authors. Accepts manuscripts directly from authors. Requires email submission with Author's Proposal Document on the website. Variable royalty on net; no advance. Average first printing varies. Publication within eight months. Responds within three months or isn't interested.
> **Types and topics:** Christian living, stewardship, reference titles, church ministry, family issues, some materials in Spanish
> **Guidelines:** *www.nlpg.com/submissions*
> **Tip:** "Always follow our online guidelines before submitting."

NORTH WIND PUBLISHING

PO Box 3655, Brewer, ME 04412 | 207-922-8435
info@northwindpublishing.com | *www.northwindpublishing.com*
Janet Robbins, publisher

Submissions: Email or mail proposal. Publishes two titles per year; trade paperbacks, e-books, POD. Receives ten submissions annually. 50% of books from first-time authors. Royalty, no advance. Publication within six to twelve months.

Guidelines: *northwindpublishing.com/about.php*

NORTHWESTERN PUBLISHING HOUSE

1250 N. 113th St., Milwaukee, WI 53226 | 800-662-6022
414-615-5710 | www.nph.net
Rev. John Braun, braunj@nph.wels.net

Denomination: Wisconsin Evangelical Lutheran Synod

Types and topics: devotions, family and personal guidance, church history, Scripture studies like the popular People's Bible commentary series and the People's Bible Teachings series on doctrine

OLIVIA KIMBRELL PRESS

PO Box 470, Fort Knox, KY 40121-0470 | 859-577-1071
admin@oliviakimbrellpress.com | www.oliviakimbrellpress.com
G. B. Williams, submissions | Heather McCurdy, editor | Gregg Bridgeman, editor-in-chief

Submissions: Specializes in true-to-life, meaningful Christian fiction and nonfiction titles intended to uplift the heart and engage the mind. Primary focus on "Roman Road" small-group guides or reader's guides to accompany nonfiction and fiction. Fiction: finished manuscript only. Nonfiction: primarily completed and an outline. Email submission.

Types and topics: adult devotionals, family, Christian living, healthy living, cookbooks, fasting/feasts; fiction: speculative/science fiction, fantasy

Imprints: CAVË (historical fiction from the periods immediately before, during, or after the time of Christ), Sign of the Whale (biblical and/or Christian fiction primarily with speculative fiction, science fiction, fantasy, or other futuristic and/or supernatural themes), House of Bread (biblical and/or traditional foods; clean foods; fasting; feasts; and healthy, nutritious information presented in an educational and entertaining manner)

Guidelines: *www.oliviakimbrellpress.com/submission.html*

Tip: "Must meet our stated editorial standards. Follow our submission guidelines. Fiction series preferred over standalone titles. Complete manuscripts only."

OUR SUNDAY VISITOR, INC.
200 Noll Plaza, Huntington, IN 46750-4303 | 260-356-8400
800-348-2440 | www.osv.com

Submissions: To assist Catholics to be more aware and secure in their faith and capable of relating their faith to others. Submit proposal through the website. Publishes thirty to forty titles per year; hardcover, trade paperbacks. Receives 500+ submissions annually. 10% of books from first-time authors. Prefers not to work through agents. Royalty 10-12% of net; average advance, $1,500. Average first printing 5,000. Publication within one to two years. Responds in six to eight weeks. Also does pamphlets and booklets.

Types and topics: prayer—books and devotionals that help readers draw nearer to God; scripture—books about how to read, understand, pray, and apply Scripture; family and marriage—books that reflect on the nature of marriage and practical books on family life; saints and heritage—informative and inspiring stories about Mary, the saints, and Catholic identity; faith and culture—books about the intersection of faith and contemporary culture; service—practical application of the call to serve the needy and love our neighbor; evangelization, apologetics, and catechetics—books that help readers explain, defend, and share their faith with others; worship—books about understanding and experiencing the graces of the sacraments, especially the eucharist; parish—books that help pastors, leaders, and parishioners conduct parish life more effectively

Guidelines: *osv.submittable.com/submit/55853/submit-a-query-or-manusript-to-osv-books*

Tip: "All books published must relate to the Catholic Church; unique books aimed at our audience. Give as much background information as possible on author qualification, why the topic was chosen, and unique aspects of the project. Follow our guidelines. We are expanding our religious education product line and programs."

P&R PUBLISHING
1102 Marble Hill Rd., Phillipsburg, NJ 08865 | 908-454-0505
editorial@prpbooks.com | www.prpbooks.com
Ian Thompson, vice president

Denomination: Reformed

Submissions: Devoted to stating, defending, and furthering the gospel in the modern world. Download the submission form from the website, and email it with an outline and two or three chapters. Publishes forty-five titles per year; hardcover and trade paperbacks. Receives 400 submissions annually. Fewer than 10% of books from first-time authors. Prefers 140-240 pages. Royalty 10-15% of net; advance. Average first printing 3,500. Publication within a year. Responds in one to four months.

Types and topics: apologetics, Bible study aids, biography, Christian issues and ethics, Christian living, church history, church resources, commentary, counseling, fiction for children and teens, theology, women's resources, youth resources

Guidelines: *www.prpbooks.com/manuscript-submissions*

Tip: "Direct biblical/Reformed content. Clear, engaging, and insightful applications of Reformed theology to life. Offer us fully developed proposals and polished sample chapters. Check our website to see the categories we publish."

PACIFIC PRESS

PO Box 5353, Nampa, ID 83653-5353 | 208-465-2500
booksubmissions@pacificpress.com | *www.pacificpress.com*

Denomination: Seventh-day Adventist

Submissions: Books of interest and importance to Seventh-day Adventists and other Christians of all ages. Publishes thirty-five to forty titles per year; hardcover, trade paperbacks. Receives 500 submissions annually. 5% of books from first-time authors. Email or mail query. Accepts manuscripts directly from authors. Prefers 40,000-90,000 words, 128-320 pages. Royalty: 12-16% of net; advance $1,500. Average first printing 5,000. Publication within six months. Responds in one to three weeks. Requires requested proposal with three chapters by email or mail, manuscript by email. Also does booklets.

Types and topics: Adults: inspiration/Christian life, prayer, doctrine and Bible study, church history, Ellen White, topics and issues, biographies and true stories, story collections, cookbooks, health and nutrition, marriage and parenting, books for sharing and gospel outreach. Children: picture books illustrating a distinctive Adventist belief for ages 1–3; true or based-on-truth, contemporary or historical stories with Christian themes (usually in a series) for ages 6-8 and 9-12; sets of Bible stories for ages 8–108.

Guidelines: *www.pacificpress.com/index.php?pgName=newsBookSub #PPPAPubs*

Tip: "Most open to spirituality, inspirational, and Christian living. Our website has the most up-to-date information, including samples of recent publications. For more information, see www.adventistbookcenter.com. Do not send full manuscript unless we request it after reviewing your proposal."

PARSONS PUBLISHING HOUSE

850-867-3061
info@parsonspublishinghouse.com | *www.parsonspublishinghouse.com*
Diane Parsons, chief editor

Submissions: We have a mandate to assist authors in releasing their voices to their world to impact it for Jesus Christ. No manuscripts through agents; accepts directly from authors. Email the manuscript submission form from the website, along with the manuscript. Responds in two months. Publishes six to twelve titles per year; hardcover, trade paperbacks, e-books, POD. Receives fifty to seventy-five submissions annually. 50% of books from first-time authors. Prefers 35,000-60,000 words, 160-200 pages. Royalty 10% on net and e-books; no advance. Average first printing varies. Publication within nine months.

Types and topics: spiritual growth, Christian living

Guidelines: on the website

Tip: "Most open to a book about victory in Christ and that is positive about the saving grace of Christ and his delivering power. Author should have some type of platform, i.e., ministry, online presence (blog, newsletter, Facebook, Twitter), speaking, etc.

PAULINE BOOKS & MEDIA

50 Saint Paul's Ave., Boston, MA 02130-3491 | 617-522-8911
editorial@paulinemedia.com | *www.pauline.org*
Sean Mayer, FSP, acquisitions editor, adults | *Marilyn Monge, FSP, and Jaymie Stuart Wolfe, editors, children and teens*

Denomination: Catholic/Daughters of St. Paul

Submissions: Publishes twenty titles per year; hardcover and trade paperbacks. Receives 350-400 submissions annually. 10% of books from first-time authors. Accepts manuscripts directly from authors. Prefers 10,000-60,000 words. Royalty 5-10% on net; offers an advance. Average first printing 2,000-5,000. Publication within two years. Email proposal as an attachment or mail it. Responds in two months. Prefers NRSV.

Types and topics: Adults: spirituality, prayer, lives of saints, faith formation, theology, family life. Children: prayer books, lives of saints, Bible stories, activity books, easy reader and middle-grade fiction, board books, picture books. YA: fiction and nonfiction.

Guidelines: *www.pauline.org/Publishing/Submit-a-Manuscript*

Tip: Looking for well-documented historical fiction and graphic novels for middle grade and YA.

PAULIST PRESS

997 Macarthur Blvd., Mahwah, NJ 07430-9990

submissions@paulistpress.com | www.paulistpress.com

Denomination: Catholic

Submissions: Email proposal and sample chapters, pages for children's chapter books, or full manuscript for other children's books. Responds in two months.

Types and topics: academic, children's, popular, and professional or clergy books

Guidelines: *www.paulistpress.com/Pages/Center/auth_res_0.aspx*

PELICAN BOOK GROUP

See Harbourlight Books, Pure Amore, Watershed Books, and White Rose Publishing.

PRAYERSHOP PUBLISHING

3525 S. 3rd Pl., Terre Haute, IN 47802 | 812-238-5504

jong@harvestprayer.com | www.prayershoppublishing.com

Jonathan Graf, publisher

Parent company: Harvest Prayer Ministries, Church Prayer Leaders Network

Submissions: Our ministry is to disciple people in prayer and grow praying churches. We only do resources that will move an individual or church deeper in prayer. Publishes four to six titles per year; trade paperbacks, e-books. Receives ten to fifteen submissions annually. 15% of books from first-time authors. Accepts manuscripts directly from authors. Prefers 30,000-50,000 words, 128-144 pages. Email or mail proposal with sample chapters. Royalty 10-15% of net for print and e-books; no advance. Average first printing 3,500. Publication in nine months. Reports in six to eight weeks. Bible version: prefers NIV.

Types and topics: practical books on prayer that show how to pray or provide guides to help people learn to pray, Bible studies/small-group resources, short booklets on one practical prayer topic, media packs that might include teaching seminar CD/DVD plus booklet

Guidelines: *harvestprayer.com/about-us/ministries/prayershop-publishing/submission-guidelines*

Tip: "Currently looking for book manuscripts, booklets, and materials that can be formatted via CD and print into training kits. We are mostly interested in products that will in some way enhance the prayer life of a local church."

PRISM BOOK GROUP

contact@prismbookgroup.com; www.prismbookgroup.com
Jacqueline Hopper, acquisitions editor, jhopper@prismbookgroup.com |
Susan Baganz, acquisitions editor, sbaganz@prismbookgroup.com | Paula
Mowery, acquisitions editor, pmowery@prismbookgroup.com

Submissions: Publishes clean and wholesome fiction. Publishes twenty-four to sixty titles annually, e-books and POD trade paperbacks. Royalties paid quarterly. Query by email only. Proofread your finished manuscript thoroughly before querying the general address. When submitting at their request, it is important to include your real name and email on your manuscript's title page; manuscripts without this information may be deleted.

Types and topics: fiction: romance, Christian romance, Christian fiction, young adult

Imprints: Diamond (clean and wholesome romance), Inspired (Christian romance), Illuminate (Christian fiction), Shine (uplifting young-adult fiction)

Tip: "Our books offer clean and compelling reads for the discerning reader. We will not publish graphic language or content and look for well-written, emotionally charged stories, intense plots, and captivating characters. We are especially interested in western/cowboy romances, regency romance, romantic suspense, and contemporary romance in both Diamond and Inspired imprints. We would also love to see more historical, biblical fiction."

PURE AMORE

PO Box 1738, Aztec, NM 87410
customer@pelicanbookgroup.com | pelicanbookgroup.com
Nicola Martinez, editor-in-chief

Parent company: Pelican Book Group

Submissions: Length: 40,000-45,000 words. Pays advance plus royalties. Accepts unagented submissions. Responds to queries in one month, full manuscripts in four months. Email submissions only through the website.

Types and topics: Only contemporary Christian romance. Pure Amore romances are sweet in tone and in conflict. These stories are the emotionally driven tales of youthful Christians between the ages of 21 and 33 who are striving to live their faith in a world where Christ-centered choices may not fully be understood.

Guidelines: *pelicanbookgroup.com/ec/index.php?main_ page=page&id=69*

Tip: "Pure Amore romances emphasize the beauty in chastity, so physical interactions, such as kissing or hugging, should focus on the characters' emotions, rather than heightened sexual desire; and scenes of physical intimacy should be integral to the plot and/or emotional development of the character or relationship."

RAINBOW PUBLISHERS

See RoseKidz.

RANDALL HOUSE PUBLICATIONS

PO Box 17306, Nashville, TN 37217 | 800-877-7030, 615-361-1221
michelle.orr@randallhouse.com | *www.randallhouse.com*
Michelle Orr, senior acquisitions editor

Denomination: Free Will Baptist

Submissions: Publishes books to make Christ known, from a conservative perspective. Email or mail proposal. Responds in ten to twelve weeks. Publishes ten to fifteen titles per year; hardcover, trade paperbacks, e-books. Receives 300-500 submissions annually. 40% of books from first-time authors. Accepts manuscripts directly from authors. Prefers 40,000 words. Royalty 12-18% on net; pays an advance. Average first printing 5,000. Publication within eighteen months.

Types and topics: Christian living, parenting, family ministry, theology, academic

Guidelines: download from the website at *www.randallhouse.com/contact*

Tip: "We are expanding our book division with a conservative perspective. We have a very conservative view as a publisher."

REGNERY FAITH

300 New Jersey Ave., N.W., Ste. 500, Washington, DC 20001
submissions@regnery.com | *www.regnery.com*
Gary Tereshita, editor-in-chief, Regnery Faith

Parent company: Regnery Publishing, Salem Media Group

Submissions: Regnery Faith imprint is dedicated to developing new faith-based projects for Christian readers. Only accepts manuscripts and proposals from agents.

RESOURCE PUBLICATIONS
See entry for Wipf and Stock Publishing.

RESURRECTION PRESS
77 West End Rd., Totowa, NJ 07572 | 973-890-2400
info@catholicbookpublishing.com | *www.catholicbookpublishing.com*
Anthony Buono, editor

Denomination: Catholic
Parent company: Catholic Book Publishing Corp.
Submissions: Mail proposal and two chapters. Responds in four to six weeks. Royalties are negotiable. Publication in twelve to eighteen months.
Types and topics: prayer, healing, spirituality, pastoral and liturgical resources
Guidelines: *www.catholicbookpublishing.com/faq.php#manuscript*

REVELL BOOKS
PO Box 6287, Grand Rapids, MI 49516 | 616-676-9185
www.revellbooks.com
Lonnie Hull Dupont, nonfiction, lhulldupont@bakerpublishinggroup.com |
Kelsey Bowen, fiction, kbowen@bakerpublishinggroup.com

Parent company: Baker Publishing Group
Submissions: Publishes inspirational fiction and nonfiction for the broadest Christian market. Accepts proposals only through agents, meeting an editor at a writers conference, or *ChristianManuscriptSubmissions.com.*
Types and topics: apologetics/world religions, Bible study, biography/ memoir, Christian living, Christianity and culture, church life, marriage and family, Spirit-filled, fiction, children and youth fiction and nonfiction
Guidelines: *bakerpublishinggroup.com/contact/submission-policy*

ROSE PUBLISHING
17909 Adria Maru, Carson, CA 90746 | 800-532-4278
info@rose-publishing.com | *www.rose-publishing.com*

Submissions: Publishes resources that help believers love God by deepening their understanding of who God is. Submit through ChristianManuscriptSubmissions.com.
Types and topics: reference products packed with charts, timelines, and simple summaries to make the Bible and its teachings easy to understand; also does pamphlets and wall charts

Imprints: Rose Bible Reference, Aspire Publishing (see separate listing), RoseKidz (see separate listing)

ROSEKIDZ

17909 Adria Maru, Carson, CA 90746 | 800-532-4278
info@rose-publishing.com | www.rose-publishing.com
Jean Christen, publisher

Parent company: Rose Publishing

Submissions: Submit manuscripts through *ChristianManuscriptSubmissions.com.*

Types and topics: reproducible Bible lesson material for children, including age-appropriate Sunday-school activities, instant Bible lessons, girls and boys devotionals, fiction; nursery, toddler, preschool, kindergarten, elementary, and preteen.

SAINT CATHERINE OF SIENA PRESS

4812 N. Park Ave., Indianapolis, IN 46205 | 888-232-149
tzander@indy.rr.com | www.saintcatherineofsienapress.com

Denomination: Catholic

Types and topics: small-group study guides that put the reader in contact with the sources of Catholic doctrine: The Holy Bible, the Fathers of the Church, papal and conciliar documents, and the Catechism of the Catholic Church

SCEPTER PUBLISHERS

PO Box 360694, Strongsville, OH 44136 | 800-322-8773, 212-354-0670
info@scepterpublishers.org | www.scepterpublishers.org
Nathan Davis, editor

Denomination: Catholic

Submissions: Publishes Catholic books that help men and women find God in ordinary life and to realize sanctity in their work, family life, and everyday activities. Send a one- or two- page proposal with cover letter by mail or email.

SERENADE BOOKS

340 S. Lemon Ave. #1639, Walnut, CA 91789
info@serenadebooks.com | www.serenadebooks.com
Erin Taylor Young, managing editor, erin@serenadebooks.com | Regina Jennings, managing editor

Submissions: Uses innovative marketing and adaptive strategies to help published authors connect with readers who want more romance from voices they love. Publishes six to eight titles per year, e-books only. 10% of books from first-time authors. Hometown Romance, 20,000-65,000 words; Timeless, 45,000-110,000 words. Royalties paid monthly; no advance. Publication within nine months. Responds in two months. Published authors email a proposal with three sample chapters; debut authors email a proposal with the complete manuscript.

Types and topics: Frontier romance, historical romance, and romance. Timeless: Features previously published books brought back to the market for a new generation of readers. Primary consideration is the power of a memorable story. The romance thread needs to be strong, but that doesn't mean the book has to fit squarely into the romance genre. A bent toward romantic suspense or historical, etc., would not exclude a great story from consideration. Hometown Romance: Story needs to be original, memorable, and of exceptional craftsmanship, with a strong sense of setting and community. While stories can be contemporary or historical, the romance must be the primary focus. Slots for debut authors are extremely limited.

Guidelines: *www.serenadebooks.com/about-us*

Tip: "We only accept submissions at certain times of the year. Please check our website before submitting."

SERVANT BOOKS

See Franciscan Media.

SMYTH & HELWYS BOOKS

6316 Peake Rd., Macon, GA 31210-3960 | 478-757-0564
proposal@helwys.com | *www.helwys.com*

Submissions: Submit both a hard and digital copy of the complete proposal and two to four sample chapters. Responds in several months.

Types and topics: Christian living, ministry/leadership, biblical studies

Guidelines: *www.helwys.com/submit-a-manuscript*

SONFIRE MEDIA PUBLISHING, LLC

PO Box 6, Galax, VA 24333 | 276-233-0276
www.sonfiremedia.com
Vie Herlocker, editor, vie.herlocker@sonfiremedia.com | Mary Beth Dahl, editor, mbdahl@taberahpress.com

Submissions: Publishes two to five titles per year, POD. Receives 50 per year. 95% from first-time authors. Length: 40,000-80,000 for nonfiction; 70,000-100,000 for fiction. Email query letter only. Replies in one to two months. Royalty 10-20%. Preferred Bible version: NIV but open to others.

Types and topics: devotionals, Christian living, writing instruction, YA and adult fantasy, science fiction, speculative, open to others types of fiction except romance

Imprints: Sonfire Media (nonfiction), Taberah Press (Christian fiction)

Guidelines: *www.sonfiremedia.com/submit.html*

Tip: "We are open to new writers if they are serious about their craft, understand the need for author marketing, and have a 'message that matters.'"

SPARKHOUSE FAMILY

PO Box 1209, Minneapolis, MN 55440 | 800-960-9705
submissions@wearesparkhouse.org | *www.sparkhouse.org*

Parent company: 1517 Media

Denomination: Evangelical Lutheran Church in America

Submissions: Email proposal as an attachment with a sample of fifteen to twenty-five pages or full manuscript, depending on the type of book.

Types and topics: board books for ages birth-3, picture books for ages 3-8, activity books for ages 3-8, early-reader and first-chapter books for ages 5-9, nonfiction books for ages 5-9 and 8-12, fiction for ages 8-12, activity books for families, devotionals for children ages 0-12 and families

Guidelines: *promo.sparkhouse.org/submissions*

Tip: "We are seeking writers and illustrators who want to create books that delight, entertain, and teach children and their parents."

SUNPENNY PUBLISHING

Urbanització Tossal Gross, 90-1, La Font d'en Carròs, 46717, Valencia Communidad, Spain (based in England too)
writers@sunpenny.com | *www.sunpenny.com*
Jo Holloway, editor

Submissions: Email brief synopsis and short author bio included in the body of the email with a one- to two-page synopsis attached. Publishes fifteen to twenty titles per year; hardcover, trade paperbacks, mass-market paperbacks, e-books. 50% of books from first-time authors. Accepts manuscripts directly from authors. Royalty on sliding scale, beginning at 15% of margin. Responds in one to two weeks to queries, one to two months to proposals, two to three months to manuscripts.

Types and topics: wit and humor, entertainment, travel, adventure, historical novels, romance, women's fiction, courage, challenges, overcoming, gift books, coffee-table books, children and young teens, self-help, memoir, biography

Imprints: Rose & Crown Books (Christian romance), ChristLight Books (Christian fiction and nonfiction in all genres)

Guidelines: *www.sunpenny.com/#!submissions*

TAU-PUBLISHING

4806 S. 40th St., Phoenix, AZ 85040 | 602-625-6183
www.tau-publishing.org

Parent company: Vesuvius Press, Inc.

Denomination: Catholic

Submissions: Email (preferred) through the website or mail proposal with one or two sample chapters. Responds in six weeks.

Types and topics: inspirational, biography, children's, books related to the Franciscans

Guidelines: *www.tau-publishing.org/showPage.aspx?pageID=276*

THOMAS NELSON PUBLISHERS

PO Box 141000, Nashville, TN 37214-1000 | 615-889-9000
www.thomasnelson.com
Amanda Bostic, associate publisher, fiction | Meaghan Porter, senior editor, W Publishing | Jessica Wong, acquisitions, Thomas Nelson Publishers

Parent company: HarperCollins Christian Publishing

Submissions: Only accepts proposals through agents or direct contact with editors. Does not accept or review any unsolicited queries, proposals, or manuscripts. Publishes fewer than 100 titles per year; hardcover, trade, e-book.

Types and topics: Christian living, church and ministry resources, Bible reference, commentaries, Bible book studies, business and leadership, biography, women's devotionals, fiction for adults and YA, gift books

Imprints: Nelson Books (spiritual growth and practical living), W Publishing Group (memoirs, help and hope for doing life better, and leading pastoral voices, with select practical living), Grupo Nelson (Spanish), Tommy Nelson (see separate entry)

Guidelines: *www.harpercollinschristian.com/write-for-us*

TOMMY NELSON

PO Box 141000, Nashville, TN 37214-1000 | 615-889-9000
www.tommynelson.com

Mackinzie Howard, children's acquisitions editor

Parent company: Thomas Nelson Publishers

Submissions: Only accepts proposals through agents or direct contact with editors. Does not accept or review any unsolicited queries, proposals, or manuscripts.

Types and topics: board books, picture books, Bible story books, devotionals for middle grade and teens

Guidelines: *www.harpercollinschristian.com/write-for-us*

TRAIL MEDIA

1320 Ynez Pl. 181585, Coronado, CA 92178 | 760-212-6519
submissions@ChisholmTrailMedia.com | *www.ChisholmTrailMedia.com*
Dana S. Chisholm, publisher

Submissions: Publishes twenty manuscripts per year. Receives 100 manuscripts per year; paperbacks, e-books. 100% first-time authors. Royalty 20%. Only email query with sample chapter or two. Publication within six months.

Types and topics: Christian living, children's books, historical fiction, young-adult fiction, Americana literature (getting back to the founders' intent)

Guidelines: chisholmtrailmedia.com/Submission-Guidelines.htm

Tip: "We generally seek new Christian authors and illustrators who have never professionally published or they tried self-publishing and are looking for a more professional, hands-on experience with editors, graphic designers, mentor authors, and support to work together on their piece to get it to print and in the hands of readers."

THE TRINITY FOUNDATION

PO Box 68, Unicoi, TN 37692 | 423-743-0199
tjtrinityfound@aol.com | *www.trinityfoundation.org*
Thomas W. Juodaitis, president

Submissions: Publishes books to promote the logical system of truth found in the Bible. Publishes three to five titles per year; hardcover, trade paperbacks, e-books. Receives ten submissions annually. 5% of books from first-time authors. Prefers 100-200 pages. Outright purchases up to $2,000; free books; no advance. Average first printing 1,000-2,000. Email or mail a proposal with sample chapters. Publication within six months. No simultaneous submissions. Responds within a week. Bible version: KJV, NKJV.

Types and topics: Calvinist/Clarkian books, Christian philosophy, economics, and politics; also does pamphlets, booklets, and tracts

Tip: "Most open to doctrinal books that conform to the Westminster Confession of Faith; nonfiction, biblical, and well-reasoned books, theologically sound, clearly written, and well organized. Must be biblical."

TRIPLE J PUBLISHING, LLC

115 Wicker St., Sanford, NJ 27330 | 919-208-8736
triplejpublishing@gmail.com | www.triplejp.com
Ophelia Livingston, acquisitions editor

Denomination: Baptist
Submissions: Publishes ten books per year. Receives thirty proposals per year. 100% from first-time authors. Preferred book length: 170 pages. Email or mail proposal with sample chapters. Responds in fifteen days. Royalty 60%; no advance. Average first print run: 200. Preferred Bible version: KJV.
Types and topics: African-American, Christian living; also does T-shirts, promotional products
Guidelines: via email
Tip: "Finished manuscript; know your targeted audience; willing to expand storyline."

TYNDALE HOUSE PUBLISHERS

351 Executive Dr., Carol Stream, IL 60188 | 630-668-8300
www.tyndale.com

Submissions: Publishes 150-200 titles per year; hardcover, trade paperbacks, e-books. 5% of books from first-time authors. Only reviews manuscripts submitted by professional literary agents, Tyndale authors, authors known to us from other publishers, or other people in the publishing industry. Average first printing 5,000-10,000. Publication within nine months. Responds in three to six months. Bible version: prefers NLT. Fiction: 75,000-100,000 words with an evangelical Christian message.
Types and topics: practical Christian books for home and family, Christian beliefs, finance, leadership, career, parenting, marriage, memoir, biography, devotionals, counseling; fiction: biblical, contemporary, futuristic, historical, romance, suspense/thriller, picture books, fiction and nonfiction for kids and teens
Imprint: Tyndale Kids, Tyndale Español (Spanish)
Guidelines: *www.tyndale.com/faq*

WARNER PRESS

1201 E. 5th St., Anderson, IN 46012 | 800-741-7721
www.warnerpress.org

Karen Rhodes, senior editor, krhodes@warnerpress.org | Robin Fogel, product editor, rfogle@warnerpress.org

Denomination: Church of God

Submissions: Email manuscript. Publishes hardcover, paperback, and e-books. Receives 100+ submissions annually. Accepts manuscripts directly through authors. Royalty and advance based on the author and type of book. Responds in six to eight weeks. Publication within one year. Bible version: KJV, NIV.

Types and topics: evangelism, discipleship, missions, pastoral leadership, Christian living, devotionals, Bible-study guides on specific subjects or a Bible book, teaching resource books; short books that are inspirational, devotional, and encouraging and help others deal with life's challenging situations; also see entry in chapter 15.

Guidelines: *www*.warnerpress.org/custom.aspx?id=3

WATERBROOK PRESS

10807 New Allegiance Dr. #500, Colorado Springs, CO 80921
719-590-4999 | info@waterbrookmultnomah.com
www.waterbrookmultnomah.com
Laura Barker, editorial director

Parent company: Crown Publishing Group, a division of Penguin Random House

Submissions: Publishes sixty titles per year; hardcover, trade paperbacks, e-books. Royalty on net; advance. Currently not accepting unsolicited manuscripts, proposals, or queries. Queries will be accepted through literary agents and at writers conferences at which a WaterBrook representative is present.

Types and topics: practical life, inspiration and encouragement, devotional, relationships and parenting, biography, memoir, topical Bible study, justice, spiritual warfare, fiction, children's books, Fisherman Bible study guides

Guidelines: *waterbrookmultnomah.com/submissions*

WATERFALL PRESS

waterfall-inquiries@brilliancepublishing.com
www.brilliancepublishing.com/waterfall.html
Sheryl Zajchowski, acquisitions

Parent company: Brilliance Publishing, Amazon.com

Submissions: Publishes twenty to thirty titles per year.

Types and topics: fiction (romance, mystery, suspense), Christian living

WATERSHED BOOKS

PO Box 1738, Aztec, NM 87410
customer@pelicanbookgroup.com | *www.pelicanbookgroup.com*
Nicola Martinez, editor-in-chief

Parent company: Pelican Book Group
Submissions: Email submissions only through the website. Length: 25,000-60,000 words. Limited-edition hardback, trade paperbacks, and e-book. Royalty 40% on download, 7% on print. Pays nominal advance. Accepts unagented submissions. Responds to queries in one month, full manuscript in three months. Email submissions only.
Types and topics: young-adult fiction that features young-adult characters; action-adventure, mystery (amateur sleuth or other), romance, science fiction, fantasy, supernatural, suspense, crime drama, police procedural, teen angst, coming-of-age, westerns; interested in series ideas
Guidelines: *pelicanbookgroup.com/ec/index.php?main_page=page&id=60*

WESLEYAN PUBLISHING HOUSE

PO Box 50434, Indianapolis, IN 46250-0434 | 317-774-7900
wph@wesleyan.org | *www.wesleyan.org/wph*

Denomination: Wesleyan
Submissions: No longer accepting unsolicited queries, proposals, or manuscripts. Only publishing "the voices of emerging leaders in The Wesleyan Church."

WESTMINSTER/JOHN KNOX PRESS

100 Witherspoon St., Louisville, KY 40202-1396
submissions@wjkbooks.com | *www.wjkbooks.com*
Bridgett Green, acquisitions editor, Biblical studies, bgreen@wjkbooks.com | *Dan Braden, acquisitions editor, academic books, dbraden@wjkbooks.com* | *Jessica Miller Kelley, acquisitions editor, jkelley@wjkbooks.com*

Denomination: Presbyterian
Parent company: Presbyterian Publishing Corporation
Submissions: Publishes approximately sixty new books and other resources each year. Prefers emailed proposals but will take them by mail. Responds in two to three months.
Types and topics: theology, biblical studies, preaching, worship, ethics, religion and culture, and other related fields for four main markets: scholars and students in colleges, universities, seminaries,

and divinity schools; preachers, educators, and counselors working in churches; members of mainline Protestant congregations; and general readers.

Imprint: Geneva Press (books specifically related to the Presbyterian Church U.S.A.)

Guidelines: *www.wjkbooks.com/Pages/Item/1345/Author-Relations.aspx*

WHITAKER HOUSE

1030 Hunt Valley Cir., New Kensington, PA 15068 | 724-334-7000
publisher@whitakerhouse.com | *www.whitakerhouse.com*
Tom Cox, managing editor, tomc@whitakerhouse.com | *Christine Whitaker, fiction acquisitions editor, christinew@whitakerhouse.com*

Denomination: Charismatic

Submissions: Only reviews proposals from agents or by request from a house representative. Email a proposal or mail to Author Liaison. Responds in six months. Publishes seventy titles per year; hardcover, trade paperbacks, e-books, POD. Receives 50-100 submissions annually. 15-20% of books from first-time authors. Prefers 40,000-70,000 words, 96-336 pages. Royalty 6-20% on net, 25% on e-books; variable advances. Average first printing 5,000.

Types and topics: biography/autobiography, Charismatic interest, Christian living, devotions, fiction, gender-specific issues for men or women, inspiration, marriage, family, relationships, prayer, spiritual growth, spiritual warfare, theology, African-American, Hispanic

Imprints: Banner Publishing, Resolute Books

Guidelines: *WhitakerManuscriptSubmissionGuidelines.pdf*

Tip: "Looking for quality nonfiction and fiction by authors with a national marketing platform. Most open to high-quality, well-thought-out, compelling pieces of work. Review the guidelines and submit details as thoroughly as possible for publication consideration."

WHITE ROSE PUBLISHING

PO Box 1738, Aztec, NM 87410
customer@pelicanbookgroup.com | *www.pelicanbookgroup.com*
Nicola Martinez, editor-in-chief

Parent company: Pelican Book Group

Submissions: Email submissions only through the website. Length: short stories, 10,000-20,000 words (e-book); novelettes, 20,000-35,000 words (e-book); novellas, 35,000-60,000 words (e-book); novels, 60,000-80,000 words (e-book and print). Limited-edition hardback, trade paperbacks, and e-book. Royalty 40% on download, 7% on print. Pays nominal advance. Accepts unagented submissions. Responds to queries in one month, full manuscript in three months. Email submissions only.

Types and topics: only romance, interested in series ideas

Guidelines: *pelicanbookgroup.com/ec/index.php?main_page=page&id=58*

WHITEFIRE PUBLISHING

13607 Bedford Rd. N.E., Cumberland, MD 21502 | 866-245-2211
www.whitefire-publishing.com
Roseanna White, senior editor, r.white@whitefire-publishing.com | Wendy Chorot, senior nonfiction editor, w.chorot@whitefire-publishing.com

Submissions: Publishes nine to twelve POD titles per year; receives 100 per year. 50% from first-time authors. Length: 60,000-125,000. Email query letter only. Replies in two to four weeks. Royalty: 50% on ebooks, 10% on print; sometimes gives advance. Preferred Bible version: KJV for historicals; no preference for contemporaries.

Types: memoir, Christian living, inspirational; fiction: historical, historical romance, romantic suspense, contemporary romance, contemporary, suspense, open to speculative and young adult

Guidelines: *whitefire-publishing.com/wordpress/sample-page/what-were-looking-for*

Tip: "Embrace the motto of 'Where Spirit Meets the Page.' Looking for stories or nonfiction with a unique angle; don't shy away from difficult subjects."

WILLIAM CAREY LIBRARY

626-720-8210
submissions@WCLBooks.com | www.missionbooks.org
Aidan Lewis, editor

Submissions: Publishes scholarly and professional or educational books, all related to missions. "We especially seek to assist the work of the mission executive, field missionary, church leader, and the student of world mission." Responds in three to six months. Send a maximum two-page query letter initially. No unsolicited manuscripts.

Types and topics: Ethnography, biography, educational, nonfiction, missions, missiology

Guidelines: *missionbooks.org/submissions*

Tip: "Read our publishing focus carefully. We only publish literature promoting world missions, specifically among unreached and unengaged peoples."

WIPF AND STOCK PUBLISHERS

199 W. 8th Ave., Ste. 3, Eugene, OR 97401-2960 | 541-344-1528
proposal@wipfandstock.com | *www.wipfandstock.com*
Rodney Clapp, editor, rodney@wipfandstock.com | *Dr. Chris Spinks, editor, chris@wipfandstock.com*

Submissions: Email proposal with proposal form from the website. Responds in eight weeks. It is your responsibility to submit a manuscript that has been fully copyedited by a professional copy editor. Publishes more than 400 books per year, short-run and e-books.

Types and topics: primarily academic

Imprint: Resource Publications (for leaders and pastors in ministries, faith-based resources for personal growth and use by educators)

Guidelines: *wipfandstock.com/submitting-a-proposal?hl=1*

WORTHY KIDS / IDEALS

6100 Tower Cir., Ste. 210, Franklin, TN 37067 | 615-932-7600
IdealsInfo@worthypublishing.com | *www.idealsbooks.com*
Kristi West, associate editor

Parent company: Worthy Publishing Group

Submissions: Publishes thirty titles per year; receives 600 per year. Fewer than 1% from first-time authors. Length: 200 words for board books, 800 words for picture books. Email proposal with full manuscript. Responds only to manuscripts of interest. Royalty: 5-7%; sometimes gives an advance. Average first print run: 10,000. Preferred Bible version: NLT.

Types and topics: Fiction and nonfiction children's books for birth through age 8: inspiration/faith, patriotism, and holidays, particularly Easter and Christmas; relationships and values; and general fiction. Annual issues of Ideals Christmas and Ideals Easter for all ages. We accept submissions for poetry and prose for these holiday issues. Submissions should be optimistic and can be nostalgic, inspirational, or humorous.

Guidelines: via email

Tip: "Editors review complete manuscripts only; do not send query letters or proposals. Previous publications, relevant qualifications or background, and a brief synopsis of your manuscript may be included in a cover letter. Please send copies only—we cannot be responsible for an original manuscript."

WORTHY PUBLISHING GROUP

134 Franklin Rd., Ste 200, Brentwood, TN 37027 | 615-932-7600
www.worthypublishing.com
Jeana Ledbetter, acquisitions, Worthy Publishing | Pamela Clements,
Worthy Inspire

> **Submissions:** Publishes thirty-six titles per year; hardcover, trade paperbacks, e-books. Requires submission by agents; unsolicited manuscripts returned unopened. Offers advance.
>
> **Types and topics:** Worthy Books: broad spectrum of genres, including current events, pop culture, biography, fiction, spiritual growth, and Bibles. Worthy Inspired: felt-need personal growth, inspirational, and devotional.
>
> **Imprints:** Worthy Books, Worthy Inspired, Worthy Kids/Ideals (see separate listing), Ellie Claire (gifts)

WRITE INTEGRITY PRESS

PO Box 702852, Dallas, TX 75370
WriteIntegrity@gmail.com | www.WriteIntegrity.com
Marji Laine Clubine, publisher

> **Submissions:** Publishes clean, wholesome fiction with a thread of Christian faith; POD, trade paperbacks, e-books. Publishes six to eight titles per year; Pix-N-Pens, three to five. Receives 200+ proposals per year. 75% from first-time authors. Generous royalties; no advance. Email proposal with first three chapters for nonfiction, first three and last chapters for fiction. Responds in two months. Publication in six to eight months. Check website for updates on current needs.
>
> **Types and topics:** fiction for children, teens, and adults; strong preference for contemporary, mystery/suspense, and others that don't fit a formula; children's picture books; nonfiction: Bible studies (geared toward men, women, couples, or teens), self-help, inspiration, Christian living
>
> **Imprints:** Pix-N-Pens Publishing (evangelical fiction and nonfiction with a strong gospel message)
>
> **Guidelines:** on the website; click on "Submissions."
>
> **Tip:** "We view our authors as family—we team together to support, promote, and pray for one another. Be professional and have a teachable spirit. Those traits and a rich dose of enthusiasm go a long way. Have a website and social media presence."

YOUTH SPECIALTIES

5320 W. 23rd St., Ste. 130, Minneapolis, MN 55416 | 888.346.4179
Ideas@YouthSpecialties.com | youthspecialties.com

> **Submissions:** Send proposal and sample chapters by email as attached file to *publishing@youthspecialties.com*. Responds in three months.
> **Types and topics:** youth ministry, parenting, meeting plans and programming ideas for middle school and high school, game books
> **Guidelines:** *youthspecialties.com/about/write-for-us*

YWAM PUBLISHING

PO Box 55787, Seattle, WA 98155 | 800-922-2143
books@ywampublishing.com | www.ywampublishing.com

> **Parent company:** Youth With A Mission
> **Submissions:** Email or mail proposal, following the template on the website; will not respond to submissions that deviate from proposal guidelines.
> **Types and topics:** evangelism, mission adventures, missions for kids, Bible studies, devotionals, leadership, relationships; no longer accepts fiction or children's literature
> **Guidelines:** *www.ywampublishing.com/t-submission.aspx*

ZONDERKIDZ

3900 Sparks Dr. S.E., Grand Rapids, MI 49512 | 616-698-6900
ZonderkidzSubmissions@harpercollins.com | www.zonderkidz.com
Robyn Burwell, acquisitions editor, Robyn.Burwell@harpercollins.com

> **Parent company:** Zondervan, HarperCollins Christian Publishing
> **Submissions:** Requires submissions only through agents.
> **Types and topics:** children's fiction and nonfiction, teen fiction and nonfiction, children's Bibles
> **Guidelines:** *www.harpercollinschristian.com/write-for-us*
> **Tip:** "We are seeking fresh fiction and nonfiction for children ages 0-18. Under our Zonderkidz and Zondervan imprints, we look for engaging picture books and board books, timeless storybook Bibles, faith-centric fiction from established authors, and nonfiction from key voices in the Christian sphere."

ZONDERVAN

3900 Sparks Dr. S.E., Grand Rapids, MI 49512 | 616-698-6900
www.zondervan.com
Carolyn McCready, trade acquisitions, Carolyn.McCready@harpercollins.com |
Molly Hodgin, gift books

Parent company: HarperCollins Christian Publishing

Submissions: Requires submissions only through agents. Publishes 120 trade titles per year; hardcover, trade paperbacks, e-books. Publication within twelve to eighteen months. Bible version: prefers NIV.

Types and topics: spiritual growth, marriage, family, social issues, leadership, finance, biography, commentaries, church and ministry, fiction (contemporary, mystery, historical, romance, science fiction, fantasy, suspense)

Imprints: Zonderkidz (see separate listing), Blink (see separate listing), Editorial Vida (Spanish), Zondervan Academic

Guidelines: *www.harpercollinschristian.com/write-for-us*

PART 2

INDEPENDENT BOOK PUBLISHING

2

INDEPENDENT BOOK PUBLISHERS

PUBLISHING A BOOK YOURSELF NO LONGER CARRIES THE STIGMA self-publishing has had in the past—if you do it right. Even some well-published writers are now hybrid authors, with independently published books alongside their royalty books. Others have built their readerships with traditional publishers, then moved to independent publishing where it is possible to make more money per sale.

Independent book publishers require the author to pay for part of the publishing costs or to buy a certain number of books. They call themselves by a variety of names, such as book packager, cooperative publisher, self-publisher, custom publisher, subsidy publisher, or simply someone who helps authors get their books printed. Services vary from including different levels of editing and proofreading to printing your manuscript as is.

Whenever you pay for any part of the production of your book, you are entering into a nontraditional relationship. Some independent publishers also offer a form of royalty publishing, so be sure you understand the contract they give you before signing it.

Some independent publishers will publish any book, as long as the author is willing to pay for it. Others are as selective about what they publish as a royalty publisher is. Some independent publishers will do as much promotion as a royalty publisher—for a fee. Others do none at all.

If you are unsuccessful in placing your book with a royalty publisher but feel strongly about seeing it published, an independent publisher can make printing your book easier and often less expensive than doing it yourself. POD, as opposed to a print run of 1,000 or more, could save you upfront money, although the price per copy is higher. Having your manuscript produced only as an e-book is also a less-expensive option.

Entries in this chapter are for information only, not an endorsement of publishers. For every complaint about a publisher, there can be several other authors who sing the praises of it. Before you sign with any company, get more than one bid to determine whether the terms you are offered are competitive. A legitimate independent publisher will provide a list of former clients as references. Also buy a couple of the publisher's previous books to check the quality of the work—covers, bindings, typesetting, etc. See if the books currently are available through any of the major online retailers.

Get answers before committing yourself. You may also want someone in the book-publishing industry to review your contract before you sign it. Some experts listed in the "**Editorial Services**" chapter review contracts.

If you decide not to use an independent publisher but do the work yourself, at least hire an editor, proofreader, cover designer, and interior typesetter-designer. The "**Editorial Services**" and "**Design and Production Services**" chapters will help you locate professionals with skills in these areas, as well as printing companies. Plus the "**Distribution Services**" and "**Publicity and Marketing Services**" chapters can help you solve one of the biggest problems of independent publishing: getting your books to readers.

AARON BOOK PUBLISHING

1104 Bristol Caverns Hwy., Bristol, TN 37620 | 423-212-1208
info@aaronbookpublishing.com | www.AaronBookPublishing.com
Lidany Rouse, acquistions editor
> **Types:** hardcover, paperback, gift book, POD
> **Services:** book covers, formatting, editing, printing, marketing, 100% net royalty from sales
> **Tip:** Prefers manuscript by email. Submission guidelines are on the website.

ACW PRESS

American Christian Writers, PO Box 110390, Nashville, TN 37222
800-21-WRITE | acwriters@aol.com | www.acwpress.com
Reg A. Forder, publisher
> **Types:** hardcover, paperback, gift book, POD
> **Services:** design, substantive editing, copyediting, proofreading
> **Production time:** two to four months
> **Tip:** "We offer a high-quality publishing alternative to help Christian authors get their material into print. High standards, high quality. If authors have a built-in audience, they have the best chance to make self-publishing a success."

ALTEN INK

1888 Montara Way, San Jacinto, CA 92583 | 951-327-3698
AltenInk3@gmail.com | www.AltenInk.com
Deborah L. Alten

> **Types:** paperback, e-book, picture book
> **Services:** substantive editing, proofreading, promotional materials, online bookstore, publishing packages of services, illustrations, book covers
> **Production time:** six months
> **Tip:** "Email us. You will get a quicker response."

AMPELOS PRESS

951 Anders Rd., Lansdale, PA 19446 | 484-991-8581
mbagnull@aol.com | writehisanswer.com/ampelospress
Marlene Bagnull, acquisitions editor

> **Types:** trade paperback, e-book, POD
> **Services:** Offers critiquing, editing, proofreading, typesetting, cover design. Especially interested in helping authors independently publish books about missions and the needs of children. Not actively soliciting manuscripts, but accepts them from writers she meets at conferences. Author receives 100% royalty.
> **Publication time:** six months.

BK ROYSTON PUBLISHING, LLC

PO Box 4321, Jeffersonville, IN 47131 | 502-802-5385
bkroystonpublishing@gmail.com | www.bkroystonpublishing.com
Julia A. Royston, CEO

> **Types:** POD, hardcover, paperback, e-book
> **Services:** editing, ghostwriting, coaching
> **Production time:** one to four months
> **Also does:** royalty publishing with a focus on books that inform, inspire, and entertain

BOOKBABY

7905 N. Crescent Blvd., Pennsauken, NJ 08110 | 877-961-6878
info@bookbaby.com | www.bookbaby.com

> **Types:** paperback, hardcover, e-book, POD, gift book, picture book, cookbook, comic book, yearbook, many other formats
> **Services:** manuscript evaluation, design, substantive editing, copyediting, proofreading, promotional materials, marketing, distribution, author websites, online bookstore

Production time: as quick as five days

Tip: E-book and printed book distribution network for self-published authors around the globe.

BOOKLOCKER.COM INC.

5726 Cortez Rd. W. #349, Bradenton, FL 34210 | 305-768-0261
angela@booklocker.com | *www.booklocker.com*
Angela Hoy, publisher

Types: hardcover, paperback, gift book, e-book, POD

Services: We break even on set-up fees and earn profits on book sales. Every BookLocker author receives a free copy of 90+ Days of Promoting Your Book Online: Your Book's Daily Marketing Plan. Pays 15% royalty on wholesale orders, 35% on *booklocker.com* orders, and 50-70% for e-book.

Production time: one month

Also does: royalty publishing through Abuzz Press, *www.AbuzzPress.com*, with exclusive three-year contract and higher royalties

Tip: "According to attorney Mark Levine, author of *The Fine Print*, BookLocker is: 'as close to perfection as you're going to find in the world of ebook and POD publishing. The ebook royalties are the highest I've ever seen, and the print royalties are better than average. BookLocker understands what new authors experience, and have put together a package that is the best in the business. You can't go wrong here. Plus, they're selective and won't publish any manuscript just because it's accompanied by a check. Also, the web site is well trafficked.'"

BOOKS BY THE BUNDLE

9217 W. River Rd., Brooklyn Park, MN 55444 | 612-968-9301
Jamie@booksbythebundle.org | *www.booksbythebundle.org*
Jamie Morrison, executive publisher | *Kelly, office manager*

Types: paperback, hardcover, e-book, POD, picture book

Services: manuscript evaluation, design, substantive editing, copyediting, proofreading, distribution, à la carte options, typesetting/interior design

Production time: six weeks to nine months

Tip: "We make publishing your book easy."

BROWN CHRISTIAN PRESS

16250 Knoll Trail Dr., Ste. 205, Dallas, TX 75248 | 972-381-0009
publisher@brownbooks.com | *www.brownchristianpress.com*
Chesle Blair

Types: hardcover, paperback, gift book, e-book
Services: editing, ghostwriting, graphic design, public relations services, marketing, warehousing, distribution, website options, e-commerce capabilities, and more; average first printing 3,000-5,000
Publication time: six months
Tip: "We are a relationship publisher and work with our authors from beginning to end in the journey of publishing."

CHRISTIAN BOOK SERVICES

307 Verde Meadow Dr., Franklin, TN 37067 | 615-472-1128
larry@christianbookservices.com | *www.christianbookservices.com*
www.carpenterssonpublishing.com
Larry Carpenter, president/CEO, editor

Types: POD, hardcover, paperback, e-book, audiobook
Services: Offers à la carte, including editing, proofreading, illustration, cover design, printing, marketing, and distribution, 63% of net revenue. Imprint: Carpenter's Son Publishing.
Production time: three to five months
Tip: "Larry is one of the few people who have worked in all aspects of book publishing, having worked for a publisher, a wholesale distributor, and a full-service distributor. Starting out in sales and marketing and eventually heading up two major companies, Larry knows all parts of the publishing industry well. Through Carpenter's Son Publishing, he can make that experience work for you!"

CHRISTIAN WRITER'S EBOOK NET

PO Box 446, Ft. Duchesne, UT 84026 | 435-772-3429
editor@writersebook.com | *www.writersebook.com*
Linda Kay Stewart Whitsitt, editor-in-chief, linda@webtechdg.com

Types: e-book
Services: Gives first-time authors the opportunity to bring their God-given writing talent to the Christian market. Pays royalty of 35-50% for sales on its site.
Production time: six months
Tip: "Make sure your work is polished and ready for print. The books we publish are sold in our online store at Amazon and eBay."

CLM PUBLISHING CO. LTD.

Building G, Ste. 5, Countryside Village Shopping Village, Box 1217 GT, Grand Cayman, Cayman Islands KY11108 | 345-926 2507
production@clmpublishing.com | *www.clmpublishing.com*
Karen E. Chin, managing editor

Types: paperback, hardcover, e-book, POD, gift book, picture book

Services: manuscript evaluation, design, substantive editing, copyediting, proofreading, promotional materials, marketing, distribution, author websites, online bookstore, publishing packages of services, à la carte options

Production time: three months

Also does: royalty contracts

Tip: "Even after many rejection letters, never stop writing. There is always a publisher for you."

CREATION HOUSE

600 Rinehart Rd., Lake Mary, FL 32746-4872 | 407-333-0600
creationhouse@charismamedia.com | *www.creationhouse.com*

Types: hardcover, paperback, gift book

Services: "We use the term 'co-publishing' to describe a hybrid between conventional royalty publishing and self- or subsidy publishing, utilizing the best of both worlds. We produce a high-quality book for our own inventory, market it, distribute it, and pay the author a royalty on every copy sold. In return, the author agrees to buy, at a deep discount, a portion of the first print run."

Production time: two to four months

Tip: Our purpose is "to inspire and equip people to live a Spirit-led life and to walk in the divine purpose for which they were created."

CREATIVE ENTERPRISES STUDIO

PO Box 224, Fort Worth, TX 76095 | 817-312-7393
AcreativeShop@aol.com | *CreativeEnterprisesStudio.co*
Mary Hollingsworth, publisher and managing director

Types: hardcover, paperback, gift book, e-book, audiobook, POD

Services: coaching, ghostwriting, editing, proofreading, typesetting, marketing, warehousing, shipping, website creation, video trailers

Production time: six months

Tip: "With 30 years' experience, CES is the best alternative to traditional publishing and self-publishing, offering first-class, custom publishing services from manuscript through printed books to help Christian authors powerfully glorify God in print."

CREDO HOUSE PUBLISHERS

3148 Plainfield Ave. N.E., Ste. 111, Grand Rapids, MI 49525-3285
616-363-2686 | *publish@credocommunications.net*
www.credohousepublishers.com
Timothy J. Beals, founder and publisher

Types: hardcover, paperback, gift book, e-book, POD

Services: Exists to "bring words to life" by working with Christian ministry leaders and organizations to develop life-changing books, Bible-related products, and other Christian resources. Can assist you in all phases of the publishing process—from concept sheets and prototypes to simple proofreading or complex content editing. Looking for fiction, children's, young adult, thoughtful nonfiction, juvenile nonfiction, women's issues titles, memoir/biography, devotional, textbooks, and special formats. Pays royalties annually on its sales. Complete the online author survey form.

CROSSHAIR PRESS

PO Box 154, Haven, KS 67543 | 316-214-9818
acquisitions@crosshairpress.com | *www.crosshairpress.com*
Amy Davis, acquisitions manager

Types: paperbacks, e-book, audio books, POD

Services: Manuscript evaluation, design, substantive editing, copyediting, proofreading, distribution

Production time: one year

Tip: "View our submission guidelines online for our reading period dates. Email submissions only."

CROSSHOUSE PUBLISHING

2844 S. FM 549, Ste. A, Rockwall, TX 75032 | 877-212-0933
sales@crosshousepublishing.org | *www.crosshousepublishing.com*
Dr. Katie Welch, publisher

Types: hardcover, trade paperback, e-book

Services: editing, design, proofreading, back-cover copy, distribution, packages of services, royalty 25% on net

Production time: three months

Tip: "We provide authors the opportunity to have their books distributed through a wide array of Christian and general bookstores. We aspire to offer the marketplace superior Christian literature that will impact readers' lives."

DCTS PUBLISHING

PO Box 40216, Santa Barbara, CA 93140 | 805-570-3168
dennis@dctspub.com | *www.dctspub.com*
Dennis Stephen Hamilton, editor

Types: print and e-book

Services: Books are designed to enrich the mind, encourage the heart, and empower the spirit.

Production time: six to eight months

Tip: "For authors who want quality low-cost publishing, we will partner with you in producing a fantastic marketable book that will sell anywhere in the world. Please contact me for more details."

DEEPER REVELATION BOOKS

PO Box 4260, Cleveland, TN 37320-4260 | 423-478-2843
www.deeperrevelationbooks.org
Mike Shreve

Types: POD, e-book

Services: editing, proofreading, design, marketing options, global distribution contacts to both Christian and general markets, cost analysis, website design, online media kits, and more

DEEP RIVER BOOKS

220 S. Pine St., Sisters, OR 97759 | 541-549-1139
bill@deepriverbooks.com | nancie@deepriverbooks.com
www.deepriverbooks.com
Bill and Nancie Carmichael, publishers

Types: hardback, trade paperback, gift book

Services: Offers writing consultation, editing, title and cover design, printing (minimum of 2,500), marketing, and retail sales. Requires author to purchase books. Pays royalty 12-18% of net on its sales of your book. Publishes thirty-five titles per year, 90% from first-time authors. Prefers 45,000+ words or 192-400 pages. Query first by email only with proposal and two or three chapters. "Anything Christian or inspirational that is well written, especially from new authors."

Production time: nine to twelve months

Tip: "Go to our website first, and read how we partner with new authors. Then, if you feel Deep River Books would be a good fit for you, email your proposal."

DESTINY IMAGE PUBLISHERS

PO Box 310, Shippensburg, PA 17257 | 800-722-6774, 717-532-3040
manuscripts@norimediagroup.com | www.destinyimage.com
Mykela Krieg, executive acquisitions director

Types: print, e-book

Services: evaluation, editing (whatever level is necessary), proofing, cover design, pagination/layout design, printing, and marketing. Requires prepurchase of 1,000 to 3,000 copies. Major topics include dreams/dream interpretation, supernatural God encounters, healing/deliverance, and prophecy. No poetry, art, or children's stories; limited fiction. Prefers 40,000-60,000 words. Submit via email or mail with book proposal form from the website. Responds in eight to twelve weeks.

Production time: twelve months

Tip: "Most open to books on the deeper life, or of charismatic interest."

EABOOKS PUBLISHING

1567 Thornhill Cir., Oviedo, FL 32765 | 407-712-3431
Cheri@eabookspublishing.com | *www.eabookspublishing.com*
Cheri Cowell, owner/publisher

Types: paperback, e-book, audiobook, POD

Services: manuscript evaluation, design, substantive editing, copyediting, proofreading, promotional materials, marketing, distribution, author websites, online bookstore, packages of services, à la carte options

Production time: ninety days

Tip: "Fill out the contact form on our website, and we will contact you."

ESSENCE PUBLISHING

20 Hanna Ct., Belleville, ON K8P 5J2, Canada | 800-238-6376
613-962-2360 | *info@essence-publishing.com* | *www.essence-publishing.com*
Sherrill Brunton, publishing manager, s.brunton@essence-publishing.com

Types: hardcover, paperback, gift book, POD, e-book, book trailer, full-color children's book

Services: Offers editing, proofreading, design, illustrations, back-cover copy, typesetting, bookmarks, online store, distribution through Amazon.com. Provides affordable, short-run book publishing. Pays royalty of 50% from bookstore and e-book sales. Average first printing 500-1,000. Uploads e-book to Amazon, iBookstore, and KOBO.

Production time: three to five months

Also does: pamphlets, booklets, tracts, posters

FAIRWAY PRESS

5450 N. Dixie Hwy., Lima, OH 45807-9559 | 800-241-4056
419-227-1818 | *david@csspub.com* | *www.fairwaypress.com*
Missy Cotrell, acquisitions editor

Types: hardcover, paperback, POD, e-book

Services: mechanical edit (spelling, grammar, punctuation, etc.), formatting, proofreading, cover design, printing (average print run 500 copies, minimum 50), ISBN, bar coding, copyright filing. Pays royalty to 50%. No email submissions. Publishes ten to fifteen titles per year.

Production time: six to nine months

Tip: This is the subsidy division of CSS Publishing Company. No longer does color illustrations or four-color books.

FAITH BOOKS & MORE

3255 Lawrenceville-Suwanee Rd., Ste. P250, Suwanee, GA 30024
678-232-6156 | publishing@faithbooksandmore.com
www.faithbooksandmore.com
Nicole Smith, managing editor

Types: hardcover, paperback, POD, offset

Services: editing, cover and interior design, distribution, marketing copy, marketing and PR advice, monthly royalty payments

Production time: three to six months

FIESTA PUBLISHING

1219 E. Colter St. #16, Phoenix, AZ 85014 | 602-795-5868
julie@fiestapublishing.com | www.fiestapublishing.com
Julie Castro, owner

Types: paperback, e-book, POD

Services: manuscript evaluation, design, substantive editing, copyediting, proofreading, promotional materials, marketing, distribution, online bookstore, packages of services, à la carte options

Production time: six to twelve weeks

Tip: "It usually takes longer than one thinks to publish a quality book."

FILLED BOOKS

529 County Road 31, Millry, AL 36558 | 251-754-9335
editor@empoweredpublications.com | www.filledbooks.com
Bridgett Henson, book coach

Types: paperbacks, hardbacks, e-book, POD

Services: manuscript evaluation, design, substantive editing, copyediting, proofreading, promotional services, marketing, distribution, packages of services

Production time: four weeks

Tip: Free publishing for Christian ministers with the purchase of 250 paperbacks.

FRUITBEARER PUBLISHING, LLC

PO Box 777, Georgetown, DE 19947 | 302-856-6649
cfa@candyabbott.com | *www.fruitbearer.com*
Candy Abbott, managing partner

> **Types:** POD, picture books
> **Services:** editing, cover design, marketing, average first printing 100-5,000
> **Production time:** one to six months
> **Also does:** pamphlets, booklets, tracts, bookmarks, business cards
> **Tip:** Accepts limited submissions, five to ten titles per year.

HALO PUBLISHING INTERNATIONAL

1100 N.W. Loop 410, Ste. 700-176, San Antonio, TX 78213
877-705-9647 | *jodie@halopublishing.com* | *www.halopublishing.com*
Jodie Greenberg, acquistions editor

> **Types:** hardcover, paperback, POD, gift book, e-book
> **Services:** editing, design, distribution, marketing, packages of services, online bookstore with 95% royalty, book trailer
> **Production time:** sixty days
> **Tip:** Also publishes in Spanish.

HEALTHY LIFE PRESS

6700 Wadsworth Blvd., Ste. 101, Arvada, CO 80003 | 877-331-2766
info@healthylifepress.com | *www.HealthyLifePress.com*
Dr. David Biebel, publisher

> **Types:** paperback, hardcover, e-book, POD
> **Services:** manuscript evaluation, design, substantive editing, copyediting, proofreading, promotional materials, marketing, distribution
> **Production time:** eight months
> **Also does:** royalty contracts
> **Tip:** "The more finished, the faster we can get a book to market."

HOLY FIRE PUBLISHING

205 St. James Ave., Goose Creek, SC 29445 | 843-285-3130
publisher@holyfirepublishing.com | *www.christianpublish.com*
Vanessa Hensel, COO

> **Types:** hardcover, paperback, e-book
> **Services:** design, copyright service, bookstore advertising, distribution, online bookstore, pays royalties on its sales, packages of services

Tip: "Our contract can be canceled at any time for any reason with a 60-day written notice. It's that simple."

MCDOUGAL PUBLISHING

PO Box 3595, Hagerstown, MD 21742 | 301-797-6637
foundation@mcdougal.org | *www.mcdougalpublishing.com*

Types: POD, offset printing
Services: manuscript critiquing, editing, cover design, typesetting

MORGAN JAMES PUBLISHING

5 Penn Plaza, 23rd Floor, New York City, NY 10001 | 212-655-5470
terry@morganjamespublishing.com | *www.morganjamespublishing.com*
W. Terry Whalin, acquisition editor, Morgan James Faith
Karen Anderson, karen@morganjamespublishing.com

Types: hardcover, paperback, e-book
Services: General market publisher that does 45-50 Christian books per year. Offers design, distribution, marketing. Requires authors to buy up to 2,500 copies at cost plus $2 per book. Pays 20-30% royalties on its sales; may offer advance of $100. Email proposal with sample chapters or full manuscript.
Production time: three to six months
Also does: royalty publishing

NORDSKOG PUBLISHING

4562 Westinghouse St., Ste. E, Ventura, CA 93003 | 805-642-2070
nordskogpublishing.com
Desta Garrett: managing editor

Services: Offers editing, design, and marketing. Seeks to publish the best in sound theological and applied Christian faith books, both nonfiction and fiction.

NYREEPRESS PRESS

PO Box 164882, Fort Worth, TX 76161 | 972-793-3736
submissions@nyreepress.com | *www.nyreepress.com*
Cederick Stewart,COO/publishing consultant

Types: POD, e-book
Services: Offers printing and distribution. Must use the submission form on the website.

PARSON PLACE PRESS, LLC

PO Box 8277, Mobile, AL 36689-0277; 251-643-6985
info@parsonplacepress.com | *www.parsonplacepress.com*
Michael L. White, managing editor

Submissions: Nonfiction: Use the Bible as the predominant source to teach something spiritually valuable, expound on a theological or doctrinal thought, explain a prophetic insight, etc. Fiction: Stories must contain reality-based, down-to-earth characters and events that demonstrate the practical application of biblical teaching to daily living. No simultaneous submissions. Email proposal according to the guidelines on the website. Guidelines: www.parsonplacepress.com/guide.html.

Services: traditional, royalty publisher but requires the author to purchase 100 copies at a deep discount

Production time: three months

Tip: "Most open to conservative, biblically based content that ministers to Christians. Write intelligently, clearly, sincerely, and engagingly."

OAKS BOUGH PUBLISHING, LLC

9119 Highway 6 S., Ste. 230, PMB 380, Missouri City, TX 77459
832-671-8906 | marykaarto@marykaarto.com | marykaarto.com
Mary Kaarto, publisher

Types: paperback, e-book
Services: proofreading
Production time: one book at a time, one author at a time
Tip: Submit three sample chapters, a book proposal, table of contents, and SASE.

REDEMPTION PRESS

1730 Railroad St., Enumclaw, WA 98022 | 360-226-3488
info@redemption-press.com | www.redemption-press.com
Athena Dean Holtz, publisher

Types: paperback, hardcover, e-book, audiobook, POD, gift book, picture book, offset printing when it's the appropriate solution

Services: manuscript evaluation, design, substantive editing, copyediting, proofreading, promotional materials, marketing, distribution, author websites, online bookstore, à la carte options, writing and marketing coaches to work one-on-one with authors

Production time: three to four months, unless extensive editing or coaching is required

Tip: "Do your due diligence before accepting a publishing offer, and be sure to contact authors who've been published and see if their experience matches the claims of the publisher. Find out how the publisher rates in *The Fine Print of Self-Publishing* 6th edition by Mark Levine."

REVIVAL WAVES OF GLORY BOOKS & PUBLISHING

PO Box 596, Litchfield, IL 62056 | 217-851-0361
bill.vincent@yahoo.com | *www.revivalwavesofgloryministries.com*
Bill Vincent, publisher

> **Types:** hardcover, paperback, e-book, audiobook
> **Services:** editing, design, distribution, packages of services, marketing campaigns
> **Production time:** one to six months

SALVATION PUBLISHER AND MARKETING GROUP

PO Box 40860, Santa Barbara, CA 93140 | 805-252-9822
opalmaedailey@aol.com
Opal Mae Dailey, editor-in-chief

> **Types:** hardcover, paperback, POD
> **Services:** Specializes in turning taped messages into book form for pastors. Average first printing 1,000. Only publishes five to seven titles per year. No simultaneous submissions. Query by email.
> **Production time:** three to four months
> **Tip:** "We do not accept any manuscript that we would be ashamed to put our name on."

SERMON TO BOOK • SPEAK IT TO BOOK

424 W. Bakerview Rd., Ste. 105 #215, Bellingham, WA 98226 | 360-223-1877
info@sermontobook.com | *www.sermontobook.com*
Caleb Breakey, lead book director

> **Types:** paperback, e-book, audiobook, POD
> **Services:** design, substantive editing, copyediting, proofreading, promotional materials, marketing, distribution, author websites, online bookstore, packages of services, à la carte options, turn sermons into books
> **Production time:** six to ten months
> **Tip:** To schedule a call with Caleb Breakey, go to *calendly.com/ sermontobook/30min*

SPLASHDOWN BOOKS

4/11 Hall Rd, Glenfield, Auckland, New Zealand 0629
+6-422-472-2301 | *grace@splashdownbooks.com* | *www.splashdownbooks.com*
Grace Bridges, managing editor

> **Types:** paperback, e-book, POD
> **Services:** manuscript evaluation, design, substantive editing, copyediting, proofreading, distribution, à la carte options, hybrid publishing

Production time: depends on how much editing is needed and how long the author needs to implement changes and learn about publishing, etc.

Tip: Speculative genres only: science fiction, fantasy, paranormal, or a combination. No preaching or excessively overt content.

STONEHOUSE INK
Boise, ID | 208-608-8325
stonehousepress@hotmail.com | stonehouseink.net
Aaron Patterson, editor-publisher

Types: paperback, e-book

Services: Specializes in fiction, including thrillers, mystery, and young adult. Interested in published authors looking to publish backlist titles or to rebrand and relaunch titles.

STRONG TOWER PUBLISHING
PO Box 973, Milesburg, PA 16863
strongtowerpubs@aol.com | www.strongtowerpublishing.com
Heidi L. Nigro, publisher

Types: paperback, e-book, POD

Services: Offers manuscript evaluation, copyediting, proofreading, substantive editing, cover and interior design, online bookstore. Specializes in books on end-times topics from the prewrath rapture perspective. Pays 25% royalty on sales. Publishes only one or two titles per year.

Production time: three to four months

Tip: "We recommend that all first-time authors have their manuscripts professionally edited. We will consider putting first-time authors into print, but by invitation only. That invitation comes only after the manuscript has been thoroughly evaluated and we have discussed the pros and cons of our unique on-demand publishing model with the author."

TATE PUBLISHING & ENTERPRISES, LLC
127 E. Trade Center Ter., Mustang, OK 73064-4421 | 888-361-9473
publish@tatepublishing.com | www.tatepublishing.com
Dr. Richard Tate, founder

Types: hardcover, paperback, e-book, audiobook, music, video

Services: distribution, marketing, book trailer, website, advertising, pays 15-40% net royalty

Production time: as short as three months if certain criteria are met

TEACH SERVICES, INC.

8300 Hwy. 41, Unit 107, PO Box 954, Ringgold, GA 30736
800-367-1844 | Publishing@teachservices.com | www.teachservices.com
Timothy Hullquist, author advisor, T.Hullquist@TEACHServices.com

Types: POD, e-book

Services: Only publishes materials that are in accordance with Seventh Day Adventist beliefs. Offers editing, design, typesetting, distribution, marketing. Pays royalty of 10-12% on print books and 25-50% on e-book.

Production time: three to six months

Tip: "Books that discuss biblical ideas or insights must be reviewed and approved by at least two Adventist ministers, retired or currently serving. Likewise books that recommend medical treatment, diet, or nutrition must be reviewed and approved by at least two medical doctors or dietitians."

TESTIMONY PUBLICATIONS

5625 Pearl Dr., Ste. F-123, Evansville, IN 47712 | 812-602-3031
mkough@testimonypublications.com | www.testimonypublications.com
Marj Kough, CEO

Types: paperback, hardcover, e-book, POD

Services: manuscript evaluation, design, substantive editing, copyediting, proofreading, promotional materials, marketing, distribution, author websites, online bookstore, packages of services, à la carte options

Production time: three to six months

Also does: royalty contracts

Tip: "We publish fiction or nonfiction books or materials with a Christian focus."

TMP BOOKS

2631 Holly Springs Pkwy., Box 35, Holly Springs, GA 30142
info@tmpbooks.com | www.TMPbooks.com
Tracy Ruckman, publisher

Types: POD, e-book

Services: Offers packages of services and à la carte pricing for editing, formatting, and design. Royalties paid quarterly. Accepts fiction, nonfiction, and children's books. Publishes ten plus titles per year.

Tip: "Affordable and professional self-publishing that allows authors to retain control of their projects."

TOTAL FUSION PRESS
PO Box 123, Strasburg, OH 44680 | 330-737-1031
contact@totalfusionpress.com | *www.totalfusionpress.com*
Rob Coburn, president
> **Types:** paperback, hardcover, e-book, audiobook, POD, gift book, picture book
> **Services:** manuscript evaluation, design, substantive editing, copyediting, proofreading, promotional materials, marketing, distribution, author websites, online bookstore, packages of services, à la carte options
> **Production time:** six to eight weeks with a completed manuscript
> **Tip:** Created to help the average person have a platform to share his or her story.

T2PNEUMA PUBLISHERS LLC
PO Box 230564, Centreville, VA 20120 | 703-973-8898
T2Pneuma@gmail.com | *www.T2Pneuma.com*
Stephen W. Hiemstra, publisher
> **Types:** paperback, e-book
> **Services:** manuscript evaluation
> **Production time:** one year
> **Tip:** "We focus on nonfiction, Christian books in English and Spanish. Check website for details before submitting manuscript ideas."

TRUTH BOOK PUBLISHERS
824 Bills Rd., Franklin, IL 62638 | 217-675-2191
truthbookpublishers@yahoo.com | *www.truthbookpublishers.com*
JaNell Lyle, editor
> **Types:** POD, e-book
> **Services:** editing, design, proofreading, printing, marketing, e-book distribution, transcription, online bookstore
> **Production time:** one month
> **Tip:** "We are missionary minded and desire to help the body of Christ mature."

TULPEN PUBLISHING
11043 Depew St., Westminster, CO 80020 | 303-438-7276
tulpenpublishing@gmail.com | *TulpenPublishing.com*
Sandi Rog, acquisitions editor
> **Types:** paperback, e-book, POD
> **Services:** manuscript evaluation, design, substantive editing, copyediting, proofreading, distribution, online bookstore, marketing tips to authors, books in brick and mortar stores

Production time: twelve to twenty months
Tip: Only accepts submissions via email. See the website for submission guidelines.

WESTBOW PRESS

1663 Liberty Dr., Bloomington, IN 47403 | 866-928-1240
www.westbowpress.com

Types: hardcover, paperback, e-book, audiobook
Services: Independent publishing division of Thomas Nelson and Zondervan. Offers manuscript evaluation, substantive editing, copyediting, cover and interior design, illustrations, indexing, Spanish translation, marketing, video trailer, distribution. Pays royalties on copies sold.

WORD ALIVE PRESS

131 Cordite Rd., Winnipeg, MB R3W 1S1, Canada | 866-967-3782
204-777-7100 | publishing@wordalivepress.ca | www.wordalivepress.ca

Types: hardcover, paperback, e-book, gift book, POD, offset
Services: packages of services, editing, design, marketing, distribution, online bookstore, quarterly royalties of 10-20%
Production time: four to five months

XULON PRESS

2301 Lucien Way, Ste. 415, Maitland, FL 32751 | 407-339-4217
866-381-2665 | www.xulonpress.com
Donald Newman, director of sales

Types: hardcover, paperback, e-book, POD
Services: manuscript review, editorial critique, developmental editing, copyediting, design, packages of services, à la carte options, color illustrations, back-cover copy, ghostwriting, translation, marketing, promotional materials, publicity, video trailer, 100% net royalty, online bookstore
Production time: three to six months

ZOË LIFE PUBLISHING

PO Box 871066, Canton, MI 48187 | 888-400-4922
authoradvocate@zoelifepub.com | www.zoelifepub.com
Sabrina Adams, publisher, sabrina.adams@zoelifepub.com

Types: hardcover, paperback, e-book
Services: packages of services, editing, cover design, layout, quality control, rights and registrations, book production, warehousing, promotion, distribution and fulfillment, online bookstore, 50% royalty
Production time: one year
Also does: royalty publishing

3

DESIGN AND PRODUCTION SERVICES

AUTHOR SUPPORT SERVICES | RUSSELL SHERRARD

Carmichael, CA | 916-967-7251

*russellsherrard@reagan.com | www.sherrardsebookresellers.com/WordPress/
author-support-services-professional-services-affordable-prices-by-russell-
sherrard-june-21-2016*

> **Contact:** email
> **Services:** Kindle e-book formatting, e-book linked table of contents, PDF creation, book-cover design, copyediting, proofreading
> **Charges:** flat fee
> **Credentials/experience:** Writing and editing since 2009; currently providing freelance services for multiple clients.

BETHANY PRESS INTERNATIONAL

6820 W. 115th St., Bloomington, MN 55438 | 888-717-7400

info@bethanypress.com | www.bethanypress.com

> **Contact:** email, phone, website form
> **Services:** short-run digital printing and long-run (minimum 500 copies) printing, only with files created by a professional book designer; e-book conversion, only with corresponding print order
> **Charges:** flat fee
> **Credentials/experience:** Printer for the majority of Christian publishing houses since 1997. We partner with publishers and ministries to create, produce, and distribute millions of life-changing Christian books each year. We invest our proceeds in training and sending missionaries through Bethany International.

BLUE LEAF BOOK SCANNING

618 Crowsnest Dr., Ballwin, MO 63021 | 314-606-9322

blue.leaf.it@gmail.com | www.blueleaf-book-scanning.com

Contact: email, phone, website form

Services: book and document scanning to multiple formats, e-book and audio conversions

Charges: flat fee

Credentials/experience: The first book-scanning service for consumers. Accurate optical character recognition (more than 99.6% accurate on ideal conditions) with excellent format retention. Can scan nearly 200 languages.

BRAYV | ROBERT CRUM

8617 66th St., Kenosha, WI 53142 | 719-351-4968

bob@brayv.co | brayv.co

Contact: email, phone

Services: book-cover design, book-interior design, illustrations

Charges: flat fee

Credentials/experience: A full-time illustrator and designer for more than 20 years experience with authors in the young-adult fiction market, as well as graphic novels and comics.

CASTELANE, INC. | KIM MCDOUGALL

Whitehall, PA | 647-281-1554

kimm@castelane.com | www.castelane.com

Contact: email

Services: book-cover design, e-book conversion, book video trailers

Charges: flat fee

Credentials/experience: Have made more than 500 book video trailers and 300 book covers since 2009. Samples and references are available on the website.

CELEBRATIONWEBDESIGN.COM BY SKWD | BRUCE SHANK

PO Box 34747, Celebration, FL 34747

info@celebrationwebdesign.com | CelebrationWebDesign.com

Contact: email, phone

Services: book-cover design, book-interior design, e-book conversion, website design

Charges: flat fee, hourly rate

Credentials/experience: Designing, developing, and hosting websites for Christian authors for more than 10 years. Fully customized website development service.

CHRISTIANPRINT.COM

6820 W. 115th St., Bloomington, MN 55438 | 888-201-1322

info@bethanypress.com | www.christianprint.com

Contact: email, phone, website form
Services: prints ancillary products, such as business cards, brochures, booklets, banners, postcards, posters, and signs
Charges: flat fee
Credentials/experience: A division of Bethany Press, founded in 1997. The revenue generated through orders helps fund important ministries of Bethany International, which takes the Gospel to some of the least-reached people groups on the planet.

CROWN LAID DOWN DESIGNS | HOLLY SMITH

College Station, TX | 719-482-5523
chrishollysmith@msn.com | *www.crownlaiddowndesigns.com*

Contact: email
Services: website design
Charges: hourly rate
Credentials/experience: Seven years' experience as a designer/developer for WordPress and Blogger sites for publications and entrepreneurs.

DESIGN CORPS | JOHN WOLLINKA

Colorado Springs, CO | 719-260-0500
john@designcorps.us | *designcorps.us*

Contact: email
Services: book-cover design, book-interior design, typesetting, e-book conversion, illustrations, website design, printing, marketing collateral
Charges: flat fee
Credentials/experience: Design Corps has been serving Christian publishers, denominations, ministries, and organizations for more than 20 years.

THE DESIGN IN YOUR MIND · FINDLEY FAMILY VIDEO PUBLICATIONS | MARY C. FINDLEY

Tulsa, OK | 918-805-0669
mjmcfindley@gmail.com | *elkjerkyforthesoul.wordpress.com*

Contact: email
Services: book-cover design, book-interior design, e-book conversion, illustrations
Charges: flat fee
Credentials/experience: Designer and formatter for 5 years for many indie authors and many genres, including illustrated children's books, graphics in layouts, illustrated e-books, print for fiction, and curriculum.

DIGGYPOD | KEVIN OSWORTH
301 Industrial Dr., Tecumseh, MI 49286 | 877-944-7844
kosworth@diggypod.com | *www.diggypod.com*

> **Contact:** email
> **Services:** book-cover design, printing
> **Charges:** based on the number of books/pages being printed. Website has an active quote calculator that provides 100% accurate pricing.
> **Credentials/experience:** DiggyPOD has been printing books since 2001. All facets of the book printing take place in our facility.

EDENBROOKE PRODUCTIONS | MARTY KEITH
Franklin, TN | 615-415-1942
johnmartinkeith@gmail.com | *www.edenbrookemusic.com/booktrailers*

> **Contact:** email
> **Services:** book trailers with custom music
> **Charges:** flat fee
> **Credentials/experience:** Have produced music for everyone from CBS Television to Discovery Channel.

FAITH & FANTASY ALLIANCE | SCOTT AND BECKY MINOR
Pottstown, PA | 610-906-6266
scottminor@comcast.net | *www.faithandfantasyalliance.com*

> **Contact:** email
> **Services:** illustration, audiobook narration, video book trailer
> **Charges:** hourly rate
> **Credentials/experience:** Scott is a professional actor, audiobook producer/narrator, full-cast audiobook producer, and video producer/editor. Becky is a professional illustrator, animator, and author. Both have BFA degrees from The University of the Arts, Philadelphia, Pennsylvania.

FISTBUMP MEDIA, LLC | DAN KING
Sarasota, FL | 941-780-4179
dan@fistbumpmedia.com | *fistbumpmedia.com*

> **Contact:** email
> **Services:** book-cover design, book-interior design, typesetting, e-book conversion, website design
> **Charges:** flat fee, hourly rate
> **Credentials/experience:** See the website for references and portfolio. Specializes in design and formatting for print-on-demand.

FIVE J'S DESIGN | JEFF AND JOY MILLER
Aubrey, TX | 940-242-1142
info@fivejsdesign.com | *fivejsdesign.com*
> **Contact:** email
> **Services:** book-cover design, book-interior design, typesetting, e-book conversion, website design
> **Charges:** flat fee
> **Credentials/experience:** We have been designing books and websites since 2008, including the website, typesetting, and cover design for *The Christian Writers Market Guide 2017*, and The Christian Writers Institute website.

HL CREATIVE | LAURA PATTERSON
PO Box 570606, Houston, TX 77257 | 281-915-4358
laura@hl-creative.com | *www.hlcreative.com*
> **Contact:** email
> **Services:** book-cover design, book-interior design, typesetting, illustrations, website design
> **Charges:** flat fee, hourly rate
> **Credentials/experience:** Thirteen years of advertising and graphic-design experience.

JOANNA MARIE ART | JOANNA MARIE
PO Box 31652, Mesa, AZ 85275 | 520-686-1088
joanna@joannamarieart.com | *www.joannamarieart.com*
> **Contact:** email
> **Services:** book-cover design, illustrations, website design
> **Charges:** flat fee, hourly service
> **Credentials/experience:** More than 10 years in fine art/illustration work, 5 years web design.

KEN RANEY
Wichita, KS | 316-737-9724
kenraney@mac.com | *kenraneydesign.blogspot.com*
> **Contact:** email, phone
> **Services:** book-cover design, book-interior design, e-book conversion, illustrations
> **Charges:** flat fee, hourly rate
> **Credentials/experience:** More than 40 years' experience in graphic design and illustration.

LIONSGATE BOOK DESIGN | LISA HAINLINE
1317 Joplin Dr. #3, San Jose, CA | 909-436-9025
Lisa@lisahainline.com | www.lionsgatebookdesign.com | www.lisahainline.com

Contact: email
Services: book-cover design, promotional materials like postcards and bookmarks, logo and website designs (editing and interior formatting also available from the company)
Charges: flat fee, free consultation
Credentials/experience: Thirty-five years of experience in professional graphic design, art direction, and advertising. Works with new and seasoned authors, providing personal attention and custom design. See portfolios on the websites.

MADISON DESIGNS | RUTH DERBY
Hanford, CA | 559-772-2489
rmadison_1@hotmail.com | www.ruthiemadison.com

Contact: email
Services: book-cover design
Charges: according to the images I use and whether it is a premade book cover or customized work.
Credentials/experience: Designed covers for indie authors, such as JoAnn Durgin, Kari Trumbo, Debra Collins, and Caryl McAdoo.

MCLENNAN CREATIVE | ALISON MCLENNAN
1933 Geraldson Dr., Lancaster, PA 17601 | 717-572-2585
alison@mclennancreative.com | www.mclennancreative.com

Contact: email, phone, website contact form
Services: book-cover design, e-book conversion, website design
Charges: flat fee, hourly rate, customized packages
Credentials/experience: More than 20 years' experience in the publishing industry.

MELINDA MARTIN
Palestine, TX | 903-948-4893
support@melindamartin.me | melindamartin.me

Contact: email
Services: book-cover design, book-interior design, typesetting, e-book conversion
Charges: flat fee
Credentials/experience: Four years of working with clients' manuscripts to achieve a design that is best for their platforms.

ROSEANNA WHITE DESIGNS | ROSEANNA WHITE

Cumberland, MD | 410-571-1678
roseannamwhite@gmail.com | *www.RoseannaWhiteDesigns.com*

    Contact: email
    Services: book-cover design, book-interior design
    Charges: flat fee
    Credentials/experience: Designed covers for several small publishers and a slew of independent authors since 2011. Covers have been finalists in several book-cover award contests.

SCREE, LLC | LANDON OTIS

Sandpoint, ID | 208-290-4624
landon@scree.it | *scree.it*

    Contact: email
    Services: website design, website development
    Charges: hourly rate
    Credentials/experience: Professional, full-time web developer at a local design and marketing firm. Websites include veritasincorporated.com and mineralchurch.org.

STARCHER DESIGNS | KARA D. STARCHER

Magnolia, OH 44643 | 330-705-3399
info@starcherdesigns.com | *www.starcherdesigns.com*

    Contact: email
    Services: book-interior design, typesetting, e-book conversion
    Charges: flat fee, page rate
    Credentials/experience: B.A. in publishing, numerous design awards from West Virginia Press Association, taught high school graphic-design classes, proficient in Adobe software and prepress procedures, 11+ years as a freelance designer.

TLC GRAPHICS | TAMARA DEVER

Austin, TX | 512-669-5744
tamara@tlcgraphics.com | *www.TLCGraphics.com*

    Contact: email
    Services: book-cover design, book-interior design, typesetting, e-book conversion, printing, publishing consulting, editorial
    Charges: custom pricing according to project needs
    Credentials/experience: Award-winning design firm and author guidance with more than 25 years of publishing experience. Small, caring team working with you, taking your raw manuscript

through editorial, design, and printing to provide a beautiful and salable book you'll be proud to represent. Services are à la carte with design contract. Also publishers of *My Publishing Journal,* a guided, illustrated journal for authors.

TRILION STUDIOS | BRIAN WHITE
Lawrence, KS | 785-841-5500
brian@TriLionStudios.com | www.TriLionStudios.com
- **Contact:** email, phone
- **Services:** book-cover design, illustrations, web design
- **Charges:** flat fee, hourly rate
- **Credentials/experience:** Twenty years in the design/web design/ branding industry. Have worked with nonprofits and churches for more than 15 years.

VIVID GRAPHICS | LARRY VAN HOOSE
120 W. Grayson St., Ste. 350, Galax, VA 24333 | 276-233-0276
larry@vivid-graphics.com | www.vivid-graphics.com
- **Contact:** email, phone
- **Services:** book-cover design, book-interior design, e-book conversion, website design
- **Charges:** flat fee, hourly rate
- **Credentials/experience:** Graphic, web, and book designer with more than 20 years' experience.

WRITERS' TABLET, LLC | TERRI WHITEMORE
4371 Roswell Rd. #315, Marietta, GA 30062 | 770-648-4101
WritersTablet@gmail.com | www.WritersTablet.org
- **Contact:** email
- **Services:** book-cover design, book-interior design, typesetting, e-book conversion, illustrations, website design
- **Charges:** flat fee
- **Credentials/experience:** Graphic design, B.S. in computer science, testimonials from local and national businesses and authors. Copywriter for G5. Five years' experience.

Note: See **Editorial Services** and **Publicity and Marketing Services** for help with these needs.

DISTRIBUTION SERVICES

BOOKMASTERS
30 Amberwood Pkw., Ashland, OH 44805 | 877-312-3520, 419-281-5100
www.bookmasters.com

Offers a wide range of fulfillment and distribution services. Contact an account executive through the website.

CBA MAILING LISTS OF CHRISTIAN BOOKSTORES
1365 Garden of the Gods Rd. #105, Colorado Springs, CO 80907
800-252-1950 | info@cbaonline.org | www.cbaonline.org

Three different lists are available for rental, including nonmember stores: 2,500 addresses, $349; member stores, 1,075 addresses, $499; combination of all stores, 3,500 addresses, $549. Prices and numbers available are subject to change. Call for full details.

CHRISTIAN BOOK DISTRIBUTORS
PO Box 7000, Peabody, MA 01961-7000 | 800-247-4784, 978-977-5000
customer.service@christianbook.com | www.christianbook.com

Sometimes distributes independently published books.

PARTNERS PUBLISHERS GROUP
2325 Jarco Dr., Holt, MI 48842 | 800-336-3137
info@partnerspublishersgroup.com | www.partnerspublishersgroup.com

Is an exclusive national distributor. Upon contractual agreement, they place your title(s) in Ingram and Baker & Taylor, present your title(s) to other wholesalers and national buyers of chain bookstores through their sales representatives, and represent your title(s) in their catalogue and the BEA national trade show. See the website for prerequisites. No print-on-demand books.

PATHWAY BOOK SERVICE

PO Box 89, Gilsum, NH 03448 | 800-345-6665
pbs@pathwaybook.com | www.pathwaybook.com

Provides warehousing, order fulfillment, and trade distribution. It is a longtime distributor to Ingram and Baker & Taylor, the vendors of choice for most bookstores. Pathway uploads new-title spreadsheets to Ingram and Baker & Taylor, as well as to Amazon. com, Barnes & Noble, Booksamillion, and Indigo/Chapters (Canada) databases on a weekly basis. Distribution outside of North America is available through Gazelle Book Services in the United Kingdom. Also provides the option of having Pathway add titles to their Amazon Advantage account, which is at a lower discount and often a lower shipping cost per book than individual accounts.

PART 3

PERIODICAL PUBLISHERS

5

TOPICS AND TYPES

This chapter is not an exhaustive list of types of manuscripts and topics editors are looking for, but it is a starting place for some of the more popular ones. For instance, almost all periodicals take manuscripts in categories like Christian living, so they are not listed here. Plus writers guidelines tend to outline general areas, not every specific type and topic an editor will buy.

CONTEMPORARY ISSUES
Anglican Journal
Bible Advocate
Catholic New York
Catholic Sentinel
Christianity Today
Citizen Magazine
The Covenant
  Companion
Eureka Street
The Journal of Adventist
  Education
Light & Life Magazine
Ministry
New Frontier Chronicle
Now What?
Our Sunday Visitor
  Newsweekly
Perspectives
Presbyterians Today
St. Anthony Messenger
War Cry

DEVOTIONALS
FCA Magazine
Focus on the Family
Gems of Truth

Halo Magazine
Mature Living
OCACW Newsletter
ParentLife
Presbyterians Today
Shades of Romance
  Magazine
The Vision

ESSAY
America
Believers Bay
The Canadian Lutheran
Catholic Digest
The Christian Century
Christian
  Communicator
Christian Librarian
Christian Standard
Commonweal
The Cresset
CrossCurrents
Faith Today
Image
Liguorian
Our Sunday Visitor
  Newsweekly
The Penwood Review

Poets & Writers
  Magazine
Relief Journal
Sharing
U.S. Catholic
The Writer
The Writer's Chronicle
Writer's Digest

EVANGELISM
Christian Research
  Journal
CommonCall
Decision
Evangelical Missions
  Quarterly
Just Between Us
Lutheran Witness
Mature Living
Net Results
New Identity Magazine
On Mission
Outreach
War Cry

FAMILY
Boundless.org
Celebrate Life Magazine
Citizen Magazine

Columbia
CommonCall
Evangelical Missions
 Quarterly
Faith & Friends
Focus on the Family
HomeLife
Joyful Living Magazine
Ministry
The Mother's Heart
ParentLife
Power for Living
Southwest Kansas Faith
 and Family
St. Anthony Messenger
Thrive

FICTION
See Short Stories.

FILLERS
Angels on Earth
Bible Advocate
Children's Ministry
Creation Illustrated
FellowScript
Focus on the Family
 Clubhouse
Focus on the Family
 Clubhouse Jr.
Freelance Writer's
 Report
The Gem
Group Magazine
Guideposts
Lutheran Digest
Shades of Romance
 Magazine

FINANCES/MONEY
Boundless.org
Children's Ministry
Columbia
Joyful Living Magazine
Just Between Us

HOW-TO
Canada Lutheran
Catechist
Catholic Digest
Celebrate Life Magazine
Children's Ministry
Christian
 Communicator
Christian Living in the
 Mature Years
Citizen Magazine
CommonCall
Creation Illustrated
Enrichment
Evangelical Missions
 Quarterly
Faith Today
Focus on the Family
Focus on the Family
 Clubhouse
Group Magazine
Hello, Dearest
Highway News and
 Good News
Homeschooling Today
InSite
The Journal of Adventist
 Education
Joyful Living Magazine
Just Between Us
Leading Hearts
Live
Lutheran Witness
Mature Living
Ministry
Ministry Today
The Mother's Heart
MTL Magazine
Mutuality
Net Results
New Identity Magazine
The Newsletter
 Newsletter
Outreach

ParentLife
Parish Liturgy
Poets & Writers
 Magazine
Psychology for Living
SAConnects
Shades of Romance
 Magazine
Teachers of Vision
Vibrant Life
The Writer
The Writer's Chronicle
Writer's Digest
Writing Corner

INTERVIEW/PROFILE
Canada Lutheran
Catholic Sentinel
Christian
 Communicator
Creation
Creation Illustrated
The Cresset
Faith Today
Good News, Etc.
History's Women
Homeschooling Today
Image
In Part
Indian Life
InSite
Light & Life Magazine
Liguorian
Ministry Today
MTL Magazine
Our Sunday Visitor
 Newsweekly
Power for Living
Relief Journal
Testimony
Vibrant Life
The Writer
The Writer's Chronicle
Writer's Digest

MARRIAGE

Boundless.org
Catholic Digest
Faith & Friends
Focus on the Family
Joyful Living Magazine
Mature Living
St. Anthony Messenger
Thrive

NEWSPAPER

Anglican Journal
The Arlington Catholic
  Herald
Catholic New York
Catholic Sentinel
Christian Courier
The Christian Herald
Christian News
  Northwest
City Light News
The Good News
  (Florida)
The Good News
  (New York)
Good News, Etc.
The Good News Journal
Indian Life
Kansas City Metro Voice
The Messianic Times
New Frontier Chronicle
Our Sunday Visitor
  Newsweekly
Prairie Messenger
Southwest Kansas Faith
  and Family

PARENTING

Catholic Digest
Columbia
Focus on the Family
Just Between Us
Parenting Teens
ParentLife

PERSONAL EXPERIENCE

Angels on Earth
Bible Advocate
The Breakthrough
  Intercessor
Catholic Digest
Canada Lutheran
Catholic New York
Catholic Sentinel
Celebrate Life Magazine
Chicken Soup for the
  Soul Book Series
Christian Standard
Christianity Today
Converge Magazine
Creation Illustrated
Decision
DTS Magazine
EFCA Today
Faith & Friends
Faith Today
Friends Journal
Halo Magazine
Hello, Dearest
Highway News and
  Good News
The Journal of Adventist
  Education
Joyful Living Magazine
Just Between Us
Leading Hearts
Leaves
The Lutheran Digest
Lutheran Witness
Mature Living
The Mother's Heart
MTL Magazine
Mutuality
A New Heart
New Identity Magazine
Now What?
Point
Power for Living

Psychology for Living
Purpose
Refreshed
SAConnects
Sharing
Shattered Magazine
Teachers of Vision
Testimony
Thrive
Today's Christian Living
Vibrant Life
The Vision
War Cry

POETRY

America
Believers Bay
Bible Advocate
The Breakthrough
  Intercessor
Chicken Soup for the
  Soul Book Series
The Christian Century
Christian Living in the
  Mature Years
Christian
  Communicator
Christian Courier
Commonweal
Creation Illustrated
The Cresset
CrossCurrents
Eureka Street
Focus on the Family
  Clubhouse
Focus on the Family
  Clubhouse Jr.
Friends Journal
The Gem
Gems of Truth
Halo Magazine
Image
Live
Lutheran Digest
Mutuality

A New Heart
OCACW Newsletter
The Penwood Review
Perspectives
Poets & Writers
  Magazine
Power for Living
Prairie Messenger
Purpose
Relief Journal
Shine Brightly
Sojourners
Sparkle
St. Anthony's Messenger
St. Mary's Messenger
A Time of Singing
U.S. Catholic
The Vision
Weavings
Young Salvationist

PROFILES
See Interviews.

REVIEWS
America
Anglican Journal
byFaith
The Canadian Lutheran
Canadian Mennonite
Celebrate Life Magazine
Charisma
The Christian Century
Christian
  Communicator
Christian Courier
The Christian Herald
Christian Journal
Christian Librarian
Christian Retailing
Christianity Today
Creation Research
  Journal
Evangelical Missions
  Quarterly
Faith Today

Fellowscript
The Good News
  (New York)
Good News, Etc.
Indian Life
Kansas City Metro Voice
Leading Hearts
The Living Church
Message of the Open
  Bible
The Messianic Times
Ministry
MTL Magazine
Mutuality
New Frontier Chronicle
OCACW Newsletter
On Mission
Perspectives
Sojourners
U.S. Catholic
The Writer

SCIENCE
Answers
Creation
Nature Friend
  Magazine

SEASONAL
Believers Bay
Bible Advocate
Catholic Digest
Canada Lutheran
Celebrate Life Magazine
Charisma
Children's Ministry
The Christian Century
Christian Courier
Christian Living in the
  Mature Years
Columbia
Decision
DTS Magazine
EFCA Today
The Gem
Gems of Truth

Group Magazine
Halo Magazine
InSite
The Journal of Adventist
  Education
Liguorian
Live
The Lutheran Digest
The Mother's Heart
The Newsletter
  Newsletter
OCACW Newsletter
Our Little Friend
Outreach
Prairie Messenger
Presbyterians Today
Primary Treasure
St. Anthony Messenger
Testimony
Time of Singing
U.S. Catholic
The Vision
War Cry
Writer's Digest

SHORT STORY/
FICTION
Believers Bay
CrossCurrents
Eureka Street
Focus on the Family
  Clubhouse
Focus on the Family
  Clubhouse Jr.
The Gem
Gems of Truth
Halo Magazine
Havok
Image
Indian Life
The Kids' Ark
Liguorian
Live
Mature Living
Nature Friend
  Magazine

Perspectives
Relief Journal
Shades of Romance Magazine
Shine Brightly
Spark! Magazine
Sparkle
Splickity Magazine
St. Anthony Messenger
St. Mary's Messenger
U.S. Catholic
The Vision
War Cry

TAKE-HOME PAPER

The Gem
Gems of Truth
Guide
Insight
Live
Our Little Friend
Power for Living
Primary Treasure
Purpose
Seek
The Vision

THEOLOGY

America
byFaith
The Canadian Lutheran
Christianity Today
Faith & Friends
Lutheran Witness
Mature Living
Presbyterians Today

6

ADULT MARKETS

AMERICA
106 W. 56th St., New York, NY 10019-3803 | 212-581-4640
articles@americamagazine.org | *www.americamagazine.org*
Eloise Blondiau, editorial assistant, blondiau@americamedia.org |
Br. Joseph Hoover, S.J., poetry editor, jhoover@americamagazine.org

Reviews: *reviews@americamedia.org*

Denomination: Catholic

Parent company: America Media, Jesuit Conference of the United States and Canada

Type: weekly print magazine plus online content; 36 pages, circulation 46,000, subscription $56

Audience: primarily Catholic, two-thirds are laypeople, college educated

Purpose: to provide a smart Catholic take on faith and culture

Submissions: Only accepts complete manuscripts submitted via the website. 100% unsolicited freelance. Responds in two weeks.

Types: Articles 2,500 words maximum. "Faith in Focus," personal essays, 800 to 1500 words. "Generation Faith," personal essays from high school and college students, 800 and 1,200 words. Poetry 30 lines maximum.

Topics: Catholic take on a political, social, cultural, economic, or ecclesial news event or historical/cultural trend; essays on joys and challenges of living out one's faith in the midst of real life

Rights: first, electronic

Payment: competitive rates, on acceptance

Guidelines: *americamedia.submittable.com/submit*

Sample: downloadable from the website

Tip: "We are known across the Catholic world for our unique brand of excellent, relevant, and accessible coverage. From theology and spirituality to politics, international relations, arts and letters, and the economy and social justice, our coverage spans the globe."

ANGELS ON EARTH

110 William St., Ste. 901, New York, NY 10038 | 212-251-8100
submissions@angelsonearth.com | *www.guideposts.org/brand/angels-on-earth-magazine*
Colleen Hughes, editor-in-chief | *Meg Belviso, departments editor for features and fillers*

> **Parent company:** Guideposts
> **Type:** bimonthly print and digital magazine; 76 pages, circulation 550,000, subscription $19.95
> **Purpose:** to tell true stories of heavenly angels and earthly ones who find themselves on a mission of comfort, kindness, or reassurance
> **Submissions:** Submit complete manuscript through the website, by email, or by mail with SASE. Responds in two months or isn't interested. 90% unsolicited freelance. Articles to 1,500 words, 40-60 per year; short anecdotes similar to full-length articles, 50-250 words. 20% kill fee on assignments. All stories must be true.
> **Types of manuscripts:** personal experience, recipes, fillers
> **Topics:** true stories about God's angels and humans who have played angelic roles on earth; "Angel Sightings," pictures of angels
> **Rights:** all
> **Payment:** $25-500, on publication
> **Guidelines:** *www.guideposts.org/writers-guidelines*
> **Sample:** 7 x 10 SASE with four stamps
> **Tip:** "We are not limited to stories about heavenly angels. We also accept stories about human beings doing heavenly duties."

ANGLICAN JOURNAL

80 Hayden St., Toronto, ON M4Y 3G2, Canada | 416-924-9199 x307
editor@anlgicanjournal.com | *www.anglicanjournal.com*
Merites Sison, editor | *Janet Thomas, assistant editor, jthomas@national.anglican.ca (submit to)*

> **Denomination:** Anglican
> **Parent company:** Anglican Church of Canada
> **Type:** monthly (except July and August) print newspaper; circulation 128,450
> **Audience:** denomination
> **Purpose:** to covers news of the Anglican Church across the country and around the world, as well as news of other denominations and social and ethical issues
> **Submissions:** No unsolicited manuscripts; email query. Maximum length: 1,000 words. Articles should focus on theological or

spiritual issues of interest to the church or society. Stories should be of interest to a national audience.

Types of manuscripts: news, book reviews

Topics: national events or local happenings that reflect the larger picture or a local happening that is unusual

Payment: 25¢/word

Guidelines: *www.anglicanjournal.com/about-us/guidelines*

ANSWERS

PO Box 510, Hebron, KY 41048 | 859-727-2222
nationaleditor@answersmagazine.com | *www.answersmagazine.com*
Pam Sheppard, national editor

Parent company: Answers in Genesis

Type: quarterly print and digital magazine; subscription $24, takes ads

Audience: adults looking for help to defend creationism

Purpose: to illustrate the importance of Genesis in building a creation-based worldview, and to equip readers with practical answers so they can confidently communicate the gospel and biblical authority with accuracy and graciousness

Submissions: Only accepts one-paragraph article proposals with author's qualifications (300 words) by email or through the website. Once accepted, email article as an attachment. Responds in one month. Article length: 300-600 words.

Types of manuscripts: teaching

Topics: apologetics for young-earth creationism and against evolution, science, animals

Rights: all, reprint

Payment: $75-$400 for all rights, $50-$225 for reprints

Guidelines: download from *answersingenesis.org/answers/magazine/contact*

THE ARLINGTON CATHOLIC HERALD

200 N. Glebe Rd, Ste. 600, Arlington, VA 22203 | 703-841-2590
editorial@catholicherald.com | *www.catholicherald.com*
Michael F. Flach, editor

Denomination: Catholic

Parent company: Arlington, VA Diocese

Type: weekly print and digital newspaper; 24 pages, circulation 70,000, print subscription $27, takes ads

Audience: denomination

Purpose: to support the Church's mission to evangelize by providing news from a Catholic perspective

Submissions: Email a query with a story idea.

Types of manuscripts: news, feature articles, profiles
Guidelines: *www.catholicherald.com/contact_us.html*

BELIEVERS BAY

1202 S. Pennsylvania St., Marion, IN 46953 | 765-997-173
editor@BelieversBay.com | www.BelieversBay.com
Tim Russ, editor

> **Type:** weekly online magazine
> **Purpose:** to share the love of God with common sense
> **Submissions:** Articles 500-1,000 words, columns 300-500 words. Open to new columns; query type and topic. 100% freelance; accepts as many as are submitted. Seasonal at least two weeks ahead. Accepts simultaneous submissions and reprints.
> **Types of manuscripts:** articles, short stories, essays, poetry
> **Topics:** almost anything
> **Rights:** onetime electronic, permanently archives pieces
> **Payment:** none
> **Guidelines:** *www.believersbay.com/submissions*
> **Tip:** "Easy to break in with quality writing; share something that shares the love of God with common sense, or share something that would be of value to the average person."

BIBLE ADVOCATE

PO Box 33677, Denver, CO 80233 | 303-452-7973
bibleadvocate@cog7.org | baonline.org
Sherri Langton, associate editor

> **Denomination:** Church of God (Seventh Day)
> **Type:** bimonthly print magazine; 32 pages, circulation 13,000, free
> **Audience:** denomination
> **Purpose:** to advocate the Bible and represent the Church of God (Seventh Day)
> **Submissions:** Prefers emailed manuscripts and queries, but also takes them by mail. 20-25% unsolicited freelance. Length: feature articles, personal experiences, 1,000-1,500 words; short articles, 500-1,000 words; fillers, 100-400+ words; poetry, 5-20 lines (traditional, free verse, blank verse), submit maximum five poems. Responds in four to ten weeks. Seasonal six months ahead; no Christmas or Easter manuscripts. Accepts simultaneous submissions. Bible: prefers NIV 1984, NKJV.
> **Types:** teaching, poetry, personal experience
> **Topics:** see theme list; biblical topics and doctrine, current religious and cultural issues, Christian living, personal testimony

Rights: first, reprint (tell when/where appeared), electronic, noncompeting onetime
Payment: articles, $25-65; poems and fillers, $20; on publication
Guidelines and theme list: *baonline.org/write-for-us*
Sample: download from the website
Tip: "If you write well, all areas are open to freelance. Articles that run no more than 1,100 words are more likely to get in. Also, fresh writing with keen insight is most readily accepted."

THE BREAKTHROUGH INTERCESSOR

PO Box 121, Lincoln, VA 20160-0121 | 540-338-4131 | fax: 540-338-1934
breakthrough@intercessors.org | *www.intercessors.org*
Noelle Garnier, editor

Parent company: Breakthrough
Type: quarterly print magazine; 36 pages, circulation 4,000, subscription $18
Audience: adults interested in growing their prayer lives
Purpose: to encourage people to pray and to equip them to do so more effectively
Submissions: Email or fax complete manuscript. Length: articles, 600-1,000 words; poetry, 12 lines maximum.
Types of manuscripts: personal experience, teaching, poetry
Topic: prayer
Rights: first and onetime, nonexclusive electronic
Payment: none
Guidelines: download from www.*intercessors.org/our-publications*
Sample copy: download from the website

BYFAITH

1700 N. Brown Rd., Ste. 105, Lawrenceville, GA 30043 | 678-825-1005
editor@byfaithonline.com | *byfaithonline.com*
Dick Doster, editor, ddoster@byfaithonline.com

Denomination: Presbyterian Church in America
Type: online magazine
Audience: denomination
Purpose: to provide news of the PCA, to equip readers to become a more active part of God's redemptive plan for the world, and to help them respond biblically and intelligently to the questions our culture is asking
Submissions: Email complete manuscripts. Articles 500-3,000 words.
Types: profiles, teaching, reviews, news
Topics: true stories of people living out their faith, practical theology,

biblical perspective on arts and culture, reviews of current books and movies, Christian living, PCA news

Guidelines: *byfaithonline.com/about*

Tip: "Theologically, byfaithonline.com's writers are Reformed and believe the faith is practical and applicable to every part of life. Most of our writers (though not all) come from the PCA."

CANADA LUTHERAN

600—177 Lombard Ave., Winnipeg, MB R3B 0W5, Canada | 888-786-6707 *204-984-9171 | editor@elcic.ca | www.elcic.ca*
Kenn Ward, editor

Denomination: Evangelical Lutheran Church in Canada

Type: monthly print magazine (8x); 32 pages, circulation 14,000, subscription $22.60 Canadian and $49.89 U.S.

Audience: denomination

Purpose: to engage the Evangelical Lutheran Church in Canada in a dynamic dialogue in which information, inspiration, and ideas are shared in a thoughtful and stimulating way

Submissions: Especially looking for articles for "Practising Our Faith," stories and ideas about how you or the people around you handle life's challenges and opportunities through faith. Length: 650 words. Also takes documentary articles and profiles of people of interest to readers (normally ELCIC members), seasonal, advice in "how to" lists, and articles highlighting ministry in the synods. Email submissions.

Types of manuscripts: personal experience, profile, documentary, how-to

Topics: seasonal, Christian living, ELCIC ministries

Rights: onetime

Guidelines: *www.elcic.ca/clweb/contributing.html*

Tip: "As much as is possible, the content of the magazine is chosen from the work of Canadian writers. The content strives to reflect the Evangelical Lutheran Church in Canada in the context of our Canadian society."

THE CANADIAN LUTHERAN

3074 Portage Ave., Winnipeg, MB R3K 0Y2, Canada; 800-588-4226, 204-895-3433; communications@lutheranchurch.ca; www.lutheranchurch.ca

Matthew Block, editor-in-chief

Denomination: Lutheran Church—Canada

Type: bimonthly print magazine; circulation 20,000, subscription $20, takes ads

Audience: denomination

Purpose: to inspire, motivate and inform

Submissions: Email complete manuscript with "Canadian Lutheran article" in the subject line. Looking for Christian reflections on current events, teaching articles about our theology, discussions of contemporary culture in the light of faith, and more.

Types of manuscripts: news, teaching, essay

Topics: theology, contemporary culture, congregational and district news (submit to appropriate district editor and include photo)

Rights: first (but reserves the right to reprint)

Payment: none for unsolicited manuscripts

Guidelines: *www.canadianlutheran.ca/submissions*

Sample: download from the website

Tip: "All feature articles with doctrinal content must go through doctrinal review to ensure fidelity to the Scriptures. As a result, authors may occasionally be asked to rewrite some sections of their article before publication."

CANADIAN MENNONITE

490 Dutton Dr., Unit C5, Waterloo, ON N2L 6H7, Canada | 519-884-3810
submit@canadianmennonite.org | *www.canadianmennonite.org*
Ross W. Muir, managing editor

Denomination: Mennonite Church Canada

Type: biweekly print magazine

Audience: denomination

Purpose: to educate, inspire, inform, and foster dialogue on issues facing Mennonites in Canada as it shares the good news of Jesus Christ from an Anabaptist perspective

Submissions: Email query first. Email manuscripts as attachments or mail them.

Types: theological reflections, sermons, opinion pieces, letters, reviews (books, music, movies), personal stories, news

Topics: see theme list

Payment: none for unsolicited articles, 10¢/word for solicited articles

Guidelines and theme list: *www.canadianmennonite.org/submissions*

Sample: download from the website

CATECHIST

1 Montauk Ave., Ste. 2, New London, CT 06320
pat.gohn@bayard-inc.com | *www.catechist.com*
Pat Gohn, editor

Parent company: National Society of Volunteer Catechists

Type: monthly (7x during school year) print magazine; subscription $28.95

Audience: catechists in parish religious education programs and religion teachers in Catholic schools

Purpose: to support teachers of children of preschool age through high school, youth ministers, parish and religious education directors and coordinators

Submissions: Present your credentials in a cover letter. Submit hard copy by mail or email as an attachment. Articles up to 1,200 words.

Types of manuscripts: how-to

Topics: Bible, the sacraments, liturgy, prayer, ecumenism, morality, social concerns, service projects, teaching methodology, planning, multicultural trends, the lives of students and their families, lesson-plan suggestions, teaching specific age groups

Payment: negotiable, on publication

Guidelines: *www.catechist.com/guidelines.php*

Tip: "Communicate your knowledge and experience in a confident presentation of your material. Use a direct tone in your writing and emphasize practical and concrete content."

CATHOLIC DIGEST

1 Montauk Ave., New London, CT 06320
queries@catholicdigest.com | *www.catholicdigest.com*
Danielle Bean, editor-in-chief

Denomination: Catholic

Type: print magazine, 9x a year; takes ads

Audience: denomination

Purpose: to encourage and support Catholics in a variety of life stages and circumstances

Submissions: Query for feature articles. Accepts simultaneous submissions. Articles 1,500 words. Seasonal four to five months ahead. Departments: "Last Word" personal essay, 550-700 words; "Open Door" first-person stories about conversion to or recovering the Catholic faith, 350-600 words; send to opendoor@catholicdigest.com. Email complete manuscript for departments.

Types of manuscripts: how-to, essay, personal experience

Topics: marriage, practical spirituality, parish/work, parenting, grandparenting, homemaking, relationships, beauty

Rights: first

Payment: $100-500, on publication

Guidelines: *www.catholicdigest.com/writers_guidelines.html*

CATHOLIC NEW YORK

1011 First Ave., Ste. 1721, New York, NY 10022 | 212-688-2399

cny@cny.org | www.cny.org
John Woods, editor-in-chief

Denomination: Catholic
Parent company: Archdiocese of New York
Type: biweekly print newspaper; 40 pages, circulation 132,680
Audience: denomination
Purpose: to become an invaluable educational tool for teaching and living the gospel in the Archdiocese of New York
Submissions: Email query or complete manuscript. 2% unsolicited freelance. Articles 500-800 words. Responds in five weeks.
Types of manuscripts: news reports, personal experience, teaching
Topics: state news, Christian living, moral issues
Rights: onetime
Payment: $15-100, on publication
Tip: "Most open to columns about specific seasons of the Catholic Church, such as Advent, Christmas, Lent, and Easter."

CATHOLIC SENTINEL

5536 N.E. Hassalo, Portland, OR 97213 | 503-281-1191
sentinel@CatholicSentinel.org | www.CatholicSentinel.org

Denomination: Catholic
Parent company: Archdiocese of Portland
Type: bimonthly print newspaper; 20 pages
Audience: Catholics who live in Oregon
Purpose: to feature Oregon people and Oregon issues that relate to Catholics
Submissions: Articles 600-1,500 words. Query first. Feature stories about Catholics living out their faith. Columns about local, national, or international issues of interest with a local connection.
Types of manuscripts: profiles, personal experience
Topics: Christian living, issues
Payment: variable rates for articles, none for columns
Guidelines: *www.catholicsentinel.org/main.asp?SectionID=15& SubSectionID=60&ArticleID=11770*

CELEBRATE LIFE MAGAZINE

PO Box 1350, Stafford, VA 22555 | 540-659-4171
clmag@all.org | www.clmagazine.org
Bonnie Seers, managing editor

Parent company: American Life League
Type: quarterly print magazine; 32 pages, circulation 25,000, subscription $14.95, takes ads

Audience: pro-life homes

Purpose: to inspire, encourage, and educate pro-life activists

Submissions: Covers all respect-for-life matters according to the Catholic Church's teaching. Email complete manuscript as an attachment. Articles 1,800 words maximum, including sidebars. Seasonal six months ahead. Bible: Jerusalem Bible, NAB (Catholic).

Types of manuscripts: personal experience, interviews, how-to, teaching, reviews

Topics: abortion, adoption, chastity, disability, elder care, death/dying, euthanasia, eugenics, special-needs children, human cloning, infertility, organ/tissue donation, family planning, pro-life activism, pro-life activities and legislation, sex education, and other respect-for-life topics

Rights: first

Payment: on publication

Guidelines: *www.clmagazine.org/submission-guidelines*

Sample: email for copy

Tip: "We are pro-life, with no exceptions, in keeping with Catholic teaching. Looking for interviews with pro-life leaders and pro-life public figures, and nonfiction stories about pro-life activities and people who live according to pro-life ethics despite adversity. Photos are preferred for personal stories."

CHARISMA

600 Rinehart Rd., Lake Mary, FL 32746 | 407-333-0600
charisma@charismamedia.com | *www.charismamag.com*
Jennifer LeClaire, senior editor

Denomination: Pentecostal/Charismatic

Type: monthly print and digital magazine; 100+ pages, circulation 90,000, subscription $15, takes ads

Audience: passionate, Spirit-filled Christians

Purpose: to empower believers for life in the Spirit

Submissions: Query only through the online form. If accepted, prefers email submission. Responds in two to three months. Seasonal five months ahead. 80% assigned. Needs articles that reflect on the work of a particular ministry, Christian author or artist, 700 words maximum; product reviews of newly released books, music, and movies/DVDs (assigned); in-depth feature stories to 2,600 words. Bible: MEV. Prefers third-person.

Types: profiles, interviews, reviews, feature stories

Topics: prayer, healing, spiritual warfare, end times, the prophetic and Israel, Christmas, Easter

Rights: all
Payment: on publication
Guidelines: *www.charismamag.com/about/write-for-us*
Sample: on the website
Tip: "Please take time to read—even study—at least one or two of our recent issues before submitting a query. Sometimes people submit their writing without ever having read or understood our magazine or its readers, and sometimes people will have read our magazine years ago and think it's the same as it has always been, but magazines undergo many changes through the years."

CHICKEN SOUP FOR THE SOUL BOOK SERIES

PO Box 700, Cos Cob, CT 06807
www.chickensoup.com
Amy Newmark, editor-in-chief

Parent company: Chicken Soup for the Soul Publishing, LLC
Type: trade paperback books, about a dozen yearly
Purpose: to share happiness, inspiration, and hope
Submissions: Submit complete manuscript only through the website. 98% unsolicited freelance. Length: 1,200 words maximum. "A Chicken Soup for the Soul story is an inspirational, true story about ordinary people having extraordinary experiences. ... These stories are personal and often filled with emotion and drama." Poems tell a story; no rhyming. Accepts submissions from children and teens for some books. No reprints.
Types: personal experiences, poetry
Topics: *www.chickensoup.com/story-submissions/possible-book-topics*
Payment: $200, one month after publication, plus ten copies of the book
Tip: "The most powerful stories are about people extending themselves, or performing an act of love, service, or courage for another person."

CHILDREN'S MINISTRY

1515 Cascade Ave., Loveland, CO 80538 | 970-669-3836
puorgbus@group.com | *childrensministry.com/about-our-magazine*
Jennifer Hooks, managing editor, jhooks@group.com

Type: bimonthly print and digital magazine
Audience: children's ministry workers
Purpose: to help leaders encourage children to grow spiritually
Submissions: feature articles 1,000-2,200 words; teacher and parent tips, games, crafts, activities 200 words. Regular columns on age-level development, outreach, family ministry, leading volunteers,

special needs, and discipline. Email or mail full manuscript. Responds in eight to ten weeks. Seasonal ten months ahead.

Types of manuscripts: how-to, tips, crafts, activities

Topics: working with volunteers; discipline; understanding children; communicating with children about faith, morals, money, friends, grades, and choices

Rights: all

Payment: features $75-400, tips and fillers $40

Guidelines: *grouppublishingps.zendesk.com/hc/en-us/articles/ 211878258-Submissions*

THE CHRISTIAN CENTURY

104 S. Michigan Ave., Ste. 1100, Chicago, IL 60603-5901 | 312-263-7510 *submissions@christiancentury.org* | *www.christiancentury.org* *Debra Bendis, senior editor* | *Elizabeth Palmer, books editor* | *Jill Peláez Baumgaertner, poetry editor*

Type: biweekly print magazine; 48 pages, subscription $65, takes ads

Audience: ecumenical, mainline ministers, educators, and church leaders

Purpose: to explore what it means to believe and live out the Christian faith in our time

Submissions: Email query first. Responds in four to six weeks. 90% unsolicited freelance. Seasonal four months in advance. Articles 1,500-3,000 words, buys 150 per year; poetry (free verse, traditional) to 20 lines. Bible version: NRSV.

Types of manuscripts: essays, humor, interviews, opinion, book reviews (assigned), poetry

Topics: poverty, human rights, economic justice, international relations, national priorities, popular culture, critiques of individual religious communities

Rights: all, reprint (tell where and when published)

Payment: articles $100-300, poems $50, reviews to $75, on publication

Guidelines and theme list: *www.christiancentury.org/submission- guidelines*

Sample copy: $3.50

Tip: "Keep in mind our audience of sophisticated readers, eager for analysis and critical perspective that goes beyond the obvious. We are open to all topics if written with appropriate style for our readers."

CHRISTIAN COURIER

2 Aiken St., St. Catherines, ON L2N 1V8, Canada | 800-969-4838 *905-937-3314* | *editor@christiancourier.ca* | *www.christiancourier.ca*

Angela Reitsma Bick, editor-in-chief, editor@christiancourier.ca | Monica Kronemeyer deRegt, features editor, ccmonicaderegt@gmail.com | Brian Bork, review editor, bbork41@gmail.com

Denomination: Christian Reformed

Type: biweekly print newspaper; 20-24 pages, circulation 2,500, subscription $58 Canadian, takes ads

Purpose: to connect Christians with a network of culturally savvy partners in faith for the purpose of inspiring all to participate in God's renewing work with his creation

Submissions: Email queries and manuscripts to the appropriate editor. Articles 700-1,200 words, book and movie reviews 750 words. Responds in one to two weeks, only if accepted. Seasonal three months ahead. Accepts simultaneous submissions and reprints (tell when/where appeared). Uses some sidebars. Prefers NIV.

Types of manuscripts: editorials, reviews, columns, features, news, poetry

Rights: onetime, reprint

Payment: $45-$70, 30 days after publication; no pay for reprints

Guidelines: *christiancourier.ca/writeForUs.php*

Tip: "Suggest an aspect of the theme which you believe you could cover well, have insight into, could treat humorously, etc. Show that you think clearly, write clearly, and have something to say that we should want to read. Have a strong biblical worldview and avoid moralism and sentimentality."

THE CHRISTIAN HERALD

PO Box 68526, Brampton, ON L6R 0J8, Canada | 905-874-1731
info@christianherald.ca | christianherald.ca

Type: monthly print newspaper

Purpose: to present an informed Christian perspective on current local, regional, and international issues, news and events

Audience: greater Toronto area

Submissions: Email query first.

Types of manuscripts: news, profiles, reviews

Topics: newsmaker profiles, including Christians in ministry, politics, sports, media, and business; book, music, concert, theatre, and movie reviews; travel destination profiles

Guidelines: *christianherald.ca/Editorial/writingforus.html*

THE CHRISTIAN JOURNAL

1032 W. Main, Medford, OR 97501 | 541-773-4004
info@thechristianjournal.org | www.TheChristianJournal.org
Chad McComas, editor

Type: monthly print and digital magazine

Audience: both Christians and non-Christians

Purpose: to share encouragement with the body of Christ in the Rogue Valley, Oregon

Submissions: Each article needs to inspire the reader to reconnect with God and his or her faith. Length: 300–500 words, average around 400 words. Email manuscript.

Types of manuscripts: feature articles, testimonies, profiles, reviews

Topics: hope, encouragement, theme-related articles, profiles of local ministries and Christian personalities, children's stories

Rights: onetime

Payment: none

Guidelines: *thechristianjournal.org/writers-information/guidelines-for-writers*

CHRISTIAN LIBRARIAN

7318 N. Pittsburg St., Spokane, WA 99217 | 937-766-2255
trobinson@whitworth.edu | www.acl.org
Tami Robinson, managing editor

Parent organization: Association of Christian Librarians

Type: print journal; subscription $30

Audience: primarily Christian librarians in institutions of higher learning

Purpose: to publish articles, provide a membership forum, and encourage writing

Submissions: Mail or email manuscripts. Shorter articles, 1,000-3,000 words, are generally preferable for practical and nonresearch papers; scholarly articles to 5,000 words, some longer. Include a 100-word abstract.

Types of manuscripts: teaching, reviews, bibliographies

Topics: Christian interpretation of librarianship, theory and practice of library science, bibliographic essays, reviews, and human-interest articles relating to books and libraries

Rights: first, with signed grant of license

Payment: none

Guidelines: *www.acl.org/index.cfm/publications/the-christian-librarian/guidelines-for-authors*

CHRISTIAN LIVING IN THE MATURE YEARS

PO Box 17890, Nashville, TN 37228 | 615-749-6512
matureyears@umpublishing.org | www.cokesbury.com/curriculum/7640/mature-years
Pamela Dilmore, editor

Denomination: United Methodist
Type: quarterly print magazine; 96 pages
Audience: ages 50 and older
Purpose: to help persons in and nearing retirement years understand and appropriate the resources of the Christian faith in dealing with specific problems and opportunities related to aging
Submissions: Email complete manuscript. Responds in six to seven months. Seasonal fourteen months in advance. Length: 900-2,000 words. Buys seventy-five to eighty per year. 80% freelance.
Types of manuscripts: how-to, travel, poems, puzzles, daily meditations, Bible lessons, poetry
Topics: how-to, health, retirement, aging, travel, finance
Payment: 7¢ per word, on acceptance
Guidelines: by email
Sample: $6 and 9 x 12 SAE

CHRISTIAN MOTORSPORTS ILLUSTRATED

PO Box 790, Quinlan, TX 75474 | 607-742-3407
www.christianmotorsports.com
Roland Osborne, publisher

Type: print magazine
Audience: people interested in all types of motorsports racing, bike rallies, aftermarket manufacturers, car clubs, auto museums, sanctioning bodies, tracks, and event sites
Purpose: to meet the spiritual needs of the motorsports community
Submissions: Articles 650-1,200 words. Query through the website.
Topics: uplifting and positive stories relating to all forms of motorsports
Payment: none
Guidelines: *www.christianmotorsports.com/index.php/from-the-editor*

CHRISTIAN NEWS NORTHWEST

PO Box 974, Newberg, OR 97132 | 503-537-9220
cnnw@cnnw.com | www.cnnw.com
John Fortmeyer, editor

Type: monthly print newspaper
Audience: people living in western and central Oregon and southwest Washington
Purpose: to inform about ministry news in the target area
Submissions: Email news and commentaries pertinent to ministry concerns in the Northwest. Length: 700 words.
Payment: none
Tip: "Top priority is given to writers living in Oregon and Washington."

THE CHRISTIAN ONLINE MAGAZINE

PO Box 262, Wolford, VA 24658
submissions@christianmagazine.org | *www.ChristianMagazine.org*
Darlene Osborne, publisher, darlene@christianmagazine.org

Type: monthly e-zine; free
Audience: general
Purpose: to bring readers the best Christian information on the net
Submissions: Email manuscript. Length: 700 words maximum. Articles should be practical, having a distinct Christian perspective throughout.
Topics: anything that builds faith
Rights: electronic
Payment: none
Guidelines: *www.christianonlinemagazine.com/submit_an_article_writer_guidelines*
Tip: "Most open to solid Christian articles founded on the Word of God."

THE CHRISTIAN RANCHMAN

PO Box 7557, Fort Worth, TX 76111 | 817-236-0023
ranchman@cowboysforchrist.net | *www.CowboysforChrist.net*
Dr. Dave Harvey, editor

Parent company: Cowboys for Christ
Type: bimonthly print tabloid; 16 pages, circulation 15,000, free
Purpose: to share the gospel with cowboys and cowgirls and those who are drawn by the cowboy image and way of life
Submissions: Email query or complete manuscript. Length: 350-1,000 words.
Types of manuscripts: testimonies, profiles
Topics: related to the cowboy way of life
Payment: none
Sample: download from *www.cowboysforchrist.net/christianranchman.htm*

CHRISTIAN RESEARCH JOURNAL

PO Box 8500, Charlotte, NC 28271-8500 | 704-887-8200
elliot.miller@equip.org | *www.equip.org*
Elliot Miller, editor-in-chief | Melanie Cogdill, managing editor

Parent company: Christian Research Institute
Type: bimonthly print journal
Audience: thoughtful laypeople, academics, scholars
Purpose: to equip Christians with the information they need to discern doctrinal errors; to evangelize people of other faiths; to present a strong defense of Christian beliefs and ethics; and to

provide comprehensive, definitive responses to contemporary apologetic concerns

Submissions: Email query or a manuscript that follows formatting guidelines. Responds in four months. Articles should reflect a command of the subject at hand, including its history, the key personalities involved, the beliefs and/or practices surrounding the controversy, and the criticisms that have been made concerning the subject. Feature articles 800, 1,200, 2,200, or 3,500 words; include 250-300-word synopsis with main facts and arguments. Summary critique review 1,800 words, effective evangelism 1,700 words, viewpoint 1,700 words, movie and book reviews 700 or 1,800 words. All articles must be within 25 words of these word counts. Kill fee 50%.

Types of manuscripts: feature articles, news stories, viewpoint, book reviews, and summary critiques

Topics: apologetics, evangelism, cults and new religions, the occult, **New** Age movement, aberrant Christian movements and teachings

Rights: first, reprint

Payment: $125-500

Guidelines: *www.equip.org/PDF/WriterGuidelinesJune2012.pdf*

Tip: "Almost nothing can better prepare you to write for the Christian Research Journal than familiarity with the Journal itself. If you are not a regular reader of the Journal, you should read all the articles in recent issues that correspond to the type of article you wish to write."

CHRISTIAN RETAILING

600 Rinehart Rd., Lake Mary, FL 32746 | 407-333-0600
retailing@charismamedia.com | *www.christianretailing.com*
Christine D. Johnson, editor, chris.johnson@charismamedia.com

Parent company: Charisma Media

Type: bimonthly print and digital trade journal

Audience: retailers, church bookstores, publishers, music labels, distributors, and others working and volunteering in the Christian products industry

Purpose: to champion the world of Christian resources and to provide critical information and insight to advance business and ministry

Submissions: Query only. Prefers third-person point of view. Bible: MEV.

Types of manuscripts: features, news stories, columns, reviews

Topics: all aspects of running a bookstore, trends in publishing, new product reviews

Payment: varies by assignment

Guidelines: *christianretailing.com/index.php/general/28335-writers-guidelines*

CHRISTIAN STANDARD

8805 Governor's Hill Dr., Ste. 400, Cincinnati, OH 45249
christianstandard@christianstandardmedia.com | *www.christianstandard.com*
Mark A. Taylor, editor

Denomination: Christian Churches/Churches of Christ
Type: monthly print magazine, 66 pages
Audience: volunteer and paid church leaders
Purpose: to inform and challenge, help leaders do their jobs, allow them to learn what other leaders in this fellowship are doing, and provide a place for them to share their successes
Submissions: Email (preferred) queries and manuscripts as attachments. Length: maximum 1,600 words, prefer 800-1,300 words. Needs: feature stories telling how and why local congregations in this fellowship are serving in their communities, with pictures; personal stories from leaders showing how they grappled with a personal or church-related leadership problem; and essays examining issues or trends of special significance to all kinds of leaders in Christian churches and churches of Christ.
Types of manuscripts: feature stories, personal experience, essays
Topics: church outreach, leadership, issues, trends
Payment: unspecified
Guidelines: *christianstandard.com/contact-us/submit-articles*
Theme list: link from guidelines
Sample: on the website

CHRISTIANITY TODAY

465 Gundersen Dr., Carol Stream, IL 60188-2498 | 630-260-6200
cteditor@christianitytoday.com | *www.christianitytoday.com*

Mark Galli, editor-in-chief
Type: monthly (10x) print and digital magazine; subscription $24.99, takes ads
Audience: intentional Christians who seek to thoughtfully integrate their faith with responsible action in the church and world
Purpose: to provide evangelical thought leaders a sense of community, coherence, and direction through thoughtful, biblical commentary on issues and through careful, caring reporting of the news
Submissions: Email query in the body of the message. Requires published credits. Responds in three weeks or not interested. Articles must be well supported, provide a fresh perspective, and connect the eternal message of the gospel with current trends, culture, events, and news. First-person articles should apply your personal experience to a broader concept of faith and biblical truth.

Types of manuscripts: profiles, interviews, feature stories, book reviews, opinion pieces, personal experience

Topics: Christians living out their faith in unique ways that impact the world for the better and communicate truth in a way that is deep, nuanced, and challenging

Rights: first, electronic

Payment: not specified

Tip: "We publish articles by and for evangelical Christians. Our readers are typically in some form of leadership or ministry—whether volunteer or professional—in their churches and communities."

THE CHURCH HERALD & HOLINESS BANNER

7407 Metcalf, Overland Park, KS 66212
editor@heraldandbanner.com | www.heraldandbanner.com
Dr. Gordon L. Snider, editor

Denomination: Church of God (Holiness)

Parent company: Herald and Banner Press

Type: monthly print and digital magazine

Audience: denomination

Submissions: Email through the website for current needs. Includes various teaching articles each month that will inspire you in your Christian walk, help you understand more about a biblical topic, etc. Also featured are various articles promoting Christian ideals, such as the importance to live with gratitude, etc.

Types of manuscripts: teaching

Topics: biblical teaching, Christian living from a holiness perspective

CITIZEN MAGAZINE

8605 Explorer Dr., Colorado Springs, CO 80920 | 719-531-3400
citizeneditor@focusonthefamily.com | www.focusonthefamily.com/socialissues/citizen-magazine
Karla Dial, editor

Parent company: Focus on the Family

Type: monthly (10x) print magazine

Audience: to equip today's Christian with often-unreported facts and the resources to dig deeper; inspire subscribers "to love and good works"; and provide ways to engage with friends, colleagues, and neighbors who may have an opposing worldview

Submissions: Balancing truth and grace, each article is carefully researched and reported on from a biblical worldview.

Types of manuscripts: teaching, profiles, news

Topics: contemporary issues, popular culture, government policy

Sample: link at *www.focusonthefamily.com/socialissues/promos/ subscribe-to-citizen-magazine*

Tip: "Our working agenda has been 'hope, how-to, and hot national topics.' We aim to provide hope by telling the stories of people and organizations that have successfully made a difference in their sphere of influence—and how they did it—so others can follow their example. When it comes to hot national topics, we provide an in-depth perspective from a Christian point of view that readers can't get from the mainstream media."

CITY LIGHT NEWS

459 Astoria Cres. S.E., Calgary, AB T2J 0Y6, Canada | 403-640-2011
editor@Calgarychristian.com | *www.calgarychristian.com*
Peter McManus, editor

Type: monthly print newspaper, 20 pages

Audience: youth to seniors who live in Southern and Central Alberta

Purpose: to report on newsworthy activities, ministries, and issues from a Christian perspective; provide thought-provoking commentary; advance the Kingdom of God by uniting and strengthening the Body of Christ through encouraging and informative stories, events, and testimonies

Submissions: 50% freelance. Deadline: no later than the 15th of the month prior to publication date.

Types of manuscripts: news reports, commentary, columns, profiles, testimonies

Topics: anything of interest to Christians in Alberta

Guidelines: www.calgarychristian.com/adventures/guidelines.htm

Sample: *www.calgarychristian.com/archives.htm*

COLUMBIA

1 Columbus Plaza, New Haven, CT 06510-3326 | 203-752-4398
columbia@kofc.org | *www.kofc.org/Columbia*
Alton J. Pelowski, editor-in-chief

Denomination: Catholic

Parent company: Knights of Columbus

Type: monthly print and digital magazine

Audience: general Catholic family

Submissions: Query first by email or mail. Length: 700-1,500 words. Seasonal six months in advance.

Types of manuscripts: feature articles, profiles

Topics: current events, social trends, family life, parenting, social problems, health and nutrition, finances, Catholic practice and teaching, church programs, institutions, personalities

Rights: first, electronic
Payment: varies, on acceptance
Guidelines: *www.kofc.org/un/en/columbia/guidelines.html*
Sample: *www.kofc.org/en/columbia/cover/201610.html*

COMMONCALL

PO Box 259019, Plano, TX 75025 | 214-630-4571 x1012
kencamp@baptiststandard.com | *www.baptiststandard.com*
Ken Camp, managing editor

Denomination: Baptist
Type: quarterly print magazine
Purpose: to aid and support the denomination on such topics as missions, evangelism, family life, leadership, effective church ministry, and Texas Baptist history
Submissions: Looking for stories about everyday Christians who are putting their faith into action.
Types of manuscripts: profiles, how-to
Topics: missions, evangelism, family life, leadership, effective church ministry

COMMONWEAL

475 Riverside Dr., Rm. 405, New York, NY 10115 | 212-662-4200
editors@commonwealmagazine.org | *www.commonwealmagazine.org*
Paul Baumann, editor

Denomination: Catholic
Type: biweekly (20x) print and digital magazine
Audience: educated, committed Catholics, as well as readers from other faith traditions
Purpose: to provide a forum for civil, reasoned debate on the interaction of faith with contemporary politics and culture
Submissions: Email queries and manuscripts as attachments or through the website. Mail poetry; buys thirty per year. Articles fall into these categories: (1) "Upfronts," 1,000-1,500 words, brief, newsy, and reportorial, giving facts, information, and some interpretation behind the headlines of the day. (2) Longer articles, 2,000-3,000 words, reflective and detailed, bringing new information or a different point of view to a subject, raising questions, and/or proposing solutions to the dilemmas facing the world, nation, church, or individual. (3) "Last Word" column, a 750-word reflection, usually of a personal nature, on some aspect of the human condition: spiritual, individual, political, or social.
Types of manuscripts: essays, features, news with interpretation, poetry

Topics: public affairs, religion, literature, the arts
Rights: all
Payment: on publication
Guidelines: *www.commonwealmagazine.org/contact-us*
Sample: $5
Tip: "Articles should be written for a general but well-educated audience. While religious articles are always topical, we are less interested in devotional and churchy pieces than in articles which examine the links between 'worldly' concerns and religious beliefs."

CONVERGE MAGAZINE

301-291 2nd Ave., Vancouver, BC V5T 1B8, Canada | 604-558-1982
info@convergemagazine.com | *www.convergemagazine.com*
Leanne Janzen, editor

Type: quarterly print and digital magazine
Audience: millennials
Purpose: to influence a growing number of people through daily content that is intelligent, authentic, and that stimulates hope in God
Submissions: Email queries and manuscripts. Articles 500-1,000 words. If no response in six weeks, assume no interest.
Types of manuscripts: personal experience
Topics: life, relationships, experiences, work, culture, faith
Guidelines: *convergemagazine.com/write*
Sample: see link at *convergemagazine.com/magazine*
Tip: "We write for those in transition: between school and work, singleness and marriage, freedom and responsibility, doubt and faith. We write as friends on the journey together, rather than one coaching another down the path. We share what we've learned through experience, rather than what we've heard or been taught. Our stories, like our lives, don't need to be tidy, with all the right answers."

THE COVENANT COMPANION

8303 W. Higgins Rd., Chicago, IL 60631 | 773-907-3328
editor@covchurch.org | *covenantcompanion.com*
Cathy Norman Peterson, managing editor

Denomination: Evangelical Covenant Church
Type: monthly (10x) print magazine
Audience: denomination
Purpose: to inform, stimulate thought, and encourage dialogue on issues that impact the church and its members
Submissions: Email or mail. Length: 1,200-1,800 words.
Types of manuscripts: news, profiles

Topics: Christian life, the church (local, denominational, and universal), spirituality, contemporary issues, social justice, outreach ministry
Rights: onetime
Payment: $35-100, two months after publication
Guidelines: *covenantcompanion.com/submit-story*
Tip: "We are interested in what is happening in local churches, conferences, and other Covenant institutions and associations, as well as reports from missionaries and other staff serving around the world. Human interest stories are also welcome."

CREATION

PO Box 4545, Eight Mile Plains, QLD 4113, Australia
editors@creation.info | creation.com/creation-magazine
Carl Wieland, managing director

Parent company: Creation Ministries International
Type: quarterly print and digital magazine; 56 pages
Audience: families, homeschoolers
Purpose: to refute evolution and give answers to defend your faith and uphold the true history of the world found in Genesis
Submissions: Email manuscript as an attachment in .rtf format. Length: maximum 1,800 words, prefers 250 to 1,600 words.
Types of manuscripts: interviews with creationists, teaching
Topics: creation science, evolution's errors, nature, Genesis, Noah's Ark, the Flood
Rights: all
Payment: none
Guidelines: *creation.com/creation-magazine-writing-guidelines*
Sample: on the website
Tip: "Except in technical articles, we like to see simple words, short sentences, and short paragraphs."

CREATION ILLUSTRATED

PO Box 7955, Auburn, CA 95604 | 530-269-1424
ci@creationillustrated.com | www.creationillustrated.com
Tom Ish, editor

Type: quarterly print magazine
Audience: families
Purpose: to share the wonders of God's creation
Submissions: Email (preferred) queries and manuscripts. Length: 1,500-2,000 words; children's stories 500-1,000 words. Kill fee 25% for assigned manuscripts. Bible: KJV, NKJV.
Types of manuscripts: teaching, personal experience, children's

stories, poetry, profile, fillers (crafts, games, puzzles, hikes, activities), how-to

Topics: nature, outdoor adventures, creatures, a creation day from Genesis

Rights: first, electronic, reprint

Payment: articles $100, children's stories $50-75, poetry $15; 30 days after publication

Guidelines: *www.creationillustrated.com/article/8/writer-and-photographer-guidelines*

Tip: "Write for the reader. Inspire the reader to be in awe of the Creator. Help generate a worshipful spirit. Glorify God the Creator. Make your story uplifting and positive, rather than confrontive or argumentative."

THE CRESSET

The Cresset, Lindwood House, Valparaiso University, 1320 S. Campus Dr., Valparaiso, IN 46383

cresset@valpo.edu

Heather Grennan Gary, editor | Marci Rae Johnson, poetry editor

Type: print journal (5-6x per year)

Audience: general readers interested in religious matters, mostly college teachers

Purpose: to comment on literature, the arts, and public affairs and explore ideas and trends in contemporary culture from a perspective grounded in the Lutheran tradition of scholarship, freedom, and faith while informed by the wisdom of the broader Christian community

Submissions: Email query first. Prefers submissions through the website but also takes them by email or mail.

Types of manuscripts: essays, poetry, interviews

Guidelines: *thecresset.org/submissions.html*

Tip: "The Cresset is not a theological journal, but a journal addressing matters of import to those with some degree of theological interest and commitment. Authors are encouraged to reflect upon the religious implications of their subject."

CROSSCURRENTS

475 Riverside Dr., Ste. 1945, New York, NY 10115 | 212-864-5439

cph@crosscurrents.org | www.aril.org

Charles Henderson, managing editor

Parent company: The Association for Religion and Intellectual Life

Type: quarterly print magazine

Audience: thoughtful activists for social justice and church reform

Submissions: Accepts emailed and mailed submissions with SASE. Responds in four to eight weeks. No unsolicited book reviews, reprints. Articles 3,000-5,000 words.
Types of manuscripts: essays, poetry, fiction
Payment: none
Guidelines: *www.aril.org/submissions.htm*
Sample: on the website

CRW MAGAZINE

1710 Evergreen St., Duarte, CA 91010 | 800-309-4466
managing.editor@ptm.org | *www.ptm.org/magazine.htm*
Greg Albrecht, senior editor

Parent company: Plain Truth Ministries
Type: quarterly print and digital magazine
Audience: general
Purpose: to combat legalism and give hope, inspiration, and encouragement to those burned out by religion
Submissions: Queries only.
Types of manuscripts: teaching
Guidelines: by email
Sample: on the website

DECISION

1 Billy Graham Pkwy., Charlotte, NC 28201 | 704-401-2246
decision@bgea.org | *billygraham.org/decision-magazine*
Bob Paulson, editor

Parent company: Billy Graham Evangelistic Association
Type: monthly (11x) print and digital magazine
Audience: general
Purpose: to set forth the Good News of salvation in Jesus Christ with such clarity that readers will be drawn to make a commitment to Christ; to encourage, teach, and strengthen Christians to walk daily with Christ and reach out to others for Christ; and to inform readers about the ministry of the Billy Graham Evangelistic Association
Submissions: Query first. 5% freelance. Articles 400-1,500 words. "Finding Jesus" (people who became Christians through Billy Graham ministries), 500-900 words. Prefers queries. Seasonal six months in advance.
Types of manuscripts: testimonies, personal experience
Topics: salvation, evangelism
Payment: $200-500, on publication

DTS MAGAZINE (FORMERLY KINDRED SPIRIT)

3909 Swiss Ave., Dallas, TX 75204
dtsmagazine@dts.edu | www.dts.edu/magazine
Raquel Wroten, editor

> **Parent company:** Dallas Theological Seminary (DTS)
> **Type:** quarterly print and digital magazine
> **Audience:** evangelical laypeople, students, alumni, donors, and friends
> **Purpose:** to offer articles rich in biblical and theological exposition, tell stories of how God is working through students and alumni, and update friends on God's work at DTS
> **Submissions:** Email query first; email or mail submission. Responds in six to eight weeks. Seasonal six months in advance. Articles: alumni profiles; exposition, usually authored by DTS faculty or similarly qualified individuals; Christian living, personal experience that encourages average Christians in how to live out their faith in the world and includes some exposition that ends with application of truth. Length: 2,000 words with 200-word sidebar.
> **Types:** profiles, teaching, personal experience
> **Rights:** first, reprint
> **Payment:** up to $500 for first, $150 for reprints, $50 for sidebars
> **Guidelines:** *www.dts.edu/magazine/policy*
> **Sample:** see the link on the website
> **Tip:** "DTS Magazine is a ministry of Dallas Theological Seminary. We prefer articles written by our alumni, faculty, students, staff, board members, donors and their families."

EFCA TODAY

PO Box 315, Charlottesville, VA 22902 | 434-961-2500
editor@efca.org | www.efcatoday.org
Diane McDougall, editor

> **Denomination:** Evangelical Free Church in America
> **Type:** quarterly digital magazine
> **Audience:** EFCA pastors, elders, Sunday-school teachers, ministry volunteers
> **Purpose:** to unify church leaders around the overall mission of the EFCA by bringing its stories and vision to life and to sharpen those leaders by generating conversations over topics pertinent to faith and life
> **Submissions:** Email query with published clips. 30% freelance. Seasonal six months in advance. Length: 500-2,000 words.
> **Types of manuscripts:** teaching, personal experience

Topics: theme-related
Rights: first, reprint
Payment: 23¢ per word, on acceptance after editing; less for reprints
Guidelines: *go.efca.org/resources/document/writing-guidelines*
Sample: *www.efcatoday.org*

ENRICHMENT: A JOURNAL FOR PENTECOSTAL MINISTRY

1445 N. Boonville Ave., Springfield, MO 65802 | 417-862-2781, x4095
enrichmentjournal@ag.org | *www.enrichmentjournal.ag.org*
George P. Wood, editor

Rick Knoth, managing editor
Denomination: Assemblies of God
Type: quarterly print journal; 128-144 pages, circulation 33,000,
subscription $24
Audience: Assembly of God ministers and other Pentecostal/
Charismatic leaders
Purpose: to enrich and encourage Pentecostal ministers to equip and
empower Spirit-filled believers for effective ministry
Submissions: Email or mail complete manuscript with SASE. 15%
unsolicited freelance. Responds in eight to twelve weeks. Articles
1,200-2,100 words, program and ministry how-tos 200-500 words.
Prefers NIV.
Types of manuscripts: how-to, sermon outlines and illustrations
Topics: preaching, pastoral practice, ministry
Rights: first
Payment: up to 10¢ per word, on publication
Guidelines: *www.enrichmentjournal.ag.org/extra/EJ_Writer_*
Guidelines.pdf
Sample copy: download from the website for a fee

EUREKA STREET

PO Box 553, Richmond, VIC 3121, Australia
editor@eurekastreet.com.au | *www.eurekastreet.com.au*
Michael Mullins, editor | Poetry editor, poetry@eurekastreet.com.au

Denomination: Catholic
Parent company: Australian Jesuits
Type: bimonthly digital journal
Audience: denomination
Purpose: to analyze, comment on, and reflect on current issues in the
worlds of politics, religion, and culture
Submissions: Submit articles using the online form. Email poetry.
Articles should provide humane, ethical analysis or commentary

on politics, religion, popular culture, or current events in Australia or the world. Length: 800 words. Short fiction and creative nonfiction up to 1,000 words. Simultaneous submissions for poetry only.

Types of manuscripts: feature articles, poetry
Topics: politics, religion, popular culture, current events
Rights: first
Payment: $200 AUD; poetry, portion of $50 allotted per week
Guidelines: *eurekastreet.com.au/article.aspx?aeid=33927#.
WB5nsvQoFUU*
Sample: download from the website

EVANGELICAL MISSIONS QUARTERLY

PO Box 794, Wheaton, IL 60187 | 630-752-7158
emq@wheaton.edu | www.emqonline.com
A. Scott Moreau, editor | Marcus Dean, book review editor

Parent company: Billy Graham Center for Evangelism
Type: quarterly print journal
Audience: missionaries; mission executives, scholars, professors, students, pastors, and supporters; missionary candidates; lay leaders
Purpose: to increase the effectiveness of the evangelical missionary enterprise
Submissions: Email query first. Articles 3,000 words; book reviews 400 words.
Types of manuscripts: reports, profiles, how-to, book reviews
Topics: world missions, evangelism, trends, missionary family life
Rights: first
Payment: $100, on publication.
Guidelines: *emqonline.com/submit-an-article*

FACTS & TRENDS

1 Lifeway Plaza, Nashville, TN 37234 | 615-251-2000
carol.pipes@lifeway.com | www.factsandtrends.net

Carol Pipes, editor
Parent company: LifeWay Christian Resources
Type: quarterly print magazine; 48 pages, circulation 65,000, free
Audience: pastors, church staff, and denominational leaders
Purpose: to provide information, insight, and resources for effective ministry
Submissions: Query only. Email for current needs.
Sample: click Archives page on the website

FAITH & FRIENDS

The Salvation Army, 2 Overlea Blvd., Toronto, ON M4H 1P4, Canada
*416-422-6226 | faithandfriends@can.salvationarmy.org | salvationist.ca/
category/faith-and-friends*
Giselle Randall, features editor

Denomination: Salvation Army
Type: monthly print magazine
Audience: general
Purpose: to show Jesus Christ at work in the lives of real people
and to provide spiritual resources for those who are new to the
Christian faith
Submissions: Email query or manuscript as attached file. Looking for
stories about people whose lives have been changed through an
encounter with Jesus: conversion, miracles, healing, faith in the
midst of crisis, forgiveness, reconciliation, answered prayers, and
more. Profiles of people who have found hope and healing through
their ministries, including prisoners, hospital patients, nursing-
home residents, single parents in distress, addicts, the unemployed,
or homeless. Length: 750-1,200 words. Ten departments with 750-
word narratives. Bible: TNIV.
Types of manuscripts: testimonials, personal experience, profiles
Topics: changed lives, marriage, family relationships, missionaries,
theology
Payment: none
Guidelines: *salvationist.ca/editorial/writers-guidelines*
Sample: on the website

FAITH TODAY

PO Box 5885, West Beaver Creek, Richmond Hill, ON L4B 0B8, Canada
905-479-5885 | editor@faithtoday.ca | www.faithtoday.ca

Bill Fledderus, senior editor
Karen Stiller, senior editor
Parent company: Evangelical Fellowship of Canada
Type: bimonthly print and digital magazine
Audience: wide spectrum of evangelical Christian men and women,
many of them in their 40s, 50s and 60s
Purpose: to connect, inform, and profile evangelicals, equipping them
with expert research and insight into Canadian culture, Christian
life, and ministry
Submissions: Email query first. Looking for articles for Kingdom
Matters, short items that reflects how God is at work in the church
in Canada, 150-450 words; and Books & Culture, reviews of

books, music, theatre, and art, 280 words. Features that provide analysis and interpretation, 800-1,800 words. Articles of more than 1,000 words require submitting an outline two weeks before due date; with sidebars that are part of the word count. Essays are 650-1,500 words. News features are 750 words. Cover stories are 2,000 words. Kill fee: 20-30%.

Types of manuscripts: profiles, analysis, opinions, book and music reviews, how-to, news, essays, personal experience

Rights: first, electronic, reprint

Payment: 15-25¢ per word CAD, six weeks after acceptance

Guidelines: *www.faithtoday.ca/writers*

Sample: *digital.faithtoday.ca/faithtoday/20160910?pg=1#pg1*

FOCUS ON THE FAMILY

8605 Explorer Dr., Colorado Springs, CO 80920
focusmagazine@family.com | *www.focusonthefamily.com/magazine*
Sheila Seifert, editorial director

Parent company: Focus on the Family

Type: bimonthly print magazine

Audience: parents, primarily of ages 4-12

Purpose: to encourage, teach, and celebrate God's design for the family

Submissions: Email or mail to Submissions Editor. Responds in eight weeks or not interested. Departments: "Family Stages," 50-200 words, practical applications for parents of preschoolers, school-aged children, tweens, and teens; send complete manuscript. "Family Faith," 150 words, devotionals that explore how a biblical principle applies to marriage, 1,200-word articles that show how to help kids understand important biblical truths; send complete manuscript. Features, 1,200-1,500 words; send complete manuscript. "Family Living," 450 words on marriage and parenting; query.

Types of manuscripts: how-to, devotional, teaching

Topics: marriage, parenting

Rights: first

Payment: 25¢ per word, $50 for "Family Stages," on acceptance

Guidelines: *www.focusonthefamily.com/magazine/call-for-submissions*

FRIENDS JOURNAL

1216 Arch St., Ste. 2A, Philadelphia, PA 19107 | 215-563-8629
martink@friendsjournal.org | *www.friendsjournal.org*
Martin Kelly, senior editor

Denomination: Religious Society of Friends

Type: monthly (11x) print and downloadable journal
Audience: denomination
Purpose: to communicate Quaker experience in order to connect and deepen spiritual lives
Submissions: Submit poetry through the website; maximum three. Feature articles 1,200-2,500 words, related to themes. Departments, around 1,500 words or fewer: Celebration, Earthcare, Faith and Practice, First-day School, Friends in Business, History, Humor, Life in the Meeting, Lives of Friends, Pastoral Care, Q&A, Reflection, Religious Education, Remembrance, Service, Witness.
Types of manuscripts: poetry, testimonies, teaching, profiles, personal experience
Topics: most issues are themed
Rights: first
Payment: none
Guidelines: *www.friendsjournal.org/submissions*
Theme list: on the website

THE GEM

PO Box 926, Findlay, OH 45839-0926 | 419-424-1961
communications@cggc.org | www.cggc.org
Rachel Foreman, editor

Denomination: Churches of God, General Conference
Type: weekly take-home paper, 8 pages
Audience: adolescents through senior citizens
Purpose: to encourage and motivate people in their Christian walk
Submissions: Articles 1,000-1,500 words, authentic experiences of God's help, of healed relationships, and of growing maturity in faith. For fiction, it is important that characters are true to life and solutions to problems are genuine.
Types of manuscripts: short stories, personal experiences, Scripture lessons, puzzles, poetry
Topics: related to theme list, seasonal
Rights: one time
Payment: $15 for articles and stories, $5-10 for fillers, after publication
Guidelines and theme list: *www.cggc.org/ministries/denominational-communications/the-gem*

GEMS OF TRUTH

7407-7415 Metcalf Ave., Overland Park, KS 66204 | 913-432-0331
www.heraldandbanner.com

Denomination: Church of God (Holiness)
Type: weekly take-home paper; 8 pages
Audience: denomination
Submissions: Send complete manuscript or query. Email through the website. Fiction 1,000-2,000 words. Seasonal six to eight months in advance. Bible: KJV.
Types of manuscripts: biographies, profiles, short stories, devotionals, poetry, teaching

THE GOOD NEWS (FLORIDA)

PO Box 670368, Coral Springs, FL 33067 | 954-564-5378
www.goodnewsfl.org
Shelly Pond, editor

Type: monthly print and digital newspaper
Audience: Dade, Broward and Palm Beach, Florida areas
Submissions: Query with clips. Articles 500-800 words.
Payment: 10¢ per word

THE GOOD NEWS (NEW YORK)

PO Box 18204, Rochester, NY 14618 | 585-271-4464
thegoodnewsrochester@frontiernet.net | *www.thegoodnewswny.com*
Alexandre V. Boutakov, editor

Type: bimonthly print newspaper
Audience: New York state
Submissions: Email query. Articles and reviews.
Sample: download from the Contact page

GOOD NEWS, ETC.

PO Box 2660, Vista, CA 92085 | 760-724-3075
goodnewseditor@cox.net |*www.goodnewsetc.com*

Rick Monroe, editor
Type: monthly print and digital newspaper
Audience: San Diego area
Purpose: to provide local Christian news and features to believers and seekers in San Diego County
Submissions: Articles 500-900 words. Query first.
Types of manuscripts: interviews, news, reviews
Payment: $40-150
Sample: on the website

THE GOOD NEWS JOURNAL

PO Box 170069, Austin, TX 78717-0069 | 512-461-2964
goodnewsjournal10@gmail.com | *www.thegoodnewsjournal.net*
Evelyn W. Davison, publisher

Type: bimonthly print and digital newspaper; 24 pages
Audience: Capital MetroPlex and Central Texas areas
Purpose: to provide leadership to individuals and corporations with a positive, patriotic, godly perspective
Submissions: Articles 350 words. Email query first.
Payment: none
Sample: on the website

GOOD NEWS MAGAZINE

PO Box 132076, The Woodlands, TX 77393-2076 | 832-813-8327
info@goodnewsmag.org | www.goodnewsmag.org
Steve Beard, editor-in-chief

Denomination: United Methodists
Type: bimonthly print magazine
Audience: Methodists seeking spiritual renewal
Purpose: to encourage United Methodist renewal
Submissions: Articles 1,500-1,850 words. Email for current needs.
Rights: onetime
Payment: $100-150, on publication

GRACECONNECT

PO Box 544, Winona Lake, IN 46590 | 574-268-1122
lcgates@bmhbooks.com | www.graceconnect.us
Liz Cutler Gates, editor

Denomination: Grace Brethren
Type: quarterly print and digital magazine
Audience: pastors, elders, and other leaders
Purpose: to build bridges of communication between the people and churches of the denomination
Submissions: Email query. Feature stories should have a Grace Brethren connection. Length: 1,000-1,500 words, sometimes 600-800 words or up to 2,000 words.
Topics: theme-related
Sample: on the website

GROUP MAGAZINE

1515 Cascade Ave., Loveland, CO 80538 | 970-669-3836
puorgbus@group.com | youthministry.com/group-magazine
Rick Lawrence, executive editor, rlawrence@group.com

Type: bimonthly print and digital magazine; 92 pages, circulation 15,000, subscription $24.95
Audience: youth workers and leaders
Purpose: to help leaders encourage teens to grow spiritually

Submissions: Email or mail full manuscript. Responds in eight to ten weeks. Seasonal ten months ahead. Articles 500-2,000 words. Fillers (games, fund-raisers, crowdbreakers, Bible studies, helpful hints, outreach ideas, discussion starters, tips) 175-300 words.

Types of manuscripts: how-to, lesson plans, fillers, Bible studies

Topics: youth ministry, understanding kids and youth culture, recruitment, training, family ministry, professionalism, spiritual growth, time management, leadership skills, worship, handling problems

Rights: all

Payment: $50-350, on acceptance

Guidelines: *grouppublishingps.zendesk.com/hc/en-us/articles/ 211878258-Submissions*

Sample: link from About page

GUIDEPOSTS

110 William St., Ste. 901, New York, NY 10038 | 212-251-8100
submissions@guideposts.com | *www.guideposts.org/brand/guideposts-magazine*
Rick Hamlin and Amy Wong, executive editors

Type: bimonthly print and digital magazine, 70 pages, subscription $16.97

Audience: general

Purpose: to help readers find peace of mind, solve tough personal problems, and build satisfying relationships

Submissions: Publishes true, first-person stories about people who have attained a goal, surmounted an obstacle, or learned a helpful lesson through their faith. A typical story is a first-person narrative with a spiritual point the reader can apply to his or her own life. Buys forty to sixty per year. Length: 1,500 words. Submit queries and manuscripts through the online form. If no answer in two months, not interested. 40% freelance. Kill fee: 20% but not to first-time freelancers. Short anecdotes similar to full-length articles, 50-250 words, for departments: "Someone Cares," stories of kindness and caring, sc@guideposts.com; "Mysterious Ways," "Family Room," "What Prayer Can Do." Also takes inspiring quotes for "The Up Side, upside@guideposts.com.

Types of manuscripts: personal experiences

Rights: all

Payment: $100-500, on acceptance

Guidelines: *www.guideposts.org/writers-guidelines*

Tip: "Be able to tell a good story, with drama, suspense, description, and dialog. The point of the story should be some practical spiritual help that the subject learns through his or her experience. Use unique spiritual insights, strong and unusual dramatic details."

HALO MAGAZINE

PO Box 1402, Sterling, VA 20167 | 540-877-3568
halomag@aol.com | *www.halomag.com*
Marian Newman Braxton, senior editor

Type: quarterly print magazine; subscription $20, takes ads
Audience: Christians and unbelievers
Purpose: to minister to the unsaved and encourage the Christian
Submissions: Articles 500-1,000 words, devotionals 200-500 words, poems no more than six stanzas with four lines per stanza, fiction 2,500 words maximum. 100% freelance. Email manuscript (prefers attached file). Accepts submissions from teens. Responds in two weeks. Seasonal two months ahead. Accepts simultaneous submissions and reprints. Some sidebars. Bible version: NIV, NASV, KJV.
Types of manuscripts: testimonies, personal experience, poetry, Bible study, quizzes, short stories, recipes, devotionals
Topics: prayer, salvation, encouragement, spiritual growth, practical Christian living, vacation spots, church activities, counseling
Rights: one-time, reprint (tell when and where it appeared)
Payment: none
Guidelines: *www.halomag.com/HM_Writingguidelines.html*
Sample: large envelope with $3 postage
Tip: "We welcome submissions in any category. We urge writers to submit their best, not their first draft."

HAVOK

submissions@splickety.com | *www.splickety.com*
Avily Jerome, editor

Parent company: Splickety Publishing Group
Type: quarterly print and digital magazine
Audience: speculative fiction fans
Purpose: to provide quick reading for fiction fans
Submissions: Publishes concise, speculative fiction; stories must cut through the day's troubles and grip readers with short attention spans. Length: 300-1,000 words; prefers 700 words or fewer. Nano-fiction stories in 100 words or fewer. All stories must fit quarterly theme. Send email submissions as attachment only.
Types of manuscripts: short stories

Topics: speculative
Rights: all for six months after publication
Payment: 2¢ per word
Guidelines: *splickety.com/submission-guidelines*
Theme list: *splickety.com/submission-guidelines/upcoming-themes*
Tip: "The best way to get published is to write compelling fiction with a beginning, middle, and an end that elicits a strong emotional response in readers. Make sure there is substantial conflict in the story, both internal and external. And above all else, make sure the story adheres to our submission guidelines and fits the prescribed theme for the issue you're submitting to."

HEARTBEAT

PO Box 9, Hatfield, AR 71945 | 870-389-6196
heartbeat@cmausa.org | *www.cmausa.org/cma_national/heartbeat.asp*
Misty Bradley, editor

Parent company: Christian Motorcyclists Association
Type: monthly print and digital magazine
Purpose: to inspire leaders and members to be the most organized, advanced, equipped, financially stable organization, full of integrity in the motorcycling industry and the Kingdom of God
Submissions: Email manuscript.
Topics: related to motocycling

HELLO, DEAREST (FORMERLY HELLO, DARLING)

2370 S. Trenton Way, Denver, CO 80231-3822 | 303-733-5353\
888-910-6677 | *content@mops.org* | *www.MOPS.org/blog*
Candice Santaferraro, editorial project manager

Parent Company: MOPS International (Mothers of Preschoolers)
Type: quarterly print magazine; 32 pages, circulation 100,000, subscription $24.95
Audience: mothers of preschoolers and school-age kids
Purpose: to inspire moms and nurture the woman who still exists inside the mother
Submissions: Email complete manuscript as an attachment.
Types of manuscripts: how-to, personal experience
Topics: Calls for submissions quarterly based on the needs of the magazine. Go to *www.hellodearest.org/we-love*, and look for "Call for Submissions."
Rights: first, reprint (tell when and where it appeared)
Guidelines: www.mops.org/writers-guidelines
Tip: "We always love a good laugh or tearjerker!"

HIGHWAY NEWS AND GOOD NEWS

PO Box 117, Marietta, PA 17547-0117 | 717-426-9977
editor@transportforchrist.org | *www.transportforchrist.org/highway*
Inge Koenig, managing editor

Parent company: Transport for Christ, International
Type: monthly print and digital magazine
Audience: truck drivers and their families
Purpose: to lead truck drivers, as well as the trucking community, to Jesus Christ and help them grow in their faith
Submissions: Especially looking for human interest stories concerning truck drivers. Length: 600-800 words. Rarely publishes poetry or fiction (600-800 words), but on occasion considers both if they focus on the trucking life. Prefers email submissions.
Types of manuscripts: personal experience, reports, how-to
Topics: spiritual growth, salvation, testimonies
Rights: first, reprint
Payment: none
Guidelines: download from the website
Sample: download from the website
Tip: "Articles submitted for publication do not have to be religious in nature; however, they should not conflict with or oppose guidelines and principles presented in the Bible."

HISTORY'S WOMEN

22 Williams St., Batavia, NY 14020 | 585-297-3009
submissions@historyswomen.com | *www.historyswomen.com*
Patti Chadwick, editor

Type: monthly print newsletter; circulation 21,000
Audience: women
Purpose: to make history come alive for women from a Christian worldview
Submissions: Looking for articles highlighting the extraordinary achievements of women throughout history which have made life better for their families and the societies in which they lived. Articles 400-1,200 words. Requires email submissions with no attachments; put "Article Submission" in the subject line.
Types of manuscripts: profiles, interviews
Topics: women of faith, social reformers, the Arts, early America, women rulers, life lessons for women, amazing moms, women in sports
Payment: none but offers alternative compensation
Guidelines: *historyswomen.com/writers-guidelines*

Tip: "Interviews or features about women who are making a difference in their world today are also welcomed and probably the most sought after."

HOLINESS TODAY
17001 Prairie Star Pkwy., Lenexa, KS 66220 | 913-577-0500
holinesstoday@nazarene.org | *www.holinesstoday.org*
Carmen Ringhiser, managing editor

> **Denomination:** Nazarene
> **Type:** bimonthly print and digital magazine; 40 pages
> **Audience:** denomination
> **Purpose:** to keep readers connected with the Nazarene experience and provide tools for everyday faith
> **Submissions:** Query through the website on Contact page.

HOMELIFE
1 Lifeway Plaza, Nashville, TN 37234-0172 | 615-251-2196
homelife@lifeway.com | *www.lifeway.com/n/Product-Family/Home-Life-Magazine*
Michael Kelly, executive editor

> **Parent company:** LifeWay Christian Resources
> **Denomination:** Southern Baptist
> **Type:** monthly print magazine; 72 pages
> **Audience:** families
> **Purpose:** to equip and challenge families to experience dynamic, healthy, Christ-centered homes
> **Submissions:** Manuscripts by assignment. Email résumé, bio, and clips. Offers practical, real world solutions toward maintaining the spiritual health of family members amid school, sports, work, play, and more.
> **Payment:** unspecified
> **Guidelines:** by email
> **Sample:** on the website

HOMESCHOOLING TODAY
PO Box 1092, Somerset, KY 42502 | 606-485-4105
editor@homeschoolingtoday.com | *homeschoolingtoday.com*

> **Ashley** Wiggers, executive editor
> **Type:** quarterly print and digital magazine; circulation 5-6,000, subscription $29.99, takes ads
> **Audience:** homeschooling parents
> **Purpose:** to encourage the hearts of homeschoolers and give them tools to instill a love of learning in their children

Submissions: Does not accept queries; email full manuscript as an attachment with "Article Submission" in the subject line. Responds in six months or not interested. Feature articles include information about a topic, unit study, encouragement, challenge, or an interview, 900-1,200 words. Departments: "Faces of Homeschooling," true stories about real homeschooling families, 600-900 words; "The Home Team," physical education, 600-900 words; "Homeschooling around the World," 600-900 words; "Language Learning," foreign languages, 600-900 words; "Thinking," logic, critical thinking, 600-900 words; "Unit Study," 800-1500 words; "Family Math," 600-900 words.

Types of manuscripts: how-to, unit studies, profiles, interviews
Topics: education, homeschooling
Rights: first, nonexclusive electronic, reprint
Payment: 10¢ per published word
Guidelines: *homeschoolingtoday.com/write-for-us*

IMAGE

3307 Third Ave. W., Seattle, WA 98119 | 206-281-2988
mkenagy@imagejournal.org | *imagejournal.org*
Mary Kenagy Mitchell, managing editor

Type: quarterly print literary journal
Purpose: to demonstrate the continued vitality and diversity of contemporary art and literature that engage with the religious traditions of Western culture
Submissions: Accepts email queries. Submit manuscripts through the website or by mail. Responds in three months. Accepts simultaneous submissions. Poetry: no more than five poems or ten pages total. Fiction, essays, and other nonfiction: 3,000-6,000 words.
Types of manuscripts: poetry, fiction, essays, interviews, artist profiles
Topics: related to art and literature
Rights: first
Payment: unspecified
Guidelines: *imagejournal.org/journal/submit*
Tip: "All the work we publish reflects what we see as a sustained engagement with one of the western faiths—Judaism, Christianity, or Islam. That engagement can include unease, grappling, or ambivalence as well as orthodoxy; the approach can be indirect or allusive, but for a piece to be a fit for Image or Good Letters, some connection to faith must be there."

IN PART

431 Grantham Rd., Mechanicsburg, PA 17055 | 717-697-2634
inpart@bic-church.org | *www.inpart.org*
Scott McFadden, editor

> **Denomination:** Brethren in Christ
> **Type:** biannual print magazine; 16 pages
> **Audience:** denomination
> **Purpose:** to communicate the life, teachings, and mission of the
> denomination
> **Submissions:** Email for current needs. Articles need to have a tie to
> the denomination.
> **Types of manuscripts:** news reports, profiles, interviews, teaching,
> testimonies
> **Sample:** download at *www.inpart.org/issue*

INDIAN LIFE

188 Henderson Hwy., Winnipeg, MB R2L 1L6, Canada
PO Box 32, Pembina, ND 58271 | *204-661-9333* | *ilm.editor@indianlife.org*
www.indianlife.org
Jim Uttley, editor

> **Parent company:** Indian Life Ministries
> **Type:** bimonthly print newspaper; 20 pages, takes ads
> **Audience:** Native North Americans
> **Purpose:** to present positive news and stories of what is happening
> among Native North Americans (First Nations, Aboriginal, and
> Indian) communities in the US and Canada
> **Submissions:** Query for current needs. 30% unsolicited freelance,
> 40% assigned. Bible: prefers New Life Version, MSG.
> **Types of manuscripts:** profiles, interviews, news features, reviews,
> historical short stories, testimonies
> **Topics:** related to Native North Americans
> **Tip:** "A writer should have understanding of some Native American
> history and culture. We suggest reading some Native American
> authors. Native authors preferred, but some others are published.
> Aim at a 10th-grade reading level."

INSITE

PO Box 62189, Colorado Springs, CO 80962-2189 | 888-922-2287
editor@ccca.org | *www.ccca.org*
Kris Hardy, editor

> **Parent company:** Christian Camp and Conference Association

Type: bimonthly print magazine; 60 pages, circulation 8,500
Audience: professionals serving in the Christian camp and conference community
Purpose: to help our members maximize their ministries by learning and staying inspired while serving God's people
Submissions: Email query first. Responds within one month. Seasonal six months ahead. Profiles and features 1,200-1,500 words; how-to articles 1,000-1,200 words; sidebars 250-500 words. 15% unsolicited freelance; 85% assigned. Bible: NIV.
Types of manuscripts: profiles, interviews, how-to
Topics: all aspects of camping ministry, business, relationships
Rights: first, electronic
Payment: 20¢ per published word, on publication
Guidelines and theme list: *www.ccca.org/ccca/Publications.asp*
Sample: $4.99
Tip: "Profiles/interviews are the best bet for newcomers and freelancers. It is crucial to study a sample copy first and then query."

INTERNATIONAL JOURNAL OF FRONTIER MISSIOLOGY

1605 E. Elizabeth St., Pasadena, CA 91104; 734-765-0368
editors@ijfm.org | *www.ijfm.org*
Brad Gill, editor

Parent company: International Society for Frontier Missiology
Type: quarterly print journal; subscription $18
Audience: mission professors, executives, and researchers; missionaries, young-adult mission mobilizers
Purpose: to cultivate an international fraternity of thought in the development of frontier missiology
Submissions: Query first. Articles 2,000-6,000 words.
Types: profiles, teaching
Topics: missiological perspective and principles, calls to commitment and involvement in frontier missions
Payment: none
Guidelines: *www.ijfm.org/author_info.htm*
Sample: download from website

THE JOURNAL OF ADVENTIST EDUCATION

12501 Old Columbia Pike, Silver Spring, MD 20904-6600 | 301-680-5069
mcgarrellf@gc.adventist.org | *jae.adventist.org*
Faith-Ann McGarrell, editor

Denomination: Seventh-day Adventist
Type: bimonthly (five per year) print journal; 48 pages, circulation 13,500, subscription $18.25

Audience: Seventh-day teachers and educational administrators in the church's school system, kindergarten to university level

Purpose: to support Seventh-day educators with informational and practical articles on a variety of topics

Submissions: Email a query first. Responds in six to seventeen weeks. Seasonal six months ahead. Accepts reprints (tell when/where appeared). All manuscripts must be submitted to the Journal through the online editorial manager at www.editorialmanager. com/jae/default.aspx. Articles six to eight pages, up to ten; buys two to twenty per year.

Types of manuscripts: how-to, persuasive, teaching, personal experience

Topics: including but not limited to classroom climate, interpersonal skills, counseling, discipline; students with special needs, learning disabilities, physical handicaps; new methods and approaches, such as cooperative learning, multiple intelligences, individualized instruction, thematic instruction; professional enrichment, staff development, teacher training; legal issues in schools

Rights: first, reprint

Payment: varies, on publication

Guidelines: *jae.adventist.org/authors.htm*

Sample: copy for 10 x 12 SASE with five stamps

Tip: "The Journal's constituency is international, a fact writers should keep in mind as they explore the implications or applications of a given topic. Special attention, where applicable, should be given to the concerns of minorities and students with special needs."

JOYFUL LIVING MAGAZINE

PO Box 311, Palo Cedro, CA 97073 | 530-247-7500
Cathy@joyfullivingmagazine.com | joyfullivingmagazine.com
Cathy Jansen, editor-in-chief

Type: quarterly print and digital magazine; 28 pages, takes ads

Audience: general

Purpose: to share encouragement and hope; to help readers grow spiritually and emotionally; and to help them in their everyday lives with practical issues

Submissions: Email articles as attachments. Length: 200-700 words.

Types of manuscripts: profiles, personal experience, recipes, how-to

Topics: making dreams come true, family, marriage, work, singleness, recovery, finances, health, dealing with loss, depression, aging, physical fitness, overcoming obstacles, healthy eating, and more

Payment: none
Guidelines: *joyfullivingmagazine.com/writers-info.html*
Sample: download from website

JUST BETWEEN US
777 S. Barker Rd., Brookfield, WI 53045 | 262-786-6478
www.justbetweenus.org
Shelly Esser, executive editor, jbu@justbetweenus.org
Parent organization: Elmbrook Church
Type: quarterly print magazine; circulation 8,000, subscription $19.95
Audience: women
Purpose: to encourage and equip women for a life of faith and service
Submissions: Prefers emailed manuscripts as attachments but also takes them by mail. Responds in six to eight weeks. Articles 500-1,500 words, testimonies 450 words. Bible version: NIV.
Types of manuscripts: how-to, testimony, personal experience
Topics: balance, intimacy with Christ, handling criticism, friendship, conflict, faith, church life, prayer, evangelism, change, spirit-filled living, finances, forgiveness, God's will, spiritual warfare, staying committed to Christ no matter what, parenting, pain, fighting weariness, church wounds, ministry helps
Payment: none
Guidelines: *justbetweenus.org/writers-guidelines*
Sample: *justbetweenus.org/sample-issue*
Tip: "Articles should be personal in tone, full of real-life anecdotes as well as quotes/advice from noted Christian professionals, and be biblically based. Articles need to be practical and have a distinct Christian and serving perspective throughout."

KANSAS CITY METRO VOICE
PO Box 1114, Lee's Summit, MO 64063 | 816-524-4522
dwight@metrovoicenews.com | *www.metrovoicenews.com*
Dwight Widamon, editor
Type: monthly print and PDF newspaper; takes ads
Audience: Kansas City metropolitan area and Topeka/Northeast Kansas
Purpose: to inform and encourage the evangelical community in the area
Submissions: Email for current needs. Takes articles and reviews.
Types of manuscripts: profiles, reviews, opinion pieces, news reports
Sample: download from the website

LEADING HEARTS

PO Box 6421, Longmont, CO 80501 | 303-835-8473
amber@leadinghearts.com | *leadinghearts.com*
Amber Weigland-Buckley, editor

> **Parent company:** Right to the Heart Ministries
> **Type:** bimonthly digital magazine; 50 pages, circulation 60,000, free, takes ads
> **Audience:** women who lead hearts at home, church, work, and community; ages 35-50
> **Submissions:** Articles on assignment only. To audition for an assignment, email an article of 1,200 words maximum and a short résumé. Gives preferred consideration to members of AWSA. Articles 800 words maximum. Columns 250-500 words. Bible version: NIV.
> **Types of manuscripts:** personal experience, how-to, profiles, reviews
> **Topics:** based on theme list
> **Rights:** first, reprint
> **Payment:** none
> **Guidelines:** *leadinghearts.com/?page_id=32*
> **Sample:** download from the website

LEAVES

PO Box 87, Dearborn, MI 48121-0087 | 313-561-2330
editor.leaves@mariannhill.us | *www.mariannhill.us/leaves.html*
Father Thomas Heier, CMM, editor-in-chief

> **Denomination:** Catholic
> **Type:** bimonthly print magazine; free
> **Audience:** Catholics, primarily in the Detroit, Michigan, area
> **Purpose:** to promote devotion to God and His saints
> **Submissions:** Articles about personal, spiritual experiences; petitions and thanksgivings; lives of saints and other holy people; timely spiritual topics; and prayers and edifying poems. Length: 500 words. 25% unsolicited freelance.
> **Types of manuscripts:** personal experience, profiles, prayers, poetry
> **Rights:** onetime
> **Payment:** none
> **Guidelines:** *www.mariannhill.us/leaves.html*
> **Sample:** write, email, or call for a copy

LEBEN

2150 River Plaza Dr., Ste. 150, Sacramento, CA 95833 | 916-473-8866

editor@leben.us | www.leben.us
Wayne C. Johnson, editor

Parent company: City Seminary of Sacramento, California
Type: quarterly print journal
Audience: general
Purpose: to tell the stories of the people and events that make up the Reformation tradition
Submissions: We are a popular history publication that aims at a general readership. Query first. Length: 500-2500 words.
Types of manuscripts: profiles
Topics: Protestant Reformers and those who have followed in their footsteps
Payment: not specified
Guidelines: *www.leben.us/writers*
Tip: "Focus on lesser-known events and people. We have no shortage of submissions about Luther, Calvin, Zwingli, etc."

LIGHT & LIFE MAGAZINE

770 N. High School Rd., Indianapolis, IN 46214 | 317-244-3660
jeff.finley@fmcusa.org | fmcusa.org/lightandlifemag
Jeff Finley, managing editor

Denomination: Free Methodist
Type: monthly print magazine
Audience: general
Purpose: to offer encouragement, provide resources, deal with contemporary issues, share denominational news, and offer faith to unbelievers
Submissions: Articles: main article that provides a more detailed examination of the issue's theme, approximately 2,100 words, primarily in third person; action article that shares the story of someone living out the theme and sometimes serves as an instructional piece detailing how to take action, 1,000 words; discipleship, for use by a weekly small group or for individual study, 800 words reflecting the theme plus two or three group discussion questions. Query first. Responds in two months. 50% unsolicited freelance. Bible: NIV.
Types of manuscripts: teaching, profile, Bible study
Topics: theme-related
Rights: first, onetime, occasional reprint (tell when and where appeared)
Payment: $100 for feature articles, $50 for others, on publication

157

Guidelines: *fmcusa.org/lightandlifemag/writers*
Themes: email *mark.crawford@fmcusa.org*
Tip: "We search for authors who write competently, provide clear information, and employ contemporary style and illustrations."

LIGUORIAN

1 Liguori Dr., Liguori, MO 63057 | 636.223.1538
liguorianeditor@liguori.org | *www.liguorian.org*
Elizabeth Herzing, editor

Denomination: Catholic
Type: monthly print and digital magazine
Audience: denomination
Purpose: to reinforce spiritual beliefs with inspiration and insight
Submissions: Articles must not exceed 2,200 words. Personal essays should be limited to 1,000. Fiction submissions should be approximately 2,000 words. Seasonal articles and stories must be received eight months in advance. Email query. Email manuscripts as attachments or mail them on a CD. Responds in two to three months.
Types of manuscripts: essay, feature, short stories, interviews
Topics: explanations of Church teachings, theological insights, Christian living
Rights: first
Payment: 12-15¢ per published word, on acceptance
Guidelines: *www.liguorian.org/submissions-and-rights-and-permissions*
Sample: 9 x 12 SASE with three stamps

LIVE

1445 N. Boonville Ave., Springfield, MO 65802-1894 | 417-862-2781
rl-live@gph.org | *www.gospelpublishing.com*
Wade Quick, editor

Denomination: Assemblies of God
Type: weekly take-home paper; 8 pages, circulation 30,000
Audience: denomination
Purpose: to encourage Christians in living for God through stories that apply biblical principles to everyday problems
Submissions: Prefers emailed submissions as attachments but will accept mailed manuscripts. Stories should be encouraging, challenging, and/or humorous. Even problem-centered stories should be upbeat. Stories should not be preachy, critical, or moralizing. They should not present pat, trite, or simplistic answers to problems. No Bible fiction or sci-fi. Length: cover stories 800-1,200 words, inside stories 200-600 words, poetry 12-25 lines. Seasonal eighteen months in advance.

Types of manuscripts: personal experiences, short stories, how-to, poetry, first-person anecdotes, short humor
Topics: all kinds of stories that show how God works in people's lives
Rights: first, reprint
Payment: 10¢ per word for first, 7¢ per word for reprint, $35-60 for poetry
Guidelines: *gospelpublishing.com/store/startcat.cfm?cat=tWRITGUID #Live*
Tip: "Make sure the stories have a strong Christian element, are written well, have strong takeaways, but do not preach."

THE LIVING CHURCH

PO Box 510705, Milwaukee, WI 53203-0121 | 414-292-1240
cwells@livingchurch.org | *www.livingchurh.org*
Christopher Wells, editor

Denomination: Episcopal
Type: biweekly print magazine
Audience: denomination
Purpose: to seek and serve the Catholic and evangelical faith of the one Church, to the end of visible Christian unity throughout the world
Submissions: Email for current needs. Takes articles and reviews.

THE LOOKOUT

8805 Governor's Hill Dr., Ste. 400, Cincinnati, OH 45249 | 513-931-4050
lookout@christianstandardmedia.com | *www.lookoutmag.com*
Kelly Carr, editor

Parent company: Christian Standard Media
Type: weekly print magazine; 16 pages, circulation 40,000
Audience: ordinary Christians who want to grow in their faith
Purpose: to provide Christian adults with true-to-the-Bible teaching about current topics to help them mature as believers and live in the world as faithful witnesses of Christ
Submissions: Query only by email; put issue number in the subject line. Email requested manuscript as an attachment. Length: 600-1,400 words. Bible: NIV.
Topics: theme-related
Rights: first
Payment: up to 11¢ per word
Guidelines and theme list: *www.lookoutmag.com/about-us/write-for-us*
Sample: *www.lookoutmag.com/sample*
Tip: "We publish strictly according to our theme list. All articles we purchase will address one of the weekly themes we have scheduled for the year."

THE LUTHERAN DIGEST

PO Box 100, Princeton, MN 55371
editor@lutherandigest.com | *www.lutherandigest.com*

Denomination: Lutheran
Type: quarterly print magazine
Audience: denomination
Purpose: to entertain and encourage believers and to subtly persuade nonbelievers to embrace the Lutheran-Christian faith
Submissions: Prefers manuscripts by mail with SASE but will look at emailed submissions as attachments and respond only if accepted. 30% unsolicited freelance. Will consider simultaneous submissions but prefers not to. Length: 3,000-7,000 characters. Popular stories show how God has intervened in a person's life to help solve a problem. Seasonal six months in advance. Poetry one or two stanzas. Interested in poems that can be sung to the melodies of familiar hymns. Submit maximum three poems in a month. Fillers: recipes, jokes.
Types of manuscripts: personal experience, seasonal, poetry, recipes
Topics: Christian living, God's presence in nature
Rights: onetime, reprint (tell when and where last appeared)
Payment: $35, on publication; none for poetry and fillers
Guidelines: *lutherandigest.com/write-for-us*
Tip: "Stories frequently reflect a Lutheran-Christian perspective but are not intended to be 'lecturing' sermonettes."

LUTHERAN FORUM

PO Box 327, Delhi, NY 13753-0327 | 607-746-7511
editor@lutheranforum.org | *lutheranforum.org*
Sarah Hinlicky Wilson, editor

Denomination: Lutheran
Parent company: American Lutheran Publicity Bureau
Type: quarterly print journal; 64 pages, subscription $28.45
Submissions: Articles 2,000-3,000 words. Email query or complete manuscript. Responds in three months.
Rights: first
Payment: none
Guidelines: *alpb.org/writers-guidelines*
Tip: "Prospective writers are encouraged to reflect on what moves them most, intellectually and spiritually, and then, armed with adequate research and forethought, put their ideas to paper."

THE LUTHERAN JOURNAL

PO Box 28158, Oakdale, MN 55128 | 651-702-0176
christianad2@msn.com | *thelutheranjournal.com*

Denomination: Lutheran
Type: annual print magazine
Audience: families
Purpose: to provide wholesome and inspirational reading for the enjoyment and enrichment of Lutherans
Submissions: Email for current needs.
Types of manuscripts: articles, poetry, prayers
Payment: none
Sample: *online.fliphtml5.com/adnv/nksx/#p=1*

LUTHERAN WITNESS

1333 S. Kirkwood Rd., St. Louis, MO 63122-7226 | 800-248-1930
lutheran.witness@lcms.org
Adriane Heins, editor

Denomination: Luthern Church Missouri Synod (LCMS)
Type: monthly (11x) print magazine; circulation 185,000
Audience: denomination
Purpose: to provide Missouri Synod laypeople with stories and information that complement congregational life, foster personal growth in faith, and help interpret the contemporary world from a Lutheran Christian perspective
Submissions: Prefers complete manuscript instead of a query. Submit by email or mail. Length: 500, 1,000, or 1,500 words. Bible: ESV.
Types of manuscripts: profiles, how-to, teaching, humor, personal experience, Bible studies
Topics: current events; theology; LCMS missions, ministries, members, history; evangelism, outreach, spiritual growth
Rights: first, electronic
Guidelines: *blogs.lcms.org/the-lutheran-witness/writers-guidelines-for-the-lutheran-witness*
Tip: "Because of the magazine's long lead time, and because many features are planned at least six months in advance of the publication date, your story should have a long-term perspective that keeps it relevant several months from the time you submit it."

MATURE LIVING

1 Lifeway Plaza, MSN 136, Nashville, TN 37234-0175 | 615-251-2000
matureliving@lifeway.com | *www.lifeway.com/n/Product-Family/*

Mature-Living-Magazine
Mike Glenn, executive editor

> **Parent company:** LifeWay Christian Resources
> **Denomination:** Southern Baptist
> **Type:** monthly print magazine; 72 pages
> **Audience:** ages 55 and older
> **Purpose:** to equip mature adults as they live a legacy of leadership, stewardship, and discipleship
> **Submissions:** Email for current needs. Buys articles and slice-of-life accounts addressing various issues like marriage, adult children, and caregiving.
> **Types of manuscripts:** personal experience, how-to, teaching, devotional, short stories, recipes
> **Topics:** marriage, caregiving, evangelism, theology, relationship with adult children, grandchildren
> **Sample:** on the website

MESSAGE OF THE OPEN BIBLE

2020 Bell Ave., Des Moines, IA 50315 | 515-288-6761
message@openbible.org | *www.openbiblemessage.org*
Andrea Johnson, editor

> **Denomination:** Open Bible Standard Churches
> **Type:** bimonthly print magazine
> **Audience:** denomination
> **Purpose:** to celebrate all the wonderful things God is doing through His people in Open Bible Churches
> **Submissions:** Email for current needs.
> **Types of manuscripts:** testimonies, news-related stories, inspirational articles, reviews
> **Payment:** none

THE MESSENGER

440 Main St., Steinbach, MB R5G 1Z5, Canada | 204-326-6401
messenger@emconf.ca |*www.emconf.ca/Messenger*
Terry M. Smith, editor

> **Denomination:** Evangelical Mennonite Conference (EMC)
> **Type:** monthly print and digital magazine
> **Audience:** generally, but not exclusively, EMC members and adherents with a range of educational and cultural backgrounds
> **Purpose:** to inform concerning events and activities in the denomination, instruct in godliness and victorious living, and inspire to earnestly contend for the faith

Submissions: Prefers email query first. Length: 1,200 words maximum. Kill fee: 50%.
Topics: open
Rights: first
Payment: $135 for 1,200 words
Guidelines: *www.emconference.ca/the-messenger/submission-guidelines*
Sample: download from Past Issues on the website

THE MESSIANIC TIMES

PO Box 10943, Pensacola, FL 32524 | 866-612-7770
editor.messianictimes@gmail.com | *www.messianictimes.com*
David Tokajer, Dylan Mathew, managing editors

Parent company: Times of the Messiah Ministries
Denomination: Messianic
Type: bimonthly print and digital newspaper
Audience: Messianic community
Purpose: to provide accurate, authoritative, and current information to unite the international Messianic Jewish community, teach Christians the Jewish roots of their faith, and proclaim that Yeshua is the Jewish Messiah
Submissions: Query preferred. Email for current needs.
Types of manuscripts: analysis; opinion pieces; book, music, and film reviews; news
Guidelines: *www.messianictimes.com/about*

METHODIST HISTORY

36 Madison Ave., Madison, NJ 07940 | 973-408-3189
atday@gcah.org | *www.gcah.org*
Alfred T. Day, III, general secretary

Denomination: United Methodist
Type: annual print journal
Audience: denomination
Submissions: Only email manuscripts as attachments. Articles on the history of other denominations and subjects will be considered when there are strong ties to events and persons significant to the history of the United Methodist tradition. Manuscripts pertaining to strictly local, as opposed to national or international interest, are not accepted. Length: maximum 5,000 words.
Topics: United Methodist history
Payment: none
Guidelines: *www.gcah.org/resources/guidelines-for-publication*

MINISTRY

12501 Old Columbia Pike, Silver Spring, MD 20904 | 301-680-6518
ministrymagazine@gc.adventist.org | *www.ministrymagazine.org*
Dr. Willie Hucks, editor

Denomination: Seventh-day Adventist
Type: monthly print and digital magazine; 28 pages, circulation
18,000, subscription $33
Audience: pastors, professors, administrators, chaplains, pastoral
students, lay leaders of all denominations
Purpose: to deepen spiritual life, develop intellectual strength, and
increase pastoral and evangelistic effectiveness of all ministers in
the context of the three angels' messages of Revelation 14:6-12
Submissions: For all submissions, include completed biographical
information form. Send all submissions as email attachments.
Articles to 2,500 words; book and resources reviews to 500 words.
Types of manuscripts: biblical studies, how-to, teaching, reviews
Topics: personal needs of the minister (spiritual, physical, emotional),
pastor-spouse team and ministry relationships, pastoral family
needs, pastoral skills, biblical studies for sermon preparation,
theological studies, worship, current issues
Rights: all
Payment: not specified, on acceptance
Guidelines: *www.ministrymagazine.org/article-submissions*
Sample: click Archives page on the website
Tip: "Writers should ask themselves: What do I expect the reader to
do with my manuscript?"

MINISTRY TODAY

600 Rinehart Rd., Lake Mary, FL 32746 | 407-333-0600
ministrytoday@charismamedia.com | *www.ministrytodaymag.com*
Christine D. Johnson, editor

Denomination: Pentecostal/Charismatic
Parent company: Charisma Media
Type: quarterly print and digital magazine, 112 pages, circulation
30,000, subscription $14.97, takes ads
Audience: pastors, ministry leaders, business leaders
Purpose: to inspire and assist ministry leaders
Submissions: Email query through the online submission form.
If no response in two weeks, assume they're not interested.
Email (preferred) or mail manuscript after query if requested.
Bible version: MEV. Most open to departments: Ministry Life,

Leadership, Outreach, and Facilities. Length: to 700 words. Also buys more in-depth features; length to 2,500 words.

Types of manuscripts: how-to, interviews, teaching

Topics: anything related to church ministry and leadership

Rights: all

Payment: unspecified, on publication

Guidelines: ministrytodaymag.com/index.php/write-for-us

Sample: download at *www.ministrytodaymag.com/index.php/ministry-today-digital*

Tip: "Most open to departments. Please take time to read—even study—at least one or two of our recent issues before submitting a query."

THE MOTHER'S HEART

PO Box 275, Tobaccoville, NC 27050
Kym@TMHMag.com | *www.the-mothers-heart.com*
Kym Wright, editor

Parent company: Living Life on Purpose

Type: bimonthly digital magazine; free, takes ads

Audience: stay-at-home and homeschool mothers

Purpose: to serve and encourage mothers in the many facets of staying at home and raising a family

Submissions: Email manuscript as attachment (preferred) or in the body of the message. Seasonal six months ahead. Length: 750-1,750 words. Takes simultaneous submissions.

Types of manuscripts: personal experience, how-to

Topics: motherhood, homeschooling, organization, living in God's strength, encouragement, homemaking, child-raising, getting it all done, father's viewpoint and roles, and other topics related to Titus 2 and Proverbs 31 living

Rights: first

Payment: $10-75 or 1/8 page advertising space

Guidelines: *www.the-mothers-heart.com/Writers%20Guidelines%20 2016-2019.pdf*

Sample: on the website

Tip: "Please keep the tone positive, real-life, with hope and a good ending. Personal experiences or other anecdotes which relate to the article topic make great lead-ins."

MTL MAGAZINE

200 W. Bay Dr., Largo, FL 33770 | 727-596-7625
ideas@mtlmagazine.com | *mtlmagazine.com*
Andrea Stock, editor

Parent company: Munce Marketing Group
Type: online magazine with five print issues a year
Audience: women
Purpose: to address the felt needs of women and connect those needs
   to products at local Christian bookstores
Submissions: Query ideas.
Types of manuscripts: interviews, reviews, how-to, testimonies,
   personal experience
Sample: on the website

MUTUALITY

122 W. Franklin Ave., Ste. 218, Minneapolis, MN 55404 612-872-6898
cbe@cbeinternational.org | *www.cbeinternational.org/content/mutuality-
magazine*
Tim Krueger, editor

Parent company: Christians for Biblical Equality
Type: quarterly print magazine
Audience: evangelicals in professional and volunteer ministry,
   seminary faculty and students, male and female leaders, and
   laypeople interested in egalitarian theory (Bible and theology) and
   practice (application in churches and homes)
Purpose: to provide inspiration, encouragement, and information
   on topics related to a biblical view of mutuality between men and
   women in the home, church, and world
Submissions: Query first through the online contact form. Also
   submit requested manuscript through that form. Responds in one
   month or more. Length: first-person narratives and feature articles,
   800-1,800 words; book, movie, or music reviews, 500-800 words.
   Bible: NIV.
Types of manuscripts: personal experience, how-to, biblical reflection,
   poetry, reviews
Topics: theme-related
Rights: first with electronic
Payment: one-year CBE membership ($49–$59 value) or up to three
   CBE recordings (up to $30 value)
Guidelines: *www.cbeinternational.org/content/mutuality-writers-guidelines*
Theme list: *www.cbeinternational.org/content/upcoming-mutuality-themes*
Sample: download PDF from guidelines page

MYSTERIOUS WAYS

110 William St., Ste. 901, New York, NY 10038 | 212-251-8100
www.guideposts.org/brand/mysterious-ways-magazine
Adam Hunter, editor

Parent company: Guideposts
Type: bimonthly print and digital magazine
Audience: general
Purpose: to encourage through true stories of extraordinary moments and everyday miracles that reveal a spiritual force at work in our lives
Submissions: Submit complete manuscript through the online form. Looking for true stories of unexpected and wondrous experiences that reveal a hidden hand at work in our lives. The best stories are those that present a credible, well-detailed account that can even leave skeptics in awe and wonder. Length: 750-1,500 words. Also buys news stories and short material, 50-350 words, for recurring features like "Wonderful World," "His Humorous Ways," and "Dreams & Premonitions."
Types of manuscripts: personal experiences
Payment: varies, after scheduled for publication
Guidelines: *www.guideposts.org/write-for-mysterious-ways*
Tip: "A typical Mysterious Ways story is written in dramatic style, with an unforeseen twist that inspires the reader to look for miracles in his or her own life. It may be told from a 1st-person or 3rd-person perspective, and can be your own experience or someone else's story. We are also on the lookout for recent experiences."

NET RESULTS

308 West Blvd. N., Columbia, MO 65203 | 888-470-2456
bill@netresults.org |*netresults.org*
Bill Tenny-Brittian, managing editor

Parent company: The Effective Church Group
Type: bimonthly print and digital magazine; subscription $29.95
Audience: pastors, church volunteers, and Christian organizations
Purpose: to share great ideas for vital ministry among leaders
Submissions: Email query first; email manuscripts as attached file. Responds in eight weeks. Practical and relevant articles on innovative ways to do mission and ministry, 1,750 words. Bible: TNIV. Takes reprints from noncompetitive periodicals with letter of release from original publication.
Types of manuscripts: how-to, teaching
Topics: evangelism, service, planning, trust-building, leadership and organizational development, worship, preaching, hospitality, Christian education, faith formation, mentoring, training, partnerships, property and technology development, fund-raising, financial planning, stewardship, communications, marketing

Rights: all print and electronic
Payment: on publication
Guidelines: *netresults.org/writers*
Theme list: *netresults.org/writers/upcoming-themes*
Sample: on the website
Tip: "We look for practical, hands-on ministry ideas that an individual can put into practice. The best ideas are those the author has actually used successfully."

NEW FRONTIER CHRONICLE

180 E. Ocean Blvd., 4th Fl., Long Beach, CA 90802 | 562-491-8723
new.frontier@usw.salvationarmy.org | *www.newfrontierchronicle.org*
Christin Davis Thieme, editor-in-chief

Parent company: The Salvation Army Western Territory
Type: monthly print newspaper
Audience: denomination in the territory
Purpose: to empower Salvationists to communicate and engage with the Army's mission
Submissions: Query first. Accepts articles and reviews. Shares information from across The Salvation Army world, reports that analyze effective programs to identify the unique features and trends for what works, tips to help local congregations better engage in the issues of today, and influential voices on relevant (and sometimes controversial) matters.

A NEW HEART

PO Box 4004, San Clemente, CA 92674-4004 | 949-496-7655
HCFUSA@gmail.com | *www.HCFUSA.com*
Aubrey Beauchamp, editor

Parent company: Hospital Christian Fellowship
Type: quarterly print magazine; 16 pages
Audience: healthcare givers
Submissions: Query or submit complete manuscripts. Length: 600-1,800 words. 20% unsolicited freelance, 10% assigned. Limited poetry.
Types of manuscripts: personal experiences, poetry
Rights: onetime
Payment: none
Tip: "Most open to real-life situations which may benefit and encourage healthcare givers and patients. True stories with medical and evangelical emphasis."

NEW IDENTITY MAGAZINE

PO Box 1002, Mount Shasta, CA 96067 | 310-947-8707
submissions@newidentitymagazine.com | *www.newidentitymagazine.com*
Cailin Briody Henson, editor-in-chief

Type: quarterly print and digital magazine

Audience: new believers

Purpose: to provide diverse, Bible-centered content to help lead new believers and seekers to a fuller understanding of the Christian faith

Submissions: Query first; prefers by email. Email requested manuscript. Responds in two to four weeks. Length: 500-3,500 words. Departments: "Grow," teaching new believers and seekers about different Christian perspectives on topics, understanding Christian concepts, jargon, disciplines, practical application of Scripture, etc.; "Connect," encouraging new believers and seekers with testimonies, articles about relationships, fellowship, church, community, discussions and expressions of faith; "Live," engaging new believers and seekers to live out their faith in the real world, with stories of people actively pursuing God and their passions, organizations and resources to apply ones gifts, talents and desires to serve God and others, sharing the love of Christ in everyday arenas.

Types of manuscripts: personal experience, teaching, testimonies, how-to, opinion

Topics: spiritual growth, applying Scripture, relationships, salvation, church, service, evangelism

Rights: first, electronic, sometimes reprint (tell when and where appeared)

Payment: none

Guidelines: *www.newidentitymagazine.com/WritersGuidelines.pdf*

Sample: on the website

Tip: "Articles need creative, well thought-out ideas that offer new insight. We value well researched, factually and biblically supported content."

THE NEWSLETTER NEWSLETTER

PO Box 36269, Canton, OH 44735 | 800-992-2144
service@newsletternewsletter.com | *www.newsletternewsletter.com*
Stephanie Martin, senior editor

Parent company: Communication Resources

Purpose: to help church secretaries and newsletter editors prepare high-quality publications

Type: monthly print and online newsletter; 14 pages, print subscription $89.95

Submissions: Query via editor email through the website. Requires requested manuscript by email. Responds in four weeks. Articles 800-1,000 words, buys 12 per year. Seasonal four months ahead.
Types of manuscripts: how-to
Rights: all
Payment: $50-150, on acceptance
Sample: risk-free trial
Tip: "Most open to how-to articles on various aspects of producing newsletters and e-newsletters—writing, layout and design, distribution, etc."

NOW WHAT?

PO Box 33677, Denver, CO 80233 | 303-452-7973
nowwhat@cog7.org | nowwhat.cog7.org
Sherri Langton, associate editor

Denomination: Church of God (Seventh Day)
Type: monthly e-zine
Audience: seekers
Purpose: to address the felt needs of the unchurched
Submissions: Each issue is built around a personal experience, with articles related to the topic. Personal experiences show a person's struggle that either led him to faith in Christ or deepened his walk with God. 100% unsolicited freelance. Prefers emailed manuscripts and queries, but also takes them by mail. Responds in four to ten weeks. Accepts simultaneous submissions. Length: 1,000-1,500 words. Bible: prefers NKJV. Avoid unnecessary jargon or technical terms. No Christmas or Easter pieces.
Types of manuscripts: personal experiences
Topics: salvation, Jesus, social issues, life problems, that are seeker sensitive
Rights: electronic, reprint (tell when/where appeared)
Payment: $25-65, on publication
Guidelines: *nowwhat.cog7.org/send_us_your_story*
Tip: "Think how you can explain your faith, or how you overcame a problem, to a non-Christian. It's a real plus for writers submitting a personal experience to also submit an objective article related to their story."

OMS OUTREACH

941 Fry Rd., Greenwood, IN 46142 | 317-881-3333
editor@onemissionsociety.org | onemissionsociety.org/give/outreach
Susan Griswold Loobie, editor, sloobie@onemissionsociety.org

Parent company: One Mission Society

Type: triannual print and digital magazine; $10 print (for two years), free digital

Purpose: to equip Christians to make disciples of Jesus Christ through informative, inspiring, and involvement-driven articles, which leads to deeper mission participation by serving, giving, and praying

Submissions: Articles 500-600 words to inform the public of ministry opportunities and report on ministry of various mission teams. Email for current needs. Bible version: ESV.

Sample: click link on the website

ON MISSION

4200 N. Point Pkwy., Alpharetta, GA 30022-4176 | 770-410-6000
jconway@namb.net | *www.onmission.com*
Joe Conway, editor

Denomination: Southern Baptist

Parent company: North American Mission Board

Type: quarterly magazine, free

Audience: Christians who are impacting their world for Christ

Purpose: to highlight the work of missionaries and help readers be on mission where they work and live

Submissions: Open to freelance articles and reviews. Email for current needs.

Topics: missions, evangelism

Sample: download from website

OUR SUNDAY VISITOR NEWSWEEKLY

200 Noll Plaza, Huntington, IN 46750 | 800-348-2440, 260-356-8400
oursunvis@osv.com | *www.osv.com/OSVNewsweekly.aspx*
Gretchen R. Crowe, editor-in-chief

Denomination: Catholic

Type: weekly print and digital newspaper

Audience: denomination

Purpose: to provide timely coverage of important national and international religious events reported from a Catholic perspective

Submissions: Query and send manuscript only through the online form. Responds in four to six weeks. Articles: news analysis, 950-1,100 words, including sidebars, but occasionally as short as 500 words or as long as 2,000 words; "In Focus," a package of articles totaling 3,000-4,000 words by one or more authors, query first; features linked to current events and trends of the day, 1,350 words; essays on relevant issues of the day, 500-750 words; profiles, 500-750 words; Q&A interviews, 1,200 words. Bible: RSV.

Types of manuscripts: news, essays, interviews

Topics: Catholic perspective on issues and news

Payment: unspecified, within four to six weeks of acceptance

Guidelines: *www.osv.com/OSVNewsweekly/More/WritersGuidelines.aspx*

Tip: "Our mission is to examine the news, culture, and trends of the day from a faithful and sound Catholic perspective—to see the world through the eyes of faith. Especially interested in writers able to do news analysis (with a minimum of 3 sources) or news features."

OUTREACH

Story Ideas, 5550 Tech Center, Colorado Springs, CO 80919
tellus@outreachmagazine.com | *www.outreachmagazine.com*
James P. Long, editor

Type: bimonthly magazine, subscription $19.95

Audience: senior pastors and church leadership, as well as laypeople who are passionate about outreach

Purpose: to be the gathering place of ideas, insights, and stories for churches focused on reaching out to their community—locally and globally—with the love of Christ

Submissions: Email or mail query or complete manuscript with cover letter and published clips. Seasonal six months ahead. Responds in eight weeks. Accepts reprints (tell when and where published). Articles 1,200-2,500 words; features 1,500-2,500 words; "Pulse" stories of what churches and individuals are doing, 200-300 words; ideas for outreach events, 300 words; and "Soulfires" profiles of people who are passionate about reaching others for Christ, 600 words.

Types of manuscripts: profiles, how-to

Topics: what's new in ministry, tips for evangelism training, focus on retention, small groups, keeping visitors engaged

Payment: $700-1,000 for feature articles

Guidelines: *www.outreachmagazine.com/magazine/3160-writers-guidelines.html*

Tip: While most articles are assigned, we do accept queries and manuscripts on speculation. Please don't query us until you've studied at least one issue of Outreach.

PARENTING TEENS

1 Lifeway Plaza, Nashville, TN 37234-0172 | 615-251-2196
lwt@lifeway.com | *www.lifeway.com/n/Product-Family/HomeLife-Magazine*
Mike Wakefield, team leader

Parent company: LifeWay Christian Resources
Denomination: Southern Baptist
Type: monthly print magazine
Audience: parents of teens
Purpose: to give parents encouragement and challenge them in their relationship with Christ so that they, in turn, can guide their teens
Submissions: Manuscripts by assignment. Email résumé, bio, and clips. Offers timely information, encouragement, expert insight, and practical advice to parents of teens. Bible: HCSB.
Payment: unspecified
Guidelines: by email
Sample: on the website

PARENTLIFE

1 Lifeway Plaza, Nashville, TN 37234-0172 | 615-251-2196
parentlife@lifeway.com | *www.lifeway.com/n/Product-Family/ParentLife-Magazine*
William Summey, editor-in-chief

Parent company: LifeWay Christian Resources
Denomination: Southern Baptist
Type: monthly print magazine
Audience: parents of children birth to preteen
Purpose: to encourage and equip parents with biblical solutions that will transform families
Submissions: Serves as a springboard for parents who may feel exasperated or overwhelmed with information by offering a biblical approach to raising healthy, productive children. Offers practical ideas and information for individual parents and couples. Query first by email. Email requested manuscript as an attachment. Include one to three sidebars. Responds in six to twelve months. Length: 500-1,500 words. Bible: HCSB.
Types of manuscripts: how-to, teaching, family devotional
Topics: parenting, health, development, education, discipline, and spiritual growth
Payment: unspecified
Guidelines: by email
Sample: on the website

PARISH LITURGY

16565 S. State St., South Holland, IL 60473 | 708-331-5485
acp@acpress.org | *www.americancatholicpress.org*
Rev. Michael Gilligan, executive director

Denomination: Catholic
Parent company: American Catholic Press
Type: quarterly magazine; 48 pages, circulation 950, subscription $26
Audience: parish priests and musicians
Purpose: to support parish leaders in planning the liturgy, resources for Sunday Mass
Submissions: Query by email or mail. Responds in eight weeks. 10% unsolicited freelance. Articles 400 words. Bible: NAB. Email for current needs.
Types of manuscripts: teaching, how-to, profiles
Topics: liturgy, sermons, petitions, music suggestions
Rights: all
Payment: not specified, on publication
Tip: "We use articles on the liturgy only—period. Send us well-informed articles on the liturgy."

PENTECOSTAL MESSENGER

PO Box 211866, Bedford, TX 76095 | 817-554-5900
communications@pcg.org | *www.pcg.org/pentecostal-messenger*
Laura Salazar, editor, lsalazar@pcg.org

Denomination: Pentecostal Church of God (PCG)
Type: quarterly print magazine
Audience: denomination
Purpose: to impart the message of Jesus Christ, strengthen believers, resource the church, and promote the essential values of the PCG
Submissions: Email for current needs. Open to freelance submissions.

THE PENWOOD REVIEW

PO Box 862, Los Alamitos, CA 90720-0862
submissions@penwoodreview.com | *www.penwoodreview.com*
Lori M. Cameron, editor

Type: biannual journal
Audience: general
Purpose: to embrace high quality poetry of all kinds and to provide a forum for poets who want to write intriguing, energetic, and disciplined poetry as an expression of their faith in God
Submissions: Email only; no attachments. 100% unsolicited freelance. Submit up to five poems or two essays at a time. Poems may be up to two pages in length, essays five pages.
Types of manuscripts: poetry, essays
Payment: $4 off a subscription
Guidelines: *www.penwoodreview.com/submissions*

Tip: "We want serious, disciplined, high quality poetry. We do not want light verse, doggerel, or greeting card-style poetry. Avoid religious platitudes, preaching, and simplistic answers."

PERSPECTIVES: A JOURNAL OF REFORMED THOUGHT

4500 60th St. S.E., Grand Rapids, MI 49512
submissions@perspectivesjournal.org | *www.perspectivesjournal.org*
Sara Sybesma Tolsma, Jason Lief, editors | *Deborah Van Duinen, Jon Witt, review editors* | *Rose Postma, poetry editor*

Denomination: Reformed
Type: bimonthly print journal
Audience: academics; pastors; and thoughtful, literate laypeople
Purpose: to express the Reformed faith theologically and to engage issues that Reformed Christians meet in personal, ecclesiastical, and societal life
Submissions: Articles: scholarly and general-interest articles, including spiritual autobiography 3,000 words maximum, editorial commentary 1,500 words maximum, fiction 3,000 words maximum, and book and film reviews 1,200 words maximum. Departments: "Inside Out," brief biblical reflection/commentary, 600 words maximum, and "As We See It," reflections on faith/culture, 500-750 words. Email manuscripts as attachments or mail on a CD.
Types: feature articles, opinion, autobiography, short stories, reviews, poetry
Guidelines: *perspectivesjournal.org/writers-guidelines*
Tip: "Because we are committed to mentoring and guiding future leaders in the church and academy, we encourage thoughtful contributions from students and emerging writers. It is part of our theological tradition to value good writing and thought, and as such we seek to encourage both rigor and freshness."

THE PLAIN TRUTH

1710 Evergreen St., Duarte, CA 91010 | 800-309-4466
managing.editor@ptm.org | *www.ptm.org*
Greg Albrecht, editor

Parent company: Plain Truth Ministries
Type: quarterly digital magazine
Audience: general
Purpose: to discover authentic Christianity without all the religious "stuff"
Submissions: Queries only.
Types of manuscripts: teaching

Guidelines: by email
Sample: on the website

POINT

11002 Lake Hart Dr., Orlando, FL 32832 | 407-563-6083
bob.putman@converge.org | *www.converge.org/point-magazine*
Bob Putman, editor

Denomination: Baptist General Conference
Type: quarterly print and digital magazine
Audience: denomination
Purpose: to increase movement awareness, ownership, and involvement by publishing captivating God-stories of Converge people and regional ministries
Submissions: Open to freelance submissions. Email query with clips. Articles 300-1,400 words.
Types: personal experiences, profiles, reports
Rights: first, reprint, electronic
Payment: $60-280, on publication
Sample: on the website

POWER FOR LIVING

4050 Lee Vance View, Colorado Springs, CO 80918 | 800-708-5550
719-536-0100 | *Powerforliving@davidccook.com* | *www.cookministries.org*
Catherine DeVries, senior managing editor

Parent company: David C. Cook
Type: weekly take-home paper; 8 pages
Audience: general
Purpose: to connect God's truth to real life
Submissions: Looking for inspiring stories and articles about famous and ordinary people whose experiences and insights show the power of Christ at work in their lives. Publishes stories covering a diverse range of subjects, from world missions to simple, relatable experiences with family and life. Length: 750-1,000 and 1,400-1,600 words. Poetry related to matters of faith and biblically based, twenty lines. Accepts reprints but prefers original work. Accepts simultaneous submissions provided the dates of publication are different. Bible: NIV, KJV.
Types of manuscripts: personal experiences, interviews, poetry
Rights: first, onetime, reprint
Payment: $125-$375 for articles, $50 for poems, on acceptance
Guidelines: *www.davidccook.com/About/jobs/index.cfm?N=7,166,2,1*
Sample: download from guidelines page

PRAIRIE MESSENGER

PO Box 190, Muenster, SK S0K 2Y0, Canada | 306-682-1772
pm.canadian@stpeterspress.ca | *www.prairiemessenger.ca*
Maureen Weber, Canadian news editor

Denomination: Catholic
Parent company: Benedictine Monks of St. Peter's Abbey
Type: weekly print newspaper; 16-20 pages
Audience: primarily prairie Catholics but ecumenical and interfaith with a liberal slant
Purpose: to make the people of God aware of their local, national, and international presence and responsibilities and to keep them informed of the concerns of all the church—its laity, teachers, scholars, and pastors
Submissions: Looking for well-written human-interest stories about a person, program, place, or experience, accompanied by several good photos. Length: 850 words maximum. Buys a few seasonal manuscripts, poetry, comment, and features. Email query and manuscripts. Responds to submissions only if accepted. 10% unsolicited freelance, 90% assigned. Accepts simultaneous submissions. Prefers NRSV.
Types of manuscripts: profiles, poetry
Topics: ecumenism, social justice, news, prairie concerns
Rights: first, reprint (tell when and where appeared)
Payment: $60, $85 with photo, $25 for reprint or poem, on publication
Guidelines: *www.prairiemessenger.ca/writers_guidelines.html*
Sample: on the website

PRESBYTERIANS TODAY

100 Witherspoon St., Louisville, KY 40202-1396 | 800-728-7228
editor@pcusa.org | *www.pcusa.org/today*
Patrick David Heery, editor

Denomination: Presbyterian Church (USA)
Type: bimonthly print and digital magazine
Audience; denomination
Purpose: to explore practical issues of faith and life, tell stories of Presbyterians who are living their faith, and cover a wide range of church news and activities
Submissions: Query first. Responds in two weeks. Prefers to work with published writers. Length: 1,000-1,800 words. Seasonal three months in advance. 25% freelance. Bible: NRSV.

Topics: features about Presbyterians, theology, Bible study, devotional helps, church's role in society

Payment: $75-300, on acceptance

PSYCHOLOGY FOR LIVING

PO Box 661900, Arcadia, CA 91066-1900

editor@ncfliving.org | ncfliving.org

Cynthia Hibma, editor

Parent company: Narramore Christian Foundation

Type: annual print journal

Audience: general

Purpose: to apply sound biblical and psychological principles to everyday issues of life

Submissions: Publishes articles that cover a wide range of personal and relational needs. Submit complete manuscript. Length: 1,200-1,700 words or fewer.

Types of manuscripts: how-to, teaching, personal experience

Topics: relationships, psychology, communication, emotions

Rights: first, reprint

Payment: $75-200

Guidelines: *ncfliving.org/psychology-for-living-literature/writers-guidelines.html*

Sample: *ncfliving.org/psychology-for-living-literature/psychology-for-living-magazine.html*

Tip: "Articles need to be written with laypeople in mind; technical terminology needs to be kept to a minimum. Also please avoid 'Christianeze' and suggestions that have a 'preachy' tone. Instead, give insight and understanding with practical applications that are well illustrated."

PURPOSE

718 N. Main St., Newton, KS 67114 | 316-281-4412

PurposeEditor@mennomedia.org | www.faithandliferesources.org/periodicals/purpose

Mary Ann Weber, editor

Denomination: Mennonite

Type: monthly take-home paper

Audience: denomination

Purpose: to encourage discipleship living

Submissions: Buys short, personal true stories, 450-700 words, and poems/verse, 12 lines maximum. Both should illustrate practical ways Christians apply their faith in daily life; biblical understandings that support discipleship; and stress loyalty to the church and its peacemaking, missional, and related ministries. Prefers email submissions.

Types of manuscripts: personal experience, poetry
Topics: theme-related
Rights: onetime
Payment: $25-$50, $10-$20 for poetry
Guidelines and theme list: download from the website

REFRESHED

PO Box 2606, El Cajon, CA 92021 | 619-567-7811
editor@refreshedmag.com | www.refreshedmag.com
Lori Arnold, editor

Parent company: Selah Media Group
Type: monthly print magazine
Purpose: to generate vibrant cultural dialogue within the framework of faith and to present engaging, real stories and features that offer our readers practical solutions to the challenges and complexities of life
Submissions: Specifically looking for local stories about people in San Diego County. Email query through the website. Responds in four to six weeks or not interested.
Types of manuscripts: personal experience, profiles
Guidelines: *refreshedmag.com/connect*, email for more details
Sample: *refreshedmag.com/digital-editions*

RELEVANT

900 N. Orange Ave., Winter Park, FL 32789 | 407-660-1411
submissions@relevantmediagroup.com | relevantmediagroup.com
Jesse Carey, senior editor, jesse@relevantmediagroup.com

Type: bimonthly print and digital magazine
Audience: millennials
Purpose: to challenge people to go further in their spiritual journey, live selflessly and intentionally, care about positively impacting the world around them, and find the unexpected places God is speaking in life, music, and culture
Submissions: Email query and complete manuscript as attachment. Responds in one to two weeks or not interested. Covers faith, culture, and intentional living. Length: 750-1,000 words.
Payment: $100-400
Guidelines: *www.relevantmagazine.com/how-write-relevant*

RELIEF JOURNAL

8933 Forestview, Evanston, IL 60203
editor@reliefjournal.com | www.reliefjournal.com
Aaron Housholder, fiction editor, aaron@reliefjournal.com | John Ballenger,
poetry editor, JohnB@reliefjournal.com | Jo Anna Gaona, creative nonfiction
editor, joanna@reliefjournal.com

> **Type:** biannual print literary journal
> **Audience:** general
> **Purpose:** to promote full human flourishing in faith and art
> **Submissions:** Looking for poetry and stories that reflect reality as
> honestly as Scripture reflects reality. Submit manuscript through
> the website. Query first for author/artist interview. Accepts
> simultaneous submissions. Costs $2 to submit a manuscript. Length:
> stories 8,000 words maximum; poetry 1,000 words maximum;
> creative nonfiction, exploratory essays with an emotional arc that
> may or may not be narrative, 5,000 words maximum
> **Types of manuscripts:** short stories, creative nonfiction, poetry,
> interviews
> **Rights:** first, electronic
> **Payment:** none
> **Guidelines:** *www.reliefjournal.com/submit-your-work*

SACONNECTS

440 W. Nyack Rd., West Nyack, NY 10994-1739 | 845-620-7200
saconnects.org
Robert Mitchell, managing editor

> **Denomination:** Salvation Army
> **Type:** monthly digital magazine
> **Audience:** denomination in the eastern territory
> **Submissions:** Manuscripts only from people who live in the eastern
> territory. Email manuscripts as attachments through the website.
> **Types of manuscripts:** news, how-to, personal experience
> **Guidelines:** *saconnects.org/submission-guidelines-magazine*

SCP JOURNAL

PO Box 40015, Pasadena, CA 91114 | 510-540-0300
scp@scp-inc.org | www.scp-inc.org
Tal Brooks, editor

> **Parent company:** Spiritual Counterfeits Project
> **Type:** quarterly print journal
> **Audience:** general

Purpose: to provide a biblical perspective on new religions and spiritual trends

Submissions: Query only. Articles analyze and discern the inside workings of new spiritual trends.

SEEK

4050 Lee Vance View, Colorado Springs, CO 80918 | 800-323-7543
seek@standardpub.com | *www.Standardpub.com.*

Type: weekly take-home paper; 8 pages

Audience: young and middle-age adults

Purpose: to encourage adults in their walk with Jesus Christ

Submissions: Buys articles and stories tied to specific Scriptures. Bible: KJV.

Topics: related to Sunday-school Scripture passages/themes. See details on the website.

Guidelines: *store.standardpub.com/pages/seek-writers-guidelines*

SHARING

PO Box 780909, San Antonio, TX 78278-0909 | 877-992-5222
sharing@orderofstluke.org | *orderofstluke.org/en/sharing-magazine.html*

Parent company: International Order of St. Luke the Physician

Type: bimonthly print magazine

Audience: general

Purpose: to inspire, educate, and inform about Christian healing of body, soul, and spirit

Submissions: Share your stories, experiences, thoughts, insights, inspirational poems, and testimonies of God's amazing power to heal. Length: articles 200-1,500 words, poetry 30-50 words. Prefers emailed submissions as attachments but will take them by mail.

Types of manuscripts: personal experience, testimonies, teaching, essays, poetry

Topics: theme-related

Rights: onetime

Payment: none

Guidelines: *orderofstluke.org/en/submit-article.html*

Theme list: by email

SHATTERED MAGAZINE

101 Stone River Rd., Huntsville, AL 35811 | 256-783-8350
rachael@shatteredmagazine.net | *shatteredmagazine.net*
Rachael Jackson, editor-in-chief

Type: quarterly print and digital magazine

Audience: general

Purpose: to celebrate our unique, God-given stories

Submission: Looking for testimonies of encountering Jesus to use in our features, life, community, and mission sections. "Where did He meet you? Where does He continue to meet you? How has He used what others intended for evil in your life for good? How has He taken what you have screwed up and redeemed for His glory? How has He used community to be a part of your story? Or, how has your community been a part of a larger story? Has God moved you to share Him with others? What has that looked like?" Query through the website.

Types of manuscripts: personal experience

Guidelines: *shatteredmagazine.net/want-to-write-for-shattered*

SOJOURNERS

3333 14th St. N.W., Ste. 200, Washington, DC 20010 | 202-328-8842
sojourners@sojo.net | *www.sojo.net*
Jim Rice, editor

Type: monthly print and digital magazine

Audience: community influencers

Purpose: to explore the intersections of faith, politics, and culture; uncover in depth the hidden injustices in the world around us; and tell the stories of hope that keep us grounded, inspired, and moving forward

Submissions: Query only with no attachments. Responds in six to eight weeks. Feature articles are typically 1800-2000 words. Send reviews to reviews@sojo.net. Mail poetry to 408 C St. N.E., Washington, D.C. 20002. Length: 25-40 lines. Often tries to use poetry geared toward particular seasons.

Types of manuscripts: feature articles, reviews, poetry

Topics: social justice, popular culture, spirituality

Rights: all

Payment: unspecified, $25 per poem, on publication

Guidelines: *sojo.net/about-us/what-we-cover/write-us*

SOUTHWEST KANSAS FAITH AND FAMILY

PO Box 1454, Dodge City, KS 67801 | 620-225-4677
stan@swkfaithandfamily.org | *www.swkfaithandfamily.org*
Stan Wilson, publisher

Type: monthly print newspaper

Audience: residents of the area

Purpose: to share the Word of God and news and information that honors Christian beliefs, family traditions, and values that are the cornerstone of our nation

Submissions: Email query or complete manuscript.

Topics: any Christian or family issue

Guidelines: *www.swkfaithandfamily.org/submitarticle.html*

SPARK! MAGAZINE (FORMERLY SPLICKETY LOVE)

submissions@splickety.com | www.splickety.com
Kimberly Duffy, editor

Parent company: Splickety Publishing Group

Type: quarterly print and digital magazine

Audience: romance readers

Purpose: to provide quick reading for fiction fans

Submissions: Publishes concise, poignant romance-themed fiction under 1,000 words; stories must cut through the day's troubles and grip readers with short attention spans. Short stories 300-1,000 words, prefers 700 words or fewer; nano-fiction 100 words maximum. All stories must fit quarterly theme. Send email submissions as attachment only.

Types of manuscripts: short stories

Rights: all for six months after publication

Payment: 2¢ per word

Guidelines: *splickety.com/submission-guidelines*

Theme list: *splickety.com/submission-guidelines/upcoming-themes*

Tip: "The best way to get published is to write compelling fiction with a beginning, middle, and an end that elicits a strong emotional response in readers. Make sure there is substantial conflict in the story, both internal and external. And above all else, make sure the story adheres to our submission guidelines and fits the prescribed theme for the issue you're submitting to."

SPLICKETY MAGAZINE

submissions@splickety.com | www.splickety.com
Catherine Jones Payne, editor

Parent company: Splickety Publishing Group

Type: quarterly print and digital magazine

Audience: flash fiction fans

Purpose: to provide quick reading for fiction fans

Submissions: Stories must cut through the day's troubles and grip readers with short attention spans. Short stories 300-1,000 words, prefers 700 words or fewer; nano-fiction 100 words maximum. All stories must fit quarterly theme. Send email submissions as attachment only.

Types of manuscripts: short stories
Rights: all for six months after publication
Payment: 2¢ per word
Guidelines: *splickety.com/submission-guidelines*
Theme list: *splickety.com/submission-guidelines/upcoming-themes*
Tip: "The best way to get published is to write compelling fiction with a beginning, middle, and an end that elicits a strong emotional response in readers. Make sure there is substantial conflict in the story, both internal and external. And above all else, make sure the story adheres to our submission guidelines and fits the prescribed theme for the issue you're submitting to."

SPORTS SPECTRUM

PO Box 2037, Indian Trail, NC 28979 | 866-821-2971
editor@sportsspectrum.com | sportsspectrum.com
Brett Honeycutt, managing editor

Type: quarterly print and digital magazine
Audience: sports fans, predominantly male, ages 20-55
Purpose: to reach non-Christians with the gospel through the testimonies and experiences of sports figures
Submissions: If you are an experienced sports writer, send information about yourself with clips to get an assignment. Query only for article ideas. Articles generally run 1,500-2,000 words plus one or two sidebars of 150 words. Works five months in advance. Bible: NIV.
Rights: all
Payment: at least 21¢ per word plus reasonable expenses
Guidelines: *www.sportsspectrum.com/about/writers-guide.php*
Tip: "It is essential that the athletes featured in Sports Spectrum demonstrate a strong Christian testimony. The fact that they occasionally talk about God or attend chapel is not enough to go on."

ST. ANTHONY MESSENGER

28 W. Liberty St., Cincinnati, OH 45202-6498 | 513-241-5615
MagazineEditors@Franciscanmedia.org | www.FranciscanMedia.org
John Feister, editor-in chief

Denomination: Catholic
Type: monthly print and digital magazine; 64 pages
Audience: family-oriented, majority are women ages 40-70
Purpose: to offer readers inspiration from the heart of Catholicism—the Gospels and the experience of God's people
Submissions: Query only by email. Responds in eight weeks. Email

manuscripts as attachments. Seasonal one year in advance. Length: about 2,000 words or shorter pieces. Fiction 2,000-2,500 words; buys twelve per year. Stories should be about family relationships and about people struggling and coping with problems, triumphing in adversity, persevering in faith, overcoming doubt, or coming to spiritual insights. Poetry 20 lines maximum. Bible: NAB.

Types of manuscripts: profiles, biblical teaching, short stories

Topics: church, sacraments, education, spiritual growth, family, marriage, social issues

Rights: first, electronic

Payment: 20¢ per word, $2 per line for poetry with minimum of $20, on acceptance

Guidelines: *www.franciscanmedia.org/writers-guide*

TEACHERS OF VISION

PO Box 45610, Westlake, OH 44145 | 888-798-1124
tov@ceai.org | www.ceai.org
Doreen Madere, editorial director | Dawn Molnar, managing editor

Parent organization: Christian Educators Association International

Type: quarterly magazine, circulation 6,500, subscription to non-CEAI members $29.95

Audience: Christian educators, primarily in public school

Purpose: to encourage, equip, and empower Christians serving in public and private schools and to demonstrate God's love to the educational community

Submissions: Email submission as attached file. Minifeatures 400-800 words, theme-based features 800-1,000 words, personal interest and methodology 400-1,000 words.

Types of manuscripts: personal experience, how-to, poetry, inspirational

Topics: theme-based, educational success story, teaching techniques, news

Rights: first, including web copy

Payment: not specified

Guidelines: *ceai.org/wp-content/uploads/2016/01/2016-writers-guidelines.pdf*

TESTIMONY

2450 Milltower Ct., Mississauga, ON L5N 5Z6, Canada | 905-542-7400
testimony@paoc.org | www.testimonymag.ca
Stephen Kennedy, editor

Parent company: Pentecostal Assemblies of Canada

Audience: general

Purpose: to celebrate what God is doing in and through the Fellowship, while offering encouragement to believers by providing a window into the struggles that everyday Christians often encounter

Type: bimonthly print magazine; 24 pages

Submissions: Query first by email. Length: 800-1,000 words. Responds in six to eight weeks. Seasonal four months ahead. Regularly uses sidebars. Bible: NIV.

Types of manuscripts: personal experience, interviews

Rights: first

Payment: unspecified

Guidelines: testimony.paoc.org/submit

Tip: "Our readership is 98% Canadian. We prefer Canadian writers or at least writers who understand that Canadians are not Americans in long underwear. We also give preference to members of this denomination, since this is related to issues concerning our fellowship."

THRIVE

PO Box 151297, Lakewood, CO 80215 | 303-985-2148
thriveministry.org/magazine

Type: digital magazine, circulation 10,000, free

Audience: women in cross-cultural work overseas

Purpose: to empower and encourage women in cross-cultural work

Submissions: Articles 500-1,000 words. All submissions must be sent through the website. Writers must be women who are or have been in cross-cultural missions.

Types of manuscripts: personal experience, recipes

Topics: cross-cultural experiences, singleness, marriage, family, spiritual formation, relationships; see subtopics on the website

Rights: first, onetime (with permission to archive permanently)

Payment: none

Guidelines: *thriveconnection.com/write-for-us*

Sample: on the website

TIME OF SINGING: A JOURNAL OF CHRISTIAN POETRY

PO Box 5276, Conneaut Lake, PA 16316
timesing@zoominternet.net | *www.timeofsinging.com*
Lora Homan Zill, editor

Parent organization: Wind & Water Press

Type: quarterly print journal; 44 pages, circulation 200+, subscription $17

Audience: general

Submissions: Prefers poems without religious jargon, that "show" and don't "tell" and take creative chances with faith and our walk with God. 95% unsolicited freelance, 5% assigned. Send complete manuscript by mail or email. Responds in twelve weeks. Seasonal six months ahead. Accepts simultaneous submissions. Accepts submissions from teens. Length: three to forty lines. Submit maximum of five. Accepts 150 per year. Avant-garde, free verse, haiku, light verse, traditional forms (sonnets, villanelles, triolets, etc.) with Christian themes. Looking for fresh rhyme.

Types of manuscripts: poetry

Rights: first, one-time, reprint (tell when and where appeared)

Payment: none

Guidelines: *www.timeofsinging.com/guidelines.html*

Sample: copy $4 each or 2/$7 (checks, money orders payable to Wind & Water Press)

Tip: "Study poetry, read widely—both Christian and non-Christian. Work at the craft. Be open to suggestions and critique. If I have taken time to comment on your work, it is close to publication. If you don't agree, submit elsewhere. I appreciate poets who take chances and a fresh look at abstract, but substantive, Christian concepts like grace, faith, etc. Time of Singing is a literary poetry journal, so I'm not looking for greeting card verse or sermons that rhyme. The best way to know what I'm looking for is to purchase and study a back issue."

TODAY'S CHRISTIAN LIVING

PO Box 5000, Iola, WI 54945 | 800-223-3161, 715-445-5000
editor@todayschristianliving.org | *www.todayschristianliving.org*
Dan Brownell, editor, danb@dan@cross-life.us

Type: bimonthly print and digital magazine

Audience: general

Purpose: to challenge Christians in their faith so they may be strengthened to fulfill the call of God in their lives

Submissions: Prefers complete manuscripts; discourages queries. Personality and ministry profiles, 1,400-1,600 words plus sidebar of 150-250 words. Personal story/anecdote 670-700 words. "Grace Notes," how important biblical principles and attributes are illustrated in everyday life, 650-700 words. Hospitality, inspirational story plus recipe, 700-1,500 words. Humorous anecdotes, 50-200 words.

Types of manuscripts: personal experience, profiles, recipes, humor

Rights: all
Payment: $25-150, after publication
Guidelines: *todayschristianliving.org/writers-guidelines*

U.S. CATHOLIC
205 W. Monroe St., Chicago, IL 60606 | 312-544-8169
submissions@uscatholic.org | *www.uscatholic.org*
Meghan Murphy-Gill, managing editor
Denomination: Catholic
Type: monthly print magazine
Audience: denomination
Submissions: Email manuscripts. Responds in six to eight weeks. Seasonal six months in advance. Features go beyond basic reporting by offering analysis and interpretation of the issues, 2,500-3,500 words. Essays, 800 to 1,600 words, present thoughtful reflections or opinions on concerns Catholics face in everyday life. "Practicing Catholic," 1,100 words with short sidebar, reflects on the meaning of a particular prayer practice. "Sounding Board" opinion piece, 1,400 words. Profiles 800 words, reviews 315 words, fiction 1,500 words, poetry.
Types of manuscripts: essays, profiles, features, short stories, poetry
Payment: $75-$500
Guidelines: *www.uscatholic.org/writers-guide*

VIBRANT LIFE
PO Box 5353, Nampa, ID 83653-5353 | 208-465-2584
vibrantlife@pacificpress.com | *www.vibrantlife.com*
Heather Quintana, editor
Denomination: Seventh-day Adventist
Type: bimonthly print magazine
Audience: general
Purpose: to promote physical health, mental clarity, and spiritual balance from a practical, Christian perspective
Submissions: Send complete manuscript by email as attachment or by mail. Short articles 450-650 words; feature articles to 1,000 words plus a sidebar if informational.
Types of manuscripts: teaching, interviews, profiles, personal experiences, how-to
Topics: health, exercise, nutrition
Rights: first, reprint
Payment: $100-300, on acceptance
Guidelines: *www.vibrantlife.com/?page_id=1369*

Tip: "Information must be reliable—no faddism. Articles should represent the latest findings on the subject, and if scientific in nature, should be properly documented. (References to other lay journals are generally not acceptable.)"

THE VISION

8855 Dunn Rd., Hazelwood, MD 63042-2299 | 314-837-7300
wasubmission@upci.org | pentecostalpublishing.com

Denomination: United Pentecostal
Type: weekly take-home paper, four pages
Audience: denomination
Submissions: Articles 500-1,600 words, fiction 1,200-1,600 words, devotionals 350-400 words, traditional poetry 12-16 lines. Seasonal nine months in advance. Accepts simultaneous submissions. 95% unsolicited freelance. Submit complete manuscript by mail or by email as an attachment. Bible: KJV.
Types of manuscripts: personal experience, short stories, devotionals, poetry
Payment: $8-30, on publication
Guidelines: *pentecostalpublishing.com/t-vision.aspx*
Tip: "Whether fiction or nonfiction, we are looking for stories depicting everyday life situations and how Christian principles are used to solve problems, resolve issues, or enhance one's spiritual growth. Be sure manuscript has a pertinent, spiritual application."

WAR CRY

615 Slaters Ln., Alexandria, VA 22314 | 703-684-5500
war_cry@usn.salvationarmy.org | www.thewarcry.org
Lt. Colonel Allen Satterlee, editor-in-chief

Denomination: Salvation Army
Type: monthly print magazine plus two special issues
Audience: denomination
Purpose: to represents the Army's mission; to bring people to Christ, help believers grow in faith and character, and promote redemptive cultural practices from the perspective of Salvation Army programs, ministries, and doctrines
Submissions: Manuscripts 800-1,250 words. Seasonal six months in advance. Submit complete manuscript through online form. Seasonal six months ahead. Bible: NLT.
Types of manuscripts: news, personal experience, teaching, limited fiction, profiles
Topics: Christian growth, evangelism, news, contemporary issues, profiles

Rights: first, one-time, reprint
Payment: 35¢ per word, 15¢ per word for reprints, on publication
Guidelines: *www.sanationalpublications.org/submission-guidelines*
Tip: "Most open to holiday material, theme-related features, and articles for the unchurched."

WEAVINGS

PO Box 340004, Nashville, TN 37203-0004 | 615-340-7254
weavings@upperroom.org | www.weavings.org

Denomination: United Methodist
Parent organization: The Upper Room
Type: quarterly print magazine
Audience: clergy, lay leaders
Purpose: to promote spiritual formation
Submissions: Open to freelance that relates to a specific, upcoming theme. Send complete manuscript by email as attachment or by mail. Responds within thirteen weeks. Articles 1,000-2,000 words, shorter vignettes 750-1,000 words.
Types of manuscripts: articles, sermons, meditations, poetry, prayers
Topics: spirituality, spiritual disciplines and formation
Payment: starts at 12¢ per word
Guidelines: *www.upperroom.org/about/writer-guidelines/weavings*
Sample: copy for 6.5 x 9.5 SASE with five stamps

7

TEEN/YOUNG ADULT MARKETS

THE BRINK
See entry in "**Daily Devotional Booklets and Websites.**"

BOUNDLESS.ORG
8605 Explorer Dr., Colorado Springs, CO 80920 | 719-531-3400
editor@boundless.org | www.boundless.org
Joy Beth Smith, editor, JoyBeth.Smith@fotf.org

> **Parent company:** Focus on the Family
> **Type:** website and articles; circulation 300,000 visitors per month, free
> **Audience:** single young adults in 20s and 30s
> **Purpose:** to help Christian young adults grow up, own their faith, date with purpose, and prepare for marriage and family
> **Submissions:** Rarely accepts unsolicited articles but open to considering new writers. To get an assignment, send a sample or two of your writing, a link to your blog, and a proposal of what you're interested in writing about. Length: 1,200-1,800 words. Accepts unsolicited blog posts 500-800 words; email manuscript. Bible: ESV.
> **Types:** articles and posts
> **Topics:** fit in these three categories: (1) adulthood: being single, career, family, money; (2) faith: spiritual growth, ministry; (3) relationships: dating, marriage, sexuality, community
> **Rights:** all
> **Guidelines:** *www.boundless.org/about/write-for-us*
> **Tip:** "Aim to engage our readers' hearts, as we're primarily in the business of affecting lives, not changing society. Use personal stories as illustrations and to spark our readers' imaginations."

DEVOZINE
See entry in "**Daily Devotional Booklets and Websites.**"

FCA MAGAZINE

8701 Leeds Rd., Kansas City, MO 64129 | 800-289-0909
mag@fca.org | *www.fca.org/magazine*
Clay Meyer, editor

> **Parent company:** Fellowship of Christian Athletes
> **Type:** bimonthly magazine, subscription $16.99
> **Audience:** teen and college athletes and their coaches
> **Purpose:** to serve as a ministry tool of the Fellowship of Christian Athletes by informing, inspiring and involving coaches, athletes, and all whom they influence, that they may make an impact for Jesus Christ
> **Submissions:** Email manuscripts through the website.
> **Types** of manuscripts: sports stories for these sections: "Community," "r12 Coach," "Fields of Faith," or "One Way 2 Play"; devotionals
> **Topics:** stories applicable to campus, camps, or coaches; devotionals that apply biblical truths to the competitive mindset and sports atmosphere
> **Guidelines:** *www.fca.org/quick-links/submit-a-devotional*

INSIGHT

PO Box 5353, Nampa, ID 83653-5353 | 301-393-4038
insight@rhpa.org | *www.insightmagazine.org*
Omar Miranda, editor, omiranda@rhpa.org

> **Denomination:** Seventh-day Adventist
> **Parent company:** Pacific Press Publishing Association
> **Type:** weekly take-home paper; 18 pages, subscription $57.68, takes ads
> **Audience:** ages 13-19
> **Purpose:** to help teenagers grow in a friendship with God, solve life's problems, and choose positive Christian values and principles to live by
> **Submissions:** Articles 1,200-1,700 words. Email submissions. Seasonal six months ahead.
> **Rights:** first
> **Payment:** $50-85, on publication
> **Guidelines:** send SASE

TAKE FIVE PLUS

See entry in "**Daily Devotional Booklets and Websites.**"

YOUNG SALVATIONIST

615 Sisters Ln., Alexandria, VA 22314 | 703-684-5500
YS@usn.salvationarmy.org | *www.youngsalvationist.org*
Captain Pamela Maynor, editor

Denomination: The Salvation Army.
Type: monthly (10x) print and digital magazine; 28 pages,
   subscription $5
Audience: teens and young adults
Purpose: to help young people develop a mature faith, a personal
   ministry, and a Christian perspective on everyday life
Submissions: Email complete manuscript through the website.
   Articles to 500 words. Responds in six weeks or isn't interested.
   Submit at least two months in advance of theme issue. Bible: NLT.
Types of manuscripts: articles, poems
Topics: related to theme
Rights: first, one-time
Payment: 35¢/word, 15¢ for reprints
Guidelines and theme list: *www.youngsalvationist.org/?s=submissions
   &submit=GO*

8

CHILDREN'S MARKETS

CADET QUEST
1333 Algers St. S.E., Grand Rapids, MI 49507 | 616-241-5616
submissions@CalvinistCadets.org | www.CalvinistCadets.org
G. Richard Broene, editor

>**Parent company:** Calvinist Cadet Corps
>**Type:** print magazine, 7x/year; 24 pages, circulation 7,000, subscription $16.45, takes ads
>**Audience:** boys ages 9-14
>**Purpose:** to show how God is at work in boys' lives and in the world around them; helping boys to grow more Christlike in all areas of life
>**Submissions:** 50% unsolicited freelance. Mail or email (no attachements) complete manuscript. Responds in eight to ten weeks. Accepts simultaneous submissions. Some sidebars. Bible: NIV.
>**Types of manuscripts:** articles 700-1,100 words, buys seven to ten per year; fiction 1,000-1,300 words, buys fourteen to fifteen per year; games, word puzzles, 20-200 words, buys 14 per year
>**Topics:** see theme list
>**Rights:** first, one-time, reprint (tell when/where appeared)
>**Payment:** 4-5¢/word, $5 for fillers; on acceptance
>**Guidelines and theme list:** *counselors.calvinistcadets.org/ submissionshelp/quest-authors-info*
>**Sample:** 9 x 12 SASE with three stamps
>**Tip:** "Most open to fiction or fillers tied to themes; request new theme list in January of each year (best to submit between February and April each year). Also looking for simple projects/crafts and puzzles (word, logic)."

COMPASSION EXPLORER
12290 Voyager Pkwy., Colorado Springs, CO 80921 | 800-336-7676
compassionmagazine@us.ci.org | www.compassion.com/kids-magazine.htm
Leanna Summers, editor-in-chief | Willow Welter, managing editor

Parent company: Compassion International

Type: triannual magazine, PDF download, online; circulation/traffic 28,000, free

Audience: children

Purpose: to broaden American children's perspective as they learn about children from the developing world in a fun, engaging way, creating a desire to help those in need

Submissions: email for current needs

DEVOKIDS

See entry in "**Daily Devotional Booklets and Websites.**"

FOCUS ON THE FAMILY CLUBHOUSE

8605 Explorer Dr., Colorado Springs, CO 80920 | 719-531-3400

www.clubhousemagazine.com

Jesse Florea, editor | Kate Jameson, editor assistant (submit to)

Parent company: Focus on the Family

Type: monthly print magazine with online extras; 32 pages, circulation 70,000, subscription $23.99, takes limited ads

Audience: children ages 8-12

Purpose: to help kids know more about God and the Bible

Submissions: 25% unsolicited freelance, 40% assigned. Complete manuscript by mail only. Responds in three months. Seasonal eight months ahead. Accepts simultaneous submissions; no reprints. Kill fee. Uses some sidebars. Bible: HCSB.

Types of manuscripts: nonfiction 400-500 or 800-1,000 words, buys five per year; fiction 1,800-2,000 words, buys thirty per year; fillers, quizzes, crafts, word puzzles, recipes 200-800 words, buys six to eight per year

Topics: personality features of ordinary kids doing extraordinary things; activity theme pages; short, humorous how-to stories with a point; quizzes that teach a biblical concept or character trait, fun-filled animal factoids; factual stories about apologetics, biblical archeology, or Christian values; craft or recipe ideas around a central theme or holiday; interviews with noteworthy Christians or Christians who experienced noteworthy events

Rights: nonexclusive license

Payment: 15-25¢ per word for articles and fillers, up to $300 for fiction; on acceptance

Guidelines: *www.clubhousemagazine.com/en/submission-guidelines.aspx*

Sample: call 800-232-6459

Tip: "Most open to fiction, personality stories, quizzes, and how-to pieces with a theme. Avoid stories dealing with boy-girl relationships; poetry; and contemporary, middle-class family settings. We look for fiction in exciting settings with ethnic characters. True stories of ordinary kids doing extraordinary things and historical fiction are good ways to break in. Send manuscripts with list of credentials. Read past issues."

FOCUS ON THE FAMILY CLUBHOUSE JR.

8605 Explorer Dr., Colorado Springs, CO 80920 | 719-531-3400
jesse.florea@fotf.org | *www.clubhousejr.com*
Jesse Florea, editor | Kate Jameson, editor assistant (submit to)

Parent company: Focus on the Family

Type: monthly print magazine with online extras; 32 pages, circulation 46,000, subscription $23.99, minimal ads

Audience: ages 3-7

Purpose: to inspire, entertain, and teach Christian values

Submissions: 30% unsolicited freelance, 30% assigned. Complete manuscript by mail only. Responds in three months. Seasonal nine months ahead. Accepts simultaneous submissions; no reprints. Kill fee. Uses some sidebars. Bible: NIRV.

Types of manuscripts: articles 100-600 words, buys one or two per year; fiction 250-800 words, buys ten per year; Bible stories 250-400 words; one-page rebus stories to 150 words; traditional poetry, 10-25 lines, to 150 words, buys four to eight per year; fillers, recipes, crafts 100-500 words, buys four to eight per year

Topics: science and nature, real children or adults with interesting experiences, modern-day and historical heroes of the faith, retold Bible stories

Rights: nonexclusive license

Payment: articles $30-200, fiction $50-200, poetry $50-100, fillers $30-100; on acceptance

Guidelines: *www.clubhousejr.com/en/submission-guidelines.aspx*

Sample: call 800-232-6459

Tip: "Most open to short, nonpreachy fiction, beginning reader stories, and read-to-me. Looking for true stories of ordinary kids doing extraordinary things. Be knowledgeable of our style, and try it out on kids first. Stories set in exotic places; nonwhite, middle-class characters; historical pieces; humorous quizzes; and craft and recipe features are most readily accepted."

GUIDE

PO Box 5353, Nampa, ID 83653-5353
guidemagazine@pacificpress.com | www.guidemagazine.org
Randy Fishell, editor

Denomination: Seventh-day Adventist
Parent company: Pacific Press Publishing Association
Type: weekly take-home paper; 32 pages, circulation 26,000, takes ads
Audience: ages 10-14
Purpose: to show readers, through stories that illustrate Bible truth, how to walk with God now and forever
Submissions: 75% unsolicited freelance, 20% assigned. Prefers complete manuscripts, rather than queries. Submit online, by email, or mail with SASE.
Types of manuscripts: articles 1,000-1,200 words (some shorter pieces 450 words and up), games, and puzzles. Sometimes accepts quizzes and other unique nonstory formats; must include a clear spiritual element. Responds in four to six weeks. Seasonal eight months in advance. Accepts submissions from teens 14 and older. Bible: NIV.
Topics: adventure, personal growth, humor, inspiration (answers to prayer, biblical narratives, mission stories, and examples of young people living out their Christian beliefs), biography, nature
Rights: first, reprints (tell when and where published)
Payment: 7-10¢ per word, $25-40 for games and puzzles; on acceptance
Guidelines: *www.guidemagazine.org/writers-guidelines*; theme list online
Sample: download from guidelines page
Tip: "Use your best short-story techniques (dialogue, scenes, a sense of plot) to tell a true story starring a kid ages 10-14. Bring out a clear spiritual/biblical message. We publish multipart true stories regularly, two to twelve parts, 1,200 words each. All topics indicated need to be addressed within the context of a true story."

KEYS FOR KID

See entry in "**Daily Devotional Booklets and Websites**."

KIDS ANSWERS

PO Box 510, Hebron, KY 41048
nationaleditor@answersmagazine.com
answersingenesis.org/kids/answers/magazine
John UpChurch, editor | Pam Sheppard, national editor (submit to)

Parent company: Answers in Genesis

Type: quarterly mini print magazine in Answers magazine; 8 pages

Audience: children

Purpose: to highlight the wonders of God's creation with kid-friendly information and images

Submissions: Only accepts one-paragraph article proposals with author's qualifications (300 words) via email or through the website. Once accepted, email article as an attachment. Responds in one month.

Types of manuscripts: nonfiction

Topics: themed

Rights: all

Payment: $75-125

Guidelines: download from *answersingenesis.org/answers/magazine/contact*

THE KIDS' ARK

PO Box 3160, Victoria, TX 77903 | 800-455-1770, 361-485-1770
thekidsarksubmissions@yahoo.com | *thekidsark.com*
Beth Haynes, senior editor

Type: quarterly print magazine; 36 pages, subscription $20, takes limited ads

Audience: ages 6-12

Purpose: to enlighten children with the love and power of God through Jesus Christ and to provide children with a solid biblical foundation on which to base their choices in life

Submissions: Email complete manuscript as an attachment. Responds in eight to ten weeks. 100% unsolicited freelance. Fiction 650 words maximum, buys sixteen per year. Also accepts submissions from children and teens. Bible: NIV.

Types of manuscripts: short stories

Topics: must relate to the theme

Rights: first, electronic, reprint

Payment: $100 for first plus electronic, $25 for reprints; on publication

Guidelines and theme list: *thekidsark.com/guidelines.htm*

Tip: "Open to fiction only (any time period). Think outside the box! Must catch children's attention and hold it, be biblically based and related to theme. We want to teach God's principles in an exciting format. Every issue contains the Ten Commandments and the plan of salvation."

NATURE FRIEND MAGAZINE

4253 Woodcock Ln., Dayton, VA 22821 | 540-867-0764
editor@naturefriendmagazine.com | www.naturefriendmagazine.com
Kevin Shank, editor, Kevin@naturefriendmagazine.com

Parent company: Dogwood Ridge Outdoors

Type: monthly print magazine; 28 pages, circulation 10,000, subscription $40

Audience: ages 6-16

Purpose: to increase awareness of God and appreciation for God's works and gifts, to teach accountability toward God's works, and to teach natural truths and facts

Submissions: 50-80% freelance. Mail complete manuscript with SASE or email with attachment. Articles 500-800 words, buys fifty per year; fiction 500-800 words, buys forty per year. Seasonal four months in advance. Accepts simultaneous submissions. Bible: KJV only.

Rights: first, reprint

Payment: 5¢/edited word, 3¢ for reprints; on publication

Types: crafts, projects, experiments, fiction, articles, photo features

Topics: nature-related, science experiments, stories about people interacting with nature or about an animal, nature-friendly gardening, nature photography lessons, survival/wilderness first-aid, weather, astronomy, flowers, marine life

Guidelines: *www.naturefriendmagazine.com/index.pl?linkid=12;class=gen*

Tip: "We would like more nature stories (as opposed to articles). Also, we would like more wintertime stories and activities. We would like more craft projects—for instance, making bird houses and feeders."

OUR LITTLE FRIEND

PO Box 5353, Nampa, ID 83653
www.ourlittlefriend.com
Anita Seymour, managing editor, anita.seymour@pacificpress.com

Denomination: Seventh-day Adventist

Parent company: Pacific Press Publishing Association

Type: weekly take-home paper

Audience: ages 1-5

Purpose: to help children understand their infinite value to Jesus, learn how to respond to God, show love to their family and friends, and serve others in their world

Submissions: One- to two-page true stories. Email complete manuscript with attached file. Seasonal seven months ahead. Responds in one month.

Payment: $25-50; on acceptance

Rights: one-time, electronic, reprint

Topics: See list in guidelines. Also Christmas, Thanksgiving, Valentine's Day, Mother's Day, Father's Day, Grandparents Days, nature

Guidelines: *www.primarytreasure.com/?page=authors*

POCKETS

See entry in "**Daily Devotional Booklets and Websites**."

PRIMARY TREASURE

PO Box 5353, Nampa, ID 83653
www.primarytreasure.com
Anita Seymour, managing editor, anita.seymour@pacificpress.com

Denomination: Seventh-day Adventist

Parent company: Pacific Press Publishing Association

Type: weekly take-home paper

Audience: ages 7-9

Purpose: to help children understand their infinite value to Jesus, learn how to respond to God, show love to their family and friends, and serve others in their world

Submissions: Four- to five-page true stories. Email complete manuscript with attached file. Seasonal seven months ahead. Responds in one month.

Payment: $25-50, on acceptance

Rights: one-time, electronic, reprint

Topics: See list in guidelines. Also Christmas, Thanksgiving, Valentine's Day, Mother's Day, Father's Day, Grandparents Days, nature

Guidelines: *www.primarytreasure.com/?page=authors*

SHINE BRIGHTLY

1333 Alger St. S.E., Grand Rapids, MI 49507 | 616-241-5616, ext. 3035
shinebrightly@gemsgc.org | www.gemsgc.org
Kelli Gilmore, managing editor, kelli@gemsgc.org

Parent company: GEMS Girls Clubs

Type: monthly (September--May) print magazine; 28 pages, circulation 14,500, subscription $13.95

Audience: girls grades 4-8

Purpose: to equip, motivate, and inspire girls to become activists for Christ

Submissions: 25% unsolicited freelance. Email complete manuscript; no attachments. Accepts simultaneous submissions. Responds in six to eight weeks. Seasonal five months ahead. Bible: NIV.

Types of manuscripts: articles 200-800 words, buys five per year; fiction 700-900 words, buys eight per year; poetry, haiku, light verse, traditional, buys two to three per year; games and puzzles 50-200 words; crafts and recipes

Topics: see theme list

Rights: first, reprint (tell when/where published), or nonoverlapping simultaneous

Payment: articles $35 or 3-5¢/word, poetry $5-15, games and puzzles $5-15.00; on publication

Guidelines and theme list: *www.gemsgc.org/main/shine_guidelines.html*

Sample: $1 plus 9 x 12 SASE with three stamps

Tip: "Be realistic—we get a lot of fluffy stories with Pollyanna endings. We are looking for real-life-type stories that girls relate to. We mostly publish short stories but are open to short reflective articles. Know what girls face today and how they cope in their daily lives. We need angles from home life and friendships, peer pressure, and the normal growing-up challenges girls deal with."

SPARKLE

1333 Alger St. S.E., Grand Rapids, MI 49507 | 616-241-5616
sparkle@gemsgc.org | gemsgc.org/sparkle-magazine
Kelli Gilmore, managing editor, kelli@gemsgc.org

Parent company: GEMS Girls Clubs

Type: monthly (October--March) print magazine; 16 pages, circulation 9,000, subscription $10.70

Audience: girls grades 1-3

Purpose: to discover who God is and how He works in His world and their lives; to help girls sparkle Jesus' light into the world

Submissions: 20% unsolicited freelance, 20% assigned. Email complete manuscript, no attachments. Accepts simultaneous submissions. Responds in six to eight weeks. Seasonal five months ahead. Bible: NIV. Accepts submissions from teens.

Types of manuscripts: articles 100-400 words, buys two to three per year; fiction 100-400 words, buys three to five per year; rhyming poetry 5-15 lines, buys two to three per year; games, crafts, recipes 50-200 words

Topics: see theme list

Rights: first, reprint (tell when/where published), or nonoverlapping simultaneous

Payment: articles $35 or 3¢/word; poetry $5-15; games, crafts, recipes $5-15; on publication

Guidelines and theme list: *www.gemsgc.org/main/sparkle_guidelines.html*

Sample: $1 plus 9 x 12 SASEwith three stamps

Tip: "Send in pieces that teach girls how to be world-changers for Christ or that fit our annual theme. We also are always looking for games, crafts, and recipes. Keep the writing simple. Keep activities short. Engage a third grader, while being easy enough for a first grader to understand."

ST. MARY'S MESSENGER

310 Birch St., Green River, WY 82935 | 270-325-3061
submissions@stmarysmessenger.com | *stmarysmessenger.com*
Kris Weipert, senior editor

Denomination: Catholic

Type: quarterly print magazine, 32 pages, subscription $19.95

Audience: ages 7-12

Purpose: a Catholic version of Highlights

Submissions: Email or mail query for nonfiction, complete manuscript for fiction. Responds to queries in one to two weeks, to manuscripts in two to four weeks. Articles 300-900 words, fiction 700-900 words. Seasonal four months in advance. Takes simultaneous submissions.

Types of manuscripts: nonfiction articles, short stories, poems, especially funny poems; puzzles, games, activities, crafts, projects, recipes

Topics: biographies of saints, historical figures, or Catholic leaders in today's world; personal stories from kids, their families, or teachers, especially about works of mercy or helping other kids live their faith; articles about individuals who exemplify humility, Christ's love, and other virtues; articles about fun, interesting things that kids are doing; Catholic traditions in different cultures, rites, and countries; interviews or profiles of Catholics who are famous or well-known but also live their faith; crafts, projects, activities, recipes.

Rights: nonexclusive first, reprint

Payment: $25-100 for article or story

Guidelines and theme list: *tmarysmessenger.com/submissions*

Tip: "Not every piece needs to be religious."

9

WRITERS MARKETS

CHRISTIAN COMMUNICATOR

9118 W. Elmwood Dr., Ste. 1G, Niles, IL 60714-5820 | 847-296-3964
ljohnson@wordprocommunications.com | *www.ACWriters.com*
Lin Johnson, managing editor | *Sally Miller, poetry editor,*
sallymiller@ameritech.com | *Reg Forder, publisher (American Christian*
Writers, PO Box 110390, Nashville, TN 37222 | *ACWriters@aol.com—*
for samples, advertising, and subscriptions)

Description: To help Christian communicators improve their writing craft and speaking ability, provide practical information about the business/publishing/freelance side of writing, keep them informed about markets, and encourage them in their ministries. Bimonthly magazine, 20 pages, circulation 1,000. Subscription $29.95. Ads.

Submitting: 50% unsolicited freelance. Queries or complete manuscript (prefers attachment) by email only. Pays $5-10 on publication for first or reprint (tell when/where appeared) rights. Responds in eight weeks. Seasonal six months ahead. No simultaneous submissions. Guidelines by email or on the website. Copy for 9 x 12 SASE with three stamps to Nashville address.

Manuscripts: How-to articles, 750-1,000 words, twenty-five per year. Reviews of books on writing, publishing, and speaking, 250-350 words; query title first. Some sidebars. Prefers NIV. Poems to twenty lines on writing, publishing, and speaking only, fifteen per year; send maximum of three poems. Interviews with well-published authors with unique angles or with editors, 750-1,000 words, six per year, query first. Anecdotes for "A Funny Thing Happened on the Way to Becoming a Communicator" humor column, 75-300 words, twenty per year.

Tips: Greatest needs are anecdotes for the "Funny Thing Happened" column and articles on research, creativity, and writing nonfiction.

FELLOWSCRIPT

PO Box 99509, Edmonton, AB T5B 0E1, Canada
fellowscripteditor@gmail.com | *www.inscribe.org/fellowscript*
Sheila Webster, editor

Description: For, by, and about writers and writing. Quarterly
newsletter, 30 pages, circulation 150-200. Subscription with
InScribe membership. Ads.

Submitting: Submit complete manuscript by email. Pays 2.5¢ per
word (Canadian funds) for onetime rights, 1.5¢ per word for
reprint rights, extra .5¢ for publication with author's permission
on the website for no more than three months. Pays by PayPal on
publication. Guidelines on the website.

Manuscripts: Feature articles, 750-1,000 words; columns, 500-750
words; reviews, 150-300 words; fillers/tips, 25-500 words; general
articles, 700 words. Responds in four weeks. Submissions deadlines
are January 1, April 1, July 1, and October 1. Plans six months ahead.

Tips: We always prefer material specifically slanted toward the needs
and interests of Canadian Christian writers. We do not publish
poetry except as part of an instructional article, nor do we publish
testimonials. We give preference to members and to Canadian writers.

FREELANCE WRITER'S REPORT

45 Main St., PO Box A, North Stratford, NH 03590-0167 | 603-922-8338
editor@writers-editors.com | *www.writers-editors.com*
Dana K. Cassell, editor

Description: To help serious, professional freelance writers— whether
full-time or part-time—improve their earnings and profits from
their editorial businesses. The bulk of the content is market news
and marketing information. Monthly newsletter, 8 pages.

Submitting: 25% freelance. Complete manuscript via email as
attachment or copied into message. Pays 10¢ per word on
publication for onetime rights. Responds within one week.
Seasonal two months ahead. Accepts simultaneous submissions
and reprints (tell when/where appeared). Guidelines are on
the website at *www.writers-editors.com/Writers/Membership/
Writer_Guidelines/writer_guidelines.htm*. Sample copy for 6 x 9
SASE with two stamps for back copy, $4 for current copy; or free
downloadable PDF copy at danasuggests.info/FWR.

Manuscripts: Articles to 900 words, 50 per year. Prose fillers to
400 words.

Tips: No articles on the basics of freelancing since readers are established freelancers. Looking for marketing and business-building for freelance writers, editors, and book authors.

OCACW NEWSLETTER

5042 E. Cherry Hills Blvd., Springfield, MO 65809 | 417-832-8409
Ozarks@yahoo.com | www.ozarksacw.org
James Cole-Rous, managing editor

Description: To encourage, inspire, and train Christians to write well and maximize publication opportunities. Published by Ozarks Chapter of American Christian Writers. Bimonthly newsletter, 8 pages, circulation 60. Subscription $10. Ads.

Submitting: 90% freelance. Query or send complete manuscript via email only, manuscript as attachment. Also attach a brief bio and digital photo. No payment for onetime and reprint rights. Responds in three weeks. Seasonal two months ahead. Accepts simultaneous submissions and reprints (tell when/where appeared). Copy for SASE with two stamps. Guidelines on the website at *www.ozarksacw.org/guidelines.php*.

Manuscripts: Feature articles, 1000-2000 words; general articles, 650-850 words; writing-book reviews, 450 words, query first; short articles related to writing, conference reviews, etc., 300-600 words; poetry about inspiration, purpose, writing, and some seasonal topics. Any Bible version. Also needs devotions that encourage, inspire, and teach (not preach) for the website.

Tips: "We want content that speaks to Christian writers by teaching and encouraging them. We welcome new writers and advertise you on our website as part of your payment."

POETS & WRITERS MAGAZINE

90 Broad St., Ste. 2100, New York, NY 10004-2272 | 212-226-3586
editor@pw.org | www.pw.org
Melissa Faliveno, senior editor

Description: Professional trade journal for poetry, fiction, and nonfiction writers. Bimonthly magazine, circulation 100,000. Subscription $19.95. Ads.

Submitting: Query with clips via email or mail. Pays $150-500 for exclusive worldwide, periodical publication and syndication rights in all languages and nonexclusive reprint rights shared 50/50 thereafter. Pays when scheduled for production. Responds in four to six weeks. Seasonal four months ahead. Some kill fees at 25%. Guidelines are on the website at *www.pw.org/about-us/about_magazine*. Sold at large bookstores and online.

Manuscripts: News and trends, 500-1,200 words; "The Literary Life," essays, 1,500-2,500 words; "The Practical Writer," how-to and advice, 1,500-2,500 words; profiles and interviews, 2,000-3,000 words (35 per year).

Tip: Most open to "News & Trends," "The Literary Life," and "The Practical Writer."

SHADES OF ROMANCE MAGAZINE

7127 Minnesota Ave., St. Louis, MO 63111
sormag@yahoo.com | *sormag.com*
LaShaundra Hoffman, editor

Description: Caters to readers and writers of multicultural literature. Quarterly online magazine. Subscription $34.95.

Submitting: Query first with "Query: (subject)" in the subject line. Responds in two to four weeks. Pays $15-25 on publication. Guidelines are on the website.

Manuscripts: Devotionals, 200-500 words; articles on marketing and the business of writing, 500-800 words; fillers, 200-500 words; short romance stories, 500-1,500 words.

THE WRITER

Editorial, Madavor Media, 25 Braintree Hill Office Park, Ste. 404, Braintree, MA 02184
tweditorial@madavor.com | *www.writermag.com*
Nicki Porter, senior editor

Description: Dedicated to expanding and supporting the work of professional and aspiring writers with a straightforward presentation of industry information, writing instruction, and professional and personal motivation. Monthly magazine, 60-68 pages; circulation 30,000. Subscription $32.95. Ads.

Submitting: 80% unsolicited freelance. Query first with short bio. Query for features six months ahead. No reprints. Pay varies by type and department on acceptance for first rights. If no response in two weeks, they probably aren't interested. Guidelines are on the website at www.writermag.com/the-magazine/submission-guidelines.

Manuscripts: Primarily looking for how-to articles on the craft of writing but also has a variety of columns and departments: "Breakthrough," first-person articles about a writer's experience in breaking through to publication, 700 words. "Freelance Success," tips on the business of freelancing, 1,000 words. "Writing Essentials," basics of the craft of writing, 800 words plus a short sidebar of resources. "How I Write," interviews with authors, 600 words. "Literary Spotlight," history and theme of a literary journal, 500 words. "Market Focus," reports on specific market areas, 1,000 words. "Off the Cuff," essays on a particular aspect of writing or the writing life, 1,000 words. "Poet to Poet," how-to on writing poetry, 500-750 words. "Take Note," topical items of literary interest, 200-500 words. "Writer at Work," specific writing problem and how it was successfully overcome on the way to publication, 750-1,500 words. "Write Stuff," reviews of books on the craft and business of writing as well as other products of interest to writers, 500-750 words. Uses some sidebars.

Tips: Personal essays must provide takeaway advice and benefits for writers. Include plenty of how-to, advice, and tips on techniques. Be specific. All topics must relate to writing.

THE WRITER'S CHRONICLE

The Association of Writers & Writing Programs, George Mason University, MSN 1E3, 4400 University Dr., Fairfax, VA 22030-4444 | 703-993-4301
chronicle@awpwriter.org | *www.awpwriter.org*
Supriya Bhatnagar, editor

Description: Provides diverse insights into the art of writing that are accessible, pragmatic, and idealistic for serious writers. Articles are used as teaching tools. Magazine published six times during the academic year, 96 pages, circulation 35,000. Subscription $20 for oneyear, $34 for two years. Ads.

Submitting: 90% unsolicited freelance. Submit only from February 1 through September 30. Submit via website portal or mail. Pays $18 per 100 words for first and electronic rights on publication. Responds in three months. No simultaneous submissions. Guidelines on the website.

Manuscripts: Interviews, 4,000-7,000 words; essays on teaching writing, 2,500-7,000 words; appreciations of contemporary writers, 2,000-5,000 words; essays on the craft of writing, 2,000 to 6,000 words; news features, 500-2,000 words; essays on careers for writers, 1,000-3,000 words. Uses some sidebars. Also buys blog posts year round for *The Writer's Notebook*, 500-1,500 words, $100 per post.

Tip: Keep in mind that 18,000 of our 35,000 readers are students or just-emerging writers.

WRITER'S DIGEST

10151 Carver Rd., Ste. 200, Cincinnati, OH 45242 | 513-531-2690, ext. 11483
wdsubmissions@fwmedia.com | *www.writersdigest.com*
Jessica Stravser, editorial director

Description: Celebrates the writing life and what it means to be a writer in today's publishing environment. Magazine, eight times per year, 72 pages, circulation 110,000. Print subscription $19.96. Copies are available at newsstands and through *www.writersdigestshop.com*. Ads.

Submitting: 20% unsolicited; 60% assigned. Email query or manuscript in the message or as a Microsoft Word attachment. Responds in two to four months. Pays 30-50¢ per word on acceptance for first and electronic rights. Guidelines are on the website at *www.writersdigest.com/submission-guidelines*. Theme list at *www.writersdigest.com/advertise/editorialcalendar*.

Manuscripts: "Inkwell," opinion pieces, 800-900 words, and short how-to pieces, trends, humor, 300-600 words; "5-Minute Memoir," 600-word essay reflections on the writing life; author profiles, 800-2,000 words; articles on writing techniques, 1,000-2,400 words. Seasonal eight months ahead. Requires requested manuscript by email, copied into message. Kill fee at 25%. Regularly uses sidebars.

Tip: Although we welcome the work of new writers, we believe the established writer can better instruct our readers. Please include your publishing credentials related to your topic with your submission.

WRITERSWEEKLY.COM

15726 Cortez Rd. W. #349, Bradenton, FL 34210 | 305-768-0261
Angela@writersweekly.com | *www.writersweekly.com*
Angela Hoy, publisher

Description: Features new and updated markets and articles on selling the written word (making more money through writing), as well as information on publishing and self-publishing. Weekly free electronic magazine.

Submitting: 20% freelance. Query letters only; don't send manuscript until requested. Email (no attachments) or use the website form. Pays $40-60 on acceptance and only via PayPal for first nonexclusive electronic rights and $20-40 for reprint rights. Responds in one week.

Manuscripts: Feature articles on ways writers can make money from their writing, how to successfully market your books, warnings about industry scams, 600 words; freelance success stories, 400 words. Guidelines on the website.

Tips: Humor is always appreciated. Our readers want to work for themselves and be able to support their families with their writing. Most write for the magazine industry and are looking for other ways to supplement or enhance their writing careers.

WRITING CORNER

410-536-4610

editor@writingcorner.com | writingcorner.com

Description: As a readers' and writers' community, *WritingCorner.com* is comprised of input from both those who read and those who write (and those of you who do both). Website.

Submitting: Responds in two weeks; feel free to nudge after that. Send queries and manuscripts via email only. Accepts reprints. No payment for nonexclusive rights; regular contributors get free sidebar ads on the site. Guidelines are on the website.

Manuscripts: Open to how-to articles on writing fiction and nonfiction, writing life, tips and tricks, basic and advance writing techniques, 600-900 words.

Tip: We like articles that provide concrete, useful advice from those who have been in the trenches and made a successful journey with their writing.

PART 4

SPECIALTY MARKETS

10

DAILY DEVOTIONAL BOOKLETS AND WEBSITES

Note that most of these markets assign all manuscripts. If there is no information listed on getting an assignment, request a sample copy and writers guidelines if they are not on the website. Then write two or three sample devotionals to fit that particular format, and send them to the editor with a request for an assignment.

THE BRINK
114 Bush Rd., Nashville, TN 37217 | 800-877-7030, 615-361-1221
thebrink@randallhouse.com | *www.thebrinkonline.com*
David Jones, editor
> **Denomination:** Free Will Baptist
> **Parent company:** Randall House
> **Audience:** college students and young adults
> **Type:** print, quarterly
> **Details:** Devotions are by assignment only to coordinate with the curriculum. For feature articles, such as interviews, stories, and opinion pieces, email query with 100-200-word excerpt if available. Does not respond unless interested. Buys all rights.
> **Tip:** "Pitch articles that are specific and relevant to twentysomethings."

CHRISTIANDEVOTIONS.US
PO Box 6494, Kingsport, TN 37663 | 423-384-4821
christiandevotionsministries@gmail.com | *www.ChristianDevotions.us*
Cindy Sproles, executive editor

Parent company: Christian Devotions Ministries
Audience: adults
Type: website
Details: Accepts freelance submissions. Follow guidelines listed under Write for Us tab. Length: 400 words, less Scripture reference. No payment. Authors keep the rights to their work. Bible version: author's choice; must be referenced.
Also accepts: 800-word posts for *InspireaFire.com*, an encouragement site for Christian service.
Tip: Follow the guidelines. Have a teachable spirit and willingness to learn.

DAILY DEVOTIONS FOR THE DEAF

21199 Greenview Rd., Council Bluffs, IA 51503 | 712-322-5493
JoKrueger@deafmissions.com | www.deafmissions.com
Jo Krueger, editor

Audience: adults
Type: print and online
Details: Nondenominational. Accepts freelance submissions. Length: 225 words. No payment. Rights: all. Bible version: Easy-to-Read or NIV.
Tip: This booklet is for deaf people for whom English is a second language. So please keep the words and sentence structure simple.

DEVOKIDS

renee@devokids.com | devokids.com
Renee McCausey, executive editor

Parent company: Christian Devotions Ministries
Audience: kids ages 7-10
Type: website
Details: Takes freelance submissions. Length: 75-250 words. Email as an attached Word document. No payment. Authors retain rights to their work.
Also accepts: submissions from kids

DEVOZINE

PO Box 340004, Nashville, TN 37203-0004 |615-340-7252
devozine@upperroom.org | devozine.org
Sandy Miller, editor

Parent company: Upper Room Ministries
Audience: teens, ages 14-19

Type: print, bimonthly

Details: Accepts freelance submissions of meditations. Themes and deadlines are posted on the website. Length: 150-250 words. Payment: $25 ($10-15 if part of a group). Weekend feature articles: 500-600 words; pays $100; query for an assignment.

Also accepts: poetry to 20 lines, submissions from teens

FORWARD DAY BY DAY

412 Sycamore St. #2, Cincinnati, OH 45202-4110 | 513-721-6659
editorial@forwardmovement.org | www.forwardmovement.org
Richelle Thompson, managing editor

Denomination: Episcopal

Audience: adults

Type: print and online

Details: Devotions are written on assignment. To get an assignment, send three sample meditations based on three of the following Bible verses: Psalm 139:21; Mark 8:31; Acts 4:12; Revelation 1:10. Likes author to complete an entire month's worth of devotions. Length: 210 words, including Scripture. Pays $300 for a month of devotions.

Tip: *Forward Day by Day* is not the place to score points on controversial topics. Occasionally, when the Scripture passage pertains to it, an author chooses to say something about such a topic. If you write about a hot-button issue, do so with humility and make certain your comment shows respect for persons who hold a different view.

FRUIT OF THE VINE

211 N. Meridian St. #101, Newberg, OR 97142 | 800-962-4014
emuhr@barclaypress.com | www.barclaypress.com
Eric Muhr, publisher

Parent company: Barclay Press

Audience: adults

Type: print, quarterly

Details: Assignment only; send writing sample and assignment request by email. Length: 250 words. Payment: contributor copies. Rights: one-time. Bible version: NRSV.

Tip: We rarely accept unsolicited submissions. Please make initial contact by email.

GOD'S WORD FOR TODAY

1445 N. Boonville Ave., Springfield, MO 65802 | 417-862-2781
GWFT@gph.org | ag.org/top/devotional
Wade Quick, team leader for dated curriculum projects

> **Denomination:** Assemblies of God
> **Audience:** adults
> **Type:** print, quarterly
> **Details:** Assignment only. Contact us for a sample assignment. We do not publish samples, and we do not pay for them. Length: 210 words. Payment: $25/devotion. Rights: all. Bible version: NIV.
> **Also accepts:** poetry, less than 20 lines
> **Tip:** Read *God's Word for Today* on the website. Become familiar with it before seeking a sample assignment. Read and follow the guidelines.

JOHN IN THE JOHN

109 W. Bridge St., Redwood Falls, MN 46283 | 218-310-2156
devointhejohn@gmail.com | johninthejohn.my-free.website
Christopher Schmitz, editor

> **Audience:** teens and adults
> **Type:** print, bimonthly
> **Details:** Accepts freelance devotionals. Each daily entry features a one- or two-page devotional reading with humorous and serious pieces similar to Chicken Soup for the Soul books. Looking especially for personal stories or reflections on facts, events, culture, popular media, etc. Humor is highly encouraged as long as it's not forced. Use reference texts from any of the four Gospels. Length: 500 words maximum but will consider longer manuscripts. No payment. Accepts reprints.

KEYS FOR KIDS

PO Box 1001, Grand Rapids, MI 49501-1001 | 616-647-4500
editorial@keysforkids.org | www.keysforkids.org
Courtney Lasater, editor

> **Parent company:** Keys for Kids Ministries
> **Audience:** children ages 8-12, often used for family devotions
> **Type:** print, quarterly and online
> **Details:** Takes only freelance submissions. Payment: $25 on acceptance. Rights: all. Length: 350-375 words, including short fiction story. Buys 30-40 per year. Seasonal four to five months ahead. Bible version: NKJV.

Tips: Avoid Pollyanna-type children—make them normal, ordinary kids, not goody-goodies. Don't be afraid of down-to-earth subjects kids face today. Divorce, abuse, pornography, racism, bullying, violence, substance abuse, and peer pressure can all be handled carefully and clearly.

LIGHT FROM THE WORD

PO Box 50434, Indianapolis, IN 46250-0434 | 317-774-7900
submissions@wesleyan.org | www.wesleyan.org/wg

Denomination: Wesleyan
Audience: adults
Type: print, quarterly
Details: Email a couple of sample devotions to fit the format and request an assignment. Write "Devotion Samples" in the subject line. Length: 200-250 words. Pays $100 for seven devotions. Guidelines at *www.wesleyan.org/wg*.
Tip: We look for clean, tight, inspirational writing that makes minimal use of first person. Writing must lead readers to discover a biblical truth and apply that truth to their lives.

POCKETS

PO Box 340004, Nashville, TN 37203-0004
pockets@upperroom.org | pockets.upperroom.org
Lynn W. Gilliam, editor

Parent company: Upper Room Ministry
Audience: children ages 6-12
Type: print, monthly (except in February)
Details: Primarily accepts unsolicited freelance manuscripts, only via mail. See the theme list and deadlines on the website. Payment on acceptance. Bible version: NRSV.
Types of manuscripts: Fiction and Scripture stories that can help children deal with real-life situations, 600-1,000 words, pays 14 cents/word. Poems, 16 lines maximum, pays $25 and up. Articles about children involved in environmental, community, and peace/justice issues, 400-1,000 words, pays 14 cents/word. Activities, puzzles, games, recipes: pays $25 and up.
Also accepts: submissions from children through age 12
Tips: We do not accept stories about talking animals or inanimate objects. Fictional characters and some elaboration may be included in Scripture stories, but the writer must remain faithful to the story.

THE QUIET HOUR

4050 Lee Vance, Colorado Springs, CO 80919
thequiethour@davidccook.com | *www.davidccook.com*

> **Parent** company: David C Cook
> **Audience:** adults
> **Type:** print, quarterly
> **Details:** By assignment only. Submit a sample devotional according
> to the description on *www.davidccook.com/About/jobs/index.*
> *cfm?N=7,166,2,2.* Length: 200 words. Payment: $140 for seven
> devotionals. Rights: all. Bible version: NIV.
> **Tip:** See the website for complete guidelines.

REFLECTING GOD

2923 Troost Ave., Kansas City, MO 64109 | 816-931-1900
dcbrush@wordaction.com | *reflectinggod.com*
Duane Brush, editor

> **Denomination:** Nazarene
> **Audience:** adults
> **Type:** print and online
> **Details:** Send a couple of sample devotions to fit the format and
> request an assignment. Length: 180-200 words. Pays $115 for
> seven devotions.
> **Tip:** Our purpose is the pursuit to embrace holy living. We want to
> foster discussion about what it means to live a holy life in the 21st
> century.

REJOICE!

35094 Laburnum Ave., Abbotsford, BC V2S 8K3, Canada | 540-434-6701
DorothyH@mennomedia.org | *www.faithandliferesources.org/periodicals/rejoice*
Dorothy Hartman, editor

> **Denomination:** Anabaptist
> **Audience:** adults
> **Type:** print, quarterly
> **Details:** Prefers that you send a couple of sample devotions and
> inquire about assignment procedures. Pays $100-125 on
> publication for seven assigned meditations. Length: 250-300
> words. Rights: first. Bible version: prefers NRSV.
> **Also** accepts: Testimonies: 500-600 words, eight per year. Poems: free
> verse, light verse, 60 characters, eight per year. Submit maximum of
> three poems. Pays $25.
> **Tip:** Don't apply for assignment unless you are familiar with the
> publication and Anabaptist theology.

THE SECRET PLACE

PO Box 851, Valley Forge, PA 19482-0851 | 800-458-3766
thesecretplace@abc-usa.org | *www.judsonpress.com*
Ingrid and Wayne Dvirnak, editors

> **Denomination:** American Baptist
> **Audience:** adults
> **Type:** print, quarterly
> **Details:** Accepts freelance submissions; does not give assignments.
> Length: 150-200 words. Payment: $20 per published submission.
> Rights: first. Bible version: NRSV.
> **Also** accepts: poems of 30 lines or fewer, $20 per poem
> **Tip:** Use less-familiar Scriptures.

TAKE FIVE PLUS

1445 N. Boonville Ave., Springfield, MO 65802 | 417-862-2781
rl-take5plus@gph.org
Wade Quick, team leader for dated curriculum projects

> **Denomination:** Assemblies of God
> **Audience:** teens
> **Type:** print, quarterly
> **Details:** Assignment only. Request a sample assignment. Length: 225
> words. Payment: $25 per devotion. Rights: all. Bible version: NIV.
> **Tip:** Read and follow the guidelines. Become familiar with *Take 5*
> before seeking a sample assignment. We do not publish sample
> assignments, and we do not offer payment for them.

THESE DAYS

100 Witherspoon St., Louisville, KY 40202 | 800-624-2412
lcheifetz@presbypub.com | *www.ppcbooks.com*
Rev. Laura M. Cheifetz, editor

> **Denomination:** Presbyterian Church (USA)
> **Audience:** adults
> **Type:** print, quarterly
> **Details:** Submissions by assignment; also accepts freelance
> devotionals. Requirements to get an assignment: Preference
> is for members of the Cumberland Presbyterian Church, The
> Cumberland Presbyterian Church in America, the Presbyterian
> Church (USA), the United Church of Christ, United Church of
> Canada, Presbyterian Church of Canada. Submission must fit the
> word count, use inclusive and expansive language for people and
> (preferably also) for God, and be appropriate and accessible for

a general church audience. Length: 180 words. Payment: $100 or $150 worth of books for seven devotions. Rights: first. Bible version: NRSV.

Also accepts: "These Moments," 475 words, devotional and prayer; pays $30 or $75 worth of books. "These Times": 850 words, devotional, five reflection questions, and prayer; pays $45 or $100 worth of books.

Tip: Be succinct and clear, and consider using lectionary texts. Address seasonal topics when appropriate.

THE UPPER ROOM

PO Box 340004, Nashville, TN 37203-0004 | 615-340-7252
ureditorial@upperroom.org | *www.devotional.upperroom.org*
Susan King, associate editor | *Andrew Breeden, associate/acquisitions editor*

Denomination: United Methodist
Audience: adults
Type: print, quarterly
Details: Accepts freelance submissions. Length: 300 words, which include everything on the printed page. Payment: $30. Rights: first. Bible versions: NIV, NRSV, CEB, KJV.
Tip: Use concrete, rather than abstract, language and a welcoming tone.

THE WORD IN SEASON

PO Box 1209, Minneapolis, MN 55440 | 414-963-1222
rochelle@writenowcoach.com | *www.augsburgfortress.org*
Rev. Rochelle Melander, editor

Denomination: Evangelical Lutheran Church in America
Audience: adults
Type: print, quarterly
Details: Gives assignments based on samples. Request guidelines, and write trial devotions. Length: 180-200 words. Payment: $20 per devotion; $75 for series of nine prayers. Rights: all. Bible version: NRSV.
Tip: Be familiar with Lutheran (ELCA) theology, and be willing to revise.

DRAMA

CHRISTIAN PUBLISHERS
(FORMERLY CONTEMPORARY DRAMA SERVICE)
PO Box 248, Cedar Rapids, Iowa 52406 | 844-841-6387
editor@christianpub.com | *www.christianpub.com*
Rhonda Wray, editor

> **Details:** Leading source of Christmas and Easter plays and musicals for all ages and all denominations. Many of them are used in schools and youth groups. Always looking for Christmas and Easter plays. Also publishes drama-related books, liturgies, and banners. Submit complete play, preferably through the website form. Guidelines are on the website.
>
> **Types:** full-length plays and musicals, one-act plays and musicals, dinner theater, children's programs and liturgies, liturgical dance programs, and banner liturgies
>
> **Tips:** People have short attention spans, and if the story is too bogged down in excessive dialogue, or if the play wonders aimlessly, they will simply tune out. If the comedy or suspense doesn't build from scene to scene, if we're not involved with the main character(s) or the dramatic question, then the play isn't going anywhere.

CSS PUBLISHING GROUP, INC.
See entry in **"Book Publishers."**

DRAMA MINISTRY
2814 Azalea PL., Nashville, TN 37204 | 866-859-7622
service@dramaministry.com | *www.dramaministry.com*
Vince Wilcox, general manager

> **Details:** The website offers more than 800 scripts. Open to all topics, including seasonal/holidays, for children, youth, and adults. Email or mail script. Buys all rights.
>
> **Types:** only short skits of 2-10 minutes, comedy, drama, monologue, readers theater

DOVE CHRISTIAN PUBLISHERS
See entry in **"Book Publishers."**

ELDRIDGE PLAYS AND MUSICALS
PO Box 4904, Lancaster, PA 17804 | 850-385-2463
newworks@histage.com | *www.95church.com*
Susan Shore, editor

> **Details:** Publishes fifteen to twenty scripts per year, receives 500 submissions annually. Length: 30 minutes—2 hours. Submit complete script via email. Simultaneous OK. Payment: 50% of royalties and 10% of copy sales. No advance. Guidelines are on the website.
>
> **Types:** full-length plays, one-act plays, compilations of skits, musicals, readers theater, childrens, teens
>
> **Tip:** We welcome shows on all subjects, but Christmas plays are very popular.

GROUP PUBLISHING
See entry in **"Book Publishers."**

PLAYERS PRESS, INC.
PO Box 1132, Studio City, CA 91614-0132 | 818-789-4980
playerspress@att.net | *www.ppeps.com*
Robert W. Gordon, editor

> **Details:** Publishes one to six religious plays per year, receives fifty to eighty religious submissions annually. Query letter only. Payment: 10% on net, advances on some titles. Publication within twelve months. No simultaneous submissions. No email submissions. Responds in one to three weeks to query, three to twelve months to manuscript. Guidelines by mail. Catalog for 9 x 12 SASE with eleven stamps or $4.50. Also sometimes reprints quality theater titles and costume books.
>
> **Types:** full-length plays and musicals for all ages
>
> **Tip:** Especially likes religious, romantic, comic, and children's plays.

12

GREETING CARDS
AND GIFTS

ABBEY PRESS
1 Hill Dr., St. Meinrad, IN 47577; 800-621-1588
service@abbeytrade.com | abbeytrade.com
> **Products:** religious and inspirational cards and gifts
> **Submissions:** Not currently taking submissions, but check the website for changes in this situation.

BLUE MOUNTAIN ARTS
Editorial Dept., PO Box 1007, Boulder, CO 80306 | 303-449-0536
editorial@sps.com | www.sps.com
> **Products:** general card publisher with some inspirational cards
> **Submissions:** Looking for original, fresh, creative submissions on love, friendship, family, philosophies, and any other topic that one person might want to share with another. No rhyming poetry, overtly religious verse, one-liners, or humor. For guidelines, send a blank email to *writings@sps.com* with "Send Me Guidelines" in the subject line. Submit by email (no attachments) or mail to Editorial Department. Responds in four months if interested. Holiday deadlines: Christmas and general holiday, July 15; Valentine's Day, September 12; Easter, November 8; Mother's Day, December 13; Father's Day, February 7.
> **Payment:** $300 per poem for worldwide, exclusive rights to publish it on a greeting card and other products. $50 per poem for one-time use in a book.

DAYSPRING
PO Box 1010, 21154 Hwy. 16 E., Siloam Springs, AR 72761
info@dayspring.com | www.dayspring.com
Trieste Van Wyngarden, editorial director, triestev@dayspring.com

Products: Christian cards, journals, and gifts

Submissions: Currently only accepting submissions from writers who have previously had work published or whom an editor meets at a conference. Uses several writing styles, but the majority is conversational. If emailing, put "write" in the subject line. If mailing, send to Editorial Department. Guidelines are on the website at *www.dayspring.com/contact/editorial*.

Payment: $75 per card for all rights

Tips: "Each DaySpring card is an opportunity, given by God, to speak something positive, wholesome, and redemptive into the life of someone else. The use of Scripture is a vital part of DaySpring product. Through it we communicate the heart of God to others."

DESIGNER GREETINGS

11 Executive Ave., Edison, NJ 08817
www.designergreetings.com

Products: general card company that does some religious cards for all occasions and holidays

Submissions: Rhyming verse and prose. Mail only, on index cards or full-size paper, to Editorial Department. Guidelines are on the website under "Opportunities."

DICKSONS, INC.

709 B Ave E., Seymour, IN 47274
submissions@dicksonsgifts.com | *www.dicksonsgifts.com*

Products: Christian gifts

Submissions: Two to eight lines, maximum sixteen, suitable for plaques, bookmarks, etc. Subjects can cover any gift-giving occasion and Christian, inspirational, and everyday social-expression topics. Phrases or acrostics of one or two lines for bumper stickers are also considered. Guidelines are on the website at *www.dicksonsgifts.com/t-contact.aspx*.

GALLANT GREETINGS

5730 N. Tripp Ave., Chicago, IL 60646 | 800-621-4279, 847-671-6500
info@gallantgreetings.com | *gallantgreetings.com*

Products: general card company with a religious line, "Inspirational Thoughts"

Submissions: Not accepting verse submissions at this time, but check the website for changes in this situation.

WARNER PRESS

1201 E. 5th St., Anderson, IN 46018-9988 | 800-741-7721
krhodes@warnerpress.org | *www.warnerpress.org*
Karen Rhodes, senior editor

Products: boxed Christian cards

Submissions: Most accepted verses average four lines in length. Themes include birthday, anniversary, baby congratulations, sympathy, get well, kid's birthday and get well, thinking of you, friendship, Christmas. Use a conversational tone with no lofty poetic language, such as thee, thou, art. Responds in six to eight weeks. Guidelines are on the website.

13

TRACTS

The following companies publish Gospel tracts but do not have writers guidelines. If you are interested in writing for them, email or phone to find out if they currently are looking for submissions. Also check your denominational publishing house to see if it publishes tracts.

CHRISTIAN LIGHT PUBLICATIONS

PO Box 1212, Harrisonburg, VA 22803-1212
info@clp.org | www.clp.org

FELLOWSHIP TRACT LEAGUE

PO Box 164, Lebanon, Ohio 45036 | 513-494-1075
mail@fellowshiptractleague.org | www.fellowshiptractleague.org

GOOD NEWS PUBLISHERS

1300 Crescent St., Wheaton, IL 60187 | 630-682-4300
www.crossway.org
Kate Felinski, editor, kfelinski@crossway.org

GOSPEL PUBLISHING HOUSE

1445 N. Boonville Ave., Springfield, MO 65802 | 800-641-4310
newproducts@gph.org | gospelpublishing.com

GOSPEL TRACT SOCIETY

PO Box 1118, Independence, MO 64051 | 816-461-6086
gospeltractsociety@gmail.com | gospeltractsociety.org

GRACE VISION PUBLISHERS

321-745-9966 (text only)
email through the website: www.gospelvision.com

MOMENTS WITH THE BOOK

PO Box 322, Bedford, PA 15522 | 814-623-8737
email through the website: mwtb.org

TRACT ASSOCIATION OF FRIENDS

1501 Cherry St., Philadelphia, PA 19102
info@tractassociation.org | www.tractassociation.org

THE TRACT LEAGUE

2627 Elmridge Dr., Grand Rapids, MI 49534-1329 | 616-453-7695
info@tractleague.com | tractleague.com

14

BIBLE CURRICULUM

This list includes only the major, nondenominational curriculum publishers. If you are in a denominational church, also check its publishing house for curriculum products. Plus some organizations, like Awana Clubs International and Pioneer Clubs, also produce curriculum for their programs.

Since Bible curriculum is written on assignment only, you'll need to get samples for age groups you want to write for (from the company's website, large Christian bookstores, or your church) and study the formats and pieces. Look for editors' names on the copyright pages of teachers manuals, or call the publishing house for this information. Also check the websites to see if they list requirements for writers.

Then write query letters to specific editors. Tell why you're qualified to write curriculum for them, include a sample of curriculum you've written or other sample of your writing, and ask for a trial assignment. Since the need for writers varies widely, you may not get an assignment for a year or more.

Some of these companies also publish undated, elective curriculum books that are used in a variety of ministries. Plus some book publishers publish lines of Bible-study guides. (See **Book Publishers.**) These are contracted like other books with a proposal and sample chapters.

A BEKA BOOKS
www.joyfullifesundayschool.com
> **Type:** Sunday school
> **Imprint:** Joyful Life

DAVID C. COOK
www.sundayschool.com
> **Types:** Sunday school, vacation Bible school, children's worship
> **Imprints:** Accent, Bible-in-Life, David C. Cook, Echoes, Encounter, Gospel Light, HeartShaper, RIO, Scripture Press, Tru, and some denominational imprints

GROUP PUBLISHING

www.group.com

Types: Sunday school, vacation Bible school, children's worship

Imprints: Buzz, Dig In, FaithWeaver NOW, Grapple, Hands-On Bible, Hands-On Worship, Living Inside Out, Play-n-Worship, Kids Own Worship

UNION GOSPEL PRESS

uniongospelpress.com

Type: Sunday school

URBAN MINISTRIES, INC.

urbanministries.com

Types: Sunday school, vacation Bible school

15

MISCELLANEOUS

These companies publish a variety of books and other products that fall into the specialty-markets category, such as puzzle books, game books, children's activity books, craft books, charts, church bulletins, and coloring books.

BARBOUR PUBLISHING
See entry in **"Book Publishers."**

BROADSTREET PUBLISHING
See entry in **"Book Publishers."**

CARSON-DELLOSA PUBLISHING GROUP
PO Box 35665, Greensboro, NC 27425-5665
freelancesamples@carsondellosa.com | *www.carsondellosa.com*

> **Types:** books with puzzles, activities, games, and children's worship bulletins; charts
>
> **Submissions:** No unsolicited queries or manuscripts. To become an independent contractor, email or mail samples and a résumé. If you have samples from supplemental education materials, send those; however, they will accept all types of samples. Guidelines are on the website at *www.carsondellosa.com/customer-service/freelance-opportunities.*

CHRISTIAN FOCUS PUBLICATIONS
See entry in **"Book Publishers."**

DAVID C. COOK
www.sundayschool.com
See entry in **"Book Publishers."**

GROUP PUBLISHING
See entry in **"Book Publishers."**

ROSE PUBLISHING
See entry in **"Book Publishers."**

WARNER PRESS
1201 E. 5th St., Anderson, IN 46018-9988 | 800-741-7721
www.warnerpress.org
Karen Rhodes, senior editor, krhodes@warnerpress.org
Robin Fogel, product editor, rfogle@warnerpress.org

Church bulletins: Short devotionals that tie into a visual image and incorporate a Bible verse (does not have to be from King James Version). Especially interested in material for holidays and special Sundays, such as Christmas, New Year's Day, Palm Sunday, Easter, Pentecost, and Communion. General themes are also welcome. Length: 110-150 words. Deadline: September 30. Pays $35 on acceptance.

Children's coloring and activity books: Most activity books focus on a Bible story or biblical theme, such as love and forgiveness. Ages range from preschool (ages 2-5) to upper elementary (ages 8-10). Include activities and puzzles in every upper-elementary book. Coloring-book manuscripts should present a picture idea and a portion of the story for each page. Deadlines: January 31 and July 31. Payment varies.

Adult coloring books: Combine devotionals or journaling pages and Scripture with picture ideas to color. Bible version: NIV, KJV.

PART 5

SUPPORT
FOR
WRITERS

16

LITERARY AGENTS

Asking editors and other writers is a great way to find a reliable agent. You may also want to visit www.sfwa.org/other-resources/for-authors/writer-beware/agents for tips on avoiding questionable agents and choosing reputable ones.

The general market has an Association of Authors' Representatives (*www.aaronline.org*), also known as AAR. To be a member the agent must agree to a code of ethics. Their web site has a list of agents who don't charge fees, except for office expenses. The site also provides information on how to receive a list of approved agents. Some listings below indicate which agents belong to the AAR. Lack of such a designation, however, does not indicate the agent is unethical; most Christian agents are not members.

ALIVE LITERARY AGENCY
(FORMERLY ALIVE COMMUNICATIONS)
7680 Goddard St., Ste. 200, Colorado Springs, CO 80920 | 719-260-7080
submissions@aliveliterary.com | *www.aivelieterary.com*

> **Agents:** Rick Christian, Bryan Norman, Lisa Jackson, Andrea Heinecke
> **Agency:** Well-known in the industry. Established in 1989. Represents more than 125 clients. Member of Association of Authors' Representatives.
> **Types:** adult novels (20%), nonfiction (75%); crossover books, juvenile books and miscellaneous, 5%.
> **New clients:** Primarily well-established, best-selling, and career authors. Always looking for a breakout, blockbuster author with genuine talent. Contact by email. Responds in six to eight weeks to referrals only; may not respond to unsolicited submissions.
> **Commission:** 15%
> **Fees:** only extraordinary costs with client's preapproval
> **Tips:** Rewrite and polish until the words on the page shine.

Endorsements and great connections may help, provided you can write with power and passion. Network with publishing professionals by making contacts, joining critique groups, and attending writers conferences in order to make personal connections and get feedback.

AMBASSADOR AGENCY

PO Box 50358, Nashville, TN 37205 | 615-370-4700; *info@AmbassadorAgency.com* | *www.AmbassadorAgency.com*

Agent: Wes Yoder, *wes@AmbassadorSpeakers.com*
Agency: Established in 1973. Recognized in the industry. Represents twenty-five to thirty clients.
New clients: Open to unpublished authors and new clients. Contact by email. Responds in four to six weeks.
Types: adult nonfiction and fiction, crossover books, and e-books; no sci-fi or medical
Commission: 15%; foreign, 15% plus expenses
Fees: none

BK NELSON LITERARY AGENCY

1565 Paseo Vida, Palm Springs, CA 92264 | 760-778-8800 *bknelson4@cs.com* | *www.bknelson.com*

Agent: B.K. Nelson
Agency: Sold more than 2,000 books. Eighty clients. Also offers speakers bureau, manuscript evaluation and editing, and self-publishing consultation.
Types: adult and children's religious and inspirational fiction and nonfiction, self-help, how-to, movies

BANNER SERVICES, LLC

PO Box 1828, Winter Park, CO 80482 *www.mikeloomis.co*

Agent: Mike Loomis
Agency: Established 2009. Represents 12 clients.
Types: Christian nonfiction, business nonfiction, crossover
New clients: Open to new authors, specializing in unpublished authors. Contact through the website with book synopsis and your website url. Responds in four weeks.
Commission: 15%
Fees: None for representation
Tip: Especially open to new/aspiring authors.

THE BLYTHE DANIEL AGENCY, INC.

PO Box 64197, Colorado Springs, CO 80962-4197 | 719-213-3427
submissions@theblythedanielagency.com | *www.theblythedanielagency.com*

Agent: Blythe Daniel, blythe@theblythedanielagency.com; Jessica Kirkland, *jessica@theblythedanielagency.com*; Blog Content Manager, Stephanie Alton, *stephanie@theblythedanielagency.com*

Agency: Recognized in the industry. Established in 2005. Represents fifty clients. Represents bestselling nonfiction authors. Sells to general market too. Also provides publicity and blog campaigns; see listing in "Publicity and Marketing Services" chapter.

Types: adult nonfiction, young-adult nonfiction, gift books, crossover books; limited children's, devotionals, Bible studies

New clients: Open to unpublished authors with an established platform/network and previously published authors. Contact by email to the submissions address with proposal and three sample chapters. Accepts simultaneous submissions. Responds in eight weeks.

Commission: 15%; foreign, dramatic rights, television, film, video, electronic and/or commercial rights, 20%

Fees: none, other than hourly consulting rates by any writer if requested

Tips: Our agency looks for authors with more than one book. We look to build career authors, not ones who publish a single title. We are acquiring books for Christian living, spiritual growth, memoirs, current events, inspirational, business/leadership, church leadership, church-ministry areas, marriage, parenting, apologetics, political, social issues, women's issues, gift books, cookbooks, and books for millennials by new voices, ministry leaders, pastors, journalists, and other professionals.

BOOKS & SUCH LITERARY MANAGEMENT

52 Mission Cir., Ste. 122, PMB 170, Santa Rosa, CA 95409-5370
representation@booksandsuch.com | *www.booksandsuch.com*

Agents: Janet Kobobel Grant, founder and president; Wendy Lawton, vice president; Rachelle Gardner; Rachel Kent; Mary Keeley

Agency: Well recognized in the industry. Established in 1996. Member of ACFW and CBA. Represents more than 250 clients. We have established a tight-knit community among our clients and offer them training in marketing, their careers, and the writing craft. Despite being one of the largest Christian literary agencies, we work hard to be nimble in an age of publishing disruption and to think long-term for our clients as we help to build their careers.

Types: fiction and nonfiction for all ages except children, general market

New clients: Open to new or unpublished authors, only with recommendation. Contact by email with query. Accepts simultaneous submissions. Responds within six weeks if interested.

Commission: 15%; foreign, 20% if foreign-rights agent is involved

Fees: none

Tips: We concentrate our efforts on adult manuscripts, but we represent a small number of authors who write for teens, middle grade, or children. None of our agents represent speculative fiction.

CREDO COMMUNICATIONS

3148 Plainfield Ave. N.E., Ste. 111, Grand Rapids, MI 49525 | 616-363-2686
contact@credocommunications.net | *www.credocommunications.net*

Agents: Timothy J. Beals, founder and president, *tim@credocommunications.net*; Ann Byle, *ann@credocommunications.net*; Drew Chamberlin, *drew@credocommunicatons.net*; Karen E. Neumair, *karen@credocommunications.net*; David Sanford, not accepting new clients

Agency: Recognized in the industry. Established in 2005. Represents seventy clients. Also offers editorial services for nonclients and coaching for self-published authors on design, typesetting, production, printing, marketing, sales, and distribution.

Types: novels and nonfiction for all ages, picture books, e-books, crossover books

New clients: By referral only. Tim: fiction and nonfiction; Ann: fiction and children's; Drew: nonfiction and children's; Karen: nonfiction. Contact by email to connect@credocommunications. net. Accepts simultaneous submissions. Responds in one week.

Commission: 15%, foreign varies

Fees: none

Tip: Seeking creative fiction and thoughtful nonfiction by established authors who bring words to life.

CURTIS BROWN, LTD.

10 Astor Pl., New York, NY 10003-6935| 212-473-5400
info@cbltd.com | *www.curtisbrown.com*

Agents: Maureen Walters; Laura Blake Peterson, *lbp@cbltd.com*

Agency: Member of Association of Authors' Representatives. General agency that handles some religious/inspirational books.

Types: adult and children's books of all types

New clients: Query via email or mail with SASE. See the website for what each agent wants with query. Responds in six to eight weeks.

Fees: photocopying and some postage

D. C. JACOBSON & ASSOCIATES

537 S.E. Ash St., Ste. 203, Portland, OR 97214 | 503-850-4800

submissions@dcjacobson.com | *www.dcjacobson.com*

Agents: Don Jacobson, Jenni Burke, Heidi Mitchell, Tawny Johnson

Agency: Established in 2006. Represents more than 100 clients. Recognized in the industry. Don is the former owner of Multnomah Publishers and has published multiple bestselling books.

Types: adult and teen novels and nonfiction, memoirs, crossover books, children's books

New clients: Open to unpublished or self-published authors and new clients. Email submissions and queries; no mail submissions. Accepts simultaneous submissions. Responds in eight weeks.

Commission: 15%

Fees: none

Tips: Looking for fresh writing that will redeem culture and renew the church. Please review our website thoroughly before submitting your proposal.

DANIEL LITERARY GROUP

601 Old Hickory Blvd. #56, Brentwood, TN 37027

submissions@danielliterarygroup.com | *www.danielliterarygroup.com*

Agent: Greg Daniel, *greg@danielliterarygroup.com*

Agency: Established in 2007. Recognized in the industry. Represents fifty clients. Types: adult nonfiction, gift books, crossover books, general market; specializes in thoughtful nonfiction in both CBA and general markets

New clients: Open to new clients. Contact by email to the submissions address. Accepts simultaneous submissions. Responds in three to four weeks.

Commission: 15%; foreign, 20% if subagent is used

Fees: none

DYSTEL & GODERICH LITERARY MANAGEMENT, INC.

1 Union Square W., Ste. 904, New York, NY 10003; 212-627-9100;

Miriam@dystel.com | *www.dystel.com*

Agents: Jane Dystel, Miriam Goderich, Stacey Glick, Michael Bourret, Jim McCarthy, Lauren Abramo, Jessica Papin, John

Rudolph, Mike Hoogland, Sharon Pelletier, Eric Myers, and Erin Young. Each agent has a separate email address on the website.

Agency: Established in 1994. Recognized in the industry. Represents five to ten religious book clients. Member of Association of Authors' Representatives.

Types: fiction and nonfiction for adults, gift books, general books, crossover books

New clients: Open to unpublished authors and new clients. Contact with a brief e-query with bio. No simultaneous queries. Submission requirements are on the website. Responds to queries in four to six weeks, to submissions in two months.

Commission: 15%; foreign, 19%

Fees: photocopying

Tips: Send a professional, well-written query to a specific agent. You can find each agent's email address and what he or she is looking for on the website.

FINE PRINT LITERARY MANAGEMENT

115 W. 29th St., 3rd Fl., New York, NY 10001 | 212-279-1282
peter@fineprintlit.com | *www.fineprintlit.com*

Agents: Peter Rubie, Stephany Evans, and four others

Agency: General agency that handles some religion/spirituality books.

Types: nonfiction for teens and adults

New clients: Open to unpublished authors and new clients. Query with SASE or e-query. Responds in two to three months.

Commission: 15%; foreign, 20%

FOLIO LITERARY MANAGEMENT

630 9th Ave., Ste. 1101; New York, NY 10036 | 212-400-1494
fweimann@foliolit.com | *www.foliolit.com.*

Agents: Frank Weimann; Claudia Cross, *claudia@ foliolitmanagement.com*

Agency: Frank was founder of the Literary Group International that was established in 1986 and then merged with Folio in 2013. Represents more than 300 clients. Member of Association of Authors' Representatives.

Types: primarily adult nonfiction, as well as select young-adult fiction

New clients: Open to new clients and unpublished authors. Contact by email to *sonali@foliolitmanagement.com.*

Commission: 15%; foreign, 25%

Fees: postage

Tips: Email query letter and first ten pages of proposal or manuscript in body of the email. No attachments. Write QUERY in the subject line.

GARY D. FOSTER CONSULTING

733 Virginia Ave., Van Wert, OH 45891 | 419-238-4082
gary@garydfoster.com | *www.garydfoster.com*

Agent: Gary Foster

Agency: Established in 1989. Represents more than fifty clients. Recognized in the industry.

Types: religious/inspirational adult novels and nonfiction, teen/YA nonfiction and novels, gift books, crossover books; prefers overtly Christian content

New clients: Open to unpublished authors and frequently to new clients. Email with cover letter and proposal; if no proposal, send cover letter, one-page summary, introduction, first two chapters, and one other chapter you feel is strongest. Accepts simultaneous submissions. Responds in one to three weeks.

Commission: 15%; foreign varies

Fees: nominal fee on signing of representation agreement

Tip: Open to talented first-time authors, CBA or ECPA.

GLOBAL TALENT REPS, INC.

125 Corsair Cir., Parker, CO 80014
info@globaltalentreps.com | *www.globaltalentreps.com*

Agent: Andrew J. Whelchel III, a.whelchel@globaltalentreps.com

Agency: Established in 2001.

Types: religious/inspirational novels for adults, nonfiction for adults, screenplays, TV/movie scripts, e-books, crossover, no romance

New clients: Open to unpublished authors and new clients. Query through the online form. Accepts simultaneous submissions. Responds in eight weeks.

Commission: 10% film; 15% books; 5% scouting; foreign 10% plus foreign sales agents fees, if any

Fees: none

Tip: Seeking humor, parenting, edgy Christian fiction like Cursebreaker, and low-budget scripts $5 million and under.

HARTLINE LITERARY AGENCY

123 Queenston Dr., Pittsburgh, PA 15235 | 412-829-2483
www.hartlineliterary.com

> **Agents:** Joyce A. Hart, *joyce@hartlineliterary.com*; Jim Hart, *jim@hartlineliterary.com*; Cyle Young, *cyle@hartlineliterary.com*; Diana Flegal, *diana@hartlineliterary.com*; Andy Scheer, *andy@hartlineliterary.com*; Linda Glaz, *linda@hartlineliterary.com*
>
> **Agency:** Recognized in the industry. Established in 1992. Represents 200 clients.
>
> **Types:** Nonfiction, fiction, general, crossover. If crossover, books must be clean, family-friendly books with no swearing or graphic sex. No gift books or poetry. Jim: adult fiction and nonfiction; Cyle: adult fiction and nonfiction, middle grade, children's; Linda: primarily fiction but open to other genres except children's.
>
> **New clients:** Joyce: only authors met at conferences or referrals; Diana: only authors met at conferences or referrals; Andy: not open to new clients. Contact by email. Prefer queries in the body of the email, proposals as attachments in Microsoft Word. Responds in six to eight weeks.
>
> **Commission:** 15% on books, 20% on movie options greater than $100,000, 25% for options less than $100,000
>
> **Fees:** none
>
> **Tips:** Our proposal guidelines are on our website. Platform is important. For fiction, make sure the book is completed. Looking for the best in fiction and nonfiction.

HIDDEN VALUE GROUP

27758 Santa Margarita Pkwy. #361, Mission Viejo, CA 92691
njernigan@hiddenvaluegroup.com | *www.HiddenValueGroup.com*

> **Agents:** Jeff Jernigan and Nancy Jernigan
>
> **Agency:** Established in 2001. Recognized in the industry.
>
> **Types:** adult fiction and nonfiction, teen/YA nonfiction (few), picture books, gift books, e-books, crossover books
>
> **New clients:** Open to previously published authors only. Email *bookquery@hiddenvaluegroup.com*. Accepts simultaneous submissions. Responds in four to six weeks.
>
> **Commission:** 15%; foreign, 15%
>
> **Fees:** none
>
> **Tips:** Looking for inspirational nonfiction, self-help, romance and suspense fiction, women's nonfiction. Make sure the proposal includes author bio, two sample chapters, and manuscript summary. A marketing plan to promote your project is a must.

THE JEFF HERMAN AGENCY, LLC

PO Box 1522, 29 Park St., Stockbridge, MA 01262 | 413-298-0077
Jeff@jeffherman.com | *www.jeffherman.com*

> **Agent:** Jeff Herman
> **Agency:** Established in 1987. Recognized in the industry. Represents more than twenty clients with religious books.
> **Types:** adult nonfiction, general books, crossover, e-books
> **New clients:** Open to unpublished authors and new clients. Query by mail with SASE or email. Accepts simultaneous submissions. Responds in four weeks.
> **Commission:** 15%; foreign, 15% or 10% when subagent is used
> **Fees:** none
> **Tips:** I love a good book from the heart. Let your mind follow your heart.

K J LITERARY SERVICES, LLC

1540 Margaret Ave., Grand Rapids, MI 49507 | 616-551-9797
kim@kjliteraryservices.com | *www.kjliteraryservices.com*

> **Agent:** Kim Zeilstra
> **New clients:** Only taking new authors by referral at this time.
> **Commission:** 15%

KATHI J. PATON LITERARY AGENCY

PO Box 2236, Radio City Station, New York, NY 10101-2236 | 212-265-6586
KJPLitBiz@optonline.net; www.PatonLiterary.com

> **Agent:** Kathi Paton
> **Agency:** Established in 1987.
> **Types:** adult nonfiction on Christian life and issues
> **New clients:** Prefers e-query.
> **Commission:** 15%; foreign, 20%
> **Fees:** for photocopying and postal submissions

KEITH CARROLL, AGENT

PO Box 428, Newburg, PA 17257 | 717-423-6621
keith@christianliteraryagent.com | *www.christianliteraryagent.com*

> **Agency:** Established in 2009 and functioned as an author coach since 2000. Represents ninety-four clients. Specializes in helping authors prepare for publication as a coach. Accepts simultaneous submissions.
> **Types:** adult and teen nonfiction, adult fiction, picture books, e-books, crossover books

New clients: New clients welcome. Contact via the client application form on the website. Reviews in five to eight weeks.

Commission: 10%

Fees: small fee for introductory consultation with unpublished authors, which includes a review/analysis of author's material, a two-hour phone call to advise and recommend regarding publishability

KEN SHERMAN & ASSOCIATES

1275 N. Hayworth, Ste. 103, Los Angeles, CA 90046 | 310-273-3840
ken@kenshermanassociates.com | kenshermanassociates.com

Agent: Ken Sherman

Agency: Established in 1989. Represents fifty clients.

Types: adult religious/inspirational novels, nonfiction, screenplays, and TV/movie scripts; also handles film and television rights to books

New clients: Open to unpublished authors and new clients by referral only. Responds in one month.

Commission: 15%; foreign, 20%; dramatic rights, 15%

Fees: office expenses and other negotiable expenses

LESLIE H. STOBBE LITERARY AGENCY

300 Doubleday Rd., Tryon, NC 28782 | 828-808-7127
www.stobbeliterary.com | www.sally-apokedak.com | stobbeliterary.com

Agents: Les Stobbe, *lhstobbe123@gmail.com*; Sally Apokedak, *sally@sally-apokedak.com*

Agency: Well-recognized in the industry. Established in 1993. Represents more than 100 clients.

Types: Les: professional-level adult fiction and nonfiction by writers with significant platforms. Sally: fiction and nonfiction board books, picture books, early readers, chapter books, middle grade, young adult; both Christian and general markets. She is "eager to find YA and middle-grade books for the general market that are also written from a Christian worldview."

New clients: Open to unpublished authors and new clients. Contact by email. Considers simultaneous submissions. Responds within ten weeks. Our preferences are books imbued with Christian values. We will not take on books with which we disagree, either because of theological perspective or style of expression. A great voice and a fresh premise are both vital if you want Sally to represent you.

Commission: 15%; foreign, 10%

Fees: none

Tips: Because of the intense competition for the few slots open to debut authors, it is wise to hire a professional editor to polish your final version.

LEVINE GREENBERG ROSTAN LITERARY AGENCY

307 Seventh Ave., Ste. 2407, New York, NY 10001 | 212-337-0934
submit@levinegreenberg.com | *www.levinegreenberg.com*

Agent: James Levine

Agency: Established in 1989. Represents 250 clients. General agency that handles some religious/inspirational books. Member of Association of Authors' Representatives.

Types: adult nonfiction

New clients: Open to unpublished authors and new clients. Contact by using the submission form on the website.

Commission: 15%; foreign, 20%

Fees: office expenses

Tips: Our specialties include spirituality and religion.

LITERARY MANAGEMENT GROUP, LLC

PO Box 41004, Nashville, TN 37204; 615-812-4445
brucebarbour@literarymanagementgroup.com
www.literarymanagementgroup.com

Agent: Bruce R. Barbour

Agency: Established in 1995. Well-recognized in the industry. Represents more than 100 clients. Also offers book packaging and consulting.

Types: adult nonfiction, inspirational, motivational, and business

New clients: No unpublished authors. Open to new clients. Email contact preferred. Will review proposals; don't send unsolicited manuscripts. Accepts simultaneous submissions. Responds in three to four weeks.

Commission: 15%; foreign, 15%

Fees: none

Tips: Follow the guidelines, proposal outline, and submissions format on the website. Use Microsoft Word. Study the market, and know where your book will fit.

MACGREGOR LITERARY

PO Box 1316, Manzanita, OR 97124
submissions@macgregorliterary.com | *www.MacGregorLiterary.com*

Agents: Chip MacGregor, Amanda Luedeke, Brian Tibbetts

Agency: Established in 2006. Member of Association of Authors' Representatives. Recognized in the industry.

Types: adult nonfiction and fiction, crossover, general market

New clients: Not currently looking to add unpublished authors except through conferences and referrals from current authors. Contact by email query through the website. See submission guidelines on the site. Does not return unsolicited submissions, even if postage is included. Accepts simultaneous submissions. Responds in four to six weeks.

Commission: 15%

Fees: none

Tip: Doing some research will help you find the right agent—one who represents the type of project you're writing and who has done deals with the types of publishers who would contract your book.

MARK SWEENEY & ASSOCIATES

7900 Arlington Cir., Ste. 509, Naples, FL 34112 | 239-775-0044
sweeney2@comcast.net

Agents: Mark Sweeney and Janet Sweeney

Agency: Recognized in the industry. Established in 2003. Represents 120 clients.

Types: adult religious and inspirational nonfiction, selective general market, crossover books; no fiction

New clients: Open to new clients but selective. Contact by email. Accepts simultaneous submissions. Responds in one week.

Commission: 15%; foreign, 15%

Fees: none

Tip: Most of our consulting business and new-author acquisitions are by referral.

MANUS & ASSOCIATES LITERARY AGENCY

425 Sherman Ave., Ste. 200, Palo Alto, CA 94306 | 650-470-5151
manuslit@manuslit.com | *www.manuslit.com*

Agents: Jillian Manus, Janet Wilkens Manus, Penny Nelson, Jandy Nelson

Agency: Members Association of Authors' Representatives. Established in 1994.

Types: adult religious/inspirational novels and nonfiction, gift books, crossover, general books

New clients: Open to unpublished authors and new clients. Query by mail or email (no attachments). For fiction, send the first thirty pages, bio, and SASE. For nonfiction, send proposal with sample chapters. Responds in twelve weeks if interested.

Commission: 15%; foreign, 20-25%

Tip: Follow the submission guidelines on the website.

MICHAEL SNELL LITERARY AGENCY

PO Box 1206, Truro, MA 02666-1206 | 508-349-3718
snell.patricia@gmail.com | *michaelsnellagency.com*

Agents: Michael and Patricia Snell

Agency: Established in 1978. Represents 200 clients. General agency that handles some adult religious books.

New clients: Open to unpublished authors and new clients. Query by email to *query@michaelsnellagency.com* or by letter with SASE. Accepts simultaneous queries but not simultaneous submissions. Responds in one to two weeks.

Commission: 15%; foreign, 15%

Tip: See the website for guidelines to write a proposal.

NAPPALAND LITERARY AGENCY

446 E. 29th St. #1674, Loveland, CO 80539
literary@nappaland.com | *www.nappalandliterary.com*

Agent: Mike Nappa

Agency: Division of Nappaland Communications, Inc. We are committed to developing authors whose writing is authentic, relevant, and eternal. Established in 1995. Recognized in the industry. Represents twelve clients.

Types: literary fiction, suspense, young-adult fiction, literary nonfiction, history, leadership, family and parenting, pop culture, humor, religious inspiration

New clients: Prefers published authors and authors who are referred by a current Nappaland author or traditional publishing company professional. Query letter only by email. Accepts simultaneous submissions. Responds in four weeks. Unsolicited submissions are automatically rejected unless sent during March 1--May 30. If interested in seeing more, he will contact you.

Commission: 15%, 20% foreign

Fees: none

Tip: Please do not send us a query that says, "I know you don't usually represent this kind of book, but ...." We will mock your obtuseness with heartless cruelty and then reject you anyway. And we won't even feel bad about it.

NATASHA KERN LITERARY AGENCY, INC.

PO Box 1069, White Salmon, WA 98672
agent@natashakern.com | *www.natashakern.com*

Agent: Natasha Kern

Agency: Well-recognized member of Author's Guild, ACFW, RWA. Established in 1987. Represents thirty-six religious clients.

New clients: Currently closed to queries from unpublished writers. We cannot read unsolicited queries or proposals. We will continue to meet with writers at conferences and accept referrals from current clients and editors.

NUNN COMMUNICATIONS, INC.

1612 Ginger Dr., Carrollton, TX 75007 | 972-394-6866
info@nunncommunications.com | *www.nunncommunications.com*

Agent: Leslie Nunn Reed

Agency: Established in 1995. Represents twenty clients. Recognized in the industry.

Types: adult nonfiction, gift books, crossover books, general books

New clients: Not open to unpublished authors. Contact by email. Responds in four to six weeks.

Commission: 15%

Fees: office expenses if more than $100

THE QUADRIVIUM GROUP

7512 Dr. Phillips Blvd., Ste. 50-229, Orlando, FL 32819
www.TheQuadriviumGroup.com

Agents: Steve Blount, *SteveBlount@TheQuadriviumGroup.com*; Susan Blount, *SusanBlount@TheQuadriviumGroup.com*

Agency: Established in 2006. Represents twenty to thirty clients. Recognized in the industry. Also offers consulting on book sales and distribution.

Types: Christian and general fiction and nonfiction for all ages, gift books, crossover books

New clients: Open to a limited number of unpublished authors with credentials, platform, and compelling story/idea and to new clients, mostly by referral. Contact by email. Responds in two to four weeks.

Commission: 15%; foreign, 20%

Fees: only extraordinary costs with client's permission

RED WRITING HOOD INK

2075 Attala Rd. 1990, Kosciusko, MS 39090 | 662-582-1191
redwritinghoodink@gmail.com | *redwritinghoodink.net*

Agent: Sheri Williams

Agency: Established in 1997. Half of clients have Christian books. Recognized in the industry.

Types: novels and nonfiction for middle grade, young adults, and adults; crossover books. No children's books younger than middle grade.

New clients: Open to unpublished authors with strong platforms and to new clients. Contact by email. Accepts simultaneous submissions noted as such. Responds in one to six weeks.

Commission: 15%; foreign, 20%

Tips: Beta readers are priceless. Research is essential to a compelling story where readers connect with your characters. Unless specifically stated in our response, we will not accept another query on the same project once we have passed on it.

ROSS YOON LITERARY AGENCY

1666 Connecticut Ave. N.W., Ste. 500, Washington, DC 20009 | 202-328-3282
www.rossyoon.com

Agents: Gail Ross, *gail@rossyoon.com*; Howard Yoon *howard@rossyoon.com*; Anna Sproul-Latimer, *anna@rossyoon.com*

Agency: Recognized in the industry. Established in 1987. Member of Association of Authors' Representatives. General agency that handles some religious/inspirational books.

Types: adult nonfiction

New clients: Contact by e-query only. Accepts simultaneous queries.

Commission: 15%; foreign, 25%

SCHIAVONE LITERARY AGENCY, INC.

236 Trails End, West Palm Beach, FL 33413-2135 | 561-966-9294
profschia@aol.com | *www.publishersmarketplace.com/members/profschia*

Agent: Francine Edelman, *FrancineEdelman@aol.com*

Agency: Recognized in the industry. Established in 1996. Represents six clients.

Types: adult and teen/YA nonfiction; teen/YA novels, general-market books

New clients: Open to published authors only. Contact by email only with a one-page query; no attachments. No postal queries or phone calls. Accepts simultaneous submissions. Responds in four to six weeks.

Commission: 15%; foreign, 20%

Fees: none

Tips: We are highly selective. We prefer submissions from authors published by major houses.

SERENDIPITY LITERARY AGENCY, LLC

1633 Broadway, New York, NY 10019

info@serendipitylit.com | www.serendipitylit.com

Agents: Regina Brooks, *rbrooks@serendipitylit.com;* Dawn Michelle Hardy, *dawn@serendipitylit.com*; Nadeen Gayle, *nadeen@serendipitylit.com*; Rebecca Bugger, *rebecca@serendipitylit.com*; Jocquelle Caiby, *jocquelle@serendipitylit.com*

Agency: Member of Association of Authors' Representatives. Established in 2000. Represents more than 100 clients, five with religious books. General agency that handles some religious books.

Types: fiction and nonfiction for all ages, gift books, crossover books, general books, poetry, e-books. No science fiction.

New clients: Open to unpublished authors and new clients. Contact by email. Accepts simultaneous submissions. Responds in six weeks.

Commission: 15%; foreign, 20%

Fees: none

THE SEYMOUR AGENCY

475 Miner Street Rd., Canton, NY 13617 | 315-386-1831

www.theseymouragency.com

Agents: Nichole Resciniti, *nicole@theseymouragency.com*; Julie Gwinn, *julie@theseymouragency.com*; Tina Wainscott, *tina@theseymouragency.com*

Agency: Recognized in the industry. Established in 1992. Member of Association of Authors' Representatives. Represents more than thirty religious clients.

Types: fiction, nonfiction, YA/children's/middle grade, cookbooks, prescriptive, self-help, spirituality

New clients: Open to unpublished authors and new clients, although prefers published authors. Contact by email with one-page query and first five pages; no attachments. Accepts simultaneous queries. Responds in three weeks.

Commission: 15%; foreign, 20%

Fees: none

Tips: We make a conscious effort to reply to every query we receive. If you do not receive a request for additional materials within three weeks, you should assume we are not interested in that particular project.

SPENCERHILL ASSOCIATES, LTD.

8131 Lakewood Main St. #205 Lakewood Ranch, FL 34202 | 941-907-3700
submissions@spencerhillassociates.com | *www.spencerhillassociates.com*

Agent: Karen Solem

Agency: Member of Association of Authors' Representatives. Recognized in the industry. Established in 2001. General agent who represents fifteen to twenty-five clients with religious books.

Types: only adult Christian fiction

New clients: Not currently open to unpublished authors; selective of new clients. Contact by email.

Commission: 15%; foreign, 20%

Fees: photocopying and express-mail charges only

Tips: Check website for latest information and needs and how to submit. No nonfiction.

THE STEVE LAUBE AGENCY

24 W. Camelback Rd. A-635, Phoenix, AZ 85013 | 602-336-8910
info@stevelaube.com | *www.stevelaube.com*

Agents: Steve Laube, president; Tamela Hancock Murray; Karen Ball; Dan Balow

Agency: Established in 2004. Well-recognized in the industry. Represents more than 200 clients.

Types: adult Christian fiction and nonfiction, theology, how-to, health, Christian living, and selected YA; no children's picture books, cookbooks, or poetry

New clients: Open to new and unpublished authors. Email full proposal with sample chapters according to the guidelines on the website. Steve also will take proposals by mail. If guidelines are not followed, the proposal will not receive a response. Accepts simultaneous submissions. Responds in six to eight weeks.

Commission: 15%; foreign, 20%

Fees: none

Tips: Looking for fresh and innovative ideas. Make sure your proposal contains an excellent presentation.

SUITE A MANAGEMENT TALENT & LITERARY AGENCY

136 El Camino Dr., Ste. 410, Beverly Hills, CA 90212; 310-278-0801
suite-a@juno.com

Agent: Lloyd D. Robinson

Agency: Recognized in the industry. Established in 1990. Represents fifty clients. Specializes in the representation of screenplays for development as made-for-television movies and low- to mid-budget features with special focus on novels and stage plays for adaptation to film or TV. Also hires writers.

Types: novels for children, teens/YA, and adults; screenplays; TV/movie scripts; general-market books. Adaptation representation limited to adaptation of novels and true-life stories for film and television development. Work must have been published for consideration.

New clients: Open to new and unpublished clients (if published in other media). Contact by email. Limit initial query to a one-page résumé/bio, including educational background, list of published credits, and list of contest awards. One-page synopsis should include title; Writers Guild registration or U.S. copyright number; logline; and three paragraphs, including beginning, middle, and ending; not a pitch sheet.

Commission: 10%; foreign, 10%

Fees: For nonclient authors without recognized publishing credits, I attach first as a publishing consultant with a one-time fee of $3,500. On publication, I attach as a talent agent (10%) with credit as consultant. As a talent agent, I then submit the book for adaptation for film or television.

SUSAN SCHULMAN LITERARY AGENCY

454 W. 44th St., New York, NY 10036 | 212-713-1633
www.susanschulmanagency.com

Agents: Susan Schulman, *schulman@aol.com*; Linda Migalti, *schulmanagency@yahoo.com*; Christine LeBlond, *CleBlond@schulmanagency.com*

Agency: Recognized in the industry. Established in 1982. Member of Association of Authors' Representatives.

Types: adult and teen/YA religious/inspirational novels; children's, teen/YA and adult nonfiction; picture books

New clients: Open to unpublished authors and new clients. Contact by e-query. Accepts simultaneous submissions. Responds in two weeks.

Commission: 15%; foreign, 10% plus 10% to co-agent if used
Fees: none

TALCOTT NOTCH LITERARY SERVICES

31 Cherry St., Milford, CT 06460 | 203-876-4959
www.talcottnotch.net

> **Agents:** Gina Panettieri, *gpanettieri@talcottnotch.net*; Paula Munier, *pmunier@talcottnotch.net*; Saba Sulaiman, *ssulaiman@talcottnotch.net*
>
> **Agency:** Building a Christian presence in the industry. Established in 2003. Represents 150 clients, ten with religious books.
>
> **Types:** nonfiction and fiction, crossover, and general-market books for all ages
>
> **New clients:** Open to unpublished authors and new clients. Prefers e-queries sent to the agent most suited for your work. Also accepts hard copies. Accepts simultaneous submissions. Responds in eight weeks.
>
> **Commission:** 15%; foreign or with coagent, 20%
>
> **Fees:** none
>
> **Tips:** While Christian and religious books are not our main focus, we are open to unique and thought-provoking works from all writers. We are open to inspirational romances and women's fiction and young-adult and middle-grade fiction that would be appropriate for faith-based publishers. We specifically seek nonfiction in areas of parenting, health, women's issues, arts and crafts, self-help, and current events. We are open to academic/scholarly work, as well as commercial projects.

TRIDENT MEDIA GROUP, LLC

41 Madison Ave., 36th Fl., New York, NY 10010 | 212-333-1511
info@tridentmediagroup.com | *www.tridentmediagroup.com*

> **Agents:** Don Fehr, Mark Gottlieb
>
> **Agency:** General market agency which handles some religious books.
>
> **Types:** adult nonfiction
>
> **New clients:** Open to unpublished authors and new clients. Contact by query, using the submission form on the website. No unsolicited manuscripts. Send outline and sample chapters only on request. Responds to queries in three weeks, to manuscripts in six weeks.
>
> **Commission:** 15%; foreign, 20-25%

VAN DIEST LITERARY AGENCY

34947 S.E. Brooks Rd., Boring, OR 97009 | 503-676-8009
david@christianliteraryagency.com | *www.ChristianLiteraryAgency.com*

Agent: David Van Diest

Agency: Established in 2003. Represents 25 clients. Recognized in the industry.

Types: teen/YA and adult novels, nonfiction for all ages, and children's novels

New clients: Open to additional clients, including unpublished authors. Contact by email through the website. Responds in six weeks.

Commission: 15%; foreign, 15%

Fees: none

WATERSIDE PRODUCTIONS, INC.

2055 Oxford Ave., Cardiff, CA 92007 | 760-632-9190
admin@waterside.com | *www.waterside.com*

Agents: See the list on the website with specialties

Agency: Established in 1982. General agency that is interested in handling Christian books and books that challenge and engage readers from a Judeo-Christian perspective.

Types: prefers nonfiction, including spiritually oriented books, devotions, and theology; will look at fiction, although the bar is high

New clients: Query via the website form. Considers simultaneous submissions.

Commission: 15%; foreign, 25%

WENDY SHERMAN ASSOCIATES

27 W. 24th St., Ste. 700B, New York, NY 10110 | 212-279-9027
submissions@wsherman.com | *www.wsherman.com*

Agents: Wendy Sherman, Kimberly Perel

Agency: General agency that handles some religious books.

Types: adult spiritual nonfiction

New clients: Open to unpublished authors and new clients. Contact by e-query only. Guidelines on the website.

Commission: 15%; foreign, 25%

WHEELHOUSE LITERARY GROUP

Nashville, Tenn.
www.wheelhouseliterarygroup.com

Agent: Jonathan Clements

Agency: Established in 2010 after Jonathan worked five years with authors and brands for another agency. He has worked with dozens of influential writers and brands within the entertainment and publishing worlds over the years, many culminating in New York Times list best-selling books, feature films, documentaries, and television series.

Types: commercial and literary fiction in the general areas of inspirational, historical, contemporary, military, as well as biography/memoir, sports, political, current events, and pop culture nonfiction--all with a values friendly approach

New clients: Open to new clients. Email through the website form, following the requirements on the site. Responds within eight weeks if interested in more information.

WILLIAM K. JENSEN LITERARY AGENCY

119 Bampton Ct., Eugene, OR 97404 | 541-688-1612
queries@wkjagency.com | *www.wkjagency.com*

Agent: William K. Jensen

Agency: Established in 2005. Recognized in the industry. Represents thirty-eight clients.

Types: adult fiction (no science fiction or fantasy), nonfiction for all ages, picture books, gift books, crossover books

New clients: Open to unpublished authors and new clients. Contact by email only. See the website for complete query details. No attachments. Accepts simultaneous submissions. If no response in four weeks, assume he is not interested.

Commission: 15%

Fees: none

WINTERS & KING, INC.

2448 E. 81st St., Ste. 5900, Tulsa, OK 74137-4259 | 918-494-6868
dboyd@wintersking.com
wintersking.com/practice-areas/publishing-agent-services

Agent: Thomas J. Winters

Agency: Established in 1983. Represents more than 100 clients. Recognized in the industry. Part of a law firm.

Types: adult religious/inspirational novels and nonfiction for all ages, gift books, e-books, crossover, general-market with underlying Christian themes

New clients: Rarely open to unpublished authors; open to qualified new clients with a significant sales history and platform. Contact by phone, mail (c/o Debby Boyd), or online form. Submit bio and proposal or outline with at least three chatper summaries; prefers full manuscript with description of platform available to help in promotion of the book

Commission: 15%; foreign, 15%

Fees: none

Tips: Unsolicited proposals and manuscripts will not be acknowledged, considered, or returned. Solicited proposals, outlines, samples, and manuscripts that are not in proper format will not be reviewed or considered for representation.

WOLGEMUTH & ASSOCIATES

8600 Crestgate Cir., Orlando, FL 32819 | 407-909-9445
info@wolgemuthandassociates.com | *www.wolgemuthandassociates.com*

Agents: Robert Wolgemuth, Andrew D. Wolgemuth, Erik S. Wolgemuth, Austin Wilson

Agency: Well-recognized in the industry. Established in 1992. Member of Association of Authors' Representatives.

Types: teen/YA and adult nonfiction

New clients: Only authors with at least one traditionally published book or by referral from current client or close contact. Query by email. Accepts simultaneous submissions.

Commission: 15%

Fees: none

Tips: We work with authors who are either bestselling authors or newly bestselling authors. Consequently, we want to represent clients with broad market appeal. Please refer to our website for submission guidelines.

WORDSERVE LITERARY GROUP

7061 S. University Blvd., Centennial, CO 80122 | 303-471-6675
admin@wordserveliterary.com (put Query in subject line)
www.wordserveliterary.com

Agents: Greg Johnson, *greg@wordserveliterary.com*; Sarah Freese, *sarah@wordserveliterary.com*; Nick Harrison, *nick@wordserveliterary.com*

Agency: Established in 2003. Represents more than 150 clients. WordServe is also partnered with *www.faithhappenings.com* to promote their authors and books in all of their ministry and PR endeavors.

Types: novels and nonfiction for all ages, gift books, picture books, crossover, general market (memoir, military, self-help, adult fiction), e-books. No screenplays or poetry. Accepts simultaneous submissions.

New clients: Greg: adds only a few clients a year; Sarah: open to new clients. Nick: open to new clients. Contact by email. Responds in four to eight weeks.

Commission: 15%; foreign, 20-30%, depending on how many coagents are involved

Fees: none

Tips: With nonfiction, first impressions count. Make sure your proposal answers all the questions on competition, outline, audience, felt need, etc. For fiction, make sure your novel is completed before you submit a proposal with synopsis and five chapters.

WORDWISE MEDIA SERVICES

4083 Avenue L, Ste. 255, Lancaster, CA 93536 | 661-382-8083
get.wisewords@gmail.com (for general inquiries only, not submissions)
www.wordwisemedia.com/agency

Agents: Steven Hutson, David Fessenden

Agency: Recognized in the industry. Established in 2011. Represents sixty clients, half with religious books.

Types: novels and nonfiction for all ages, no poetry or picture books

New clients: New clients welcome. Prefers referrals or conference meets. For all submissions, use the query form on the website. For other inquiries, phone or email is OK. Accepts simultaneous submissions. Responds in thirty days; OK to nudge after then.

Commission: 15%; foreign, 20% if shared with another agent

Fees: maybe for printing and postage at cost for a manuscript mailed to a publisher

Tips: For all submissions, please follow the instructions on the website carefully. Specify the agent's name in the email subject line if you have a preference.

WRITERS HOUSE

21 W. 26th St., New York, NY 10010 | 212-685-2400
www.writershouse.com

Agents: Dan Lazer, *dlazar@writershouse.com*; Rebecca Sherman, *rebeccasubmissions@writershouse.com*; more listed on website

Agency: Founded 1974. General agency that handles some religious books.

Types: trade books of all types, fiction and nonfiction, children's books; film and TV rights; no screenplays, teleplays, or software

New clients: Contact by email or mail with a SASE. Queries generally responded to within six weeks and manuscripts within eight weeks.

YATES & YATES

1551 N. Tustin Ave., Ste. 710, Santa Ana, CA 92705 | 714-480-4000
email@yates2.com | *www.yates2.com*

> **Agents:** Sealy Yates, Matt Yates, Curtis Yates, Mike Salisbury
>
> **Agency:** Established in 1989. Recognized in the industry. Represents more than fifty clients. Our holistic approach combines agency representation, expert legal advice, marketing guidance, career coaching, creative counseling, and business-management consulting. We work with clients to focus their efforts, hone and sharpen their messages, obtain broad distribution, increase their influence, and build a lasting and successful career. In short, we help our clients make their ideas matter.
>
> **Types:** adult nonfiction
>
> **New clients:** No unpublished authors. Contact by email.
>
> **Commission:** negotiable

ZACHARY SHUSTER HARMSWORTH LITERARY AND ENTERTAINMENT AGENCY

535 Boylston St., Ste. 1103, Boston, MA 02116 | 617-262-2400
mchappell@zshliterary.com | *www.zshliterary.com*

> **Agent:** Mary Beth Chappell
>
> **Agency:** General agency that handles some religious books. Recognized in the industry. Represents fifteen to thirty religious clients.
>
> **Types:** adult religious/inspirational novels and nonfiction, crossover, general market
>
> **New clients:** Open to unpublished authors and new clients. Contact by email through the online form only. No unsolicited submissions.
>
> **Commission:** 15%; foreign and film, 20%
>
> **Fees:** office expenses only
>
> **Tip:** We are looking for inspirational fiction; Christian nonfiction, especially books that focus on the emerging/emergent church or would appeal to readers in their 20s and 30s; and teen/YA series.

17

WRITERS CONFERENCES AND SEMINARS

ARIZONA

AMERICAN CHRISTIAN WRITERS MENTORING RETREAT
Phoenix, AZ | September 8-9 | *acwriters.com*
> **Contact director:** Reg A. Forder, PO Box 110390, Nashville TN 37222; 800-21-WRITE; *ACWriters@aol.com*
> **Description:** Two-day intensive, hands-on work on a manuscript submitted in advance. Teachers include Dr. Dennis E. Hensley, Lin Johnson, and Jim Watkins. Attendance 6-30.

CALIFORNIA

LEVEL 10 CHRISTIAN CONFERENCE AND WORKSHOPS
Anaheim, CA | April 21-22 | *www.level10christian.com*
> **Contact director:** Antonio L. Crawford, PO Box 1458, National City, CA 91951; 619-791-5810; *ncwcsd@yahoo.com*
> **Description:** Serving infopreneurs, entrepreneurs, and experts wanting to build a book, business, and brand around their message. Special track for advanced writers. Editors and agents on faculty. Full and partial scholarships. Attendance: 200.

MOUNT HERMON CHRISTIAN WRITERS CONFERENCE
Mount Hermon, CA (near Santa Cruz) | April 7-11 (pre-conference clinics April 5-7) | *writers.mounthermon.org*
> **Contact director:** Kathy Ide, *KathyIde@MountHermon.org*
> **Description:** Editors, agents, and publishers on faculty. Speakers: Mark Batterson and Stacy Hawkins Adams. Special track for advanced writers. Partial scholarships. Attendance: 250-300.
> **Contest:** Six types of awards presented at the conference.

ORANGE COUNTY CHRISTIAN WRITERS CONFERENCE

Anaheim, CA | April 21-22 | *www.occwc.com*

> **Contact director:** Antonio L. Crawford, PO Box 1458, National City, CA 91951; 619-791-5810; *ncwcsd@yahoo.com*
>
> **Description:** Tracks for advanced writers and teens. Speakers: Kathi Macias and Mark Mikelat. Editors and agents on faculty. Full and partial scholarships. Attendance: 200.

SAN DIEGO CHRISTIAN WRITERS' GUILD FALL CONFERENCE

San Diego, CA | October | *www.sandiegocwg.org*

> **Contact director:** Jennie Gillespie, PO Box 270403, San Diego CA 92198; 760-294-3269; *info@sandiegocwg.org*
>
> **Description:** Editors and agents on faculty. Offers an advanced track. Offers partial scholarships. Attendance: 200.
>
> **Contest:** Unpublished manuscript contest.

SANTA BARBARA CHRISTIAN WRITERS CONFERENCE

Santa Barbara, CA; October | *www.cwgsb.com*

> **Contact director:** Opal Mae Dailey, PO Box 40860, Santa Barbara, CA 93140; 805-252-9822; *opalmaedailey@aol.com*
>
> **Description:** Special 20-year anniversary celebration. Full and partial scholarships. Attendance: 75.

SOCAL CHRISTIAN WRITERS' CONFERENCE

La Mirada, CA | June 22-24 | *www.SoCalCWC.com*

> **Contact director:** Kathy Ide, *KathyIde@SoCalCWC.com*
>
> **Description:** Editors and agents on faculty. Special tracks for advanced writers and teens. Full and partial scholarships. New conference. Attendance: estimate 200.

WEST COAST CHRISTIAN WRITERS CONFERENCE

Pleasanton, CA | February 17-18 | *www.westcoastchristianwriters.com*

> **Contact director:** Susy Flory, 1660 Freisman Rd., Pleasanton, CA 94588; 510-828-5360; *info@westcoastchristianwriters.com*
>
> **Description:** Editors, agents, and publishers on faculty. Speakers include Tosca Lee and Michele Cushatt. Partial scholarships. Attendance: 175.
>
> **Contest:** Story contest with prizes.

WRITER'S SYMPOSIUM BY THE SEA

San Diego, CA | Feb. 21-23 | *www.pointloma.edu/writers*

Contact director: Dean Nelson, 3900 Lomaland Dr., San Diego, CA 92106; 619-849-2592; *deannelson@pointloma.edu*

Description: Speakers include Shauna Niequist. Attendance: 1,000.

COLORADO

COLORADO CHRISTIAN WRITERS CONFERENCE

Estes Park, CO | May 17-20 | *colorado.writehisanswer.com*

Contact director: Marlene Bagnull, 951 Anders Rd., Lansdale, PA 19446; 484-991-8581; *mbagnull@aol.com*

Description: Workshops and continuing sessions for writers at all levels; special track for teens. Editors, agents, and publishers on faculty. Partial scholarships. Attendance: 210.

Contest: For registered conferees. Entries based on the conference theme of "Write His Answer" from Habakkuk 2:2. Prose (maximum 500 words) or poetry by published and not-yet-published authors. The winner in each of the four categories receives 50% off the registration fee the following year. Entry fee $10.

COLORADO WRITING RETREAT

Buena Vista, CO; September 14-17 | *www.coloradowritingretreat.com*

Contact director: Shelley Hitz, PO Box 6542, Colorado Springs, CO 80934; 719-445-6558; *shelley@shelleyhitz.com*

Description: Speaker: Shelley Hitz. Attendance: 5.

WRITE IN THE SPRINGS
(FORMERLY PEAK WRITING CONFERENCE)

Colorado Springs, CO | April 1 | *acfwcs.acfwcolorado.com*

Contact director: Mary Agius, PO Box 7862, Colorado Springs, CO 80933; 719-686-7761; acfwcs.president@acfwcolorado.com

Description: Speaker: Cara Putman. Attendance: 40.

WRITERS ON THE ROCK

Denver, CO | May | *www.RedLetterBelievers.com*

Contact director: David Rupert, 14473 W. 3rd, Golden, CO 80401; 720-237-7487; *david@davidrupert.net*

Description: Editors, agents, and publishers on faculty. Special track for teens. Attendance: 250.

CONNECTICUT

reNEW RETREAT FOR NEW ENGLAND WRITING

West Hartford, CT | October 6-8 | *www.reNEWwriting.com*

> **Contact director:** Lucinda Secrest McDowell, reNEW Writing, P.O Box 290707, Wethersfield, CT 06129; *info@reNEWwriting.com*
>
> **Description:** Speakers include Carol Kent, Christa Parrish, Tessa Afshar, Lori Roeleveld, and Christa Hutchins. Special track on speaking. Attendance: 75.

DELAWARE

VINE & VESSELS CHRISTIAN WRITERS CONFERENCE

Georgetown, DE | October 21 | *www.vineandvessels.com*

> **Contact directors:** Joyce Sessoms and Betty Ricks-Jarman, 20684 State Forest Rd., Georgetown, DE 19947; 302-382-9904 (Joyce), 302-448-5939 (Betty); *crownjewel777@comcast.net*
>
> **Description:** Editors and publishers on faculty. Partial scholarships. Attendance: 100.

FLORIDA

ACFW CENTRAL FLORIDA SPRING SEMINAR

Orlando, FL | April 15 | *www.cfacfw.org*

> **Contact director:** Kristen Stieffe, 1655 Peel Ave., Orlando, FL 32806; 407-928-7801; *treasurer@cfacfw.com*
>
> **Description:** Full-day seminar; changes yearly. Attendance: 20.

AMERICAN CHRISTIAN WRITERS MENTORING RETREAT

Orlando, FL | November 17-18 | *acwriters.com*

> **Contact director:** Reg A. Forder, PO Box 110390, Nashville TN 37222; 800-21-WRITE; *ACWriters@aol.com*
>
> **Description:** Two-day intensive, hands-on work on a manuscript submitted in advance. Teachers include Dr. Dennis E. Hensley, Lin Johnson, and Jim Watkins. Attendance 6-30.

THE DEEP THINKERS RETREAT 2017

Miramar Beach, FL | February 24-27 | *learnhowtowriteanovel.com/product/deep-thinkers-retreat-2017/#lodging*

Contact director: Susan May Warren, 15100 Marion Ln. W., Minnetonka, MN 55345; *admin@mybooktherapy.com*

Description: Five days of feedback and one-on-one mentoring for intermediate and aspiring novelists. Intense, yes. Focused, for sure. Limited to only writers who want to dig into their stories and take them from good to great. This retreat will help you realize your story and give you the tools to write it. Teachers: Susan May Warren and Rachel Hauck. Attendance: 16.

FLORIDA CHRISTIAN WRITERS CONFERENCE

Lake Yale, FL (Leesburg) | February 22-26 | *www.FloridaCWC.net*

Contact directors: Eva Marie Everson and Mark Hancock, 504 Spoonbill Ct., Winter Springs, FL 32708; 407-615-4112; *FloridaCWC@aol.com*

Description: Editors, agents, and publishers on faculty. Keynote speaker: Dr. Dennis E. Hensley. Special track for teens. Full and partial scholarships. Attendance: 250.

Contest: Thirteen categories (articles, Bible studies, children's early readers, children's picture books, devotionals, flash fiction, middle-grade books, nonfiction books, six categories of fiction, poetry, short story, YA fiction, YA nonfiction).

GEORGIA

AMERICAN CHRISTIAN WRITERS MENTORING RETREAT

Atlanta, GA | July 7-8 | acwriters.com

Contact director: Reg A. Forder, PO Box 110390, Nashville TN 37222; 800-21-WRITE; *ACWriters@aol.com*

Description: Two-day intensive, hands-on work on a manuscript submitted in advance. Teachers include Dr. Dennis E. Hensley, Lin Johnson, and Jim Watkins. Attendance 6-30.

ATLANTA CHRISTIAN WRITERS CONFERENCE

Marietta, GA | August 17-19 | *www.ChristianAuthorsGuild.org*

Contact director: Cynthia L. Simmons, 322 Homestead Cir., Kennesaw, GA 30144; 770-926-8627; *cynthialsimmons@gmail.com*

Description: Affordable two-day conference with a variety of sessions and speakers. Multiple classes offered in several writing genres. Editors, agents, and publishers on faculty. Partial scholarships. Attendance: 75.

PENCON

Atlanta, GA | May 4-6 | *thechristianpen.com/pencon*

Contact director: Jenne Acevedo, *PENCON@TheChristianPEN.com*

Description: PENCON is the only conference for editors in the Christian market. Editors and publishers on faculty. Speakers include Cecil Murphey. Full and partial scholarships. Attendance: 75. Note: This conference changes location every year.

POWER OF WORDS CHILDREN'S WRITERS CONFERENCE

Atlanta, GA | September 15-20 | *www.childrenswritersconference.com*

Contact director: Sally Apokedak, 678-744-7745, *sally@sally-apokedak.com*

Description: Editors and agents on faculty. Speakers include Gary Schmidt and Kirby Larson. Although this is not specifically a Christian conference, a Christian publisher will be represented (Zondervan), along with several general-market editors. Full and partial scholarships. Attendance: 75.

ILLINOIS

EVANGELICAL PRESS ASSOCIATION ANNUAL CONVENTION

Lombard, IL | April 9-11 | *www.evangelicalpress.com/convention*

Contact director: Lamar Keener, Executive Director, PO Box 20198, El Cajon, CA 92021; 888-311-1731; *director@evangelicalpress.com*

Description: Primarily focused on periodical editors but has a writing track. Editors on faculty. Attendance: 200. Note: This conference changes location every year.

Contest: Freelance writers may submit articles and/or blog entries into contest, which requires EPA membership.

KARITOS ART AND WORSHIP CONFERENCE

Naperville, IL | July 13-15 | *karitos.org*

Contact director: Bob Hay, 2650 Brookwood Way, Unit 217, Rolling Meadows, IL 60008; 847-925-8018; *roberthay@karitos.com*

Description: The mission of Karitos is to provide biblically based artistic and technical growth experiences to Christian artists, including writers. Attendance: 150.

WRITE-TO-PUBLISH CONFERENCE

Wheaton, IL (Chicago area) | June 14-17 | *www.writetopublish.com*

Contact director: Lin Johnson, 9118 W. Elmwood Dr., Ste. 1G, Niles, IL 60714-5820; 847-296-3964; *lin@writetopublish.com*

Description: Six to eight continuing tracks and more than thirty electives for beginning through advanced career writers. Editors, agents, and publishers on faculty. Plenary speaker: Carol Kent. Attendance: 175.

Contest: Best New Writer and Writer of the Year awards, both for alumni who attend this year.

INDIANA

TAYLOR UNIVERSITY'S PROFESSIONAL WRITING CONFERENCE

Upland, IN | August 4-5
taylorsprofessionalwritersconference.wordpress.com

Contact director: Linda Taylor, 236 W. Reade Ave., Upland, IN 46989; 765-998-5591; *taylorpwrconference@gmail.com*

Description: Editors and agents on faculty. Keynote speaker: Jerry B. Jenkins. Tracks for advanced writers and teens. Attendance: 150.

KANSAS

CALLED TO WRITE

Pittsburg, KS | March 30—April 1 | *calledtowriteconference.wordpress.com*

Contact director: Julane Hiebert, 350 Lake Rd., Council Grove, KS 666846; 785-561-0217; *julhiebert@gmail.com*

Description: Speakers: Kathy Ide and Twila Belk. Full and partial scholarships. Attendance: 70-75.

Contest: For fiction, nonfiction, poetry, devotionals, children's fiction, and children's nonfiction.

KENTUCKY

KENTUCKY CHRISTIAN WRITERS CONFERENCE

Elizabethtown, KY | June 23-24 | *www.kychristianwriters.com*

Contact director: Lisa Greer, PO Box 2719, Elizabethtown, KY 42702; 502-488-0230, 502-330-2773; email through website

Description: Keynote speaker: Twila Belk. Special tracks for fiction, nonfiction, and professional (business side of writing). Editors and publishers on faculty. Full scholarships. Attendance: 70-100.

MICHIGAN

AMERICAN CHRISTIAN WRITERS MENTORING RETREAT

Grand Rapids, MI | June 9-10 | *acwriters.com*

Contact director: Reg A. Forder, PO Box 110390, Nashville TN 37222; 800-21-WRITE; *ACWriters@aol.com*

Description: Two-day intensive, hands-on work on a manuscript submitted in advance. Teachers include Dr. Dennis E. Hensley, Lin Johnson, and Jim Watkins. Attendance 6-30.

BREATHE CHRISTIAN WRITERS CONFERENCE

Grand Rapids, MI | October 6-7 | *www.breatheconference.com*

Contact director: Ann Byle, 1765 3 Mile Rd. N.E., Grand Rapids, MI 49515; 616-389-4436; *breathewritersconference@gmail.com*

Description: A relaxed, information-filled, community-building conference for new and advanced writers of fiction, nonfiction, and poetry. We offer 36 breakout sessions, one-on-ones, two plenary workshops, and two keynote events. Speaker: Leslie Leyland Fields. Editors, agents, and publishers on faculty. Offers full and partial scholarships. Attendance: 140.

MARANATHA CHRISTIAN WRITERS' CONFERENCE

Muskegon, MI | September | *www.maranathachristianwriters.com*

Contact administrator: Bonnie Emmorey, *Bonnie@maranathachristianwriters.com*

Description: Agents, editors, and publishers on faculty. Scholarships available. Attendance: 200 maximum.

Contest: Leona Hertel Awards Contests open only to conferees. Details on the website.

WRITING FOR YOUR LIFE

Holland, MI | May 15-17 | *writingforyourlife.com/conferences*

Contact director: Brian Allain, 8 Apache Trl., Freehold, NJ 07728; 732-637-9399; *brian@writingforyourlife.com*

Description: Editors, agents, and publishers on faculty. Speakers include Barbara Brown Taylor and Rachel Held Evans. Special track for advanced writers. Attendance: 250.

MINNESOTA

AMERICAN CHRISTIAN WRITERS MENTORING RETREAT

Minneapolis, MN | August 4-5 | *acwriters.com*

Contact director: Reg A. Forder, PO Box 110390, Nashville TN 37222; 800-21-WRITE; *ACWriters@aol.com*

Description: Two-day intensive, hands-on work on a manuscript submitted in advance. Teachers include Dr. Dennis E. Hensley, Lin Johnson, and Jim Watkins. Attendance 6-30.

MINNESOTA CHRISTIAN WRITERS GUILD SPRING SEMINAR

Minneapolis, MN | March 11 | *www.mnchristianwriters.com/seminar*

Contact director: Joyce K. Ellis, 11223 Providence Ln., Eden Prairie, MN 55344; 763-443-5648

Description: This annual seminar offers something for everyone— from novice to pro, from fiction writers to nonfiction writers. Speaker: Bob Hostetler, who will focus on "Writing Masterfully." Attendance: 30-40.

MISSOURI

HEART OF AMERICA CHRISTIAN WRITERS NETWORK

Kansas City, MO | October 19-21 | *www.hacwn.org*

Contact director: Jeanette Littleton, 3706 N.E. Shady Lane Dr., Gladstone, MO 64119; 816-459-8016; *hacwn@earthlink.net*

Description: Editors, agents, and publishers on faculty. Editors tell what they're looking for; first pages. Attendance: 120.

Contests in most genres with $3 entry fee.

NEBRASKA

WORDSOWERS CHRISTIAN WRITERS CONFERENCE

Omaha, NE | April 28-29 | *www.wordsowers.com*

Contact director: Kat Crawford, 927 Homer St., Omaha, NE 68107; 402-932-4817; *kat@wordsowers.com*

Description: Twenty workshops from beginning to advanced, poetry and music composition. Editors, publishers, and agents on faculty and via Skype. Speaker: Tosca Lee. Special tracks for advanced writers and teens. Offers full and partial scholarships. Attendance: 85-100.

NEVADA

CHRISTIAN COMMUNICATORS CONFERENCE
Lake Tahoe, NV | August 30—September 3
www.ChristianCommunicators.com
> **Contact** codirectors: Tammy Whitehurst, Sherry Poundstone, Lori Boruff; email through the website
> **Description:** The goal of this conference is to educate, validate, and launch women in their speaking ministries and help speakers expand their ministries with writing. Attendance: limited to 50.

REALM MAKERS
Reno, NV | July 2017 | *www.realmmakers.com*
> **Contact director:** Becky Minor, 939 N. Washington St., Pottstown, PA 19464; info@faithandfantasyalliance.com
> **Description:** Realm Makers is for writers of faith who create science fiction, fantasy, and related subgenres. Full and partial scholarships available, based on merit and needs. Agents and editors in attendance from both CBA and general markets. Attendance: 200+. Note: This conference changes location every year.
> **Contest:** Contests for published books and book covers with cash awards.

NEW MEXICO

CLASS WRITERS CONTREAT
Albuquerque, NM | Fall | *www.classeminars.org*
> **Contact director:** Judy McLaughlin, Classeminars, PO Box 36551, Albuquerque, NM 87176; 702-882-0638; *classcontreat@gmail.com*
> **Description:** Faculty includes publishers. Full scholarships. Attendance: 50.

THE CLASSEMINAR
Albuquerque, NM | *www.classeminars.org/events.html*
> **Contact director:** Gerry Wakeland, Classeminars, PO Box 36551, Albuquerque NM 87176; 702-882-0638; *classeminars@gmail.com*
> **Description:** For anyone who wants to improve his or her communication skills for the spoken or written word, for professional or personal reasons. Attendance: 75-100.

NORTH CAROLINA

ASHEVILLE CHRISTIAN WRITERS CONFERENCE

Asheville, NC | February 17-19 | *www.ashevillechristianwritersconference.com*

Contact director: Cindy Sproles, PO Box 6494, Kingsport, TN 37663; *cindybootcamp@gmail.com*

Description: Editors and agents on faculty. Speakers: Vonda Skelton, Michelle Medlock Adams, and Les Stobbe. Track for advanced writers. Full and partial scholarships. Attendance: 120 maximum.

Contest: Badge of Honor Contest, where we look at new manuscripts. Winner's book goes before the publications board of Lighthouse Publishing of the Carolinas for a possible book contract.

BLUE RIDGE MOUNTAINS CHRISTIAN WRITERS CONFERENCE

Black Mountain, NC | May 21-25 | *BlueRidgeConference.com*

Contact directors: Edie Melson and DiAnn Mills, 1 Ridgecrest Dr., Black Mountain, NC 28770; 800-588-7222; *Edie@ediemelson.com, DiAnn@DiAnnMills.com*

Description: Editors, agents, and publishers on faculty. Speakers include Todd Starnes, Tosca Lee, Davis Bunn, and Bob Hostetler. Special track for advanced writers; various practicums as well. Partial scholarships. Attendance: 450+.

Contests: Selah Awards for published authors, Foundations Awards for unpublished attendees, Directors' Choice for former attendees.

SHE SPEAKS

Concord, NC | July 20-22 | *shespeaksconference.com*

Contact director: Lisa Allen, 630 Team Rd. #100, Matthews, NC 28105; 704-849-2270; *shespeaks@Proverbs31.org*

Description: Speaking and writing tracks. Speakers include Lysa TerKeurst. Editors and agents on faculty. Attendance: 700.

OHIO

NORTHWEST OHIO CHRISTIAN WRITERS

Holland, OH | October 21 | *nwocw.org*

Contact director: Denise Shumway, 418 Danesmoor Rd., Holland, OH 43528; 419-345-6271; *denise.shumway@gmail.com*

Description: Attendance: 35.

OREGON

OREGON CHRISTIAN WRITERS FALL CONFERENCE

Tualatin, OR (Portland area) | October 21 | *www.oregonchristianwriters.org*

> **Contact:** Sue Miholer, Business Manager, 1075 Willow Lake Rd. N., Keizer, OR 97303; 503-393-3356; *business@oregonchristianwriters.org*
>
> **Description:** Speaker: Jeff Gerke. Attendance: 125.

OREGON CHRISTIAN WRITERS SPRING CONFERENCE

Eugene, OR | May 20 | *www.oregonchristianwriters.org*

> **Contact:** Sue Miholer, Business Manager, 1075 Willow Lake Rd. N., Keizer, OR 97303; 503-393-3356; *business@oregonchristianwriters.org*
>
> **Description:** Speakers: Dan Kline and Kay Marshall Strom. Attendance: 125.

OREGON CHRISTIAN WRITERS SUMMER COACHING CONFERENCE

Portland, OR | August 15–18 | *www.oregonchristianwriters.org*

> **Contact director:** Lindy Jacobs, 1075 Willow Lake Rd. N., Keizer, OR 97303; 503-393-3356; *summconf@oregonchristianwriters.org*
>
> **Description:** Nine coaching classes for advanced, intermediate, and beginning writers. Speakers: Frank Peretti and Tessa Afshar. Editors and agents on faculty. Partial scholarships to members only. Attendance: 225.
>
> **Contest:** The winners of the Cascade Writing Contest are awarded during the conference. This is a multigenre contest open to published and unpublished work and runs February 14–March 31.

OREGON CHRISTIAN WRITERS WINTER CONFERENCE

Salem, OR | February 25 | *www.oregonchristianwriters.org*

> **Contact:** Sue Miholer, Business Manager, 1075 Willow Lake Rd. N., Keizer, OR 97303; 503-393-3356; *business@oregonchristianwriters.org*
>
> **Description:** Speaker: James L. Rupert. Attendance: 125.

PENNSYLVANIA

GREATER PHILADELPHIA CHRISTIAN WRITERS CONFERENCE

Langhorne, PA; July 26-29 | *philadelphia.writehisanswer.com*

> **Contact director:** Marlene Bagnull, 951 Anders Rd., Lansdale, PA 19446; 484-991-8581; *mbagnull@aol.com*
>
> **Description:** Workshops and continuing sessions for writers at all levels; special track for teens. Editors, agents, and publishers on faculty. Partial scholarships. Attendance: 220.
>
> **Contest:** For registered conferees. Entries based on the conference theme of "Write His Answer" from Habakkuk 2:2. Prose (maximum 500 words) or poetry by published and not-yet-published authors. The winner in each of the four categories receives 50% off their registration fee the following year. Entry fee $10.

MONTROSE CHRISTIAN WRITERS CONFERENCE

Montrose, PA | July 16-21 | *www.montrosebible.org/OurEvents.aspx*

> **Contact director:** Marsha Hubler, 1833 Dock Hill Rd., Middleburg, PA 17842; 570-837-0002; *marshahubler@wildblue.net*
>
> **Description:** Editors and agents on faculty. Speakers: Torry Martin, Barbara Scott, B. J. Taylor, and Patti Souder. Special tracks for advanced writers and teens. Partial scholarships, including Shirley Brinkerhoff Memorial Scholarship, a $150 grant toward tuition, given to a writer who's not yet secured a book contract but is actively striving to hone the craft of writing. Attendance: 105.

ST. DAVIDS CHRISTIAN WRITERS' CONFERENCE

Grove City, PA | June 21-25 | *www.stdavidswriters.com*

> **Contact director:** Susan Lower, 717-372-3303, *inspireme@susanlower.com*
>
> **Description:** Editors and agents on faculty. Speakers: Michelle Medlock Adams, Eva Marie Everson, and Suzanne and Shawn Kuhn. Special track for advanced writers. Full and partial scholarships. Attendance: 60.
>
> **Contests:** Several writing contests available to attendees to enter. See detailed list on the website.

WRITER TO WRITER CONFERENCE

Hershey, PA | February 3-5 | *www.writertowriter.com*

> **Contact:** 800-868-4388; *service@munce.com*
>
> **Description:** Allows writers to go from "think to ink." Held in

conjunction with the Christian Product Expo conducted by the Munce Group, which serves independent Christian retailers, and cohosted by SuzyQ coaching service. Offers workshops in four areas: nonfiction, fiction, publishing, and marketing. Special student rate.

Contest: PUB Board, A Shark Tank-like experience; three conferees.

SOUTH CAROLINA

CAROLINA CHRISTIAN WRITERS CONFERENCE

Spartansburg, SC | March 10-11 | *www.fbs.org/writers*

> **Contact director:** Linda Gilden, 250 E. Main St., Spartanburg, SC 29306; 864-699-1756; *linda@lindagilden.com*
>
> **Description:** Editors, agents, and publishers on faculty. Speakers include Torry Martin. Full scholarships. Attendance: 100.

LEXINGTON WORD WEAVERS CHRISTIAN WRITERS' WORKSHOP

Lexington, SC | January 21 | *www.lexingtonwordweavers.com*

> **Contact director:** Jean Wilund, 1015 Corley Mill Rd., Lexington, SC 29072; 803-422-1410; *info@lexingtonwordweavers.com*
>
> **Description:** Special tracks for beginning and advanced writers. Speaker: Eva Marie Everson. Full and partial scholarships. Attendance: 60.

WRITE2IGNITE CONFERENCE FOR CHRISTIAN WRITERS OF LITERATURE FOR CHILDREN AND YOUNG ADULTS

Tigerville, SC | March 24-25 | *write2ignite.com*

> **Contact director:** Deborah S. DeCiantis, 864-977-7731, info. *write2ignite@gmail.com*
>
> **Description:** Focus is on writing for children and youth. Special track for teens. Partial and full scholarships. Attendance: 100

TENNESSEE

AMERICAN CHRISTIAN WRITERS MENTORING RETREAT

Nashville, TN | April 21-22 and October 13-14 | *acwriters.com*

> **Contact director:** Reg A. Forder, PO Box 110390, Nashville TN 37222; 800-21-WRITE; *ACWriters@aol.com*
>
> **Description:** Two-day intensive, hands-on work on a manuscript

submitted in advance. Teachers include Dr. Dennis E. Hensley, Lin Johnson, and Jim Watkins. Attendance 6-30.

MID-SOUTH CHRISTIAN WRITERS CONFERENCE

Memphis, TN | March 18 (meet-and-greet event March 17)
MidSouthChristianWriters.com

> **Contact director:** April Carpenter, PO Box 236, Nesbit, MS 38651; 901-378-0504; *midsouthchristianwriters@gmail.com*
>
> **Description:** Editors on faculty. Keynote speaker: James Watkins. Partial scholarships. Attendance: 75-100.

WRITING FOR YOUR LIFE

Nashville, TN | July | *writingforyourlife.com/conferences*

> **Contact director:** Brian Allain, 8 Apache Trl., Freehold, NJ 07728; 732-637-9399; *brian@writingforyourlife.com*
>
> **Description:** Editors and agents on faculty. Speakers include Barbara Brown Taylor and Rachel Held Evans. Special track for advanced writers. Attendance: 250.

TEXAS

AMERICAN CHRISTIAN FICTION WRITERS (ACFW) CONFERENCE

Grapevine, TX (Dallas area) | September 21-24 | *www.acfw.com/conference*

> **Contact director:** Robin Miller, PO Box 101066, Palm Bay, FL 32910-1066; *director@acfw.com*
>
> **Description:** Continuing education sessions and workshop electives specifically geared for five levels of fiction writing experience from beginner to advanced. Track for advanced writers. Editors and agents in attendance. Full scholarships. Attendance: 650.
>
> **Contest:** The Genesis Contest is for unpublished writers whose Christian fiction manuscript is completed. The Carol Awards honor the best of Christian fiction from the previous calendar year.

TEXAS CHRISTIAN WRITERS CONFERENCE

Houston, TX | August 5 | *www.centralhoustoniwa.com*

> **Contact director:** Martha Rogers, 6038 Greenmont, Houston, TX 77092; 713-686-7209; *marthalrogers@sbcglobal.net*
>
> **Description:** Editors on faculty. Speakers include Janice Thompson, Kathleen Y'Barbo, and DiAnn Mills. Attendance: 60.
>
> **Contests:** Inspirational Writers Alive! Open Writing Competition.

WRITE NOW WORKSHOPS AND RETREATS

Granbury, TX | *www.WriteNow-Workshop.com*

> **Contact director:** Dena Dyer, 308 Bridge St., Granbury, TX 76048;
> 817-537-2715; *workshopswritenow@gmail.com*
> **Description:** Full and partial scholarships. Attendance: 25-75.

VIRGINIA

CCW SELF PUBLISHING CONFERENCE

Clifton, VA | January 28 | *capitalchristianwriters.org*

> **Contact director:** Sarah Hamaker, 12925 Braddock Rd., Clifton, VA
> 20124; 703-803-9447; *ccwriters@gmail.com*
> **Description:** Self-publishing information. Speaker: Hallee Bridgeman,
> indie author, on "Generating the Work." Attendance: 20-30.

WASHINGTON

NORTHWEST CHRISTIAN WRITERS RENEWAL

Bellevue, WA | May 5–6 | *nwchristianwriters.org*

> **Contact director:** Diana Savage, PO Box 2706, Woodinville, WA
> 98072; 425-298-3699 (text only); *renewal@nwchristianwriters.org*
> **Description:** Editors and agents on faculty. Keynote speaker: Bill
> Myers. Full scholarships. Attendance: 150.

WISCONSIN

GREEN LAKE CHRISTIAN WRITERS' CONFERENCE

Green Lake, WI | August 6-10 | *www.glcc.org/adults*

> **Contact director:** Kris Wood, Green Lake Conference Center,
> W2511 County Rd. 23, Green Lake, WI 54941; 920-420-6321;
> *KrisWood@glcc.org*
> **Description:** Editors on faculty. Partial scholarships. Attendance: 40.

CANADA

InSCRIBE CHRISTIAN WRITERS' FELLOWSHIP FALL CONFERENCE

Edmonton, AB | September 21-23 | *inscribe.org/fall-conference*

> **Contact director:** Ruth L. Snyder, PO Box 99509, Edmonton, AB
> T5B 0E1, Canada; 780-646-3068; *sun.beam3@yahoo.com*

Description: Editors on faculty. Speakers include Shelley Hitz. Special track for advanced writers. Partial scholarships. Attendance: 100.

Contest: The Fall Contest is our largest writing event, offering a variety of categories in numerous genres. Details at *inscribe.org/contests*.

WRITE CANADA

Toronto, ON | June | *thewordguild.com/write-canada*

Contact director: Andi M. Harris, The Word Guild, King George Rd., Ste. 226, 245, Brantford, ON N3R 7N7, Canada; *writecanada@thewordguild.com*.

Description: Hosted by The Word Guild, an association of Canadian writers and editors who are Christian. Offers a career track. Editors and agents on faculty. Scholarships available. Attendance: 250.

ONLINE

SOCIAL MEDIA MARKETING FOR SPIRITUAL WRITERS

January | *writingforyourlife.com/conferences*

Contact director: Brian Allain, 8 Apache Trl., Freehold, NJ 07728; 732-637-9399; brian@writingforyourlife.com

Description: Attendance: 200.

WRITING FOR YOUR LIFE ONLINE CONFERENCE

March | *writingforyourlife.com/conferences*

Contact director: Brian Allain, 8 Apache Trl., Freehold, NJ 07728; 732-637-9399; *brian@writingforyourlife.com*

Description: Editors and agents on faculty. Attendance: 200.

CONFERENCES THAT CHANGE LOCATIONS

The following conferences change locations every year but are listed with their 2017 locations:

AMERICAN CHRISTIAN FICTION WRITERS CONFERENCE

EVANGELICAL PRESS ASSOCIATION ANNUAL CONVENTION

PENCON

REALM MAKERS

18

WRITERS GROUPS

In addition to the groups listed here, check these websites for other groups in your area:

American Christian Writers chapters: *www.acwriters.com*
American Christian Fiction Writers chapters: *www.acfw.com*
Word Weavers International chapters: *www.Word-Weavers.com*

ARIZONA

CHANDLER WRITERS' GROUP

chandlerwriters.wordpress.com

> **Meetings:** member's home, near Dobson and Queen Creek, Chandler, AZ; second Friday of the month, 9:00-11:30 a.m.
> **Contact:** Jenne Acevedo, 480-510-0419, *jenneacevedo@cox.net*
> **Members:** 12

CHRISTIAN WRITERS OF THE WEST

www.christianwritersofthewest.com

> **Meetings:** Denny's, 4400 N. Scottsdale Rd., Scottsdale, AZ; last Saturday of the month, 1:00-3:00 p.m.
> **Contact:** Brenda Poulos, 480-628-6728, *mtnst14@gmail.com*
> **Members:** 30
> **Affiliation:** American Christian Fiction Writers

FOUNTAIN HILLS CHRISTIAN WRITERS' GROUP

> **Meetings:** Fountain Hills Presbyterian Church, 13001 N. Fountain Hills Blvd., Fountain Hills, AZ; second Friday of the month, 9:00 a.m. to noon
> **Contact:** Jewell Johnson, 480-836-8968, *tykeJ@juno.com*
> **Members:** 8-12

NORTHERN ARIZONA WORD WEAVERS
www.Word-Weavers.com
> **Meetings:** Spirit of Joy Church, 330 Scenic Dr., Clarkdale, AZ;
> second Saturday of the month, 9:30-11:30 a.m.
> **Contact:** Alice Klies, 928-300-9700, *alice.klies@gmail.com*
> **Members:** 30
> **Affiliation:** Word Weavers International

ARKANSAS

ACFW ARKANSAS
www.facebook.com/ACFWAR
> **Meetings:** Searcy Public Library, 113 E. Pleasure Ave., Searcy, AR;
> second Saturday of the month, 1:00 p.m.
> **Contact:** Tara Johnson, 501-821-4976, *tara@tarajohnsonministries.com*
> **Members:** 20
> **Affiliation:** American Christian Fiction Writers

CALIFORNIA

ACFW ORANGE COUNTY (OC)
> **Meetings:** location varies, Garden Grove, CA; second Thursday of
> the month, 6:30 p.m.
> **Contact:** Deborah Marino, 714-873-5609, *deborahmarino7@gmail.com*
> **Members:** 14
> **Affiliation:** American Christian Fiction Writers

ACFW SAN FRANCISCO BAY AREA CHAPTER
www.meetup.com/ACFWSFBayArea
> **Meetings:** Crosswalk Church, 445 S. Mary Ave., Sunnyvale, CA;
> third Saturday of odd months, 10 a.m. to noon
> **Contact:** Katie Vorreiter, *acfwsfbayarea@gmail.com*
> **Members:** 15
> **Affiliation:** American Christian Fiction Writers

CIRCUIT WRITERS
> **Meetings:** Grass Valley United Methodist Church, 236 S. Church St.,
> Grass Valley, CA; first Tuesday of the month, 6:15 p.m.
> **Contact:** Janet Ann Collins, 530-272-4905, *jan@janetanncollins.com*
> **Membership:** 6

INSPIRE CASTRO VALLEY (CV) WRITERS GROUP
www.inspirewriters.com
> **Meetings:** 3 Crosses Church, 20600 John Dr., Castro Valley, CA;
> Mondays, 6:30-8:30 p.m. (email first)
> **Contact:** Susy Flory, 510-828-5360, *susyflory@gmail.com*
> **Members:** 15
> **Affiliation:** Inspire Christian Writers

SAN DIEGO CHRISTIAN WRITERS' GUILD
www.sandiegocwg.org
> **Meetings:** throughout San Diego county, CA; members-only
> Internet group
> **Contact:** Jennie Gillespie, PO Box 270403, San Diego, CA 92198;
> 760-294-3269; *info@sandiegocwg.org*
> **Members:** 200

COLORADO

ACFW COLORADO SPRINGS
www.acfwcs.acfwcolorado.com
> **Meetings:** First Evangelical Free Church, 3022 W. Fontanero St.,
> Colorado Springs, CO; generally first Saturday of the month
> **Contact:** Mary Agius, 719-686-7761, *acfwcs.president@acfwcolorado.com*
> **Members:** 45
> **Affiliation:** American Christian Fiction Writers

ACFW COLORADO WESTERN SLOPE
www.westernslopeacfw.blogspot.com
> **Meetings:** The Artful Cup, 3090 N. 12th St., Grand Junction, CO;
> fourth Saturday of the month, 10:00 a.m.
> **Contact:** Niki Turner, 970-948-9547, *westernslopeacfw@gmail.com*
> **Members:** 10
> **Affiliation:** American Christian Fiction Writers

MILE HIGH SCRIBES (AKA ACFW SOUTH DENVER CHAPTER)
acfwsouthdenver.acfwcolorado.com
> **Meetings:** Highlands Ranch Library, 9292 S. Ridgeline Blvd.,
> Highlands Ranch, CO; see website for day and time
> **Contact:** Caren Boddie, 720-331-9361, *hike5837@msn.com*
> **Members:** 10
> **Affiliation:** American Christian Fiction Writers

SPRINGS WRITERS

springswriters.wordpress.com

> **Meetings:** Woodmen Valley Chapel, 250 E. Woodmen Rd., Colorado Springs, CO; second Tuesday of each month except July, August, and December, 6:00–8:00 p.m.
> **Contact:** Scoti Springfield Domeij, 719-209-9066, *springswriters@gmail.com*
> **Members:** 350

WRITERS ON THE ROCK

www.writersontherock.com

> **Meetings:** Green Mountain Recreation Center, 13198 W. Green Mountain Dr., Lakewood, CO; monthly
> **Contact:** David Rupert, 720-237-7487, *info@writersontherock.com*
> **Members:** 170

WRITERS ON THE ROCK, HIGHLANDS RANCH

www.facebook.com/groups/WritersOnTheRock

> **Meetings:** Living Way Church, 345 E. Wildcat Reserve Pkwy., Littleton, CO; second Tuesday of the month
> **Contact:** David Rupert, 720-237-7487, *info@writersontherock.com*
> **Members:** 170

CONNECTICUT

WORD WEAVERS BERKSHIRES

wordweaversberkshires.org

> **Meetings:** Sherman Church, 6 Church Rd., Sherman, CT 06784; third Saturday of the month, 9 a.m. to noon
> **Contact:** Tara Alemany, 860-946-0544, *info@wordweaversberkshires.org*
> **Members:** 15
> **Affiliation:** Word Weavers International

DELAWARE

DELMARVA CHRISTIAN WRITERS' FELLOWSHIP

www.delmarvawriters.com

> **Meetings:** Georgetown Presbyterian Church, Tunnell Hall, 203 N. Bedford St., Georgetown, DE; third Saturday of the month, 9:00 a.m. to noon

Contact: Candy Abbott, 302-856-6649, *cfa@candyabbott.com*
Members: 20

KINGDOM WRITERS FELLOWSHIP

Meetings: Atlanta Road Alliance Church, 22625 Atlanta Rd., Seaford, DE; second Thursday of the month, 6:15-8:30 p.m.
Contact: Eva Maddox, 302-628-4594, *evacmaddox@outlook.com*
Members: 10
Affiliation: Delmarva Christian Writers' Fellowship

VINE AND VESSELS CHRISTIAN WRITERS FELLOWSHIP

www.vineandvessels.com

Meetings: Seaford Library, 600 N. Market St., Seaford, DE; fourth Saturday of the month, 10 a.m. to noon
Contact: Joyce Sessoms, 302-382-9904, *crownjewel777@comcast.net*; or Betty Ricks-Jarman, 302-448-5939
Members: 10-12
Affiliation: Delmarva Christian Writers' Fellowship

FLORIDA

ACFW CENTRAL FLORIDA CHAPTER

www.cfacfw.org

Meetings: Grace Covenant Presbyterian Church, 1655 Peel Ave., Orlando, FL; third Saturday of the month, January—October, noon to 2 p.m.
Contact: Kristen Stieffel, 407-928-7801, *treasurer@cfacfw.com*
Members: 15
Affiliation: American Christian Fiction Writers

BRANDON CHRISTIAN WRITERS

www.facebook.com/BrandonChristianWriters

Meetings: St. Andres United Methodist Church, 3315 Bryan Rd., Brandon, FL; fourth Thursday of the month, 7:00-9:00 p.m.
Contact: Cheryl Johnston, 813-763-3154, *cherylbethjohnston@mac.com*
Members: 25
Affiliation: American Christian Writers

CALLAHAN CREATIVE WRITING WORKSHOP

www.callahanwriters.blogspot.com

Meetings: Callahan Branch Library, 450077 State Road 200, Ste. 15, Callahan, FL; selected Tuesdays, 6:15-8:00 p.m.

Contact: Nancy Lee Bethea, 904-403-4360, *nancyleebethea@gmail.com*
Members: 40-50
Affiliation: American Christian Fiction Writers

MAGBOOKMEDIA WRITERS
www.magbookmediatv.com
> **Meetings:** Port St. Lucie Library, Morningside Branch, 2410 S.E. Morningside Blvd., Port St. Lucie, FL; Tuesdays, 6:00-8:00 p.m.
> **Contact:** Aria Gmitter, 609-901-0670, *air@magbookmedia.com*
> **Members:** 5

NORTH JAX WORD WEAVERS
www.Word-Weavers.com
> **Meetings:** North Jacksonville Baptist Church, 8531 N. Main St., Jacksonville, FL; second Saturday of the month, 10 a.m. to 1:00 p.m.
> **Contact:** Richard New, 904-708-8072, *loco7mo@yahoo.com*
> **Members:** 8
> **Affiliation:** Word Weavers International

SOUTH FLORIDA WORD WEAVERS
> **Meetings:** Hartman Household, 1729 N.W. 36 Court, Oakland Park, FL; second Saturday of the month, 9:30 a.m.
> **Contact:** Patricia Hartman, 954-295-1103, *patricia@patriciahartman.com*
> **Members:** 15
> **Affiliation:** Word Weavers International

SPACE COAST WORD WEAVERS
www.Word-Weavers.com
> **Meetings:** Brevard County Public Libraries, 308 Forrest Ave., Cocoa, FL; second Sunday of the month, 2:00-4:30 p.m.
> **Contact:** Dylyce P. Clarke, 321-266-5627, *1royaldy@gmail.com*
> **Members:** 12
> **Affiliation:** Word Weavers International

SUNCOAST CHRISTIAN WRITERS GROUP
> **Meetings:** Panera Bread, Largo Mall, 10500 Ulmerton Rd., Largo, FL; third Thursday of the month, 10 a.m.
> **Contact:** Elaine Creasman, 727-251-3756, *emcreasman@aol.com*
> **Members:** 15

VOLUSIA WORD WEAVERS
www.Word-Weavers.com
> **Meetings:** Faith Church Fellowship Hall, 4700 S. Clyde Morris Blvd., Port Orange, FL; first Monday of the month, 7:00 p.m.

Contact: Patricia Keough-Wilson, 386-761-5994,
keoughwilson_239@msn.com
Members: 20
Affiliation: Word Weavers International

WORD WEAVERS DESTIN

www.Word-Weavers.com

Meetings: Village Baptist Church, bldg. 8, 101 Matthew Dr.,
Destin, FL; second Saturday of the month, 9:30 a.m.
Contact: Chris Manion, 850-573-3091, *Writeaway@me.com*
Members: 6
Affiliation: Word Weavers International

WORD WEAVERS GAINESVILLE FLORIDA

www.Word-Weavers.com

Meetings: alternating member homes, Gainesville, FL; fourth Sunday
of the month, 2:00-4:00 p.m.
Contact: John Brewer, 352-278-4572, *aplbytes@gmail.com*
Members: 5-10
Affiliation: Word Weavers International

WORD WEAVERS LAKE COUNTY

www.Word-Weavers.com

Meetings: Calvary Chapel, 1601 W. Main St., Leesburg, FL; second
Saturday of the month, 10 a.m.
Contact: C. Kevin Thompson or Becky Joie Oakes, 352-787-2972,
ckevinthompson@gmail.com
Members: 7
Affiliation: Word Weavers International

WORD WEAVERS OCALA CHAPTER

www.Word-Weavers.com

Meetings: Marion County Public Library, Ocala, 2720 E. Silver
Springs Blvd., Ocala, FL; third Sunday of the month, 1:30-4:00
p.m.
Contact: Jen Odom or Delores Kight, 407-615-4112,
Delores@FHRX.net
Members: 10+
Affiliation: Word Weavers International

WORD WEAVERS OF CLAY COUNTY

www.Word-Weavers.com

Meetings: Fleming Island, FL; third Saturday of the month, 10:00 a.m. to 2:00 p.m.
Contact: Shari McGriff, *Shari.McGriff@gmail.com*
Members: 5-10
Affiliation: Word Weavers International

WORD WEAVERS OF THE TREASURE COAST
www.Word-Weavers.com

Meetings: First Church Of God, 1105 58th Ave., Vero Beach, FL; first Saturday of the month or second Saturday if the first falls on a major holiday, 9:30 a.m.
Contact: Loretta Beasley, 772-202-7998 or Marene Graham, 772-321-2871; *ruhischild2@bellsouth.net*
Members: 17
Affiliation: Word Weavers International

WORD WEAVERS ORLANDO
www.facebook.com/wordweaversorlando

Meetings: Calvary Chapel, 5015 Goddard Ave., Orlando, FL; second Saturday of the month, 9:45 a.m.
Contact: Rick Whitted, 972-679-7745, *Rick@rawhitted.com*
Members: 40-45
Affiliation: Word Weavers International

WORD WEAVERS TAMPA
www.Word-Weavers.com

Meetings: Jan Powell, 1901 S. Village Ave., Tampa, FL; first Saturday of the month, 9:30 a.m. to noon
Contact: Sharron Cosby, 813-690-3021, *sharroncosby@gmail.com*
Members: 22
Affiliation: Word Weavers International

GEORGIA

ACFW NORTH GEORGIA
www.acfwnga.wix.com/home

Meetings: Sugar Hill Church, 5091 Nelson Brogdon Blvd. (Hwy. 20), Sugar Hill, GA; fourth Tuesday of each month, 7:00-9:00 p.m.
Contact: Ane Mulligan, *acfwnga@gmail.com*
Members: 20
Affiliation: American Christian Fiction Writers

CHRISTIAN AUTHORS GUILD

www.christianauthorsguild.org

Meetings: Prayer & Praise Christian Fellowship, 6409 Bells Ferry Rd.,
Woodstock, GA; first Monday of the month, 7:00 p.m.
Contact: Michael Anderson, 770-735-3020,
info@christianauthorsguild.org
Members: 50

WORD WEAVERS WOODSTOCK

www.Word-Weavers.com

Meetings: Prayer & Praise Christian Fellowship, 6409 Bells Ferry Rd.,
Woodstock, GA; third Monday of the month, 7:00 p.m.
Contact: Jennifer Henn, 470-775-2533, *JenniferHennWriter@gmail.com*
Members: 15
Affiliation: Word Weavers International

IDAHO

IDAHOPE CHRISTIAN WRITERS

www.idahopechristianwriters.com

Meetings: Meridian First Baptist Church, 428 W. Pine Ave.,
Meridian, ID; second Thursday of each month, 7:00 p.m.
Contact: Patrick Craig, 707-338-1617,
IdahopeChristianWriters@gmail.com
Members: 60

ILLINOIS

ACFW CHICAGO CHAPTER

www.acfwchicago.com

Meetings: Schaumburg Public Library, 130 S. Roselle Rd.,
Schaumburg, IL; second Friday of every month
Contact: Lara Helmling, 815-979-8614, *Lara@larahelmling.com*
Members: 20
Affiliation: American Christian Fiction Writers

AURORA ILLINOIS WORD WEAVERS

www.Word-Weavers.com

Meetings: call or email for location; second Saturday of each month,
1:00-3:00 p.m.

Contact: Cindy Huff, 630-281-0337, *cindyhuff11@gmail.com*
Members: 7
Affiliation: Word Weavers International

WORD WEAVERS LAND OF LINCOLN
www.Word-Weavers.com

Meetings: Lincoln Christian University, 100 Campus View Dr.,
   Lincoln, IL; second Saturday of every month, 10:00 a.m.
Contact: Robin McClallen, 217 732-8629, *freetofly4ever@gmail.com*
Members: 9
Affiliation: Word Weavers International

WORD WEAVERS O'FALLON
www.scribesofpraise.org

Meetings: First Baptist Church O'Fallon, 1111 E. Hwy. 50, O'Fallon,
   IL; second Saturday of each month, 1:00-2:00 p.m.
Contact: Tammika Jones, 618-509-0798, *tmdjones1@gmail.com*
Members: 4
Affiliation: Word Weavers International

WORD WEAVERS ON THE BORDER
www.Word-Weavers.com

Meetings: Lake Villa Public Library, 1001 E. Grand Ave., Lake Villa,
   IL; fourth Wednesday of the month, 7:00-8:30 p.m.
Contact: TLC Nielsen, 847-532-5015, *soulfixer13@yahoo.com*
Members: 7
Affiliation: Word Weavers International

WORD WEAVERS WEST SUBURBS
www.facebook.com/groups/wwnaperville

Meetings: near Lisle Post Office, 4507 Chelsea Ave., Lisle, IL; second
   Saturday of the month, 9:30 a.m.
Contact: Mary Sandford, 630-915-1893, *MeSandford27@gmail.com*
Members: 4-5
Affiliation: Word Weavers International

INDIANA

ACFW INDIANA CHAPTER
www.hoosierink.blogspot.com

Meetings: various places in Indiana, quarterly

Contact: Karla Akins, 260-578-1775, *acfwindianachapter@gmail.com*
Members: 50
Affiliation: American Christian Fiction Writers

BLUFFTON CHRISTIAN WRITING CLUB
www.facebook.com/groups/137239503139200

Meetings: River Terrace Retirement Community, 400 Caylor Blvd., Bluffton, IN; third Monday of the month, 6:30-8:30 p.m.
Contact: Kayleen Reusser, *kjreusser@adamswell.com*
Members: 10

FORT WAYNE CHRISTIAN WRITING CLUB

Meetings: Waynedale Public Library, 2200 Lower Huntington Rd., Fort Wayne, IN; fourth Tuesday of the month, 6:00-8:00 p.m.
Contact: Kayleen Reusser, *kjreusser@adamswells.com*
Members: 10

HEARTLAND CHRISTIAN WRITERS
www.facebook.com/Heartland-Christian-Writers-Community-181346731973054

Meetings: Mount Pleasant Christian Church's Community Life Center, 381 N. Bluff Rd., Greenwood, IN; third Monday of every month, 9:30 a.m. and 6:30 p.m.
Contact: Michele Israel Harper, 317-550-9755, *MicheleIsraelHarper@gmail.com*
Members: 45+

KANSAS

ACFW KANSAS CITY WEST
www.facebook.com/ACFWKansasCityWestChapter

Meetings: Bonner Springs City Library, 201 N. Nettleton Ave., Bonner Springs, KS; second Saturday of every month, 1:00-3:00 p.m.; optional critique group, 3:30-5:00 p.m.
Contact: Barbara Hartzler, *acfwkcwest@gmail.com*
Members: 10-15
Affiliation: American Christian Fiction Writers

MARYLAND

MOUNTAIN CHRISTIAN CHURCH WRITERS' GROUP
MountainCC.org/WritersGroup
> **Meetings:** New Life Center, Room 118/120, 1824 Mountain Rd., Bel
> Air, MD; Sundays, 2:30-4:30 p.m.
> **Contact:** Christy Struben, 410-692-6304, *cstruben711@gmail.com*
> **Members:** 20+

MICHIGAN

WORD WEAVERS WEST MICHIGAN—GRANDVILLE
www.Word-Weavers.com
> **Meetings:** Russ' Restaurant, 4440 Chicago Dr., S.W., Grandville, MI;
> first and third Tuesdays, 6:30-8:30 p.m.
> **Contact:** Kathy Bruins, 616-403-4894, *author@kathybruins.com*
> **Members:** 5
> **Affiliation:** Word Weavers International

WORD WEAVERS WEST MICHIGAN—HOLLAND
www.Word-Weavers.com
> **Meetings:** City on a Hill, 100 Pine St., Zeeland, MI; first and third
> Tuesdays of the month, 12:30-2:30 p.m.
> **Contact:** Kathy Bruins, 616-403-4894, *author@kathybruins.com*
> **Members:** 10
> **Affiliation:** Word Weavers International

WORD WEAVERS WEST MICHIGAN—MUSKEGON
www.Word-Weavers.com
> **Meetings:** Norton Shores Public Library, 705 Seminole Rd., Norton
> Shores, MI; first and third Tuesdays, 5:45-7:45 p.m.
> **Contact:** Kathy Bruins, 616-403-4894, *author@kathybruins.com*
> **Members:** 10
> **Affiliation:** Word Weavers International

WORD WEAVERS WEST MICHIGAN—NORTH GRAND RAPIDS
www.Word-Weavers.com
> **Meetings:** York Creek Community Center, 3999 Alpenhorn N.W.,
> Walker, MI; first and third Tuesday of the month, 6:30-8:30 p.m.
> **Contact:** Kathy Bruins, 616-403-4894, *author@kathybruins.com*
> **Affiliation:** Word Weavers International

MINNESOTA

ACFW MINNESOTA N.I.C.E.
www.acfwminnesotanice.com
> **Meetings:** Trinity Baptist Church, 2220 Edgerton St., Maplewood, MN; usually fourth Sunday of the month, 6:00-8:00 p.m.
> **Contact:** Brenda Anderson, *acfw.mn_nice@yahoo.com*
> **Members:** 25
> **Affiliation:** American Christian Fiction Writers

MINNESOTA CHRISTIAN WRITERS GUILD
www.mnchristianwriters.com
> **Meetings:** Oak Knoll Lutheran Church, 600 Hopkins Crossroad, Minnetonka, MN; second Monday of the month, September—May, 7:00-8:30 p.m.
> **Contact:** Beverly Snyder, *info@mnchristianwriters.com*

MISSOURI

HEART OF AMERICA CHRISTIAN WRITERS NETWORK
www.hacwn.org
> **Meetings:** Greater Kansas City area; monthly informational meetings, biweekly critique groups
> **Contact:** Jeanette Littleton, 816-459-8016, *HACWN@earthlink.net*
> **Members:** 150

OZARKS CHAPTER OF AMERICAN CHRISTIAN WRITERS
www.OzarksACW.org
> **Meetings:** University Heights Baptist Church, 1010 S. National, Springfield, MO
> **monthly** September—May
> **Contact:** Jeanetta Chrystie, 417-832-8409, *DrChrystie@mchsi.com*
> **Members:** 47
> **Affiliation:** American Christian Writers

NEBRASKA

MY THOUGHTS EXACTLY
mythoughtsexactlywriters.wordpress.com

Meetings: place varies, Fremont, NE; time varies
Contact: Cheryl, 402-727-6508, *Cheryl@seekingbalancebycheryl.com*
Members: 6

NEW JERSEY

NORTH JERSEY CHRISTIAN WRITERS GROUP
www.njcwg.blogspot.com

Meetings: Cornerstone Christian Church, 495 Wyckoff Ave.,
Wyckoff, NJ; first Saturday (usually) of each month, 10:00 a.m.
to noon
Contact: Barbara Higby, *njcwgroup@gmail.com*
Members: 12

NEW YORK

REDEEMER WRITERS GROUP
www.faithndwork.com

Meetings: Center for Faith and Work, 1166 Avenue of the Americas,
New York, NY; monthly, 7:00-9:00 p.m.
Contact: Esther Suh, 212-808-4460, *redeemerwriters@gmail.com*
Members: 20
Affiliation: Redeemer Presbyterian Church

SOUTHERN TIER CHRISTIAN WRITERS

Meetings: Olean First Baptist Church, 133 S. Union St., Olean, NY;
first and third Mondays, April—October, 7:00 p.m.; first Monday
only November—March, 6 p.m.
Contact: Deb Wuethrich, 716.379.8702, *deborahmarcein@gmail.com*
Members: 9
Affiliation: American Christian Writers

NORTH AND SOUTH DAKOTA

ACFW DAKOTAS
www.facebook.com/groups/ACFWDakotas

Meetings: location, day of week, and frequency varies by region
Contact: Shannon McNear, 843-327-0583, *sdmcnear@gmail.com*
Members: 15
Affiliation: American Christian Fiction Writers

NORTH CAROLINA

CHARLOTTE WORD WEAVERS
www.Word-Weavers.com
> **Meetings:** Carmel Presbyterian Church, Ligon Hall, 2048 Carmel Rd., Charlotte, NC; third Saturday of the month, 2:00-4:00 p.m.
> **Contact:** Kim Dent, 330-904-5130, *Kimberlyjamesdent@gmail.com*
> **Members:** 20
> **Affiliation:** Word Weavers International

WILMINGTON WORD WEAVERS
www.Word-Weavers.com
> **Meetings:** Live Oak Church, 740 S. College Rd., Wilmington, NC; first Monday of the month, 7:00 p.m.
> **Contact:** Andy Lee, 910-515-1623, *wordsbyandylee@gmail.com*
> **Members:** 20
> **Affiliation:** Word Weavers International

OHIO

ACFW OHIO
www.facebook.com/groups/220166801456380
> **Meetings:** Etna United Methodist Church, 500 Pike St., Etna, OH; first Saturday of the month, noon to 3:00 p.m.
> **Contact:** Tamera Lynn Kraft, 330-733-8007, *tkrafty@sbcglobal.net*
> **Membership:** 20
> **Affiliation:** American Christian Fiction Writers

DAYTON CHRISTIAN SCRIBES
> **Meetings:** Kettering Seventh-Day Adventist Church, 3939 Stonebridge Rd., Kettering, OH; second Thursday of the month, 7:00-9:00 p.m.
> **Contact:** Lois Pecce, 937-433-6470,*daytonchristianscribes@gmail.com*
> **Members:** 35
> **Affiliations:** Dayton Christian Writer's Guild, Middletown Area Christian Writers

MIDDLETOWN AREA CHRISTIAN WRITERS
(M.A.C. WRITERS)
middletownwriters.blogspot.com
> **Meetings:** Healing Word Assembly of God, 5303 S. Dixie Hwy., Franklin, OH; third Tuesday of each month, 7:00-8:30 p.m.

Contact: Donna J. Shepherd, 513-423-1627, *donna.shepherd@gmail.com*
Members: 25

NORTHWEST OHIO CHRISTIAN WRITERS

www.nwocw.org

Meetings: St. Mark's Lutheran Church, 315 S. College, Bowling Green, OH; fourth Friday of January, March, May, July, and September, 11:00 a.m.
Contact: Shelley Lee, 419-308-3615, *email@nwocw.org*
Members: 30

WORD WEAVERS NORTHEAST OHIO

www.Word-Weavers.com

Meetings: First Church of the Brethren, 122 E. 3rd St., Ashland, OH; first Thursday of each month, 6:30 p.m.
Contact: Tina Hunt/Shellie Arnold, 567-203-8872/330-805-4795; *neohwordweavers@gmail.com*
Members: 8
Affiliation: Word Weavers International

OKLAHOMA

FELLOWSHIP OF CHRISTIAN WRITERS

fellowshipofchristianwriters.org

Meetings: Kirk of the Hills Presbyterian Church, 4102 E. 61st, Tulsa, OK
Contact: Martha Curtis, *marthajcurtis@yahoo.com*
Members: 60

OKLAHOMA CHRISTIAN FICTION WRITERS

okcchristianfictionwriters.blogspot.com

Meetings: Henderson Hills Baptist Church, 1200 E. I-35 Frontage Rd., Edmond, OK; third Saturday of each month. 1:00-3:00 p.m.
Contact: J. J. Johnson, 405-615-9594, *ocfwchapter@gmail.com*
Members: 35
Affiliation: American Christian Fiction Writers

WORDWRIGHTS

www.wordwrights-okc.com

Meetings: Catholic Pastoral Center, Room B13, 7501 N.W. Expressway, Oklahoma City, OK; second Saturday of the month, 10:00 a.m. to noon

Contact: Lori Williams, 405-738-5336, *dewlaw@cox.net*
Members: 30

OREGON

OREGON CHRISTIAN WRITERS
www.oregonchristianwriters
> **Meetings:** Portland, OR metro area, three all-day Saturday conferences, summer coaching conference
> **Contact:** *president@oregonchristianwriters*; 1075 Willow Lake Road N., Keizer, OR 97303; 503-393-3356

WORD WEAVERS PORTLAND EAST
www.Word-Weavers.com
> **Meetings:** Panera Bread, 1017 N.W. Civic Dr., Gresham, OR; second Saturday of every month, 10:00 a.m.
> **Contact:** Tere Belcher, 503-927-5701, *talkin_tere@yahoo.com*
> **Members:** 10
> **Affiliation:** Word Weavers International

WORDWRIGHTS
> **Meetings:** Gresham/east Multnomah County, OR; two times a month, Thursday afternoons
> **Contact:** Susan Thogerson Maas, 503-663-7834, *susan.maas@frontier.com*
> **Members:** 5

PENNSYLVANIA

ACFW PENNSYLVANIA STATE CHAPTER
acfwpennsylvania.com
> **Meetings:** online, fourth Tuesday of the month, 7:30 p.m.
> **Contact:** Donna L. H. Smith, 717-201-2675, *dlhswriter@windstream.net*
> **Members:** 35
> **Affiliation:** American Christian Fiction Writers

CHRISTIAN WRITERS GUILD
> **Meetings:** Perkin's Restaurant, 505 Galleria Dr., Johnstown, PA; last Tuesday of each month except July and December
> **Contact:** Betty Rosian, 814-255-4351, *wordsforall@hotmail.com*
> **Members:** 12

GREATER PHILLY CHRISTIAN WRITERS FELLOWSHIP

www.writehisanswer.com/greaterphillychristianwriters

> **Meetings:** Marlene Bagnull's home, 951 Anders Rd., Lansdale, PA; monthly, usually the third Thursday, 10 a.m. to 12:30 p.m.
> **Contact:** Marlene Bagnull, 484-991-8581, *mbagnull@aol.com*
> **Members:** 10

LANCASTER CHRISTIAN WRITERS

lancasterchristianwriterstoday.Blogspot.com

> **Meetings:** Lancaster Alliance Church, 210 Pitney Rd., Lancaster, PA; third Saturday of the month, 9:30 a.m. to noon
> **Contact:** Jeanette Windle, *jeanette@jeanettewindle.com*
> **Affiliation:** American Christian Writers

LANSDALE, PA WOMEN'S CRITIQUE GROUP

www.writehisanswer.com/lansdalepawomenscritiquegroup

> **Meetings:** Marlene Bagnull's home, 951 Anders Rd., Lansdale, PA; every other Thursday, 7:30-10:00 p.m.
> **Contact:** Marlene Bagnull, 484-991-8581, *mbagnull@aol.com*
> **Members:** 12

POTTER COUNTY WRITER'S GROUP

> **Meetings:** Artisan center, 227 N. Main St., Coudersport, PA; second Saturday of the month
> **Contact:** Michelle Lazurek, 814-274-8165, *Michellelazurek@yahoo.com*
> **Members:** 8

SOUTH CAROLINA

SOUTH CAROLINA CHAPTER OF ACFW

scwritersacfw.blogspot.com

> **Meetings:** North Anderson Baptist Church, 2308 N. Main St., Anderson, SC; usually fourth Saturday of the month except July and December, November is third Saturday, 2:00-5:00 p.m.
> **Contact:** Elva Martin, 864/226-7024, *elvacmartin@gmail.com*
> **Members:** 20+
> **Affiliation:** American Christian Fiction Writers

WORD WEAVERS LEXINGTON CHAPTER

www.LexingtonWordWeavers.com

> **Meetings:** Riverbend Community Church, 1015 Corley Mill Rd., Lexington, SC; second Monday of every month, 6:45-9:00 p.m.

Contact: Jean Wilund, 803-422-1410, *info@lexingtonwordweavers.com*
Members: 33
Affiliation: Word Weavers International

WORD WEAVERS SUMMERVILLE

www.Word-Weavers.com

Meetings: Summerville Presbyterian Church, 407 S. Laurel St., Summerville, SC; first Monday of each month, 7:00 p.m.
Contact: Jeannine Brummett, Summerville.lady@yahoo.com
Members: 8
Affiliation: Word Weavers International

WRITING 4 HIM

Meetings: Christian Supply, 1600 Reidville Rd., Spartanburg, SC 29301; second Thursday of the month, 9:45 a.m.
Contact: Linda Gilden, *linda@lindagilden.com*
Members: 100

TENNESSEE

ACFW MEMPHIS

Meetings: Compassion Church, 3505 S. Houston Levee, Germantown, TN; third Saturday of the month except December, 10 a.m. to noon
Contact: Loretta Eidson, *Loretta@LorettaEidson.com*
Members: 15
Affiliation: American Christian Fiction Writers

CHATTANOOGA WORD WEAVERS

www.Word-Weavers.com

Meetings: McKee Library, Southern Adventist University, 4881 Taylor Cir., Collegedale, TN; second Thursday of the month, 7:00-9:00 p.m.
Contact: Roberta Fish, 407-719-4490, *robertamfish@gmail.com*
Members: 12
Affiliation: Word Weavers International

MIDDLE TENNESSEE ACFW

Meetings: Woodmont Baptist Church, 2100 Woodmont Blvd., Nashville, TN; first Saturday of every month, 10 a.m. to noon
Contact: Julie Gwinn, 615-957-3443, *julie@theseymouragency.com*
Members: 25
Affiliation: American Christian Fiction Writers

TEXAS

ACFW CENTRAL TEXAS CHAPTER
www.centexacfw.com
> **Meetings:** Georgetown Public Library, 402 W. 8th St., Georgetown, TX, second Saturday of the month, 9:30-11:30 a.m.
> **Contact:** Joy Nord, 512-626-7304, glyndajoynord@yahoo.com
> **Members:** 20
> **Affiliation:** American Christian Fiction Writers

ACFW DFW CHAPTER (AKA READY WRITERS)
www.dfwreadywriters.blogspot.com
> **Meetings:** Arlington Community Church, 1715 W. Randol Mill Rd., Arlington, TX; second Saturday of every month, 10:00 a.m.
> **Contact:** J. A. Marx, 972-841-4477, *embattledspirit@jamarx.net*
> **Members:** 25-30
> **Affiliation:** American Christian Fiction Writers

ACFW HOUSTON
www.houstonchristianauthors.com
> **Meetings:** University Baptist Church, 16106 Middlebrook Dr., Houston, TX; second Saturday of the month, 2:00-4:30 p.m.
> **Contact:** Lisa Godfrees, 713-703-5472, *houstonchristianauthors@gmail.com*
> **Members:** 7
> **Affiliation:** American Christian Fiction Writers

ALAMO CITY CHRISTIAN FICTION WRITERS (ACCFW)
> **Meetings:** La Madeleine, 722 N.W. Loop 410, San Antonio, TX; second Saturday of the month, 10 a.m. to noon
> **Contact:** Allison Pittman, 210-241-7257 (text preferred)
> **Members:** 15
> **Affiliation:** American Christian Fiction Writers

CENTRAL HOUSTON INSPIRATIONAL WRITERS ALIVE!
www.houstoncentraliwa.com
> **Meetings:** Houston's First Baptist Church, 7474 Katy Fwy. (Interstate 10), Houston, TX; second Thursday of each month except July, August, and December, 7:00 p.m.
> **Contact:** Martha Rogers, 713-686-7209, *marthalrogers@sbcglobal.net*
> **Members:** 22

CROSS REFERENCE WRITERS
sites.google.com/site/crossreferencewriters
> **Meetings:** Aldersgate United Methodist Church, 2201 Earl Rudder Fwy. S., College Station, TX; first Thursday of the month, 7:00-8:30 p.m.
> **Contact:** Tammy Hensel, 979-204-0674, *CrossRefWriters@yahoo.com*
> **Members:** 10

PINEY WOODS WRITER'S GROUP
> **Meetings:** Starbucks, 101 IH 45 South, Huntsville, TX; first Tuesday of the month, 6:00 p.m.
> **Contact:** Robin Bryce, 936-662-4285, *Robin@RobinBryce.com*
> **Members:** 4

ROCKWALL CHRISTIAN WRITERS GROUP
rcwg.blogspot.com
> **Meetings:** Lake Pointe Church, 701 E. I-30, Rockwall, TX; second Monday of each month, 7:00 p.m.
> **Contact:** Darren Sapp, 214-477-4039, *darrenlsapp@gmail.com*
> **Members:** 40

STORY HELP GROUPS
(FORMERLY NORTH TEXAS CHRISTIAN WRITERS)
www.storyhelpgroups.org
> **Meetings:** various locations in Dallas/Fort Worth, TX area; check the website
> **Contact:** Frank Ball, *frank.ball@storyhelpgroups.org*
> **Members:** 250

WRITERS ON THE STORM (WOTS)
wotsacfw.blogspot.com
> **Meetings:** The Woodlands/Shenandoah Lupe Tortilla behind Red Robin, 19437 Interstate 45, Shenandoah, TX; third Saturday of every month, 11:00 a.m. to 1:00 p.m.
> **Contact:** Janice Thompson, *wots.acfw@gmail.com*
> **Members:** 20-25
> **Affiliation:** American Christian Fiction Writers

WRITERS LIFE GROUP
> **Meetings:** Lakewood Church, 3700 Southwest Freeway, Houston, TX; second and fourth Fridays of each month, 7:00-8:30 p.m.
> **Contact:** Melanie Stiles, 832-259-9576, melstiles@aol.com
> **Members:** 125

VIRGINIA

CAPITAL CHRISTIAN WRITERS
capitalchristianwriters.org
> **Meetings:** Truro Episcopal Church, Gunnell House, 10520 Main St.,
> Fairfax, VA; second Monday of odd months
> **Contact:** Betsy Dill, 703-803-9447, *ccwriters@gmail.com*
> **Members:** 25

JOYWRITERS
www.facebook.com/JoyWriters-An-American-Christian-Writers-Chapter-146894242070595
> **Meetings:** Galax, VA area; small critique groups
> **Contact:** Vie Herlocker, 276-237-7574, *vherlock@yahoo.com*
> **Members:** 7
> **Affiliation:** American Christian Writers

RICHMOND WORD WEAVERS
www.Word-Weavers.com
> **Meetings:** Mount Vernon Baptist Church, 11220 Nuckols Rd., Glen
> Allen, VA; second Tuesday of each month, 7:30 p.m.
> **Contact:** Mary Beth Dahl, 804-270-6862, *mbdahl@marybethdahl.org*
> **Members:** 7
> **Affiliation:** Word Weavers International

WORD WEAVERS WILLIAMSBURG
www.Word-Weavers.com
> **Meetings:** James City County Library, 7770 Croaker Rd.,
> Williamsburg, VA; second Monday of the month, 5:30-8:00 p.m.
> **Contact:** Sheryl Buckner, 757-342-1460, *Sheryl@SherylBuckner.com*
> **Members:** 2
> **Affiliation:** Word Weavers International

WASHINGTON

CHRISTIAN SCRIBES
> **Meetings:** SonBridge, 1200 S.E. 12th St., College Pl., WA; second
> and fourth Tuesday of each month, 3:00 p.m.
> **Contact:** Helen Heavirland, 541-938-3838, *hlh@bmi.net*
> **Members:** 5

VANCOUVER CHRISTIAN WRITERS

Meetings: Vancouver, WA
Contact: Jon Drury, 510-909-0848, *jondrury2@yahoo.com*
Members: 5-7

WALLA WALLA CHRISTIAN WRITERS

Meetings: SonBridge, 1200 S.E. 12th St., College Place, WA; first and third Tuesday of each month, 3:00 p.m.
Contact: Helen Heavirland, 541-938-3838, *hlh@bmi.net*
Members: 5

WISCONSIN

ACFW WISCONSIN SOUTH EAST CHAPTER

www.facebook.com/wiseacfw

Meetings: Wisconsin Lutheran College, 8800 W. Bluemound Rd., Milwaukee, WI; first Thursday of the month 6:30-8:30 p.m.
Contact: Susan M. Baganz, 920-539-9311, *silygoos@gmail.com*
Members: 25
Affiliation: American Christian Fiction Writers

PENS OF PRAISE CHRISTIAN WRITERS

Meetings: Faith Church, 2201 42nd St., Manitowoc, WI; third Monday of every month, 6:30-8:30 p.m.
Contact: Becky McLafferty, 920-758-9196, *rebeccamclafferty@gmail.com* or Sue Kinney, 920-242-3631, *susanmarlenekinney@gmail.com*
Members: 8-12

WESTERN WISCONSIN CHRISTIAN WRITERS GUILD

www.wwcwg.com

Meetings: Bethesda Lutheran Church, 123 W. Hamilton, Eau Claire, WI; second Tuesday of each month, 7:00 p.m.
Contact: Sheila Wilkinson, 715-839-1207, *wwcwg.info@gmail.com*
Members: 20

WORD & PEN CHRISTIAN WRITERS

wordandpenchristianwriters.com

Meetings: St. Thomas Episcopal Church, 226 Washington St., Menasha, WI; second Monday, January—November, 7:00-9:00 p.m.
Contact: Christine Stratton, 920-739-0752, *gcefsi@new.rr.com*

Members: 20
Affiliation: American Christian Writers chapter

CANADA

THE WORD GUILD
www.thewordguild.com

Contact: Ruth Thorogood, executive director, 245 King George Rd., Ste. 226, Brantford, ON N3R 7N7, Canada; 800-969-9010; *info@thewordguild.com*

Services: Regional writers chapters across Canada. Sponsors the annual Write Canada conference in Toronto and contests and awards for Canadian Christian writers.

Members: 325

NATIONAL AND ONLINE

ACFW BEYOND THE BORDERS
www.facebook.com/groups/ACFWBeyondtheBorders

Contact: Iola Goulton, *iola@iolagoulton.com*
Members: 100
Affiliation: American Christian Fiction Writers

AMERICAN CHRISTIAN FICTION WRITERS
acfw.com

Contact: Robin Miller, executive director, PO Box 101066, Palm Bay, FL 32910; *director@acfw.com*

Services: Email loop, genre Facebook pages, online courses, critique groups, and local and regional chapters. Sponsors contests for published and unpublished writers and conducts the largest fiction conference annually.

Members: 2600+

CHRISTIAN AUTHORS NETWORK
ChristianAuthorsNetwork.com

Meetings: Online and at major writing-industry events, daily via private loop

Contact: Angela Breidenbach, president or Ava Pennington, secretary; *can_inc@yahoo.com*

Members: 125+

CHRISTIAN INDIE AUTHOR NETWORK

www.christianindieauthors.com

> **Meetings:** 24/7 on Facebook and website
> **Contact:** Mary C. Findley, 918-805-0669, *mjmcfindley@gmail.com*
> **Members:** 400+

CHRISTIAN WOMEN WRITER'S GROUP

cwwriters.com

> **Meetings:** weekly and monthly communications
> **Contact:** Jen Gentry, 918-724-3996, *jennyokiern37@gmail.com*
> **Members:** 100+
> **Affiliation:** Christian Indie Author Network

INSPIRE CHRISTIAN WRITERS

www.inspirewriters.com

> **Meetings:** regional and online critique groups
> **Contact:** Robynne Miller, 530-217-8233, *inspiredirectors@gmail.com*
> **Members:** 150
> **Affiliation:** West Coast Christian Writers

JERRY JENKINS WRITERS GUILD

www.JerrysGuild.com

> **Contact:** *WeCare@JerryJenkins.com*
> **Services:** 21-time *New York Times* bestselling author Jerry Jenkins coaches subscribers online via Live Online Workshops, (1 hour of training, 30 minutes of Q&A); *Manuscript Repair & Rewrite* sessions, in which he conducts a thorough revision of a member's first page; *Master Classes* (Jerry asks leading industry experts the questions you would ask); *Office Hours*, an extended monthly live Q&A session with Jerry; free access to *Jumpstart Courses* (Fiction and Nonfiction); all sessions recorded and archived for 24/7 member access
> **Meetings:** Unscheduled pop-ups in major cities
> **Members:** More than 2,000

PEN-SOULS

> **Meetings:** online and email; monthly reminders are emailed to members to pray for one another and share urgent, personal prayer requests and publishing announcements
> **Contact:** Janet Ann Collins, 530-272-4905, *jan@janetanncollins.com*
> **Members:** 10-12

REALM MAKERS
www.realmmakers.com
> **Meetings:** quarterly online
> **Contact:** Rebecca Minor, *members@realmmakers.com*
> **Membership:** 100

WORD WEAVERS INTERNATIONAL, INC.
www.Word-Weavers.com
> **Contact:** Eva Marie Everson, president, 504 Spoonbill Ct., Winter Springs, FL 32708; 407-615-4112; *WordWeaversInternational@aol.com*
> **Services:** Local chapters and online groups for manuscript critiquing. Sponsors Florida Christian Writers Conference.
> **Members:** 500+

WORD WEAVERS ONLINE GROUPS
www.Word-Weavers.com
> **Meetings:** via Google Hangouts; times vary, two hours
> **Contact:** Eva Marie Everson, 407-615-4112, *WordWeaversInternational@aol.com*
> **Members:** 6 per "page," currently 14 pages
> **Affiliation:** Word Weavers International

WORD WEAVERS PAGE 14 ONLINE GROUP
www.Word-Weavers.com
> **Meeting:** last Friday of the month, 8:30-10:30 a.m.
> **Contact:** Kathy Bruins, 616-403-4894, *author@kathybruins.com*
> **Members:** 6
> **Affiliation:** Word Weavers Internationa

19

EDITORIAL SERVICES

Entries in this chapter are for information only, not an endorsement of editing skills. Before hiring a freelance editor, ask for references if they are not posted on the website; and contact two or three to help determine if this editor is a good fit for you. You may also want to pay for an edit of a few pages or one chapter before hiring someone to edit your complete manuscript.

A LITTLE RED INK | BETHANY KACZMAREK
Jarrettsville, MD | 443-608-4013
editor@bethanykaczmarek.com | *www.bethanykaczmarek.com*
> **Contact:** email
> **Services:** manuscript evaluation, substantive editing/rewriting, copyediting, proofreading
> **Types of manuscripts:** short stories, novels, adult, teen/YA
> **Charges:** hourly rate
> **Credentials/experience:** An ACFW Editor of the Year finalist (2015), Bethany enjoys working with both traditional and indie authors. Several of her clients are award-winning and best-selling authors, though she does work with aspiring authors as well. She has edited for speculative fiction publishing houses Enclave Publishing and Brimstone Fiction.

A LITTLE RED INK | ERYNNE NEWMAN
Travelers Rest, SC | 919-229-1357
ALittleRedInk@gmail.com | *www.ALittleRedInk.com*
> **Contact:** email
> **Services:** manuscript evaluation, substantive editing/rewriting, copyediting, proofreading
> **Types of manuscripts:** short stories, novels, book proposals, adult, teen/YA
> **Charges:** hourly rate
> **Credentials/experience:** Rita Award-winning editor with five years of experience.

A WAY WITH WORDS WRITING AND EDITORIAL SERVICES | RENEE GRAY-WILBURN

Colorado Springs, CO | 719-271-7076
waywords@earthlink.net

Contact: email

Services: substantive editing/rewriting, copyediting, proofreading, ghostwriting, coauthoring, write website text, create small group/Bible study guides, write curriculum lesson plans, write discussion questions for books, write from transcriptions, write children's books and other material, résumé design and writing

Types of manuscripts: articles, nonfiction books, devotionals, short stories, novels, curriculum, gift books, technical material, adult, teen/YA, picture books, easy readers, middle grade

Charges: hourly rate

Credentials/experience: More than 20 years of freelance writing and editing. Wrote five children's books for Capstone Press; extensive curriculum writing for David C. Cook and Group Publishing; wrote children's articles/activities and parenting articles for Focus on the Family; developed online study guides for Wallbuilders; extensive copyediting and proofreading for NavPress (including the Remix Message Bible), David C. Cook, WaterBrook, and major international ministries, as well as numerous independent authors.

ABOVE THE PAGES | PAM LAGOMARSINO

Coulterville, CA | 209-878-0245
abovethepages@gmail.com | www.abovethepages.com

Contact: email

Services: manuscript evaluation, substantive editing/rewriting, copyediting, proofreading, create small group/Bible study guides, write discussion questions for books

Types of manuscripts: articles, nonfiction books, devotionals, short stories, curriculum, gift books, adult, teen/YA, picture books, easy readers, middle grade, homeschool and children's ministry materials

Charges: flat fee, word rate

Credentials/experience: AA in English communication; two years of editing experience for Christian nonfiction books, devotionals, sermons, workbooks, homeschool curriculum, and children's materials; certificates in essential skills for Editing nonfiction and editing children's books from The Christian PEN; Certificate for keys to effective editing from Sandhills Community College.

ACEVEDO WORD SOLUTIONS, LLC | JENNE ACEVEDO

Chandler, AZ | 480-510-0419
jenneacevedo@gmail.com | www.jenneacevedo.com

Contact: email

Services: substantive editing/rewriting, copyediting, proofreading, coauthoring, create newsletters, write website text, create small group/Bible study guides, write discussion questions for books, writing coach

Types of manuscripts: articles, nonfiction books, devotionals, query letters, book proposals, curriculum, gift books, adult, teen/YA, picture books, easy readers, middle grade

Charges: hourly rate, word rate

Credentials/experience: Co-owner of Christian Editor Network, LLC; director of The Christian PEN: Proofreaders and Editors Network; director of PENCON; member of the Christian Editor Connection; founder and director of the Chandler Writers' Group since 2011.

ACW CRITIQUE SERVICE | REG A. FORDER

PO Box 110390, Nashville, TN 37222 | 800-21-WRITE
ACWriters@aol.com | www.ACWriters.com

Contact: email

Services: manuscript evaluation, substantive editing/rewriting, copyediting, proofreading

Types of manuscripts: articles, nonfiction books, devotionals, poetry, short stories, novels, query letters, book proposals, curriculum, scripts, gift books, technical material, adult, teen/YA, picture books, easy readers, middle grade

Charges: flat fee, hourly rate, page rate, word rate

Credentials/experience: Established for 35 years. Staff of experienced editors.

ADAM MAYES

Tulsa, OH | 918-638-7282
adamemayes@gmail.com | www.mayesediting.com

Contact: email

Services: manuscript evaluation, substantive editing/rewriting, copyediting, proofreading, ghostwriting, coauthoring

Types of manuscripts: novels, query letters, adult, teen/YA

Charges: word rate, free query-letter critiques

Credentials/experience: BA in English literature from University of Tulsa; silver member of The Christian PEN.

ADIRONDACK EDITING | SUSAN UTTENDORFSKY

Port Leyden, NY

adirondackediting@gmail.com | *www.adirondackediting.com*

Contact: email

Services: manuscript evaluation, substantive editing/rewriting, copyediting, proofreading, writing coach, full-package developmental editing

Types of manuscripts: articles, nonfiction books, devotionals, short stories, novels, query letters, book proposals, adult, teen/YA, picture books, easy readers, middle grade

Charges: word rate

Credentials/experience: More than thirty years of experience in editing and writing; ACES/Poynter certified editor; ongoing continuing education; have edited more than 140 books in the past five years.

AM EDITING AND FREELANCE WRITING |
ANGELA MCCLAIN

125 Mariner Dr., Kings Mountain, NC 28086 | 704-258-6103

amediting35@gmail.com | *www.amediting.webs.com*

Contact: phone

Services: manuscript evaluation, substantive editing/rewriting, copyediting, proofreading, ghostwriting, create brochures, create newsletters, write curriculum lesson plans, write discussion questions for books, writing coach

Types of manuscripts: articles, nonfiction books, devotionals, poetry, short stories, novels, gift books, adult, teen/YA, picture books, easy readers, middle grade

Charges: page rate

Credentials/experience: As a freelance writing consultant, Angela is a contractor for hire. She has been hired to either edit or write content for various print media. Angela is highly flexible, and she can balance the business and writing requirements of multiple clients simultaneously.

AMBASSADOR COMMUNICATIONS |
CLAIRE HUTCHINSON

Sun City West, AZ | 812-390-7907

claire@clairehutchinson.net | *www.ambassadorcommunications.biz*

Contact: email

Services: manuscript evaluation, substantive editing/rewriting, copyediting, proofreading, ghostwriting, coauthoring, write website text, create small group/Bible study guides, write curriculum lesson plans, write discussion questions for books, create PowerPoint presentations, writing coach

Types of manuscripts: articles, nonfiction books, devotionals, poetry, short stories, novels, query letters, scripts, gift books, adult, teen/ YA, picture books, easy readers, middle grade

Charges: flat rate, page rate

Credentials/experience: BA, MA, two screenwriting certificates from UCLA.

AMI EDITING | ANNETTE IRBY

Tacoma, WA | 206-234-7780
editor@AMIediting.com | www.AMIediting.com

Contact: email

Services: manuscript evaluation, substantive editing/rewriting, copyediting, proofreading, critiquing

Types of manuscripts: short stories, novels

Charges: hourly rate

Credentials/experience: Annette spent five years working in acquisitions with a CBA publisher. She has more than twelve years of experience editing in the CBA marketplace and has worked with several well-known authors and publishers. She's an author and an active book reviewer. See her website for testimonials.

AMY BOEKE

Rockford, IL | 815-243-1333
abboeke@gmail.com | alight2readby.wordpress.com

Contact: email

Services: substantive editing/rewriting, copyediting, proofreading, ghostwriting, create brochures, create newsletters, write website text, create small group/Bible study guides, write curriculum lesson plans, write discussion questions for books, Create PowerPoint presentations, writing coach

Types of manuscripts: articles, nonfiction books, devotionals, short stories, novels, query letters, book proposals, curriculum, adult, teen/YA, picture books, easy readers, middle grade

Charges: hourly rate

Credentials/experience: BA English studies, Taylor University Fort Wayne; MAT secondary English education, Rockford College; three years of freelance editing experience.

AMY DROWN

Kalispell, MT | 719-244-1743
editing@amydrown.com | www.amydrown.com/editing

> **Contact:** email
> **Services:** manuscript evaluation, substantive editing/rewriting, copyediting, proofreading
> **Types of manuscripts:** novels, adult, teen/YA, back-cover descriptions, and pitch sheets
> **Charges:** flat fee, word rate
> **Credentials/experience:** Internationally recognized freelance editor specializing in inspirational fiction writing and editing since 2009. I contract with publishers, as well as directly with authors, both published and prepublished, and offer highly competitive rates.

ANDI L. GREGORY

Jasper, IN | 812-309-9865
AndiLGregory@outlook.com | www.AndiLGregory.com

> **Contact:** email
> **Services:** copyediting, proofreading, line edits
> **Types of manuscripts:** short stories, novels, book proposals, teen/YA
> **Charges:** word rate
> **Credentials/experience:** I graduated from Taylor University with a bachelor's in professional writing. I have attended multiple writing conferences and done a couple of editing internships. As an author myself, I understand the difficulties of writing for a particular audience and the things one can miss when self-editing. A polished manuscript, one without many grammar and spelling mistakes, keeps agents, editors, publishers, and readers from being pulled out of your story by a small mistake.

ANDREA MERRELL

Travelers Rest, SC | 864-616-5889
AndreaMerrell7@gmail.com | www.AndreaMerrell.com

> **Contact:** email
> **Services:** substantive editing/rewriting, copyediting, proofreading, writing coach
> **Types of manuscripts:** articles, nonfiction books, devotionals, short stories, novels, adult
> **Charges:** hourly rate
> **Credentials/experience:** Andrea is an author and freelance editor. She is an associate editor with Lighthouse Publishing of the

Carolinas and Christian Devotions Ministries. She is a member of The Christian PEN: Proofreaders and Editors Network and teaches classes at writers conferences.

ANDY SCHEER EDITORIAL SERVICES

5074 Plumstead Dr., Colorado Springs, CO 80920 | 719-282-3729
Andy@AndyScheer.com | *AndyScheer.com*

Contact: e-mail

Services: manuscript evaluations and critiques, copyediting, substantive editing/rewriting, back-cover writing and makeovers

Types of manuscripts: novels, nonfiction books, short stories, book proposals, one-sheets, adult, teen/YA

Charges: page rate; per project for critiques, back-cover copy, and one sheets.

Credentials/experience: More than thirty years of experience in Christian writing, editing, and publishing. Former editor-in-chief of Jerry B. Jenkins Christian Writers Guild. Has served as a judge for national fiction and nonfiction contests and edited fiction and nonfiction for *New York Times* best-selling authors.

ANN KROEKER

Westfield, IN | 317-763-0002
ann@annkroeker.com | *annkroeker.com*

Contact: email

Service: writing coach

Types of manuscripts: articles, nonfiction books, devotionals, poetry, short stories, query letters, book proposals, gift books, adult

Charges: flat fee, hourly rate

Credentials/experience: Coaching offered as a package of services at a monthly rate; for occasional, one-time coaching needs I charge an hourly rate. When a client requests extensive editorial services that exceed the scope of the coaching package, I quote a flat rate per project.

ANNA MOSELEY GISSING

Bethlehem, PA | 336-414-9968
annamgissing@me.com | *www.about.me/annamgissing*

Contact: email

Services: substantive editing/rewriting, copyediting, create small group/Bible study guides, write discussion questions for books, writing coach

Types of manuscripts: articles, nonfiction books, devotionals, curriculum, adult, teen/YA

Charges: hourly rate

Credentials/experience: I am a senior writing instructor at a seminary, an editor for an online publication, and an editor for a curriculum company. I have experience writing and editing curriculum, discussion guides, books, devotionals, and articles. I also have two theological degrees and experience in academic writing and editing.

ARDEO LIT | NICOLE GRANT

Crown Point, IN | 312-371-7024
nicole@ardeolit.com | www.ardeolit.com

Contact: email

Services: substantive editing/rewriting, copyediting, proofreading

Types of manuscripts: nonfiction books, devotionals, poetry, short stories, novels, curriculum, adult

Charges: flat fee, word rate

Credentials/experience: UC Berkeley Professional Sequence in Editing.

ARMOR OF HOPE WRITING SERVICES | DENISE WALKER

Covington, GA | 678-656-8930
dwalker@armorofhopewritingservices.com
www.armorofhopewritingservices.com

Contact: email

Services: copyediting, proofreading, ghostwriting, coauthoring, write curriculum lesson plans, write discussion questions for books, create PowerPoint presentations

Types of manuscripts: nonfiction books, devotionals, short stories, novels, curriculum, teen/YA, picture books, easy readers, middle grade

Charges: fees are on the website

Credentials/experience: Freelance proofreader (children's books and Christian manuscripts), middle-school language arts teacher for twelve years.

ASPIRE EDITING SERVICES | CHRISTY DISTLER

Warminster, PA | 267-231-6723
christy@aspireeditingservices.com | www.aspireeditingservices.com

Contact: email

Services: manuscript evaluation, substantive editing/rewriting, copyediting, proofreading

Types of manuscripts: nonfiction books, devotionals, poetry, short stories, novels, adult, picture books, easy readers

Charges: word rate

Credentials/experience: Educated at Temple University and University of California–Berkeley. Thirteen years of editorial experience, both as an employee and a freelancer. Currently works mostly for publishing houses but accepts freelance work as scheduling allows.

AUTHOR SUPPORT SERVICES | RUSSELL SHERRAD

Carmichael, CA | 916-967-7251
russellsherrard@reagan.com | www.sherrardsebookresellers.com/WordPress/author-support-services-the-authors-place-to-get-help

Contact: email

Services: manuscript evaluation, substantive editing/rewriting, copyediting, proofreading, Kindle e-book formatting, PDF creation, linked table of contents, Twitter and Facebook marketing, submit URL to search engines, book-cover design, blog administration, free services

Types of manuscripts: articles, nonfiction books, devotionals, short stories, novels, teen/YA, picture books, easy readers, middle grade

Charges: flat fee

Credentials/experience: Writing and editing e-books since 2009; freelance services for multiple number of clients.

BA WRITING SOLUTIONS, LLC | BLAKE ATWOOD

Dallas, TX | 512-818-5320
blake@editfor.me | www.blakeatwood.com

Contact: email

Services: manuscript evaluation, substantive editing/rewriting, copyediting, ghostwriting, coauthoring, book-contract evaluation, write website text, create small group/Bible study guides, write discussion questions for books, writing coach

Types of manuscripts: articles, nonfiction books, devotionals, novels, query letters, book proposals, adult

Charges: word rate

Credentials/experience: Prior to starting BA in writing solutions in 2014, Blake worked as an editor for three years at a Christian website startup, served for six years as director of communications for First Baptist Church Georgetown, and was a proofreader for the Texas Senate. Since 2014, he's written and released two books of his own, including *Don't Fear the Reaper: Why Every Author Needs an Editor*; coauthored two books; ghostwritten four books; edited dozens of books; and has helped clients craft well-received book proposals. Certified editor with Christian Editor Connection.

BARBARA KOIS

1007 Cherry St., Wheaton, IL 60187 | 630-532-2941
barbarakois@sbcglobal.net | *www.barbarakois.com*

Contact: email

Services: manuscript evaluation, substantive editing/rewriting, copyediting, proofreading, ghostwriting, coauthoring, write website text, write discussion questions for books, writing coach

Types of manuscripts: articles, nonfiction books, devotionals, short stories, novels, gift books, technical material, adult, teen/YA, picture books, easy readers, middle grade

Charges: hourly rate, page rate

Credentials/experience: Barbara is a writer, editor, author coach, and speaker for writers conferences. She has written or cowritten nine books. She has published more than 600 articles in the *Chicago Tribune*, as well as articles in *Today's Christian Woman*, *Moody*, *Angels on Earth*, *Psychology for Living*, and *Whispers from Heaven*. She has edited more than 400 books for several publishers. She is a regular contributor to technology and other corporate websites and serves as a corporate communications consultant.

BECKY WHITWORTH

Leitchfield, KY | 270-257-2461
blwhit@bbtel.com

Contact: email

Services: substantive editing/rewriting, proofreading, writing coach

Types of manuscripts: articles, nonfiction books, devotionals, short stories, novels, adult, teen/YA, middle grade

Charges: flat fee

Credentials/experience: Retired language arts teacher, currently working as journalist/columnist, published in several magazines, author of five books, independent editor since 1998 with more than sixty clients (worked with some several times on different projects).

BODY AND SOUL PUBLISHING, LLC | SHELLEY HITZ

PO Box 6542, Colorado Springs, CO | 719-445-6558
shelley@shelleyhitz.com | *www.shelleyhitz.com*

Contact: email

Services: author coach

Types of manuscripts: nonfiction books

Charges: monthly or yearly fee

Credentials/experience: Author of more than forty books and owner of *AuthorAudienceAcademy.com* where I help authors get their first drafts out of their heads and onto paper in record time. I teach self-publishing and book marketing.

BOOK OX | THOMAS WOMACK

165 S. Timber Creek Dr., Sisters, OR 97759 | 541-788-6503
Thomas@BookOx.com | *www.BookOx.com*

Contact: email
Services: manuscript evaluation, substantive editing/rewriting, copyediting, coauthoring, create small group/Bible study guides, write discussion questions for books, writing coach
Types of manuscripts: nonfiction books, devotionals, novels, book proposals
Charges: word rate
Credentials/experience: A veteran book editor with four decades of full-time experience.

BREAKOUT EDITING | DORI HARRELL

Yakima, WA | 509-910-2220
doriharrell@gmail.com | *www.doriharrell.wix.com/breakoutediting*

Contact: email
Services: substantive editing/rewriting, copyediting, proofreading, write website text
Types of manuscripts: articles, nonfiction books, devotionals, short stories, novels, query letters, adult, teen/YA, picture books, middle grade
Charges: word rate
Credentials/experience: Dori is a multiple award-winning writer. She freelance edits full-time and has edited more than 100 novels and nonfiction books. As an editor, she releases more than twenty-five books annually.

BRIANNA STORM HILVETY

Moweaqua, IL | 217-412-6841
brianna@theliterarycrusader.com | *theliterarycrusader.com*

Contact: email
Services: substantive editing/rewriting, copyediting, proofreading
Types of manuscripts: articles, nonfiction books, short stories, novels, adult, teen/YA, middle grade
Charges: page rate, word rate
Credentials/experience: I'm a silver member of The Christian PEN, an associate editor for Castle Gate Press, and the copy editor for Kingdom Pen magazine.

BUTTERFIELD EDITORIAL SERVICES | DEBRA L. BUTTERFIELD

St. Joseph, MO | 816-752-2171
deb@debralbutterfield.com | DebraLButterfield.com

Contact: email
Services: manuscript evaluation, substantive editing/rewriting, copyediting, proofreading, writing coach
Types of manuscripts: articles, nonfiction books, devotionals, short stories, novels, query letters, book proposals, adult
Charges: hourly rate
Credentials/experience: Six years of experience as a freelancer; two years of experience with a traditional publisher.

byBRENDA | BRENDA WILBEE

Bellingham, WA | 360-389-6895
Brenda@BrendaWilbee.com | www.BrendaWilbee.com

Contact: email
Services: manuscript evaluation; substantive editing/rewriting; copyediting; create brochures; create newsletters; write website text; writing coach; book design: typesetting and layout, cover
Types of manuscripts: nonfiction books, novels, adult
Charges: flat fee, hourly rate
Credentials/experience: MA in English, BA in professional writing: interdisciplinary, AA in graphic design. I have written ten books--both fiction and nonfiction--with more than 700,000 copies sold, was a regular contributor to Guideposts' *Daily Devotionals* for seventeen years, and somewhere along the line wrote a smattering of short stories and radio scripts. My work has appeared in Zondervan's *Women's Bible #2*, Guidepost's *Best Loved Stories*, a cowboy anthology, and the fiction chapter for *Inside Religious Writing*. I've taught all aspects of writing at writers conferences, colleges, and universities. As an editor and teacher, I help people find their voices and their places within the bigger conversation around us. As an artist and graphic designer, I help writers hone their work and package it and walk them through the process of self-publishing if this is the goal; otherwise, I help writers understand and shape their work to meet publishing demands.

C. S. LAKIN

Morgan Hill, CA | 530-200-5466
cslakin@gmail.com | www.livewritethrive.com

Contact: email

Services: substantive editing/rewriting, copyediting, proofreading, writing coach

Types of manuscripts: nonfiction books, devotionals, poetry, short stories, novels, query letters, book proposals, gift books, adult, teen/YA, picture books, easy readers, middle grade

Charges: hourly rate

Credentials/experience: More than ten years of professional experience in editing and critiquing manuscripts. (I critique more than 200 manuscripts a year for authors, agents, and publishers.) Author of twenty-two books, including sixteen novels (nine traditionally published) and six writing-craft books (The Writer's Toolbox Series). Award-winning author and blogger (*Live Write Thrive*), live and online workshop instructor (*cslakin.teachable.com*; *ChristianWritersInstitute.com*).

CARLA'S MANUSCRIPT SERVICE | CARLA BRUCE

10229 W. Andover Ave., Sun City, AZ 85351 | 612-876-4648
carlaabruce@cox.net

Contact: email

Services: manuscript evaluation, substantive editing/rewriting, copyediting, proofreading, ghostwriting, create small group/Bible study guides

Types of manuscripts: articles, nonfiction books, devotionals, short stories, novels, curriculum, technical material, adult, teen/YA

Charges: hourly rate, page rate

Credentials/experience: Thirty years experience overall, including all levels of editing for almost any kind of manuscript; more than twenty ghostwritten books; fifteen years of editing, copyediting, and typesetting for college textbook companies.

CARLA ROSSI EDITORIAL SERVICES | CARLA ROSSI

The Woodlands, TX
carla@carlarossi.com | *www.carlarossi.com*

Contact: email

Services: manuscript evaluation, substantive editing/rewriting, copyediting, writing coach, specializing in content editing of romance fiction

Types of manuscripts: short stories, novels, adult

Charges: word rate

Credentials/experience: Freelance editor for two years. Traditionally published since 2008. Independently published since 2014. Silver member of The Christian Pen. Member of Romance Writers of America and serve on the board of my local chapter.

CHRISTIAN COMMUNICATOR MANUSCRIPT CRITIQUE SERVICE | SUSAN TITUS OSBORN

3133 Puente St., Fullerton, CA 92835 | 714-313-8651
susanosb@aol.com | *www.christiancommunicator.com*

> **Contact:** email, phone
>
> **Services:** manuscript evaluation, substantive editing/rewriting, copyediting, proofreading, ghostwriting, book-contract evaluation, write website text, create small group/Bible study guides, write curriculum lesson plans, write discussion questions for books, writing coach
>
> **Types of manuscripts:** articles, nonfiction books, devotionals, poetry, short stories, novels, query letters, book proposals, curriculum, scripts, gift books, technical material, adult, teen/YA, picture books, easy readers, middle grade
>
> **Charges:** flat fee, hourly rate, page rate, word rate
>
> **Credentials/experience:** Have a staff of fourteen editors with more than 30 years of experience. Recommended by Evangelical Christian Publishers Association and a number of publishing houses and agents.

CHRISTIAN EDITOR CONNECTION | CHRISTI MCGUIRE

Lakewood Ranch, FL | 941-201-8964
Coordinator@ChristianEditor.com | *www.ChristianEditor.com*

> **Contact:** email
>
> **Services:** manuscript evaluation, substantive editing/rewriting, copyediting, proofreading, ghostwriting, coauthoring, writing coach
>
> **Types of manuscripts:** articles, nonfiction books, devotionals, poetry, short stories, novels, query letters, book proposals, curriculum, scripts, gift books, technical material, adult, teen/YA, picture books, easy readers, middle grade
>
> **Charges:** flat fee, hourly rate, page rate, word rate
>
> **Credentials/experience:** The Christian Editor Connection began in 2007 as a matchmaking service to connect authors, publishers, and agents with qualified, established, professional editorial freelancers who meet their specific needs.

THE CHRISTIAN PEN: PROOFREADERS AND EDITORS NETWORK | JENNE ACEVEDO

Lakewood Ranch, FL | 480-510-0419
jenne@christianeditor.com | *www.thechristianpen.com*

Contact: website
Service: Membership network for Christian editors
Charges: annual membership fee
Description: The Christian PEN is dedicated to equipping aspiring and established freelance editors with education, networking, and community. We offer three levels of membership: bronze, silver, and gold.

CHRISTIANMANUSCRIPTSUBMISSIONS.COM

408-966-3998
info@christianmanuscriptsubmissions.com
www.ChristianManuscriptSubmissions.com

Contact: website
Service: online manuscript-submission service
Types of manuscripts: books—all kinds and all ages
Charges: $98 for six months
Description: Operated by the Evangelical Christian Publishers Association (ECPA), it is the only manuscript service created by the top Christian publishers looking for unsolicited manuscripts in a traditional, royalty-based relationship. It allows authors to submit their manuscript proposals in a secure, online format for review by editors from publishing houses that are members of ECPA.

CM CREATIVE CONSULTING, LLC | CHRISTI MCGUIRE

Lakewood Ranch, FL | 941-201-8964
Christi@ChristiMcGuire.com | www.ChristiMcGuire.com

Contact: email
Services: manuscript evaluation, substantive editing/rewriting, copyediting, proofreading
Types of manuscripts: nonfiction books, devotionals, query letters, book proposals, curriculum, adult
Charges: hourly rate, word rate
Credentials/experience: Christi, freelance editor, writer, and consultant, has been in the Christian publishing industry for sixteen years. Currently, her primary focus is partnering with authors in the creative process to polish their nonfiction book manuscripts and help them navigate the path to publishing through her company. She is on the teaching faculty for PENCON, the only convention for Christian editors in the industry. Christi is a co-owner of the Christian Editor Network, LLC; the director for the Christian Editor Connection; and the director of The PEN Institute, an online educational institute for Christian editors; as well as a member of the Editorial Freelance Association.

COLLABORATIVE EDITORIAL SOLUTIONS | ANDREW BUSS

Green Valley, AZ
info@collaborativeeditorial.com | collaborativeeditorial.com

Contact: email
Services: copyediting, proofreading
Types of manuscripts: articles, nonfiction books
Charges: hourly rate, page rate
Credentials/experience: Member of the Editorial Freelancers Association and The Christian PEN, former member of the Society of Biblical Literature. More than two years of full-time copyediting and proofreading experience, specializing in nonfiction manuscripts.

CORNERSTONE-INK EDITING | VIE HERLOCKER

Fancy Gap, VA | 276-237-7574
vherlock@yahoo.com | www.cornerstone-ink.com

Contact: email
Services: manuscript evaluation, substantive editing/rewriting, copyediting
Types of manuscripts: articles, nonfiction books, devotionals, short stories, novels, query letters, book proposals, adult, teen/YA, middle grade
Charges: hourly rate
Credentials/experience: Member of The Christian PEN: Proofreaders and Editors Network. Certified through Christian Editors Connection. Editor for a small publisher since 2008.

THE CORPORATE PEN | CATHY STREINER

Orange Park, FL | 904-527-8117
Cathy@thecorporatepen.com | www.thecorporatepen.com

Contact: email
Services: substantive editing/rewriting, copyediting, proofreading, ghostwriting, coauthoring, create brochures, create newsletters, write website text, create small group/Bible study guides, write discussion questions for books, writing coach
Types of manuscripts: articles, nonfiction books, devotionals, short stories, novels, scripts, gift books, technical material, adult, teen/YA
Charges: flat fee, hourly rate, page rate, word rate, hourly rate with a maximum
Credentials/experience: Extensive experience with the written word. Cathy began making her living as a writer prior to 1990, and in

2001 established her own company. She self-published a Christian novel in 2009 under a pseudonym and enjoys using her writing and editing skills to help other Christians.

CREATIVE ENTERPRISES STUDIO | MARY HOLLINGSWORTH

Bedford, TX | 817-312-7393
ACreativeShop@aol.com | CreativeEnterprisesStudio.com

> **Contact:** email
> **Services:** manuscript evaluation, substantive editing/rewriting, copyediting, proofreading, ghostwriting, coauthoring, write website text, write discussion questions for books
> **Types of manuscripts:** nonfiction books, devotionals, short stories, novels, book proposals, curriculum, gift books, adult, teen/YA, picture books, easy readers, middle grade
> **Charges:** rates vary according to the work required, estimates provided
> **Credentials/experience:** CES is a publishing services company, hosting more than 150 top Christian publishing freelancers. We work with large, traditional Christian publishers on books by best-selling authors. We also produce custom, first-class books on a turnkey basis for independent authors, ministries, churches, and companies.

CREST PUBLISHER SERVICES | EDWARD BOLME

PO Box 481022, Charlotte, NC 28269 | 704-995-6739
info@crestpub.com | www.crestpub.com

> **Contact:** email
> **Services:** copyediting, proofreading, write website text, typesetting/ interior design
> **Types of manuscripts:** nonfiction books, short stories, novels, book proposals, technical material, adult, teen/YA
> **Charges:** flat fee, hourly rate, word rate
> **Credentials/experience:** Published author; award for interior design; more than twenty years of experience.

CREWS AND COULTER EDITORIAL SERVICES (FORMERLY THE WRITE WAY) | JANET CREWS AND KAY COULTER

713 Gila Trl. (Janet) or 806 Hopi Trl. (Kay), Temple, TX 76504
254-314-2600 or 254-778-6490 | janetkcrews@gmail.com
bkcoulter@sbcglobal.net | www.crewscoultereditorialservices.com

> **Contact:** email
> **Services:** manuscript evaluation, substantive editing/rewriting, copyediting, proofreading, ghostwriting, coauthoring, create

brochures, create newsletters, create PowerPoint presentations, writing coach

Types of manuscripts: nonfiction books, devotionals, short stories, novels, query letters, book proposals, curriculum, gift books, adult, teen/YA, middle grade

Charges: hourly rate

Credentials/experience: Janet and Kay have a combined thirty-six years of experience as editors. Kay is also a published author. Both are members of The Christian PEN and Christian Editor Connection and have worked for several publishers as contract editors, as well as freelance editors with individuals. Kay is experienced in ghostwriting and working with non-native English speakers. Both have experience in editing academic papers.

CROSS & DOT EDITORIAL SERVICES | KATIE VORREITER

San Jose, CA | 408-812-3562
Katie@CrossAndDot.net | www.CrossAndDot.net

Contact: email

Services: copyediting, proofreading

Types of manuscripts: articles, nonfiction books, devotionals, short stories, novels, curriculum, gift books, technical material, adult, teen/YA, middle grade

Charges: flat rate

Credentials/experience: Certificate in professional sequence in editing, U.C. Berkeley; MA in international management; BA in English and Spanish.

CYPRESS WIND | RACHEL HILLS

Mooresville, IN | 317-443-0019
emRachel@CypressWind.com | www.CypressWind.com

Contact: email

Services: substantive editing/rewriting, copyediting, proofreading, writing coach, web page and blog copyediting

Types of manuscripts: articles, nonfiction books, short stories, novels, adult, teen/YA

Charges: rates based on the project

Credentials/experience: I have sixteen years of experience editing for academics and various certifications and training in editing and writing.

DAVID E. FESSENDEN

315 3rd St., Ste. 1, New Cumberland, PA 17070| 215-767-9600
dave@fessendens.net | www.davefessenden.com

Contact: email

Services: manuscript evaluation, substantive editing/rewriting, copyediting, coauthoring, book contract evaluation, create brochures, create newsletters, write website text, create small group/Bible study guides, write curriculum lesson plans, write discussion questions for books, create PowerPoint presentations, writing coach, book-proposal revision

Types of manuscripts: articles, nonfiction books, devotionals, short stories, novels, query letters, book proposals, curriculum, gift books, technical material, adult, teen/YA, picture books, easy readers, middle grade

Charges: flat fee

Credentials/experience: More than thirty years in writing and editing, more than twenty years in editorial management for Christian publishers.

DENA DYER

Granbury, TX | 806-567-1423
denadyer@gmail.com | www.denadyer.com

Contact: email

Services: manuscript evaluation, substantive editing/rewriting, ghostwriting, coauthoring, create newsletters, write website text, writing coach

Types of manuscripts: articles, nonfiction books, devotionals, query letters, book proposals, gift books, adult

Charges: hourly rate

Credentials/experience: Multipublished, award-winning author with more than twenty-five years of experience in the Christian publishing industry.

DR. DENNIS E. HENSLEY

6824 Kanata Ct., Fort Wayne, IN 46815-6388 | 765-667-8193
Dnhensley@hotmail.com | www.dochensley.com

Contact: email, phone

Services: manuscript evaluation, substantive editing/rewriting, copyediting, proofreading, ghostwriting, coauthoring, writing coach

Types of manuscripts: articles, nonfiction books, devotionals, poetry, short stories, novels, query letters, book proposals, adult, teen/YA, new adult

Charges: page rate

Credentials/experience: PhD in English, author of sixty-two published books, college writing professor for twenty years.

DIANA BRANDMEYER

O'Fallon, IL | 314-690-3616
diana@dianabrandmeyer.com | *www.dianabrandmeyer.com*

Contact: email
Services: substantive editing/rewriting, writing coach
Types of manuscripts: short stories, novels, adult, teen/YA
Charges: word rate
Credentials/experience: CBA best-selling author, member of American Christian Fiction Writers, editing more than ten years, member of The Christian Pen.

DONE WRITE EDITORIAL SERVICES | MARILYN A. ANDERSON

127 Sycamore Dr., Louisville, KY, 40223 | 502-244-0751
shelle12@aol.com | *www.TheChristianPEN.com*

Contact: email
Services: manuscript evaluation, copyediting, proofreading
Types of manuscripts: articles, nonfiction books, devotionals, poetry, short stories, novels, curriculum, technical material, adult, picture books, easy readers, middle grade, doctoral dissertations, and theses
Charges: hourly rate
Credentials/experience: I am qualified by an MA in English and a BA in English and the humanities from the University of Louisville. I taught English grammar and literature for four years and have tutored ESL students for twelve years. I worked as a writer, editor, and proofreader of educational curriculum manuscripts, as well as in the energy, utility, and benefits industries for about eighteen years. To date, I have edited fifty-four books, a workbook, thirty-three doctoral dissertations, and a master's thesis, along with innumerable business projects. I have written a company history in three different formats and a glossary of utility terms. I conduct editing and proofreading services for both publishing houses and independent authors. I am a charter and gold member of The Christian PEN: Proofreaders and Editors Network and a member of the Christian Editor Connection.

EAGLE EYE EDITS | TOM THREADGILL

Bells, TN | 731-501-0479
tom@eagleeyeedits.com | *www.EagleEyeEdits.com*

Contact: email
Services: manuscript evaluation, substantive editing/rewriting, copyediting, proofreading, writing coach
Types of manuscripts: novels

Charges: word rate

Credentials/experience: Tom has several years of experience as both an editor and author. Ongoing training ensures the latest industry standards are applied. His editing style leans heavily toward teaching new authors, with developmental editing and mentoring his specialty.

ECHO CREATIVE MEDIA | BRENDA NOEL

Smyrna, TN | 615-223-0754
bnoel@thewordeditor.com

Contact: email

Services: substantive editing/rewriting, copyediting, proofreading, ghostwriting, write website text, create small group/Bible study guides, write curriculum lesson plans, write discussion questions for books

Types of manuscripts: articles, nonfiction books, devotionals, short stories book proposals, curriculum, gift books, adult, teen/YA, picture books, easy readers

Charges: flat fee, hourly rate

Credentials/experience: Fifteen years of experience in the Christian publishing industry.

EDIT RESOURCE, LLC | ERIC AND ELISA STANDFORD

19265 Lincoln Green Ln., Monument, CO 80132 | 719-290-0757
info@editresource.com | *www.editresource.com*

Contact: email

Services: manuscript evaluation, substantive editing/rewriting, ghostwriting, coauthoring, create small group/Bible study guides, write discussion questions for books, writing coach, copywriting

Types of manuscripts: articles, nonfiction books, devotionals, novels, book proposals, curriculum, adult, teen/YA, middle grade

Charges: flat fee, hourly rate

Credentials/experience: We are a husband-and-wife team with more than forty combined years as publishing professionals who have helped on hundreds of books, including many bestsellers. We also represent some of the best writers and editors in the business.

EDITOR FOR YOU | MELANIE RIGNEY

4201 Wilson Blvd. #110328, Arlington, VA 22203 | 703-863-3940
editor@editorforyou.com | *www.editorforyou.com*

Contact: email

Services: manuscript evaluation

Types of manuscripts: nonfiction books, devotionals, short stories, novels, query letters, book proposals, adult

Charges: hourly rate, word rate

Credentials/experience: Melanie has more than thirty years of experience as a writer, reporter, and editor. She established her consultancy in 2003 and has helped hundreds of authors, publishers, and agents. For more information on her credentials and pricing, visit the website. To learn more about Melanie's writing life, visit *www.melanierigney.com.*

eDITMORE EDITORIAL SERVICES | TAMMY DITMORE

501-I S. Reino Rd. #194, Newbury Park, CA 91320 | 805-630-6809
tammy@editmore.com | www.editmore.com

Contact: email

Services: manuscript evaluation, substantive editing/rewriting, copyediting, proofreading, write discussion questions for books, create PowerPoint presentations, writing coach

Types of manuscripts: articles, nonfiction books, devotionals, curriculum, gift books, adult

Credentials/experience: Tammy offers writing, editing, and consulting services to publishers, authors, businesses, organizations, and scholars. She has worked as an editor and writer for daily newspapers, academic journals, books, magazines, and individual authors. Her published writing includes interview-based features, research-driven reports, and first-person essays.

EDITOR WORLD, LLC | PATTI FISHER

Newport, VA | 614-500-3348
info@editorworld.com | www.editorworld.com

Contact: email

Services: copyediting, proofreading

Types of manuscripts: articles, nonfiction books, devotionals, poetry, short stories, novels, query letters, book proposals, curriculum, scripts, gift books, technical material, adult, teen/YA, picture books, easy readers, middle grade

Charges: word rate

Credentials/experience: See website. Credentials of each editor are listed in individual profiles along with client ratings.

EDITORIAL SERVICES | KIM PETERSON

1114 Buxton Dr., Knoxville, TN 37922 | 865-693-9363
peterskus@yahoo.com

Contact: email

Services: manuscript evaluation, substantive editing/rewriting, copyediting, proofreading, create brochures, create newsletters, write website text, create small group/Bible study guides, write curriculum lesson plans, write discussion questions for books, create PowerPoint presentations, writing coach coauthoring, conference speaker

Types of manuscripts: articles, nonfiction books, devotionals, poetry, short stories, novels, query letters, book proposals, curriculum, gift books, technical material, adult, teen/YA, picture books, easy readers, middle grade

Charges: hourly rate

Credentials/experience: MA in print communication. Twenty-four years as a college writing instructor.

ELAINA RAMSEY

Alexandria, VA | 703-403-3424
elainabueno@gmail.com | www.sojo.net

Contact: email

Services: substantive editing/rewriting, copyediting, proofreading, write website text, create small group/Bible study guides, write curriculum lesson plans, write discussion questions for books

Types of manuscripts: articles, devotionals curriculum, scripts

Charges: hourly rate

Credentials/experience: As a former editor of *Sojourners* magazine, I am experienced in editing religious and social-justice content from across the theological and political spectrum. Trained in Associated Press style. I am adept at developing discussion guides, toolkits, and preaching resources. MTS degree and solid experience leading campaigns. I specialize in faith-based media, messaging, and advocacy for racial justice and women's empowerment.

ELIZABETH EASTER

Choctaw, CA | 405-259-9625
FictionEditingService@yahoo.com | penworthypress.com

Contact: email

Services: manuscript evaluation, substantive editing/rewriting, copyediting, proofreading, writing coach

Types of manuscripts: devotionals, poetry, short stories, novels, query letters, book proposals, adult, teen/YA

Charges: flat fee, hourly rate, page rate, word rate

Credentials/experience: Twenty years as a freelance proofreader and editor; three years as a proofreader or an associate editor with small presses; many years as a writer (under a pseudonym) who has been edited. My job is not to make your story mine but to hunker down inside your story, get to know it, and help you tell it to the best of your ability.

ELOQUENT EDITS, LLC | DENISE ROEPER

Port Orange, FL | 386-299-8814
denise.eloquentedits@gmail.com | www.eloquentedits.com

Contact: email
Services: copyediting, proofreading
Types of manuscripts: nonfiction books, short stories, novels, teen/YA, middle grade
Charges: word rate, also review a document and provide an estimate
Credentials/experience: I have edited and proofread print matter ranging from brochures, business print, website content to fiction manuscripts. Specialties are editing fiction, motivational, and spiritual print. Accepting projects that require a short turnaround time.

FACETS EDITORIAL SERVICES | DEBORAH CHRISTENSEN

PO Box 354, Addison, IL 60107 | 630-830-5787
dcfacets@earthlink.net | www.Plowingthefields.wordpress.com

Contact: email, phone
Services: substantive editing/rewriting, copyediting, proofreading, write website text, writing coach
Types of manuscripts: articles, nonfiction books, devotionals, short stories, novels, curriculum, adult, teen/YA
Charges: hourly rate
Credentials/experience: I served as the editor and writer for Christian Service Brigade (CSB Ministries) for eighteen years and for Lighthouse Christian Products for eleven years. I mentored writers with the Jerry B. Jenkins Christian Writers Guild. I am proficient with Associated Press style, *Chicago Manual of Style*, and *The Christian Writer's Manual of Style*.

FAITH EDITORIAL SERVICES | REBECCA FAITH

Novelty, OH | 216-906-0205
rebecca@faitheditorial.com | www.faitheditorial.com

Contact: email
Services: substantive editing/rewriting, copyediting, proofreading, create newsletters, create small group/Bible study guides, write discussion questions for books, transcription
Types of manuscripts: articles, nonfiction books, technical material, adult, teen/YA, sermons

Charges: hourly rate, word rate

Credentials/experience: I was the managing editor for a Christian nonprofit newsletter for six years. I currently copyedit, proofread, and write content for a global Christian ministry that includes material for the website, study guides, and sermon synopses and outlines. In addition, I currently edit technical, peer-reviewed papers for journal publications and manage and train a team of copy editors.

FAITHFULLY WRITE EDITING | DAWN KINZER

Covington, WA | 206-235-2663
dawnkinzer@comcast.net | *www.faithfullywriteediting.com*

Contact: email

Services: substantive editing/rewriting, copyediting, proofreading

Types of manuscripts: nonfiction books, devotionals, short stories, novels

Charges: page rate

Credentials/experience: Dawn launched Faithfully Write Editing in 2010. Since then, she has edited for First Steps Publishing, Future Word Publishing, and writers pursuing publication. Serving as a judge for contests that award excellence in Christian fiction has given her additional opportunities to serve the writing community. She is a member of the Northwest Christian Writers Association and the American Christian Fiction Writers, as well as The Christian PEN and the Christian Editor Connection.

FAITHWORKS EDITORIAL & WRITING | NANETTE THORSEN SNIPES

Buford, GA | 770-945-3093
nsnipes@bellsouth.net | *www.faithworkseditorial.com*

Contact: email

Services: manuscript evaluation, copyediting, create newsletters

Types of manuscripts: articles, nonfiction books, devotionals, poetry, short stories, query letters, book proposals, adult, picture books, easy readers, middle grade, memoirs, business

Charges: hourly rate, page rate

Credentials/experience: In twenty-five years, I have published more than 500 articles and stories, with stories in more than sixty compilation books and devotionals. Member of The Christian PEN: Proofreaders and Editors Network and Christian Editors Connection. Currently edit for ghostwriters, children's fiction writers, memoir writers, and writers of adult nonfiction. Clients include self-published authors, traditionally published authors, and an award-winning author. In the business arena, I have proofread monthly newsletters for a corporate business for twelve years.

FINAL TOUCH PROOFREADING & EDITING | HEIDI MANN

Ely, MN | 701-866-4299
mann.heidi@gmail.com | *www.FinalTouchProofreadingAndEditing.com*

Contact: email
Services: copyediting, proofreading
Types of manuscripts: articles, nonfiction books, devotionals, novels, curriculum, adult, teen/YA, picture books, easy readers, middle grade, Bible studies
Charges: flat rate; hourly rate
Credentials/experience: Fourteen years of experience as a seminary-trained Lutheran pastor; excellent understanding of writing mechanics and style, honed through years of higher education and professional use; freelance editor since 2007 serving authors, publishers, and other entities; have completed multiple educational courses to enhance my knowledge and skills; passionate about writing that intersects with Christian faith. Member of The Christian PEN.

FINDLEY FAMILY VIDEO PUBLICATIONS | MARY C. FINDLEY

Tulsa, OK | 918-805-0669
mjmcfindley@gmail.com | *www.elkjerkyforthesoul.wordpress.com*

Contact: email
Services: copyediting, proofreading, create brochures, create newsletters, write website text, create small group/Bible study guides, write curriculum lesson plans, write discussion questions for books, create PowerPoint presentations
Types of manuscripts: articles, nonfiction books, devotionals, poetry, short stories, novels, curriculum, technical material, adult, teen/YA, picture books, easy readers, middle grade
Charges: word rate
Credentials/experience: Former editor at Bob Jones University Press; proofreader/copy editor for American Advertising Distributors' promotional literature from coupon to book-length; copy editor for many indie authors, fiction and nonfiction, most genres, via online contact. References available on request.

FINESSE WRITING & EDITING SERVICE | DEB PORTER

PO Box 12, St Clair, NSW, Australia, 2759 | +61 412 530 765
finessewriting.com.au

Contact: email, phone

Services: manuscript evaluation, substantive editing/rewriting, writing coach

Types: nonfiction books, devotionals, short stories, novels, adult, teen/YA

Charges: page rate

Credentials/experience: As an editor and writing coach for more than thirteen years, working with FaithWriters.com, and as a publisher for the past three years, I have helped countless people hone their writing skills.

FISTBUMP MEDIA, LLC | DAN KING

Sarasota, FL | 941-780-4179

dan@fistbumpmedia.com | fistbumpmedia.com

Contact: email

Services: manuscript evaluation, proofreading, write website text

Types of manuscripts: nonfiction books, devotionals, short stories, novels,

teen/YA

Charges: flat rate, word rate

Credentials/experience: Fistbump Media provides self-publishing support services in addition to blog/website hosting and design, email subscriber management, and social-media services. We support experienced and first-time writers and leverage the power of self-publishing. References and portfolio are on the website.

FRANKFORT WRITERS CENTER | CHARITY SINGLETON CRAIG

358 N. Jackson St., Ste. B, Frankfort, IN 46041 | 317-446-1818

charity@frankfortwriterscenter.com | www.frankfortwriterscenter.com

Contact: email

Services: manuscript evaluation, substantive editing/rewriting, copyediting, create brochures, create newsletters, write website text, writing coach

Types of manuscripts: articles, nonfiction books, devotionals, short stories, novels, query letters, book proposals, adult

Charges: combination of hourly and word rate

Credentials/experience: Bachelor's degree in communications; more than twenty years of experience with writing and editing; author of *On Being a Writer: 12 Simple Habits for a Writing Life That Lasts*; frequent workshop leader.

GALADRIEL GRACE

Lexington, KY | 859-368-8889
galadriel@galadrielgrace.com | galadrielgrace.com

Contact: email

Services: substantive editing/rewriting, copyediting, proofreading, create brochures, create newsletters, write website text, create small group/Bible study guides, write curriculum lesson plans, write discussion questions for books, query letters

Types of manuscripts: short stories, query letters, curriculum, teen/YA, picture books, easy readers, middle grade

Charges: flat rate

Credentials/experience: Several years of experience teaching English and language; writing and editing children's books, query letters, website and marketing content both personally and professionally for clients.

GINGER KOLBABA

Elgin, IL | 847-366-6547
ginger@gingerkolbaba.com | www.gingerkolbaba.com

Contact: email

Services: manuscript evaluation, substantive editing/rewriting, copyediting, proofreading, ghostwriting, coauthoring, create small group/Bible study guides, write discussion questions for books, writing coach

Types of manuscripts: articles, nonfiction books, devotionals, novels, novels, query letters, book proposals, adult, teen/YA

Charges: hourly rate for editing, flat rate for writing

Credentials/experience: More than twenty years in the industry. Former editor of *Today's Christian Woman* and *Marriage Partnership* magazines and *Kyria.com*, all national, award-winning publications of Christianity Today International. Written or contributed to more than thirty books and 500 articles, both in print and online. Clients include many publishing houses and best-selling authors.

HAYHURST EDITORIAL, LLC | SARAH HAYHURST

Grayson, GA | 715-548-1514
sarah@sarahhayhurst.com | www.sarahhayhurst.com

Contact: email

Services: substantive editing/rewriting, copyediting, proofreading, create newsletters, write website text, create PowerPoint presentations, writing coach

Types of manuscripts: articles, nonfiction books, devotionals, curriculum, adult, teen/YA, picture books, middle grade

Charges: word rate

Credentials/experience: Editor. Writer. Coach. Sarah pursued a bachelor's degree in communication arts in 2014, graduating *cum laude*. She is a gold member of The Christian PEN and is certified with the Christian Editor Connection with which she passed testing and demonstrated expertise in proofreading, copyediting, and content editing of both fiction and nonfiction manuscripts, as well as other content. Nonfiction is her #1 area of expertise. Sarah has enjoyed a variety of positions, such as editor/teacher for a publishing company, managing editor for a university, marketing director for a law firm, and computer/ESL teacher for a private school. These and other experiences make Sarah versatile today.

HENRY MCLAUGHLIN

Saginaw, TX

henry@henrymclaughlin.org | www.henrymclaughlin.org

Contact: email

Services: manuscript evaluation, substantive editing/rewriting, copyediting, ghostwriting, coauthoring, create PowerPoint presentations, writing coach

Types of manuscripts: nonfiction books, short stories, novels, adult

Charges: flat fee, hourly rate, page rate

Credentials/experience: I have been a full-time writer since 2010. My first novel won the Operation First Novel contest. I have published both traditionally and independently, as well as in magazines and anthologies. I have coached and edited eleven authors in both fiction and nonfiction. I have worked extensively with writers groups, coaching and teaching the craft of writing. I have also taught the craft at conferences, workshops, seminars, and webinars.

HESTERMAN CREATIVE | DR. VICKI HESTERMAN

PO Box 6788, San Diego, CA 92166

vhes@icloud.com

Contact: email

Services: manuscript evaluation, substantive editing/rewriting, copyediting, proofreading, coauthoring, create newsletters, write website text, create small group/Bible study guides, writing coach

Types of manuscripts: articles, nonfiction books, devotionals, novels, query letters, book proposals, gift books, adult, teen/YA

Charges: industry-standard hourly rate based on word count and work needed; binding quote given with sample chapters and synopsis

Credentials/experience: Thirty years of experience in the field, both Christian and secular: newspaper photojournalist, publishing-house book editor, university writing professor, book collaborator, and writing coach.

HOUSTONFREELANCEWRITER.COM | KATHERINE SWARTS

Houston, TX | 832-573-9501

ks@houstonfreelancewriter.com | www.HoustonFreelanceWriter.com

Contact: email

Services: ghostwriting, coauthoring, create newsletters, write website text, create small group/Bible study guides, write curriculum lesson plans, write discussion questions for books, write blog posts

Types of manuscripts: articles, nonfiction books

Charges: flat fee

Credentials/experience: I have more than ten years of experience as a freelance writer and two years as an online content writer. My publishing credits are listed in detail on my website; also see my LinkedIn profile, *www.linkedin.com/in/houstonfreelancewriter*.

INKSNATCHER | SALLY HANAN

Austin, TX | 512-351-5869

inkmeister@inksnatcher.com | www.inksnatcher.com

Contact: email, text

Services: substantive editing/rewriting, copyediting, proofreading, ghostwriting, coauthoring, write website text, write discussion questions for books

Types of manuscripts: articles, nonfiction books, short stories, novels, curriculum, gift books, adult, teen/YA, easy readers, middle grade

Charges: flat rate, hourly rate, word rate

Credentials/experience: Established in 2007, Inksnatcher has edited books and written copy for Bobby Conner, Shawn Bolz, Jon Hamill, and Dennis Cramer, among many others.

INSPIRATION FOR WRITERS, INC. | SANDY TRITT

1527 18th St., Parkersburg, WV 26101 | 304-428-1218

IFWeditors@gmail.com | www.InspirationForWriters.com

Contact: email, phone

Services: manuscript evaluation, substantive editing/rewriting, copyediting, proofreading, ghostwriting, write curriculum lesson plans, write discussion questions for books, writing coach, consulting

Types of manuscripts: nonfiction books, devotionals, short stories, novels, query letters, book proposals, curriculum, scripts, gift books, adult, teen/YA, middle grade

Charges: flat fee, word rate

Credentials/experience: We are one of the oldest and most respected editing/writing companies on the Internet today. All our editors-writers are published authors with years of editing experience who've been specially trained to edit according to our high standards.

IT'S YOUR VOICE, ONLY BETTER! | SHARMAN MONROE

Washington, DC | 240-353-8000
myjourneytome@gmail.com | *www.myjourneytome-thediscovery.com*

Contact: email

Services: substantive editing/rewriting, copyediting, proofreading

Types of manuscripts: articles, nonfiction books, devotionals, short stories, adult

Charges: hourly or flat rate, negotiable

Credentials/experience: More than twenty-five years of writing, editing, and proofreading experience. Edited more than seven published books.

JAMES PENCE

Greenville, TX | 469-730-6478
james@pence.com | *jamespence.com*

Contact: email

Services: manuscript evaluation, substantive editing/rewriting, copyediting, proofreading, coauthoring, writing coach

Types of manuscripts: nonfiction books, novels, adult, teen/YA

Charges: flat fee, page rate

Credentials/experience: Author or coauthor of nine books, including novels, nonfiction, and text/instructional. Publishers include Osborne/McGraw-Hill, Tyndale, Kregel, Baker, Thomas Nelson, and Mountainview Books.

JAMES WATKINS

jim@jameswatkins.com | *jameswatkins.com*

Contact: email

Services: manuscript evaluation, substantive editing/rewriting, copyediting, ghostwriting, coauthoring, write website text, write discussion questions for books, writing coach

Types of manuscripts: articles, nonfiction books, devotionals, book proposals, adult

Charges: page rate

Credentials/experience: Award-winning editor (four Evangelical Press Awards), developed the editing course at Taylor University, served as an editor and editorial director at Wesleyan Publishing House for more than twenty years. He is the author of twenty books and more than 2,000 articles.

JAMIE CHAVEZ

Murfreesboro, TN

jamie.chavez@gmail.com | *www.jamiechavez.com*

Contact: email

Services: manuscript evaluation, substantive editing/rewriting, copyediting, coauthoring, write website text, write discussion questions for books

Types of manuscripts: articles, nonfiction books, novels, book proposals, curriculum, gift books, adult, teen/YA, picture books, easy readers, middle grade

Charges: flat fee

Credentials/experience: Eleven years with Thomas Nelson Publishers and twelve years as a freelance editor. See website for more complete bio.

JANIS WHIPPLE

9608 Regiment Ct., Land O Lakes, FL, 34638 | 954-579-8545

janiswhipple@gmail.com

Contact: email

Services: manuscript evaluation, substantive editing/rewriting, copyediting, proofreading, coauthoring, create brochures, create small group/Bible study guides, write discussion questions for books, writing coach

Types of manuscripts: articles, nonfiction books, devotionals query letters, book proposals, curriculum, gift books, adult, teen/YA

Charges: hourly rate, sometimes do fee projects

Credentials/experience: Thirty years of editing; ten years as an in-house editor with B&H Publishers in acquisitions and managing editing; fifteen years as a freelance editor and writing coach.

JAY PAYLEITNER

629 N. Tyler Rd., Saint Charles, IL 60174 | 630-377-7899

jaypayleitner@gmail.com | *www.jaypayleitner.com*

Contact: email

Services: coauthoring
Types of manuscripts: nonfiction books, gift books, technical material, adult, teen/YA, picture books, easy readers, middle grade
Charges: flat fee, shared advance and royalties
Credentials/experience: Authored more than twenty books for six CBA publishers, including *What If God Wrote Your Bucket List?*, *Lifeology*, *52 Things Kids Need from a Dad*, and *52 Ways to Connect as a Couple.*

JEANETTE GARDNER LITTLETON, PUBLICATION SERVICES
3706 N.E. Shady Lane Dr., Gladstone, MO | 816-459-8016
jeanettedl@earthlink.net | www.linkedin.com/in/jeanette-littleton-b1b790101?trk=hp-identity-name

Contact: email
Services: manuscript evaluation, substantive editing/rewriting, copyediting, proofreading, create brochures, create newsletters, write website text, create small group/Bible study guides, write curriculum lesson plans, write discussion questions for books, consulting
Types of manuscripts: articles, nonfiction books, devotionals, short stories, novels, query letters, book proposals, curriculum, gift books, technical material, adult, teen/YA, easy readers, middle grade
Charges: flat fee, hourly rate, page rate
Credentials/experience: Thirty years of experience as editor for various publications and publishers, full-time and freelance, including Moody, Guideposts, Tyndale, Church of the Nazarene, Bethany House, Comfort Publishing, Howard Publishing, Answers in Genesis, Youth Specialties, and Barbour. Also have written more than 2,500 articles of all styles, devotionals, skits, promotional blurbs, curriculum, and a few books.

JEANETTE HANSCOME
San Ramon, CA | 925-487-7550
jeanettehanscome@gmail.com | jeanettehanscome.com

Contact: email
Services: manuscript evaluation, substantive editing/rewriting, copyediting, ghostwriting, coauthoring, write website text, write discussion questions for books, writing coach
Types of manuscripts: articles, nonfiction books, devotionals, short stories, novels, query letters, book proposals, gift books, adult, teen/YA, middle grade
Charges: flat fee, hourly rate

Credentials/experience: I have more than twenty years of writing experience and twelve years of editing, critiquing, and teaching. My publishing credits include five published books, one short fiction e-book, and more than 300 published articles, devotions, and stories.

JEFF PEPPLE

15317 Laurel Ridge, Leo, IN 46765 | 260-627-7347
jhpepple@hotmail.com

Contact: email; phone
Services: manuscript evaluation, substantive editing/rewriting, copyediting, proofreading, write website text
Types of manuscripts: articles, nonfiction books, devotionals, short stories, novels, curriculum, scripts, gift books, technical material, adult, teen/YA, easy readers, middle grade
Charges: flat fee, hourly rate, page rate, word rate
Credentials/experience: BA in professional writing, Taylor University.

JENNIFER EDWARDS WRITING & EDITING |
JENNIFER EDWARDS

Loomis, CA | 916-768-4207
mail.jennifer.edwards@gmail.com | *www.jedwardsediting.net*

Contact: email
Services: manuscript evaluation, substantive editing/rewriting, copyediting, proofreading, write website text, create small group/ Bible study guides, write curriculum lesson plans, write discussion questions for books, create PowerPoint presentations
Types of manuscripts: articles, nonfiction books, devotionals, curriculum, scripts, gift books, technical material
Charges: flat fee
Credentials/experience: Master's degree in biblical and theological studies from Western Seminary; gold member of the Christian Editor Network. Managing editor of the publishing arm of Principles To Live By (PTLB, *ptlb.com*). I also manage the marketing processes for PTLB. promoting their consultants, events, and book launches, including website, blog, email campaigns, social-media elements, and donor relations.

JHWRITING+ | NICOLE HAYES

Randleman, NC | 410-709-8549
jhwritingplus@yahoo.com | *www.jhwritingplus.com*

Contact: email

Services: manuscript evaluation, substantive editing/rewriting, copyediting, proofreading, ghostwriting, coauthoring, write website text, create small group/Bible study guides, write curriculum lesson plans, write discussion questions for books writing coach

Types of manuscripts: articles, nonfiction books, devotionals, poetry, short stories, novels, curriculum, gift books, technical material, adult, teen/YA

Charges: flat rate, word rate

Credentials/experience: Bachelor's degree in English; PhD in education. Although I do most writing, editing, and proofreading projects, my niche is creative nonfiction (engaging, dramatic, factual prose). I have been writing and editing for more than twenty-five years.

JLC EDITING SERVICES | JODY COLLINS

1403 Newport Ct. S.E., Renton, WA 98058 | 425-260-0948
heyjode70@yahoo.com | *www.jodyleecollins.com*

Contact: email

Services: manuscript evaluation, copyediting, proofreading, create small group/Bible study guides, write curriculum lesson plans, writing coach, big-picture edit of your message/vision

Types of manuscripts: articles, nonfiction books, devotionals, book proposals, curriculum, picture books, easy readers

Charges: hourly rate, page rate, word rate

Credentials/experience: BA in liberal studies, English major. Teaching credential, 1991. Post graduate work included courses in writer's workshop and teaching writing. More than twenty-five years of experience writing and editing. Blog content Editor/coordinator for Faith & Culture Writer's Community.

JOCELYN L. BAILEY

1100 Market St., Floor 6 (Society of Work), Chattanooga, TN 37402
615-270-EDIT | *jocelynlyn@gmail.com* | *www.jocelynbailey.com*

Contact: email, phone

Services: manuscript evaluation, substantive editing/rewriting, copyediting, proofreading, ghostwriting, coauthoring, write website text, write discussion questions for books, create PowerPoint presentations, writing coach

Types of manuscripts: articles, nonfiction books, devotionals, short stories, novels, query letters, book proposals, gift books, technical material, adult, teen/YA, picture books, easy readers, middle grade

Charges: flat rate, hourly rate

Credentials/experience: Ten years in publishing industry; MA and PhD in literature and composition.

JOY MEDIA | JULIE-ALLYSON IERON

Park Ridge, IL

joy@joymediaservices.com | *www.joymediaservices.com*

Contact: email

Services: manuscript evaluation, substantive editing/rewriting, copyediting, ghostwriting, coauthoring, write website text, create small group/Bible study guides, write discussion questions for books, writing coach

Types of manuscripts: articles, nonfiction books, devotionals, book proposals, gift books, adult

Charges: hourly rate

Credentials/experience: Master's degree in journalism and more than twenty-five years of experience in Christian publishing, writing, editing, and public relations. Specializes in Christian living, Bible study, and business/ministry promotions. Coaches first-time authors.

KAREN O'CONNOR COMMUNICATIONS | KAREN O'CONNOR

Watsonville, CA | 831-726-6008

karen@karenoconnor.com | *www.karenoconnor.com*

Contact: email

Services: manuscript evaluation, copyediting, write discussion questions for books, writing coach

Types of manuscripts: articles, nonfiction books, query letters, book proposals, adult

Charges: flat fee, hourly rate

Credentials/experience: Published author of more than seventy-five books, hundreds of magazine articles, business writing, blogs, newsletters, and educational writing.

KAREN SAARI

Burney, CA | 208-749-0084

karensaari144@gmail.com | *livinginserendipity.com*

Contact: email

Services: substantive editing/rewriting, copyediting, proofreading

Types of manuscripts: articles, short stories, novels, gift books, teen/YA, easy readers, middle grade

Charges: page rate

Credentials/experience: I'm currently working toward a BA in English. I've been writing for ten years and editing for three years. I've worked on projects from a quilt instruction book to a fairy tale.

KATHY IDE BOOK SERVICES | KATHY IDE

Brea, CA | 714-529-1212
Kathy@KathyIde.com | www.KathyIde.com

Contact: email

Services: manuscript evaluation, substantive editing/rewriting, copyediting, proofreading, ghostwriting, coauthoring, create small group/Bible study guides, writing coach

Types of manuscripts: articles, nonfiction books, devotionals, short stories, novels, query letters, book proposals, scripts, gift books, adult, teen/YA

Charges: hourly rate

Credentials/experience: Kathy is the author of *Proofreading Secrets of Best-Selling Authors* and the editor-compiler of the Fiction Lover's Devotional series. She has ghostwritten ten nonfiction books and a series of five novels. Kathy has been a professional freelance editor since 1998, offering a full range of editorial services for aspiring writers, established authors, and book publishers. She speaks at writers conferences across the country and is the director of the Mount Hermon Christian Writers Conference and the SoCal Christian Writers' Conference. Kathy is a co-owner of the Christian Editor Network, parent company to The Christian PEN: Proofreaders and Editors Network, the Christian Editor Connection, the PEN Institute, and PENCON.

KATHY TYERS GILLIN

Bozeman, MT
kathytyers@yahoo.com | www.kathytyers.com

Contact: email

Services: substantive editing/rewriting, copyediting, proofreading, writing coach

Types of manuscripts: articles, nonfiction books, novels, adult, teen/YA

Charges: hourly rate

Credentials/experience: *New York Times* bestselling author of ten science fiction/fantasy novels and two nonfiction books. Experience editing multiple fiction genres and nonfiction, including scholarly theological books. Thirty years writing experience. MA, Christianity and the Arts, Regent College, Canada.

KATIE MORFORD

Haven, KS | 316-293-9202
morford.katie@gmail.com | www.storyforhisglory.com

Contact: email

Services: manuscript evaluation, substantive editing/rewriting, copyediting, create brochures, create newsletters, write website text, write discussion questions for books, create PowerPoint presentations, writing coach, fiction mentorship courses

Types of manuscripts: articles, short stories, novels, scripts, adult, teen/YA

Charges: flat rate, word rate, depending on type of edit

Credentials/experience: Cofounder and primary content editor for Crosshair Press; editor of multiple published novels and numerous articles; graduate of the Jerry B. Jenkins Christian Writers Guild; member of The Christian PEN; degree in journalism from Kansas State University; experience as writer, editor, and photographer for newspapers; three years of experience managing international nonprofit communications and working as a writer, editor, photographer, social media/blogger, and documentary producer. Specializes in deep developmental/content edits for character-centric novels in the speculative, action, international thriller, and historical fiction genres.

KEELY BOEVING EDITORIAL | KEELY BOEVING

Denver, CO | 303-916-7498
keely.boeving@gmail.com | www.keelyboeving.com

Contact: email

Services: manuscript evaluation, substantive editing/rewriting, copyediting, ghostwriting, coauthoring

Types of manuscripts: nonfiction books, novels, query letters, book proposals, adult, teen/YA, middle grade

Charges: hourly rate

Credentials/experience: Experienced editor and copy editor, formerly worked in editorial for Oxford University Press. Have worked with independent clients, literary agencies, and publishers as a freelancer for the past several years.

KELLY KAGAMAS TOMKIES

Bexley, OH | 614-270-0185
kellytomkies@gmail.com | users.wowway.com/~kakwrite/About.html

Contact: email

Services: substantive editing/rewriting, copyediting, proofreading, ghostwriting, writing coach

Types of manuscripts: articles, nonfiction books, devotionals, short stories, novels, query letters, book proposals, adult, teen/YA, picture books, easy readers, middle grade

Charges: flat fee

Credentials/experience: I have nearly twenty years of editorial experience, including authoring seven books for different publishers, contributing chapters to two National Geographic books, serving as editor of three major business magazines, and years of experience writing and editing for publishers and individual authors. My client list includes HarperCollins, John Wiley & Sons, McGraw-Hill, Kirkus Editorial, Fountainhead Press, Barbour Books, Vantage Press, and Gadfly, LLC, as well as individual authors who wish to find publishers or self-publish.

KEN WALKER

729 Ninth Ave. #331, Huntington, WV 25701 | 304-525-3343
kenwalker33@gmail.com | *www.KenWalkerWriter.com*

Contact: email

Services: manuscript evaluation, substantive editing/rewriting, ghostwriting, coauthoring, write discussion questions for books, writing coach

Types of manuscripts: articles, nonfiction books, devotionals, book proposals, adult

Charges: based on complexity of work and time involved

Credentials/experience: Longtime freelancer, ghostwriter, coauthor and book editor. Certified with Christian Editor Connection.

KRISTEN STIEFFEL

Orlando, FL | 407-928-7801
kristen@kristenstieffel.com | *www.kristenstieffel.com*

Contact: email

Services: manuscript evaluation, substantive editing/rewriting, copyediting, proofreading, ghostwriting, coauthoring, writing coach

Types of manuscripts: short stories, novels, query letters, book proposals, adult, teen/YA, picture books, easy readers, middle grade, specializing in fantasy and science fiction

Charges: custom quotes per project

Credentials/experience: Certified with Christian Editor Connection. Member of the Editorial Freelancers Association and gold member of The Christian PEN: Proofreaders and Editors Network. Freelance editor since 2010; prior to that worked twenty years in business journalism.

LEE WARREN COMMUNICATIONS | LEE WARREN

Omaha, NE | 402-740-5795

leewarrenjr@outlook.com | *www.leewarren.info/editing*

Contact: email
Services: copyediting, proofreading
Types of manuscripts: nonfiction books, devotionals, novels
Charges: word rate
Credentials/experience: Lee Warren has copyedited for three publishing houses, one manuscript critique service, and a Christian newspaper. He's also copyedited and proofread dozens of manuscripts through his own service (testimonials available on the website).

LESLIE L. MCKEE EDITING | LESLIE L. MCKEE

lmckeeediting@gmail.com | *lmckeeediting.wixsite.com/lmckeeediting*

Contact: email
Services: substantive editing/rewriting, copyediting, proofreading, write discussion questions for books
Types of manuscripts: nonfiction books, devotionals, poetry, short stories, novels, adult, teen/YA, picture books, easy readers, middle grade
Charges: word rate per-project rate
Credentials/experience: Freelance editor with various publishing houses (large and small) since 2012, working with traditionally published and self-published authors. Member of The Christian PEN and American Christian Fiction Writers. See website for details on services offered, as well as testimonials.

LIBBY GONTARZ

Apache Junction, AZ | 480-278-4848

libbygontarz@gmail.com | *libbygontarz@gmail.com*

Contact: email
Services: substantive editing/rewriting, copyediting, proofreading, write website text
Types of manuscripts: articles, nonfiction books, curriculum, adult, middle grade
Charges: flat fee, hourly rate, sample edit and quote available
Credentials/experience: Following a successful career teaching at the fourth grade and middle school levels, Libby moved into corporate

training, working with school districts across the United States
to improve student test scores. Subsequently, she has written and
edited educational materials for instruction and assessment of
student learning at the elementary, junior-high, and high-school
levels. Libby has also worked for a weekly newspaper, writing and
coordinating articles on local businesses and politics, penning a
weekly column and editing the community and business sections.
Libby especially enjoys helping writers of Christian nonfiction and
personal memoir to bring their dreams of independent publication
to reality. Member of The Christian PEN.

LIGHTHOUSE EDITING | LON ACKELSON

13326 Community Rd. #11, Poway, CA 92064 | 858-748-9258
Isaiah68la@sbcglobal.net | *lighthouseedit.com*

Contact: email
Services: manuscript evaluation, substantive editing/rewriting,
   copyediting, proofreading, ghostwriting, coauthoring, book
   contract evaluation
Types of manuscripts: articles, nonfiction books, short stories, query
   letters, book proposals, curriculum, adult, easy readers; middle grade
Charges: flat fee, page rate
Credentials/experience: Published book in 2008, edited many books
   and articles all accepted by publishers for Lighthouse Editing,
   which I started in 1993; nineteen years of experience editing
   Christian curriculum for children as a senior editor; professional
   editor since 1984.

LIGHTNING EDITING SERVICES | DENISE LOOCK

Waynesville, NC | 908-868-5854
denise@lightningeditingservices.com | *www.lightningeditingservices.com*

Contact: email
Services: manuscript evaluation, substantive editing/rewriting,
   copyediting, proofreading, create newsletters, create small group/
   Bible study guides, write discussion questions for books, create
   PowerPoint presentations
Types of manuscripts: articles, nonfiction books, devotionals, gift
   books, teen/YA, middle grade
Charges: flat fee, hourly rate
Credentials/experience: Associate editor for Lighthouse Publishing
   of the Carolinas (five years); high-school English teacher and
   college instructor (twenty-nine years); editor of *The Journey
   Christian Newspaper* (three years); author of two devotional books.

LISA BARTELT

Lancaster, PA | 717-673-7236
lmbartelt@gmail.com | lisabartelt.com

Contact: email
Services: copyediting, proofreading, coauthoring create newsletters, write website text
Types of manuscripts: articles, nonfiction books, devotionals, novels, query letters
Charges: hourly rate
Credentials/experience: Eight years of writing and editing for daily newspapers; member of American Christian Fiction Writers and The Christian PEN; published articles in *Thriving Family*, *Prayer Connect*, and *The Upper Room*; wrote curriculum for Group Publishing.

LINDSAY A. FRANKLIN

Escondido, CA | 858-243-8134
Lindsay@LindsayAFranklin.com | lindsayafranklin.com

Contact: email
Services: manuscript evaluation, substantive editing/rewriting, copyediting, proofreading, ghostwriting, coauthoring, writing coach
Types of manuscripts: nonfiction books, short stories, novels, adult, teen/YA, picture books, easy readers, middle grade
Charges: hourly rate, word rate
Credentials/experience: Award-winning, published author; member of The Christian PEN.

LINORE BURKARD EDITING SERVICES | LINORE ROSE BURKARD

Waynesville, OH | 513-331-0143
Linore@LinoreBurkard.com | www.LinoreBurkard.com

Contact: email
Services: manuscript evaluation, copyediting, proofreading, write discussion questions for books
Types of manuscripts: articles, devotionals, poetry, short stories, novels, adult, teen/YA
Charges: hourly rate
Credentials/experience: Previous editor-in-chief of religious publication; *magna cum laude* degree in English lit; published author of five novels; previous editing experience.

LOGOS WORD DESIGNS, LLC | LINDA NATHAN

PO Box 735, Maple Falls, WA 98266-0735 | 360-599-3429
linda@logosword.com | www.logosword.com

Contact: email

Services: manuscript evaluation, substantive editing/rewriting, copyediting, proofreading, ghostwriting, write website text, write discussion questions for books

Types of manuscripts: articles, nonfiction books, devotionals, short stories, novels, query letters, book proposals, gift books, technical material, adult, teen/YA; apologetics, academic, law, journalism, interviews, reviews, business, the arts, health/social sciences, education, history, and marketing communications

Charges: word rate

Credentials/experience: Linda has operated Logos Word Designs since 1992. She has more than thirty years of experience as an independent freelance writer, editor, and publishing consultant, working with authors and institutions on a wide range of projects. She has ten years of experience in most areas of the legal field as a paralegal, legal secretary, and notary public. She has also edited nearly 100 college textbooks and helped numerous authors achieve publication. Member of Northwest Independent Editors Guild, Editorial Freelancers Association, American Christian Fiction Writers. Certified with Christian Editor Connection.

LOUISE M. GOUGE

Kissimmee, FL | 407-694-5765
Louisemgouge@aol.com | www.blog.Louisemgouge.com

Contact: email

Services: copyediting

Types of manuscripts: devotionals, short stories, novels, query letters, book proposals

Charges: word rate

Credentials/experience: College English professor; multi-published, award-winning author of twenty-three novels.

LUCIE WINBORNE

Longwood, FL | 321-439-7743
lwinborne704@gmail.com | www.bluetypewriter.com

Contact: email

Services: copyediting, proofreading

Types of manuscripts: articles, nonfiction books, devotionals, poetry, short stories, novels, query letters, book proposals, curriculum, scripts, gift books, adult, teen/YA, easy readers, middle grade, blog posts

Charges: hourly rate

Credentials/experience: Member of The Christian PEN and Editorial Freelancers Association. Copy editor for Global Hope Network International and Ask God Today Ministries. Proofreader for Lighthouse Publishing of the Carolinas. Experience in proofreading and copyediting fiction, nonfiction, educational, and business documents. Demonstrated adherence to deadlines and excellent communication skills.

LUCY CRABTREE

Lawrence, KS | 913-543-1782
editingbylucy@gmail.com | *editingbylucy.com*

Contact: email
Services: copyediting, proofreading
Types of manuscripts: articles, nonfiction books, short stories, novels, query letters, book proposals, adult
Charges: word rate
Credentials/experience: Polished writer and editor with nine years of professional experience in the publishing industry (seven years) and educational settings (two years). Well-versed in Microsoft Office and Adobe Creative Suite. Familiarity with Associated Press, American Psychological Association, and *Chicago Manual* style books. Experience with Drupal, WordPress, and Blogger.

LYNNE TAGAWA

San Antonio, TX | 210-544-4397
lbtagawa@gmail.com

Contact: email
Services: copyediting, proofreading
Types of manuscripts: articles, nonfiction books, short stories, novels, curriculum, scripts, adult, teen/YA, middle grade; specializing in theological, historical, and science/medicine
Charges: word rate
Credentials/experience: Copy editor with Chapel Library of Pensacola; high-school writing instructor; silver member of The Christian PEN; author of *Sam Houston's Republic*; member of American Christian Fiction Writers.

MARCY WEYDEMULLER

San Francisco, CA | 925-876-4860
marcy@sowinglightseeds.com | *www.marcyweydemuller.com*

Contact: email
Services: manuscript evaluation, substantive editing/rewriting, create

small group/Bible study guides, write curriculum lesson plans, write discussion questions for books, writing coach

Types of manuscripts: articles, nonfiction books, devotionals, short stories, novels, curriculum, adult, teen/YA, picture books, easy readers, middle grade

Charges: hourly rate

Credentials/experience: I have worked on more than forty published novels, and four of the authors I work with have published three or more series. My current edits have included historical fiction, historical Christmas novella, YA contemporary, middle-readers both historical and contemporary, suspense-mystery, woman's romance, and memoir. I have more than twenty-five years of experience writing, mentoring, and teaching, both in fiction and nonfiction, including Bible studies and college composition. I have completed a BA in history and sociology and an MFA in writing, with a special focus on fantasy, poetry, and children's literature.

MARILYN A. ANDERSON

127 Sycamore Dr., Louisville, KY | 502-244-0751
shelle12@aol.com | *www.TheChristianPEN.com*

Contact: email

Services: manuscript evaluation, copyediting, proofreading

Types of manuscripts: articles, nonfiction books, devotionals, poetry, short stories, novels, curriculum, technical material, adult, picture books

Charges: hourly rate

Credentials/experience: BA, MA in English and the humanities; worked as a writer, editor, and proofreader of educational curriculum manuscripts, as well as in the energy, utility, and benefits industries for about eighteen years. To date, I have edited fifty-four books, a workbook, thirty-three doctoral dissertations, and a master's thesis, along with numerous business projects. I have written a company history in three different formats and a glossary of utility terms. I conduct editing and proofreading services for both publishing houses and independent authors. I am a charter and professional gold member of The Christian PEN: Proofreaders' and Editors Network and a member of the Christian Editor Connection.

MARK MY WORD EDITORIAL SERVICES, LLC | VICKI ADANG

Indianapolis, IN | 317-549-5176
vadang@outlook.com | *www.mmwllc.net*

Contact: email

Services: manuscript evaluation, substantive editing/rewriting, copyediting, proofreading

Types of manuscripts: articles, nonfiction books, adult, teen/YA, easy readers, middle grade

Charges: hourly rate

Credentials/experience: I have more than twenty years of editorial experience, ranging from Christian fiction (*The Hungering Dark* by Stephen Clark) to reference works (*Comparative Religion For Dummies*) to creative nonfiction (*Busy and Blessed: 10 Simple Steps for Parents Seeking Peace* by Chuck Thompson).

MARTI PIEPER

Mount Dora, FL | 352-409-3136
marti@martipieper.com | www.martipieper.com

Contact: email

Services: manuscript evaluation, substantive editing/rewriting, copyediting, proofreading, ghostwriting, coauthoring write website text, create small group/Bible study guides, write curriculum lesson plans, write discussion questions for books, writing coach

Types of manuscripts: articles, nonfiction books, devotionals, poetry, query letters, book proposals, curriculum, adult, teen/YA

Charges: flat fee, hourly rate

Credentials/experience: BS in education, MDiv in communications. Fifteen years professional writing and editorial experience, including magazine editing and freelance editing for publishers. Have ghostwritten eight traditionally published nonfiction books, one a best-seller.

MENTOR ME CAREER NETWORK | CHERYL ROGERS

Tampa, FL | 863-288-0802
cheryl@mentormecareernetwork.com | www.mentormecareernetwork.com

Contact: email

Services: manuscript evaluation, substantive editing/rewriting, copyediting, proofreading, ghostwriting, coauthoring, create brochures, create newsletters, write website text, create small group/Bible study guides, writing coach, book interior and cover design, e-formatting

Types of manuscripts: articles, nonfiction books, adult, teen/YA, middle grade

Charges: flat rate, hourly rate, word rate

Credentials/experience: BA in journalism and sociology; more than five years of book editing/freelancing; one year of newspaper copyediting; eleven years of newspaper reporting; four years of desktop design, including brochures, booklets, and flyers.

MICHELLE BURFORD EDITORIAL SERVICES, LLC |
MICHELLE BURFORD

New York, NY | 646-883-5122

Michelle@MichelleBurford.com | www.MichelleBurford.com

Contact: email

Services: ghostwriting

Types of manuscripts: nonfiction books

Charges: flat fee

Credentials/experience: Number 1 *New York Times* best-selling ghostwriter (celebrity memoir); founding senior editor of *O, The Oprah Magazine*; Harvard-trained journalist.

MONICA SHARMAN EDITING | MONICA SHARMAN

Colorado Springs, CO | 719-373-6042

monicasharman@yahoo.com | www.monicasharman.wordpress.com/monica-sharman-editing

Contact: email

Services: copyediting, proofreading

Types of manuscripts: articles, nonfiction books, devotionals, poetry, short stories, curriculum, gift books, technical material, adult, teen/YA, picture books, easy readers, middle grade

Charges: flat fee, hourly fee

Credentials/experience: Certified with Christian Editor Connection. Monica has worked with both traditional publishers and self-publishing authors. Previous projects include Bible studies, devotionals, Christian nonfiction, fiction, poetry, blog content, and business website content. Monica is known for her technical accuracy, sharp eye, and light touch preserving the author's voice. See her website for previous clients and more information.

MWORDS | MARLENE MCCURLEY

Milcreek, WA | 425-243-4660

mwordsedit@gmail.com | www.mwords.net

Contact: email

Services: manuscript evaluation, substantive editing/rewriting, copyediting, proofreading

Types of manuscripts: articles, nonfiction books, devotionals, short stories, novels, gift books, adult, teen/YA, picture books, easy readers, middle grade

Charges: word rate

Credentials/experience: Editing credential from the Graham School at the University of Chicago. Member of Northwest Independent Editors Guild, Editorial Freelancers Association, The Christian PEN, and Northwest Christian Writers Association (NCWA). Volunteer for the Alzheimer's Association and NCWA. Fifteen years of experience in multiple genres.

NATALIE HANEMAN

Franklin, TN | 615-712-4430

nathanemann@gmail.com | www.nataliehanemannediting.com

Contact: email

Services: manuscript evaluation, substantive editing/rewriting, copyediting

Types of manuscripts: nonfiction books, novels, book proposals, adult, teen/YA, middle grade

Charges: flat fee

Credentials/experience: Eleven years in-house at publishing houses, eight of those at Thomas Nelson in the fiction division under the tutelage of Allen Arnold (2004-2012). Since 2012, I've been freelance editing fiction and nonfiction (substantive and line), as well as helping authors get their synopses ready to submit to agents. I've edited more than 300 manuscripts and particularly love working with newer authors or authors who are unsure if they should publish traditionally or indie. Certified by the Christian Editors Connection.

NATALIE NYQUIST

Chicago, IL | 773-459-8558

natalie@natalienyquist.com | natalienyquist.com/editor

Contact: email

Services: substantive editing/rewriting, copyediting, proofreading, coauthoring, book contract evaluation, create brochures, create newsletters, write website text, create small group/Bible study guides, write curriculum lesson plans, write discussion questions for books, create PowerPoint presentations, writing coach

Types of manuscripts: articles, nonfiction books, devotionals, poetry gift books, adult, teen/YA, picture books, easy readers, middle grade, academic biblical studies

Charges: hourly rate

Credentials/experience: More than 300 projects completed for Christian publishing houses, including HarperCollins Christian Publishing, P&R Publishers, and Moody Publishers. Editing certificate from the University of Chicago, bachelor's in Biblical studies from Moody Bible Institute. Specialties: academic content (biblical studies), bibliographies and citations (Chicago style), details and consistency across large projects.

NOBLE CREATIVE, LLC | SCOTT NOBLE

PO Box 131402, St. Paul, MN 55113 | 651-494-4169
snoble@noblecreative.com | *www.noblecreative.com*

Contact: email

Services: manuscript evaluation, substantive editing/rewriting, copyediting, proofreading, ghostwriting, write website text, create small group/Bible study guides, writing coach

Types of manuscripts: articles, nonfiction books, devotionals, query letters, book proposals, curriculum, adult

Charges: flat fee

Credentials/experience: Nearly twenty years of experience as an award-winning journalist, writer, editor, and proofreader. More than 1,000 published articles, many of them prompting radio and television appearances. Won several awards from Evangelical Press Association. Worked with dozens of published authors and other public figures, as well as first-time authors and small businesses. Have a BA and MS from St. Cloud State University and an MA from Bethel Seminary.

NOVEL IMPROVEMENT SERVICES | JEANNE MARIE LEACH

Hudson, CO | 303-536-4241
jeanne@novelimprovement.com | *novelimprovement.com*

Contact: email

Services: manuscript evaluation, substantive editing/rewriting, copyediting, proofreading, writing coach, speaking on fiction topics

Types of manuscripts: short stories, novels, query letters, book proposals, adult, teen/YA

Charges: flat fee, page rate

Credentials/experience: Past coordinator and current gold member of The Christian PEN: Proofreaders and Editors Network; member of Christian Editor Network; and member #46 of American Christian Fiction Writers, where she received the 2012 Member Service Award. She teaches four online courses on editing fiction (thirty-two weeks) per year to editors and authors through the PEN Institute and has mentored more than a dozen authors who have gone on to win numerous awards in the writing industry. She speaks on writing and editing fiction at conferences and Christian writers organizations.

OASHEIM EDITING SERVICES | CATHY OASHEIM

Chantilly, VA | 720-373-9486
admin@cathyoasheim.com | *www.cathyoasheim.com*

> **Contact:** email
>
> **Services:** substantive editing/rewriting, copyediting, proofreading, create newsletters, write website text, create small group/Bible study guides, write curriculum lesson plans, write discussion questions for books, create PowerPoint presentations
>
> **Types of manuscripts:** articles, nonfiction books, devotionals, short stories, novels, query letters, gift books, technical material, adult, teen/YA, picture books, easy readers, middle grade
>
> **Charges:** flat fee, hourly rate, page rate, word rate
>
> **Credentials/experience:** Copy editor providing substantial editing services for Christian fiction and nonfiction, military stories, oral history, and academia using American Psychological Association (APA), MLA, Associated Press, and *The Christian Writer's Manual* style guides. More than twelve years of technical writing experience, more than four years working with a Christian independent publishing company. Constant Contact and Mail Chimp, devotionals, newsletters, book covers, e-book formatting, I can do. Christian, former telecom engineer (technical), degree in applied psychology (APA), mediator (contracts), and Navy veteran (oral history).

ODD SOCK PROOFREADING & COPYEDITING | STEVE MATHISEN

Aberdeen, WA | 206-660-8431
scmathisen98037@hotmail.com | *oddsock.me*

> **Contact:** email
>
> **Services:** substantive editing/rewriting, copyediting, proofreading
>
> **Types of manuscripts:** nonfiction books, short stories, novels, adult, teen/YA, middle grade
>
> **Charges:** page rate
>
> **Credentials/experience:** I am a silver member of The Christian PEN: Proofreaders and Editors Network. Several of the books I have worked on have gone on to be quite successful and have won awards. See the list of books on the "Covers & Testimonials" page on my website.

OUR WRITTEN LIVES | RACHAEL HARTMAN

Universal City, TX | 318-319-6893

publisher@owlofhope.com | www.OurWrittenLives.com

>   **Contact:** email
>   **Services:** manuscript evaluation, substantive editing/rewriting, copyediting, proofreading, ghostwriting, coauthoring, book contract evaluation; create small group/Bible study guides, write curriculum lesson plans, write discussion questions for books, writing coach
>   **Types of manuscripts:** articles, nonfiction books, devotionals, curriculum
>   **Charges:** hourly rate
>   **Credentials/experience:** Member of Christian Small Publisher Association. MS in human services, specialization in counseling; BA in liberal studies with a minor in writing; and certified life coach; ten years in the writing and publishing industry; established Our Written Lives in 2013; author of three books.

PAMELA GOSSIAUX

Whitmore Lake, MI | 734-846-0112

pam@pamelagossiaux.com | www.PamelaGossiaux.com

>   **Contact:** email
>   **Services:** manuscript evaluation, substantive editing/rewriting, copyediting, proofreading, write website text, write discussion questions for books
>   **Types of manuscripts:** articles, nonfiction books, devotionals, short stories, novels, query letters, book proposals, gift books, adult, teen/YA, picture books, easy readers, middle grade
>   **Charges:** flat fee, hourly rate, depends on the project
>   **Credentials/experience:** Published author, twenty-five years of journalism experience, writing workshop teacher, dual BA degrees in creative writing and English language and literature. I have worked with writers in many genres, both fiction and nonfiction, including best-sellers.

PEGGYSUE WELLS

Roanoke, IN | 260-433-2817

peggysuewells@gmail.com | www.PeggySueWells.com

>   **Contact:** email
>   **Services:** substantive editing/rewriting, copyediting, ghostwriting, coauthoring, write website text, create small group/bible study

guides, write curriculum lesson plans, write discussion questions for books, writing coach

Types of manuscripts: articles, nonfiction books, novels, query letters, book proposals, curriculum, scripts, gift books, adult, teen/YA

Charges: flat fee, hourly rate

Credentials/experience: Producer and cohost of award-winning WBCL Mid-Morning show, PeggySue is the author of a couple dozen books, including two bestsellers, an audio finalist, and several coauthored projects, one of which is a parenting book with June Hunt because she writes well with others. PeggySue connects authors with publishers, writes proposals, and edits fiction and nonfiction.

PERFECT WORD EDITING SERVICES | LINDA HARRIS

Colorado Springs, CO | 719-464-5189

lharris@perfectwordediting.com | www.perfectwordediting.com

Contact: email

Services: substantive editing/rewriting, copyediting, proofreading, create brochures, create small group/Bible study guides, write curriculum lesson plans, write discussion questions for books, writing coach

Types of manuscripts: articles, nonfiction books, devotionals, query letters, book proposals, curriculum, gift books, adult, teen/YA, picture books, easy readers, middle grade

Charges: page rate

Credentials/experience: Freelance editor and writer with thirty-five years of experience. Gold member of The Christian PEN, certified by the Christian Editor Connection, instructor for The PEN Institute.

PICKY, PICKY INK | SUE MIHOLER

Keizer, OR | 503-393-3356

suemiholer@comcast.net

Contact: email

Services: copyediting

Types of manuscripts: articles, nonfiction books, devotionals, curriculum, gift books

Charges: hourly rate

Credentials/experience: In business since 1998 to serve the needs of the writing community. Have edited more than seventy book-length manuscripts for several Christian publishers and also for individuals.

PLOT & PROSE | MARY KEANE

Park Ridge, IL | 773-691-7477
info@plotandprose.com | www.plotandprose.com

Contact: email
Services: substantive editing/rewriting, copyediting, proofreading
Types of manuscripts: short stories, novels, adult, teen/YA, easy
readers, middle grade
Charges: word rate
Credentials/experience: Completed Fiction Editing 1, 2, 3 from
The Christian Pen. Writer and indie author. Specializing in
independent authors, debut authors, e-book publishing.

PRATHER INK LITERARY SERVICES | VICKI PRATHER

Raymond, MS | 601-573-4295
pratherINK@gmail.com | pratherink.wordpress.com

Contact: email
Services: copyediting, proofreading, coauthoring
Types of manuscripts: nonfiction books, devotionals, poetry, short
stories, novels, gift books, adult, teen/YA, picture books, middle grade
Charges: hourly rate, word rate
Credentials/experience: The Christian PEN silver member.

PROFESSIONAL PUBLISHING SERVICES | CHRISTY CALLAHAN

PO Box 461, Waycross, GA 31502 | 912-809-9062
professionalpublishingservices@gmail.com | ProfessionalPublishingSvcs.com

Contact: website
Services: manuscript evaluation, substantive editing/rewriting,
copyediting, proofreading, writer coach
Types of manuscripts: nonfiction books, devotionals, poetry, short
stories, novels, curriculum, gift books, technical material, adult,
teen/YA, picture books, easy readers, middle grade
Charges: hourly rate
Credentials/experience: MA in intercultural studies, Fuller
Theological Seminary; gold member, The Christian PEN;
Christian Editor Connection certified.

RALENE BURKE

Vine Grove, KY | 270-823-3874
raleneburke@gmail.com | www.raleneburke.com

Contact: email
Services: manuscript evaluation, substantive editing/rewriting,
copyediting, proofreading, writing coach

Types of manuscripts: articles, nonfiction books, devotionals, short stories, novels, adult, teen/YA

Charges: hourly rate, page rate

Credentials/experience: Numerous novels, short stories, and articles edited for clients, a couple who have been up for awards. Ralene has taken classes through The Christian PEN and the University of California--San Diego to sharpen her editing skills. Member of The Christian PEN, American Christian Fiction Writers, and Realm Makers.

REBECCA LUELLA MILLER

Whittier, CA | 562-907-8586

rluellam@Yahoo.com | *rewriterewordrework.wordpress.com*

Contact: email

Services: manuscript evaluation, substantive editing/rewriting, copyediting, proofreading, writing coach

Types of manuscripts: nonfiction books, novels, curriculum, scripts, adult, teen/YA, picture books, easy readers, middle grade

Charges: page rate

Credentials/experience: I have edited for more than fifty writers, some traditionally published and some self-published. I've worked with a publisher on additional projects, both fiction and nonfiction. In addition, I have a BA in literature and more than thirty years of experience as a secondary English teacher, which gave me a great deal of practice evaluating writing.

REBECCA LYLES

Boise, ID | 208-562-1592

beckylyles@beckylyles.com | *www.beckylyles.com*

Contact: email

Services: manuscript evaluation, substantive editing/rewriting, copyediting, proofreading, writing coach

Types of manuscripts: articles, nonfiction books, devotionals, short stories, novels, query letters, book proposals, adult, teen/YA

Charges: hourly rate, page rate

Credentials/experience: Rebecca is a multipublished author who has edited fiction and nonfiction for more than fifteen years, including brochures, white papers, newsletters, educational material, and Bible studies on the nonfiction side and short stories, children's books, and award-winning novels on the fiction side.

REFINE SERVICES | KATE MOTAUNG

Holland, MI | 616-422-9157

kate@refineservices.com | *www.refineservices.com*

Contact: email
Services: manuscript evaluation, substantive editing/rewriting, copyediting, proofreading, write website text, create small group/ Bible study guides, write discussion questions for books, writing coach
Types of manuscripts: articles, nonfiction books, devotionals, novels
Charges: flat fee, hourly rate, word rate
Credentials/experience: Five years of experience working with a variety of clients and projects.

REVISIONS BY RACHEL, LLC | RACHEL E. NEWMAN

Owasso, OK | 918-207-2833
Editor@RevisionsbyRachel.com | www.RevisionsbyRachel.com

Contact: email
Services: manuscript evaluation, substantive editing/rewriting, copyediting, proofreading, indexing
Types of manuscripts: nonfiction books, novels, query letters, book proposals, curriculum, adult, teen/YA, picture books, easy readers, middle grade, speculative fiction
Charges: word rate
Credentials/experience: Rachel holds a BS in paralegal studies from Northeastern State University in Oklahoma. She graduated *summa cum laude* in 2006 and was awarded the Certified Paralegal designation by the National Association of Legal Assistants. Certified with Christian Editor Connection. She is a gold member of The Christian PEN: Proofreaders and Editors Network, is an established freelance editor with Christian Editor Connection, is an instructor with The PEN Institute, serves as a judge for the Excellence in Editing Award, and has served as faculty for PENCON, the only conference for editors in the Christian market.

ROBIN'S RED PEN | ROBIN PATCHEN

Edmond, OK | 405-816-4867
robin@robinpatchen.com | www.robinsredpen.wordpress.com

Contact: email
Services: manuscript evaluation, substantive editing/rewriting, copyediting, writing coach
Types of manuscripts: short stories, novels, adult, teen/YA
Charges: page rate
Credentials/experience: Robin is one of the authors of *5 Editors Tackle the 12 Fatal Flaws of Fiction Writing*. She is a multipublished, award-winning author and freelance editor

specializing in Christian fiction. As the copy editor for Serenade Press, she has the privilege of working with exceptionally talented romance novelists. Robin loves mentoring new writers and helping established writers polish their books. She enjoys reading and editing almost every adult fiction genre.

SALLY E. STUART

15935 S.W. Greens Way, Tigard, OR 97224 | 503-642-9844
stuartcwmg@aol.com | *www.stuartmarket.com*

Contact: email; phone
Services: manuscript evaluation, book contract evaluation
Types of manuscripts: articles, nonfiction books, novels, book proposals
Charges: $40 per hour for critiques, $45 per hour for phone/personal consultations
Credentials/experience: Author of thirty-eight books, including twenty-seven editions of *The Christian Writers Market Guide* and her latest, *The Writing World Defined: A to Z.* More than forty-five years of experience as a writer, teacher, and marketing expert.

SARAH HAMAKER

Fairfax, VA | 703-691-1676
shamaker@verizon.net | *shamaker@verizon.net*

Contact: email
Services: manuscript evaluation, copyediting, proofreading, ghostwriting, coauthoring, write website text, writing coach
Types of manuscripts: articles, nonfiction books, novels, query letters, gift books, adult, picture books, easy readers, middle grade
Charges: flat fee, hourly rate
Credentials/experience: Sarah has been freelancing for more than a dozen years. Her work background includes stints at two national trade associations as part of their editorial teams (writing and editing articles, speeches, and magazines). During her freelance career, she's penned hundreds of articles for such varied clients as the National Association of Convenience Stores, National Religious Broadcasters, National Restaurant Association, National Club Association, Crosswalk.com, The Christian Post, and *The Washington Post's On Parenting* blog. Sarah has stories published in *Chicken Soup for the Soul* books, as well as two nonfiction books. She's also edited numerous publications, including both fiction and nonfiction books for both adult and children. In addition, she's ghostwritten articles and *Out of the Shadows: A Journey of Recovery from Depression.*

SCRIVEN COMMUNICATIONS | KATHIE SCRIVEN

22 Ridge Rd. #220, Greenbelt, MD 20770 | 240-542-4602
KathieScriven@yahoo.com | *www.linkedin.com/in/kathie-scriven-46981037*

Contact: email, phone
Services: manuscript evaluation, substantive editing/rewriting, copyediting, proofreading
Types of manuscripts: articles, short stories, nonfiction books, book proposals, poetry, query letters, devotionals, curriculum, scripts, adult, teen/YA
Charges: flat fee
Credentials/experience: I have edited more than seventy-five Christian nonfiction books and more than 100 shorter projects, including booklets, biographical sketches, press releases, and grant applications. Former editor of four Christian publications and freelance writer for several Christian and general-market publications. Bachelor's degree in mass communication with a concentration in journalism from Towson University. I'm happy to email a document that describes my credentials and experience in more detail.

SEACOAST SYNERGY | PATRICIA WATKINS

Imperial Beach, CA | 970-308-3188
SeacoastSynergy@outlook.com | *www.facebook.com/Seacoast SynergySD*

Contact: email
Services: proofreading, write discussion questions for books
Types of manuscripts: articles, nonfiction books, short stories, novels, adult, teen/YA, picture books, easy readers, middle grade
Charges: flat fee, page rate
Credentials/experience: Patricia is a published author and educator with extensive experience proofreading fiction and nonfiction. She enjoys creating thought-provoking discussion questions for both genres. During her eight years as a literacy instructor for gifted students, she edited, compiled, and produced a yearly student literary magazine. She is a member of the San Diego Christian Writers Guild.

SHARON HINCK

Minneapolis, MN | 952-886-0040
s.hinck@comcast.net | *www.sharonhinck.com*

Contact: email
Services: substantive editing/rewriting, copyediting

Types of manuscripts: novels

Charges: word rate

Credentials/experience: MA; ten years experience of editing dozens of authors from beginners through *New York Times* best-selling writers; experienced novelist; thorough yet encouraging.

SHERRY CHAMBLEE

Sun Valley, CA | 818-767-8765

chambleeservices@gmail.com | *www.offscript.weebly.com*

Contact: email

Services: copyediting, proofreading

Types of manuscripts: articles, nonfiction books, devotionals, poetry, short stories, novels, gift books, technical material, adult, teen/YA, picture books, easy readers, middle grade

Charges: word rate

Credentials/experience: I am a freelance editor, working directly with authors for the past four years. I have edited both fiction and nonfiction, including works ranging from illustrated children's picture books and middle-grade chapter books, to young adult and adult Christian fiction.

SHERRY MADDEN

Lake Forest Park, WA | 206 919-2203

madden58sheryl@gmail.com | *www.sheryl-madden.com*

Contact: email

Services: substantive editing/rewriting, copyediting, proofreading

Types of manuscripts: articles, nonfiction books, devotionals, short stories, novels, book proposals, gift books, adult, teen/YA

Charges: page rate

Credentials/experience: Certification in professional editing from University of Washington; three years of editing experience in fiction, nonfiction, memoirs, coffee-table books, magazine articles, blog posts, newsletters.

SHIRL'S EDITING SERVICES | SHIRL THOMAS

9379 Tanager Ave., Fountain Valley, CA 92708 | 714-968-5726

shirlth@verizon.net

Contact: email, phone

Services: manuscript evaluation, substantive editing/rewriting, copyediting, proofreading, ghostwriting, coauthoring, writing coach

Types of manuscripts: articles, nonfiction books, devotionals, poetry, short stories, novels, query letters, book proposals, scripts, gift books, technical material, adult

Charges: hourly rate
Credentials/experience: Professional writer since 1973 and editor since 1994. Complete résumé available.

SIGHTHOUND EDITORIAL SERVICES | MEGAN LEE
Herndon, VA | 703-229-2369
sighthoundeditorial@gmail.com | *www.sighthoundeditorialservices.com*

Contact: email
Services: manuscript evaluation, substantive editing/rewriting, copyediting, proofreading, write discussion questions for books, writing coach
Types of manuscripts: novels, adult, teen/YA
Charges: flat fee, hourly rate, page rate, word rate
Credentials/experience: I'm a published author with an MFA in creative writing from George Mason University. As an editor with Pelican Book Group, I evaluate manuscripts for acquisition and work closely with authors and other editors to ensure manuscripts meet their potential throughout the publication process. Additionally, I've taught English to high school and college students for the past fifteen years.

smWORDWORKS | SUSAN G. MATHIS
Colorado Springs, CO | 719-331-9352
mathis.wordworks@gmail.com | *www.SusanGMathis.com*

Contact: email
Services: manuscript evaluation, substantive editing/rewriting, copyediting, proofreading. coauthoring, book contract evaluation, writing coach
Types of manuscripts: articles, nonfiction books, novels, query letters, book proposals, adult, picture books
Charges: word rate
Credentials/experience: Susan has a BA in English and journalism. She is the founding editor of Thriving Family magazine and former editor/editorial director of twelve Focus on the Family publications. She is a versatile writer, creating both fiction and nonfiction for adults and children. Before she jumped into the fiction world, her first two books were nonfiction, coauthored with her husband. She also has written an indie-published children's book, contributions to book compilations, and hundreds of magazine and newsletter articles on a variety of topics.

SO IT IS WRITTEN | TENITA JOHNSON

Rochester, MI | 313-999-6942

info@soitiswritten.net | www.soitiswritten.net

Contact: emails

Services: copyediting, proofreading, ghostwriting, write website text, writing coach

Types of manuscripts: articles, nonfiction books, devotionals, poetry, short stories, novels, adult, teen/YA, picture books, easy readers, middle grade

Charges: page rate

Credentials/experience: More than sixteen years of writing and editing experience in all forms of media, including newspapers, magazines, and manuscripts.

STARCHER DESIGNS | KARA D. STARCHER

Magnolia, OH | 330-705-3399

info@starcherdesigns.com | www.starcherdesigns.com

Contact: email

Services: manuscript evaluation, substantive editing, copyediting, proofreading, create brochure, create small group guides, write curriculum lesson plans, write discussion questions for books

Types of manuscripts: articles, nonfiction books, devotionals, short stories, novels, adult

Charges: word rate, flat fee

Credentials/experience: BA in publishing, former high-school English teacher, more than eleven years as a freelance editor.

STEEPLE VIEW COACHING | ANDREA BOESHAAR

PO Box 33, Newberg, WI 53060 | 414-708-8930

AuthorAndreaBoeshaar@gmail.com | www.AndreaBoeshaar.com

Contact: email

Services: manuscript evaluation, substantive editing/rewriting, writing coach

Types of manuscripts: short stories, novels, teen/YA

Charges: page rate

Credentials/experience: Author of more than thirty books, certified Christian life coach.

STICKS AND STONES | JAMIE CALLOWAY-HANAUER

Annapolis, MD | 510-972-3285

snsedits@gmail.com | www.snsedits.com

Contact: email

Services: manuscript evaluation, substantive editing/rewriting, copyediting, proofreading, ghostwriting, coauthoring, book contract evaluation, write website text, create small group/Bible study guides, write curriculum lesson plans, write discussion questions for books, writing coach

Types of manuscripts: articles, nonfiction books, devotionals, poetry, short stories, novels, query letters, book proposals, curriculum, adult, teen/YA, easy readers, middle grade

Charges: flat fee

Credentials/experience: Jamie has eighteen years of experience in the editing field. Previously a full-time public interest attorney who also edited part-time, she is now the owner/operator of Sticks and Stones, where she specializes in academic, legal, and faith-based fiction and nonfiction for adults and teens; ghostwriting; and proposal and query review and development.

SUE'S SIMPLE SNIPPETS | SUE A. FAIRCHILD

Watsontown, PA | 570-939-0318
sueafairchild74@gmail.com | *suessimplesnippets.wordpress.com*

Contact: email

Services: substantive editing/rewriting, copyediting, write website text

Types of manuscripts: nonfiction books, devotionals, short stories, novels, gift books, teen/YA

Charges: hourly rate

Credentials/experience: Substantive editor for Christian Editor Network, content editor for online publisher, and published author of devotionals for *The Secret Place* and *The Upper Room*. Specializes in devotional, young adult, and fantasy books.

SUPERIOR EDITING SERVICE | JAN ACKERSON

611 S Elm, Three Oaks, MI 49128 | 269-756-9912
jan_ackerson@yahoo.com | *www.superioreditingservice.com*

Contact: email

Services: substantive editing/rewriting, copyediting, writing coach

Types of manuscripts: poetry, short stories, novels, gift books, adult, teen/YA, picture books, easy readers, middle grade

Charges: word rate

Credentials/experience: Seven years editing (both freelance and for Breath of Fresh Air Press), author of *Stolen Postcards*, short stories in multiple anthologies.

TANDEM SERVICES | JENNIFER VANDER KLIPP

PO Box 492, Belmont, MI 49306 | 414-465-2567
hello@tandemservicesjvk.com | *www.tandemservicesjvk.com.*

Contact: email

Services: manuscript evaluation, substantive editing/rewriting, copyediting, proofreading, ghostwriting, coauthoring, create small group/Bible study guides, writing coach

Types of manuscripts: articles, nonfiction books, devotionals, short stories, novels, query letters, book proposals, gift books, adult, teen/YA, picture books, easy readers, middle grade

Charges: flat rate, hourly fee, word rate, specific to each project

Credentials/experience: Tandem Services brings together a group of industry professionals with more than twenty years of experience in business, marketing, and publishing to help writers navigate the world of publishing, indie or traditional. Our staff includes experienced, in-house editors at Big Five publishers as well as published authors. Our services include complex project management, writing and editing, marketing, and graphic design. Our clients include Our Daily Bread Ministries, Credo Communications, Zondervan, HarperCollins Christian Publishing, Barbour Publishing, and Concordia, as well as many individual authors.

TISHA MARTIN

Atlanta, IL | 850-583-7051

tmartinwrites@gmail.com | www.tishamwrites.com

Contact: email

Services: manuscript evaluation, substantive editing/rewriting, copyediting, proofreading, create newsletters, write website text, write curriculum lesson plans, write discussion questions for books, create PowerPoint presentations, writing coach

Types of manuscripts: articles, nonfiction books, devotionals, short stories, novels, curriculum, technical material, adult, teen/YA, picture books, easy readers, middle grade

Charges: hourly rate, word rate

Credentials/experience: Eighteen years of experience; BA in professional writing; MS in curriculum and instruction in English education.

TLC GRAPHICS | TAMARA DEVER

Austin, TX | 512-669-5744

tamara@tlcgraphics.com | www.TLCGraphics.com

Contact: email

Services: substantive editing/rewriting, copyediting, proofreading, ghostwriting, coauthoring, indexing

Types of manuscripts: nonfiction books, devotionals, novels, gift books, adult, teen/YA, picture books, easy readers, middle grade, homeschool and children's ministry materials

Charges: flat fee based on individual project

Credentials/experience: Award-winning design firm and author guidance with more than twenty-five years of publishing experience. Small, caring team working with you, taking your raw manuscript through editorial, design, and printing to provide a beautiful and salable book you'll be proud to represent. Services are à la carte with design contract.

TOTAL FUSION PRESS | ROB COBURN

PO Box 123, Strasburg, OH 44680 | 330-737-1031

contact@totalfusionpress.com | www.totalfusiopress.com

Contact: email, phone

Services: manuscript evaluation, substantive editing/rewriting, copyediting, proofreading, ghostwriting, coauthoring, book contract evaluation, create brochures, create newsletters, write website text, create small group/Bible study guides, write curriculum lesson plans, write discussion questions for books, create PowerPoint presentations, writing coach

Types of manuscripts: nonfiction books, short stories, novels, book proposals

Charges: flat fee, hourly rate, word rate

Credentials/experience: With more than twenty years of editing and design services, the team at Total Fusion Press loves to help people reach their full potential.

TRIPLE EDGE CRITIQUE SERVICE | LINDA W. YEZAK

Nacogdoches, TX | 936-568-0565

linda.yeza@lwyezak.com | lindayezak.com

Contact: email

Services: manuscript evaluation, substantive editing/rewriting, copyediting, ghostwriting, coauthoring

Types of manuscripts: short stories, novels, adult, teen/YA, creative nonfiction

Charges: hourly rate

Credentials/experience: Ten years of experience. Content editor for two small publishers; editorial assistant for a literary agent; copy editor for an online magazine. Silver member of The Christian PEN; additional courses in editing fiction and author mentoring.

TURN THE PAGE WRITER CRITIQUES | CINDY THOMSON

Pataskala, OH | 614-354-3904

cindyswriting@gmail.com | cindyswriting.com/hire-me

Contact: email
Services: manuscript evaluation, proofreading, critiques
Types of manuscripts: articles, novels
Charges: page rate, word rate
Credentials/experience: Traditionally published author of eight books, past mentor for the Jerry B. Jenkins Christian Writers Guild, mentor for local high-school students.

URBANSKI EDITING SERVICES | JUDE URBANSKI

Muncie, IN | 765-748-6464
urbanski4u@aol.com | *www.judeurbanski.com*

Contact: email
Services: manuscript evaluation, substantive editing/rewriting, copyediting, proofreading
Types of manuscripts: articles, nonfiction books, devotionals, short stories, novels, gift books, adult
Charges: page rate
Credentials/experience: Member of The Christian Pen, Christian Editor Connection, American Christian Fiction Writers; traditionally published author.

THE VERSATILE PEN | CHRISTY PHILLIPPE

8816 S. 73rd East Ave., Tulsa, OK 74133 | 918-284-7635
christy6871@aol.com | *www.theversatilepen.com*

Contact: email
Services: manuscript evaluation, substantive editing/rewriting, copyediting, proofreading, create brochures, create newsletters, write website text, create small group/Bible study guides, write curriculum lesson plans, write discussion questions for books
Types of manuscripts: articles, nonfiction books, devotionals, short stories, novels, curriculum, gift books, adult, teen/YA
Charges: hourly rate, word rate
Credentials/experience: More than twenty years of experience as managing editor, senior editor, and editorial director of various publishing companies and as the owner of The Versatile Pen.

WHALIN & ASSOCIATES | W. TERRY WHALIN

Highlands Ranch, CO 80126 | 720-708-4953
terry@terrywhalin.com | *thewritinglife.ws*

Contact: email
Services: substantive editing/rewriting, ghostwriting, coauthoring, create small group/Bible study guides, write discussion questions for books

Types of manuscripts: nonfiction books, devotionals, book proposals, gift books, adult
Charges: flat fee
Credentials/experience: Terry has written more than sixty books for traditional publishers, including one book that has sold more than 100,000 copies. He has written for more than fifty publications and worked in acquisitions at three publishing houses.

WORD MARKER EDITS | KATHRESE MCKEE
8765 Spring Cypress, Ste. L219, Spring, TX 77379 | 281-787-6938
kmckee@kathresemckee.com | www.wordmarkeredits.com
Contact: email
Services: manuscript evaluation, substantive editing/rewriting, copyediting, proofreading, ghostwriting
Types of manuscripts:, short stories, novels adult, teen/YA, middle grade
Charges: hourly rate, page rate, word rate
Credentials/experience: Kathrese is an editor, fiction author, former middle-school reading and ESL teacher, speaker, and blogger. She specializes in editing speculative fiction written from a Christian worldview but is also available to edit other genres and fiction for the general market. She is a silver member of The Christian PEN: Proofreaders and Editors Network.

WORDMELON, INC. | MARGOT STARBUCK
Durham, NC | 919-321-5440
wordmelon@gmail.com | www.wordmelon.com
Contact: email
Services: manuscript evaluation, substantive editing/rewriting, ghostwriting, coauthoring, create small group/Bible study guides
Types of manuscripts: articles, nonfiction books, devotionals, query letters, book proposals
Charges: flat fee
Credentials/experience: Margot has an MDiv from Princeton Theological Seminary and a bachelor's degree from Westmont College. She is the author, coauthor, and collaborator on seven books and ghostwriter on others. She has lent her touch to more than fifty major publishing projects. Visit her website to see endorsements and a current CV.

WORDS FOR LIFE | GINNY L. YTTRUP
Granite Bay, CA | 916-276-7359
ginny@ginnyyttrup.com | www.ginnyyttrup.com

Contact: email
Services: manuscript evaluation, substantive editing/rewriting, proofreading, writing coach
Types of manuscripts: articles, nonfiction books, devotionals, short stories, novels, query letters, book proposals, adult, teen/YA
Charges: hourly rate, page rate
Credentials/experience: Ginny is an award-winning novelist and trained life coach who combines her skills when coaching writers and evaluating manuscripts. She works with beginning and published writers of both fiction and nonfiction.

WORDWISE MEDIA SERVICES | STEVEN HUTSON

4083 Avenue L, Ste. 255, Lancaster, CA 93536 | 661-382-8083
submit@wordwisemedia.com | *www.wordwisemedia.com*

Contact: email
Services: manuscript critique/evaluation, copyediting
Types of manuscripts: articles, nonfiction books, devotionals, short stories, novels, query letters, book proposals, curriculum, scripts, gift books, technical material, adult, teen/YA, easy readers, middle grade
Charges: see website
Credentials/experience: Twelve years of experience. See website for details.

WRITE BY LISA | LISA THOMPSON

Litchfield Park, AZ | 623-258-5258
writebylisa@gmail.com | *www.writebylisa.com*

Contact: email
Services: manuscript evaluation, substantive editing/rewriting, copyediting, proofreading, ghostwriting, coauthoring, create newsletters, write website text, create small group/Bible study guides, write curriculum lesson plans, write discussion questions for books, writing coach
Types of manuscripts: articles, nonfiction books, devotionals, short stories, novels, query letters, book proposals, curriculum, gift books, adult, teen/YA middle grade
Charges: word rate
Credentials/experience: I have a BA in elementary education with a minor in English. I have been writing and editing full-time since 2009 and have satisfied clients all over the world, many of whom return for additional business and refer other clients to me.

THE WRITE EDITOR | ERIN K. BROWN

Corvallis, MT | 406-239-5590
thewriteeditor@gmail.com | *www.writeeditor.net*

Contact: email
Services: manuscript evaluation, substantive editing/rewriting, copyediting, proofreading, write discussion questions for books
Types of manuscripts: articles, nonfiction books, devotionals, short stories, novels, query letters, book proposals, curriculum, gift books, adult, teen/YA, middle grade
Charges: flat fee, hourly rate, word rate, page rate
Credentials/experience: Erin is a full-time, professional freelance editor, proofreader, and writer (since 2001). She edits and proofreads book manuscripts, magazine articles, anthologies, short stories, textbooks, and more. Her editing specialty is nonfiction works, including self-help, how-to, devotionals, Bible studies, biography, memoir, history, apologetics, leadership, ministry, family, health and wellness, inspiration, personal growth, relationships, success, and homeschool. Erin's formal training in editorial practices and procedures, ten years in Christian retailing, twenty-six years in education, and more than ten years as a judge for a national fiction award affords her a wide knowledge and experience base that she brings to her editing. She combines her love of editing and teaching through The Pen Institute, teaching nonfiction editing skills to other professional editors.

WRITE HIS ANSWER MINISTRIES | MARLENE BAGNULL

951 Anders Rd., Lansdale, PA 19446 | 484-991-8581
mbagnull@aol.com | *writehisanswer.com*

Contact: email
Services: copyediting, proofreading
Types of manuscripts: articles, nonfiction books, devotionals, short stories, novels, adult
Charges: flat fee, hourly rate
Credentials/experience: More than thirty years of experience in publishing, leading critique groups, and directing writers conferences; author of nine books with more than 1,000 sales to Christian periodicals; editor, typesetter, and publisher of ten Ampelos Press books.

WRITE NOW EDITING & COPYWRITING | KARIN BEERY

Elk Rapids, MI | 231-350-0226
karin@karinbeery.com | *www.writenow-editing.com*

Contact: email
Services: manuscript evaluation, substantive editing/rewriting, proofreading, ghostwriting, write website text, writing coach

Types of manuscripts: short stories, novels, query letters, book proposals, adult, teen/YA

Charges: flat fees for copy work, per word for novel editing

Credentials/experience: Christian Editor Connection certified substantive fiction editor, The Christian PEN: Proofreaders and Editors Network gold member, American Christian Fiction Writers Association, American Christian Writers Association, American Writers and Artists Inc., trained copywriter.

WRITE NOW SERVICES | KAREN APPOLD

Macungie, PA | 610-351-5400
kappold@msn.com | *www.WriteNowServices.com*

Contact: email

Services: copyediting, proofreading, write website text, write magazine articles

Types of manuscripts: articles, devotionals, query letters, curriculum, adult, teen/YA, print advertisements

Charges: word rate

Credentials/experience: I've owned a writing-editing business since 2003, working independently and from home full-time. I've been published in many trade and consumer publications and have also worked in some editor positions. Check my website for testimonials and more details about my editorial services.

WRITE PATHWAY EDITORIAL SERVICES | ANN KNOWLES

Wilmington, NC | 910-231-9520
annknowles03@aol.com | *www.WritePathway.com*

Contact: email

Services: copyediting, proofreading, ghostwriting, coauthoring, writing coach, transcription, Spanish translation

Types of manuscripts: articles, nonfiction books, devotionals, poetry, short stories, novels, query letters, book proposals, curriculum, gift books, adult, teen/YA, picture books, easy readers, middle grade

Charges: project cost

Credentials/experience: Retired educator, MA in education, certified ESL and Spanish; ESL training consultant for public schools and community colleges. I joined The Christian PEN: Proofreaders and Editors Network in 2005 and started Write Pathway in 2007. I have taken numerous courses from The Christian PEN, American Christian Fiction Writers, Write Integrity Press, and Christian Writers International. Presenter at writers conferences.

WRITER'S EDGE SERVICE

info@writersedgeservice.com | www.writersedgeservice.com

Contact: website

Service: Professional editors with many years of experience in working with major Christian publishers evaluate, screen, and expose potential books to traditional Christian publishing companies

Types of manuscripts: books—all kinds except poetry and all ages

Charges: $99

Description: For more than twenty years, it has been a method of effective communication between writers and major traditional Christian publishers. Because most traditional publishers no longer accept unsolicited manuscripts, new or relatively unknown writers have little chance to be seen by a traditional publisher unless they have a credible literary agent. Writer's Edge Service, in full cooperation with more than seventy-five traditional, royalty-based Christian publishers, gives writers another option. The acquisition editors of these companies view relevant manuscripts that make the cut at Writer's Edge because they know they have been carefully screened and evaluated before being passed to them for consideration. Over the years, hundreds of authors have been successfully published because of Writer's Edge Service.

THE WRITER'S FRIEND | DONNA CLARK GOODRICH

Mesa, AZ | 480-962-6694

dgood648@aol.com | www.thewritersfriend.net

Contact: email

Services: copyediting, proofreading

Types of manuscripts: articles, nonfiction books, devotionals, short stories, novels, query letters, book proposals, gift books, adult, teen/YA, picture books, easy readers, middle grade

Charges: hourly rate, page rate

Credentials/experience: More than fifty years editing and proofreading for publishers and writers.

WRITER'S RELIEF, INC. | RONNIE L. SMITH

Wood Ridge, NJ | 866-405-3003

info@wrelief.com | www.writersrelief.com

Contact: email, phone

Services: proofreading, creative writing submissions

Types of manuscripts: poetry, short stories, novels, query letters, book proposals

Charges: flat fee, page rate, word rate

Credentials/experience: Helping authors reach their publishing goals since 1994. Writer's Relief, Self-Publishing Relief, and Web Design Relief offer a complete array of services to facilitate every step of an author's path to publishing—from making targeted submissions to traditional publishing markets, to offering self-publishing guidance and marketing support, to building author websites.

WRITER'S TABLET, LLC | TERRI WHITMIRE
4371 Roswell Rd #315, Marietta, GA 30062 | 770-648-4101
Writerstablet@gmail.com | *www.Writerstablet.org*
www.FunCreativeWriting.com

Contact: email

Services: manuscript evaluation, substantive editing/rewriting, copyediting, proofreading, coauthoring, create brochures, create newsletters, write website text, create small group/Bible study guides, write curriculum lesson plans, write discussion questions for books, create PowerPoint presentations, writing coach

Types of manuscripts: articles, nonfiction books, devotionals, poetry, short stories, novels, curriculum, adult, teen/YA, picture books, easy readers, middle grade

Charges: flat fee

Credentials/experience: Certification in children's literature, BS in computer science, literary assistant to a New York agency, communications degree, published authors. We have assisted numerous clients in website content, website design, developmental editing, manuscript critique, copyediting, manuscript formatting, Kindle publishing, self-publishing, and various other business writing requests. Our talented team also serves as writing coaches to young writers through our business *www.funcreativewriting.com*.

WRITE WAY COPYEDITING, LLC | DIANA SCHRAMER
Sun Prairie, WI | 608-837-8091
diana@writewaycopyediting.com | *www.writewaycopyediting.com*

Contact: email, phone

Services: manuscript evaluation, substantive editing/rewriting, copyediting

Types of manuscripts: articles, nonfiction books, devotionals, short stories, novels, gift books, adult, teen/YA, picture books, easy readers, middle grade

Charges: hourly rate

Credentials/experience: I have been a full-time, freelance copy editor for six years. I have edited 170 book-length manuscripts, fiction, nonfiction, and creative nonfiction, ranging from 15,000 words to more than 100,000, and have evaluated more than 850 manuscripts for editorial recommendation. References on request.

WRITING WITH GRACE | ANN SWINDELL

St. Louis, MO

Writingwithgracecourse@gmail.com | www.writingwithgrace.com

Contact: email

Services: copyediting, coauthoring, writing coach, online Christian writing courses

Types of manuscripts: articles, nonfiction books, devotionals

Charges: hourly rate

Credentials/experience: Ann holds an MA in writing and an MFA in creative nonfiction writing. She taught as a college instructor for five years before deciding to offer the same material through online Christian writing courses and coaching. Her first book, a spiritual memoir, releases with Tyndale in 2017.

WRITTEN BY A PRO | SHARLA TAYLOR

Richmond Hill, GA | 912-656-6857

writtenbyapro@msn.com | www.writtenbyapro.com

Contact: email

Services: manuscript evaluation, substantive editing/rewriting, copyediting, proofreading, ghostwriting, coauthoring, write website text, create small group/Bible study guides, write curriculum lesson plans, write discussion questions for books, create PowerPoint presentations, writing coach, résumé/CV writer, LinkedIn profile writer, job-search strategist, and facilitator of an online Bible study for job seekers

Types of manuscripts: articles, nonfiction books, devotionals, short stories, novels, query letters, book proposals, curriculum, scripts, gift books, adult, teen/YA, middle grade

Charges: flat fee, hourly rate, word rate, service options and prices for job seekers on website

Credentials/experience: Certified professional résumé writer; certified career enlightenment LinkedIn writer; experienced job-search strategist with more than twenty years in the careers industry; leads a free online Bible study for job seekers based on the Theology of Work project (*www.theologyofwork.org*).

Sharla has developed thousands of résumés for business leaders, executives, career-changers, people reentering the workforce, and recent college graduates.

YOUR TIME TO WRITE | MARY BUSHA

Ocala, FL | 517-416-0133
yourtimetowrite@gmail.com

Contact: email

Services: manuscript evaluation, copyediting, proofreading, writing coach

Types of manuscripts: nonfiction books, devotionals, book proposals, gift books

Charges: hourly rate, page rate

Credentials/experience: More than thirty-five years in publishing, including newspapers, magazines, and books. Works with author from book idea to publication and all steps in between. Full résumé available on request. First one-hour consultation at no charge.

INTERNATIONAL

AIMEE REID

Hamilton, Ontario, Canada | 905-317-9234
areid@aimeereid.com | *www.aimeereid.com*

Contact: email

Services: manuscript evaluation, substantive editing/rewriting, create small group/Bible study guides, write curriculum lesson plans, write discussion questions for books

Types of manuscripts: articles, nonfiction books, devotionals, curriculum, adult, teen/YA, picture books, easy readers, middle grade

Charges: hourly rate

Credentials/experience: Developmental and stylistic editing for all audience ages.

AOTEAROA EDITORIAL SERVICES | VENNESSA NG

PO Box 228, Oamaru, New Zealand 9444 | +6-422-434-6995
editor@aotearoaeditorial.com | *www.aotearoaeditorial.com*

Contact: email

Services: manuscript evaluation, substantive editing/rewriting, copyediting, proofreading, writing coach

Types of manuscripts: short stories, novels, adult

Charges: page rate

Credentials/experience: Fourteen years of experience working with Christian fiction authors. Member of The Christian PEN.

CELTICFROG EDITING | ALEX MCGILVERY

Flin Flon, Manitoba, Canada | 204-271-2066
thecelt.icfrog@gmail.com | *celticfrogediting.com*

Contact: email, comment on website

Services: manuscript evaluation; writing coach; character and plot arcs, tone, voice, writing quality, technical

Types of manuscripts: articles, nonfiction books, devotionals, short stories, novels, adult, teen/YA, middle grade

Charges: $300 for a 100k book, adjusted up or down for longer or shorter work; $200 minimum for novels; $25 an hour for short works and consultations. Free, no-obligation test edit of the first 5k of a book for new clients

Credentials/experience: I've been a writer and book reviewer for more than thirty years, a content editor for the past three years. I've edited more than forty books, many of which have hit best-seller status on Amazon. See the website for the titles of published books I've worked on.

CHRISTIAN EDITING SERVICES | IOLA GOULTON

Tauranga, New Zealand
igoulton@christianediting.co.nz | *www.christianediting.co.nz*

Contact: email

Services: manuscript evaluation, substantive editing/rewriting, copyediting, proofreading

Types of manuscripts: novels, adult, teen/YA

Charges: hourly rate

Credentials/experience: Iola is a member of the Christian PEN: Proofreaders and Editors Network, American Christian Fiction Writers, Romance Writers of New Zealand, and Omega Writers. She has completed fiction editing courses with The Christian PEN, as well as a range of courses through Lawson Writers Academy and American Christian Fiction Writers, and won the 2016 Genesis Award for novella.

EDIPPEN & QUILL | CALEB AJINOMOH

Lagos, Lagos 100278 | +234-703-941-1298
femmefatalelit.fiction2016@gmail.com | *edippe.skynova.io*

Contact: email

Services: substantive editing/rewriting, copyediting, ghostwriting

Types of manuscripts: nonfiction books, short stories, novels, adult, picture books

Charges: page rate

Credentials/experience: With more than four years working the editorial desk at West Africa's foremost tabloid (*The Sun Newspaper*) and copyediting for *Mustard Magazine*, Africa's biggest Christian music magazine, I set out to begin my own business last year. I have worked with one Harvard Law undergraduate and a local rapper for their nonfiction projects. Currently a member of The Christian PEN and looking for ambitious, genre-defying authors to work with.

EXTRA INK EDITS | MEGAN EASLEY-WALSH

North Co. Dublin, Ireland
www.Megan@ExtraInkEdits.com | Megan@ExtraInkEdits.com

Contact: email or form on website

Services: manuscript evaluation, copyediting, proofreading, write website text, write discussion questions for books, writing coach, title help for indie authors, synopsis critiques, submission package polishes, and more

Types of manuscripts: articles, nonfiction books, devotionals, short stories, novels, query letters, adult, teen/YA, picture books, easy readers, middle grade

Charges: flat fee, hourly rate, word rate, depending on the service

Credentials/experience: More than eight years of experience as a writing consultant and editor; previously taught writing to college students in the UNESCO literature city of Dublin, Ireland; certified English teacher; historical and international relations degrees. I am also a writer, and my writing has been requested for use in classrooms and churches.

NEXT INDEX SERVICES | JESSICA MCCURDY CROOKS

Old Harbour, St. Catharine, Jamaica | 954-406-5426
nextindexservices@gmail.com | www.next-index.com

Contact: email

Services: proofreading, write website text, indexing

Types of manuscripts: articles, nonfiction books

Charges: varies, depending on the client's needs

Credentials/experience: More than twenty years of experience in indexing and proofreading.

NEXT LEVEL EDITING AND TRANSCRIPTION |
DARLENE OAKLEY

St. Catharines, Ontario, Canada | 289-696-2382
darlene@darscorrections.com | *www.darscorrections.com*

> **Contact:** email
> **Services:** manuscript evaluation, substantive editing/rewriting, copyediting, proofreading
> **Types of manuscripts:** articles, nonfiction books, devotionals, short stories, novels, adult, teen/YA
> **Charges:** word rate
> **Credentials/experience:** Thirty-six edited books (fiction and nonfiction, variety of genres), more than fifteen years of writing and editing experience, more than 400 published articles online, editor-proofreader for Lanico Media House and Next Century Publishing.

NITPICKING WITH A PURPOSE | MARSHA MALCOLM

Savanna-la-mar, Westmoreland, Jamaica | 876-823-2092
purposefulnitpicker@gmail.com | *www.nitpickingwithapurpose.com*

> **Contact:** email
> **Services:** copyediting, proofreading
> **Types of manuscripts:** short stories, novels, picture books, easy readers, middle grade
> **Charges:** word rate
> **Credentials/experience:** Expert rating certification in Keys to Editing (2014).

SPLASHDOWN BOOKS | GRACE BRIDGES

Glenfield, Auckland, NZ 0629 | +6-422-472-2301
gracebridges1@gmail.com | *www.gracebridges.kiwi*

> **Contact:** email
> **Services:** manuscript evaluation, substantive editing/rewriting, copyediting, proofreading; accepting only those manuscripts that are already in good condition, with an appropriate corresponding discount
> **Types of manuscripts:** novels, adult, teen/YA, picture books, easy readers, middle grade, speculative genre
> **Charges:** word rate
> **Credentials/experience:** Ten years in publishing and editing; signed off on the final quality of more than forty books published under my label, with over a dozen professionally recognized. Based in New Zealand, I specialize in science fiction and fantasy and in making American concepts internationally understandable.

VINEMARC COMMUNICATIONS | MARCIA LAYCOCK
PO Box 637, Blackfalds, Alberta, Canada T0M 0J0 | 403-885-9828
vinemarc@telus.net | *www.marcialeelaycock.com*

> **Contact:** email
>
> **Services:** copyediting, proofreading
>
> **Types of manuscripts:** devotionals, poetry, short stories, novels, adult, teen/YA, middle grade
>
> **Charges:** hourly rate
>
> **Credentials/experience:** Published in several genres, indie and royalty; winner of several awards, including Best New Canadian Christian Author; have judged contests for American Christian Fiction Writers, InScribe Christian Writers, and The Word Guild; edited several books.

20

PUBLICITY AND MARKETING SERVICES

THE ADAMS GROUP | GINA ADAMS
6688 Nolensville Rd. 108-149, Brentwood, TN 37027 | 615-776-1590
gina@adamsprgroup.com | *www.adamsprgroup.com*
> **Contact:** email, phone
> **Services:** public relations, marketing, and social-media management for Christian fiction, nonfiction, and children's books
> **Charges:** flat rate
> **Credentials/experience:** In the Christian marketplace for nearly three decades, representing Christian singers, bands, films, authors, speakers, and major conference events. Membership in National Religious Broadcasters and Evangelical Press Association.

AUTHOR SUPPORT SERVICES | RUSSELL SHERRARD
Carmichael, CA | 916-967-7251
russellsherrard@reagan.com | *www.sherrardsebookresellers.com/WordPress/*
author-support-services-the-authors-place-to-get-help
> **Contact:** email
> **Services:** Twitter and Facebook marketing, submitting URL to search engines; working with Christian books, e-books, fiction, and nonfiction
> **Charges:** flat fee
> **Credentials/experience:** Writing and editing since 2009; currently providing freelance services for multiple clients.

THE BLYTHE DANIEL AGENCY, INC. | BLYTHE DANIEL
PO Box 64197, Colorado Springs, CO 80962-4197 | 719-213-3427
blythe@theblythedanielagency.com | *www.theblythedanielagency.com*
> **Other publicist:** Stephanie Alton, *stephanie@theblythedanielagency.com*, blog content manager
> **Contact:** e-mail

Services: range of publicity campaigns utilizing broadcast and print media and the Internet, including blogs, websites, online magazines, and online broadcasts; working primarily with adult and young-adult nonfiction

Charges: customized by campaign

Credentials/experience: We have personal relationships with hundreds of media outlets that we have developed over the past 20 years in the business. Through our relationships, understanding of the changing media landscape, and careful selection of content we promote, we are able to provide our clients more opportunities to bring recognition to their books. Blythe worked 5 years as the publicity director and 2 years as the marketing director for Thomas Nelson.

CHRISTIAN SMALL PUBLISHERS ASSOCIATION (CSPA) | SARAH BOLME

PO Box 481022, Charlotte, NC 28269 | 704-277-7194
cspa@christianpublishers.net | *www.christianpublishers.net*

Contact: email

Services: Founded in 2004, CSPA is an organization for small publishers producing materials for the Christian marketplace. We help small publishers and independently published authors market their books, including at trade shows for members.

EABOOKS PUBLISHING | CHERI COWELL

Oviedo, FL | 407-712-3431
Cheri@eabookspublishing.com | *www.eabookspublishing.com*

Contact: email

Services: marketing coaching that includes branding, website/blog, and social media; works with fiction, nonfiction, children's

Charges: flat fee

Credentials/experience: Traditionally published author who now owns a self-publishing company that also offers this coaching service because it is what I wish I had: one-on-one coaching.

ENLIVEN YOUR TRIBE! | BRIAN ALLAIN

Freehold, NJ | 732-637-9399
brian@enlivenyourtribe.com | *enlivenyourtribe.com*

Contact: email

Services: platform development, strategic marketing, social-media marketing, consulting

Charges: flat fee

Credentials/experience: Frederick Buechner Center, Writing For Your Life, *www.linkedin.com/in/brianallain*

LITFUSE PUBLICITY GROUP | AMY LATHROP

14820 Greenwood Ave. N., Shoreline, WA 98133 | 903-874-8363
info@litfusegroup.com | *www.litfusegroup.com*

Other publicists: Audra Jennings, *audra@litfusegroup.com*; Caitlin Wilson, *caitlin@litfusegroup.com*

Contact: email

Services: publicity, blog tours, online events, social-media management and consulting, launch teams, and author-assist services; working with fiction and nonfiction

Charges: package rates for combined services, social-media and author-assist rates vary based on needs

Credentials/experience: Our clients have included Thomas Nelson, Zondervan, Tyndale, WaterBrook Multnomah, Kregel, Abingdon, and many other Christian publishers.

MCCLURE/MUNTSINGER PUBLIC RELATIONS | PAMELA MCCLURE AND JANA MUNTSINGER

PO Box 804, Franklin, TN 37065 | 615-595-8321
info@mmpublicrelations.com | *www.mmpublicrelations.com*

Contact: email

Services: customized publicity campaigns with any book they like; rarely work with self-published authors

Charges: customized by campaign

Credentials/experience: Former clients include all major publishers. We work with all types of media from print to television to internet to radio, including mainstream and religious media. Our favorite projects are those we can promote to both religious and mainstream national media. After more than 40 combined years of book publicity, we have long and strong relationships with dozens of editors, writers, and producers. We specialize in knowing how to place religious books in Christian and general-market media, traditional outlets, and online.

MEDIA CONNECT | SHARON FARNELL

301 E. 57th St., New York, NY 10022 | 212-593-6337
sharon.farnell@finnpartners.com | *www.media-connect.com*

Contact: email

Services: full-service book publicity firm: TV and radio campaigns, print, online, book tours, etc.; primarily working with nonfiction but also children's books and some fiction titles. We have several specialties, including our Faith Division, as well as business, sports, health, parenting, etc.

Charges: flat rate

Credentials/experience: More than 50 years of experience with book publicity.

SIDE DOOR COMMUNICATIONS | DEBBIE LYKINS

Menomonee Falls, WI | 224-234-6699
deb@sidedoorcom.net | www.sidedoorcom.net

Contact: email

Services: Media relations, working with both Christian and traditional media, as well as online media and bloggers. We focus primarily on Christian nonfiction titles and the occasional novel. We primarily work on traditionally published titles but will consider self-published titles. We look for well-written, well-edited books on topics that we believe will be of interest to the media. We also consider the author's credentials on the subject. No self-published novels.

Charges: project fee

Credentials/experience: More than two decades of experience in marketing, public relations, and communications, with more than 15 years in Christian book publicity. Authors represented have been featured in numerous media outlets.

VERITAS COMMUNICATIONS | DON S. OTIS

PO Box 1505, Sandpoint, ID 83864 | 719-275-7775
don@veritasincorporated.com | www.veritasincorporated.com

Contact: email

Services: Christian publicity for authors, publishers, and not-for-profits. Specializing in Christian and conservative titles or organizations, issues-driven products, marriage and family. Emphasis on nonfiction with fiction on a case-by-case basis, depending on the issues covered by the book and expertise of the author.

Charges: flat fee

Credentials/experience: Freelance publicist since 1991. Former television and radio producer, author of six books, speaker at numerous conferences and seminars. Have booked 30,000 interviews for more than 1,000 authors and organizations.

WILDFIRE MARKETING | ROB EAGAR
3625 Chartwell Dr., Suwanee, GA 30024 | 770-887-1462
Rob@StartaWildfire.com | *www.StartaWildfire.com*

Contact: phone

Services: Trains writers to (1) build a complete marketing plan;
(2) build a website that attracts readers, grows their platform,
and increases book sales; (3) create a memorable brand that sets
them apart in a crowded marketplace; (4) develop powerful
keynote speeches to garner higher speaking fees; (5) capture more
media coverage and turn interviews into book sales; (6) establish
partnerships with high-profile organizations for exponential
growth; (7) coordinate efforts with their publishers to maximize
resources and promotional tools; and (7) create new products and
services that dramatically boost income. Does not consult with
aspiring, independent, or self-published authors.

Charges: flat fee

Credentials/experience: Rob has helped more than 400 authors,
including *New York Times* bestsellers, and has consulted with
numerous publishing houses. He's helped B-level authors become
bestsellers and helped bestselling authors expand their book sales
even more. He is the author of *Sell Your Book Like Wildfire*.

21

CONTESTS

A listing here does not guarantee endorsement of the contest. For guidelines on evaluating contests, go to *www.sfwa.org/other-resources/ for-authors/writer-beware/contests*.

Note: Dates may not be accurate since many sponsors had not posted their 2017 dates before press time.

CHILDREN AND TEENS

CORETTA SCOTT KING BOOK AWARD
www.ala.org/awardsgrants/awards/24/apply

Sponsored by Coretta Scott King Task Force, American Library Association. Annual award for children's books published the previous year by African-American authors and/or illustrators. Books must promote an understanding and appreciation of the "American Dream" and fit one of these categories: preschool to grade 4, grades 5–8, grades 9–12.

Deadline: December 1. **Prizes:** plaque and $1,000.

POCKETS FICTION-WRITING CONTEST
www.pockets.upperroom.org/write-for-us

Must be unpublished and not historical or biblical fiction. Previous winners not eligible. Length: 800-1,000 words. Send to Pockets Fiction Contest, Lynn W. Gilliam, Editor, PO Box 340004, Nashville TN 37203-0004. Designate "Fiction Contest" on outside of envelope. Send SASE for return and response.

Deadline: Submit between March 1 and August 15. **Prize:** $500 and publication in *Pockets*.

SOCIETY OF CHILDREN'S BOOK WRITERS AND ILLUSTRATORS

www.scbwi.org/awards/grants/for-authors

Sponsors a variety of contests, scholarships, and grants.

Deadline: Deadlines vary. **Prizes:** ten awards for published authors and five for unpublished authors plus grants for emerging voices and student writers.

FICTION

ALEXANDER PATTERSON CAPPON PRIZE FOR FICTION

www.newletters.org/writers-wanted/writing-contests

Sponsored by University of Missouri--Kansas City. Entries accepted in these categories: poetry, nonfiction/essay, fiction/short-story.

Deadline: May 18. **Entry fee:** $15. **Prize:** $1,500 for the best in each category.

AMERICAN CHRISTIAN FICTION WRITERS CONTESTS

www.acfw.com/contests

Genesis Contest for unpublished Christian fiction writers in a number of categories/genres. First Impressions award for unpublished writers. Carol Awards for best Christian fiction published the previous year.

Deadline: varies by contest. **Entry fee:** varies by category and membership.

ATHANATOS CHRISTIAN MINISTRIES NOVEL AND NONFICTION CONTEST

www.christianwritingcontest.com

A contest to develop a genre of fiction that might be called "literary apologetics," the use of fiction and story to communicate the gospel and the worldview associated with it. Length: 40,000–90,000 words.

Deadline: January 15. **Entry fee:** $90-100. **Prizes:** first place, $2,500 and possible book contract; two runner-up awards, $1,000 and possible book contract.

BARD FICTION PRIZE

www.bard.edu/bfp

Sponsored by Bard College. Awarded to a promising, emerging young writer of fiction, 39 years or younger and an American citizen. Entries must be previously published.

Deadline: July 15. **Entry fee:** none. **Prize:** $30,000 and appointment as writer-in-residence for one semester at Bard College, Annandale-on-Hudson, New York.

BOSTON REVIEW SHORT STORY CONTEST
www.bostonreview.net/contests

Previously unpublished short stories no longer than 5,000 words.
Deadline: Mid-October. **Entry fee:** $20. **Prize:** $1,500 plus publication.

BULWER-LYTTON FICTION CONTEST
www.bulwer-lytton.com

Sponsored by San Jose State University English Department. For the worst opening line to a novel. Each submission must be a single sentence; multiple entries allowed. Entries will be judged by categories: general, detective, western, science fiction, romance, etc. Overall winners, as well as category winners.
Deadline: June 30.

FLANNERY O'CONNOR AWARD FOR SHORT FICTION
www.ugapress.org/index.php/series/FOC

Sponsored by University of Georgia Press. For collections of short fiction. Length: 40,000–75,000 words. Contestants must be residents of North America.
Deadlines: Submit between April 1 and May 31. **Entry fee:** $30. **Prize:** $1,000 plus publication under royalty book contract.

GLIMMER TRAIN PRESS FICTION CONTESTS
www.glimmertrain.com/pages/writing_guidelines.php

Categories: short story for new writers, very short fiction, fiction open, family matters, and standard. See the website for definitions of each category. Emerging writers are welcome in all categories. Short Story Award for New Writers is exclusively open to writers whose fiction has not appeared, nor is scheduled to appear, in any print publication with a circulation greater than 5,000.
Deadlines: February 29, June 30, October 31. **Entry fee:** $18. **Prizes:** first place, $700-$3,000 plus publication in *Glimmer Train Stories*.

GRACE PALEY PRIZE FOR SHORT FICTION
www.awpwriter.org/contests/overview

Sponsored by Association of Writers and Writing Programs. Short-story collections. May contain stories previously published in periodicals. Length: 150-300 pages.
Deadlines: Submit between January 1 and February 28. **Entry fee:** $25. **Prize:** $5,000 and publication.

JACK DYER FICTION PRIZE
craborchardreview.siu.edu/dyer.html

Sponsored by Southern Illinois University Department of English. Annual competition in poetry, short story (6,000 words), and literary nonfiction (6,500 words) on a theme. Check website for current theme.

Deadline: varies from mid-February to mid-May. **Entry fee:** $15. **Prizes:** $2,000 each and publication in *Crab Orchard Review*.

JAMES JONES FIRST NOVEL CONTEST
www.wilkes.edu/pages/1159.asp

Sponsored by Wilkes University. For a first novel or novel-in-progress by a U.S. writer who has not published a novel. Submit a two-page outline and the first fifty pages of an unpublished novel.

Deadline: March 15. **Entry fee:** $30. **Prizes:** first place, $10,000; two runners-up, $1,000 each. A selection from the winning work is published in *Provincetown Arts*.

KATHERINE ANNE PORTER PRIZE FOR FICTION
untpress.unt.edu/submitting-katherine-anne-porter-prize-short-fiction

Sponsored by University of North Texas Press. Quality unpublished fiction by emerging writers of contemporary literature. Can be a combination of short-shorts, short stories, and novellas from 100 to 200 pages (27,500-50,000 words). Material should be previously unpublished in book form.

Deadline: Submit between May 1 and June 30. **Entry fee:** $25. **Prize:** $1,000 and publication.

NATIONAL WRITERS ASSOCIATION NOVEL-WRITING CONTEST
www.nationalwriters.shoppingcartsplus.com/f/Novel_Form4.pdf

To encourage development of creative skills and recognize and reward outstanding ability in the area of novel writing. Any genre or category of novel manuscript may be entered. Only unpublished works in the English language. Maximum length: 100,000 words. Must be submitted via USPS.

Deadline: postmarked by April 1. **Entry fee:** $35. **Prizes:** first place, $500 and possible representation; second place, $250; third place, $150; fourth through tenth places, book of the winner's choice; honorable mentions, certificate.

NATIONAL WRITERS ASSOCIATION SHORT-STORY CONTEST

www.nationalwriters.shoppingcartsplus.com/f/Short_Story_Contest1.pdf

Any genre of story. Length: 5,000 words maximum. Submit only unpublished works in the English language via mail.

Deadline: postmarked by July 1. **Entry fee:** $15. **Prizes:** first place, $250; second place, $100; third place, $50; fourth through tenth places: recognition.

REALM MAKERS AWARDS

www.realmmakers.com

Sponsored by The Faith and Fantasy Alliance. Realm Makers Genre Awards in these categories: debut, science fiction, fantasy, young adult, supernatural/horror, and other (for those who don't feel other categories accurately characterize their speculative work). Realm Award recognizes the most excellent speculative novel written by a Christian author in the previous calendar year. Length: 60,000 words minimum; 50,000 words minimum for young adult. Parable Award for Excellence in Cover Design is awarded to the best overall cover for a speculative novel written by a Christian author.

Deadline: Submit between January 1 and 20. **Entry fee:** $35 for books, $25 for cover designs. **Prizes:** cash.

SERENA MCDONALD KENNEDY AWARD

www.snakenationpress.org/submission-guidelines

Sponsored by Snake Nation Press. Novellas up to 50,000 words or short-story collections up to 200 pages, published or unpublished.

Deadline: August 31. **Entry fee:** $25. **Prize:** $1,000 and publication.

SILVER QUILL SOCIETY BEST SHORT FICTION CONTEST

www.thestorytellermagazine.com/contests

Sponsored by *The Storyteller* anthology/magazine. Open genre contest but must be about family in some way and suitable for a family magazine. Length: 3,000 words maximum. Can enter multiple stories with separate entry fee for each one.

Deadline: September 25. **Entry fee:** $5. **Prizes:** first place, $50; second place, $25; third place, $15; fourth place, $10.

TOBIAS WOLFF AWARD FOR FICTION

www.bhreview.org/contest-submissions-guidelines

Sponsored by Western Washington University's *Bellingham Review*. Length: 6,000 words maximum.

Deadline: Submit between December 1 and March 15. **Entry fee:** $20. **Prize:** $1,000 plus publication.

NONFICTION

ANNIE DILLARD AWARD IN CREATIVE NONFICTION
bhreview.org/contest-submissions-guidelines

Sponsored by Western Washington University's *Bellingham Review*. Unpublished essays on any subject. Length: 6,000 words maximum.

Deadline: Submit between December 1 and March 15. **Entry fee:** $20 for first submission; $10 each additional one. **Prize:** $1,000.

AWP PRIZE FOR CREATIVE NONFICTION
www.awpwriter.org/contests

Sponsored by Association of Writers and Writing Programs. Open to published and unpublished authors. Book collection of nonfiction mamuscripts. Length: 150–300 pages.

Deadline: Submit between January 1 and February 28. **Entry fee:** $15 for members, $30 for nonmembers. **Prize:** $2,500.

THE BECHTEL PRIZE
www.twc.org/publications/bechtel-prize

Sponsored by Teachers & Writers Collaborative. For unpublished essays that explore themes related to creative writing, arts education, and/or the imagination. Length: 3,500 words maximum.

Deadline: December 16. **Entry fee:** $20. **Prize:** $1,000 and publication.

EVENT NON-FICTION CONTEST
www.eventmagazine.ca/contest-nf

Unpublished creative nonfiction. Length: 5,000 words maximum.

Deadline: April 15. **Entry fee:** $34.95; includes a one-year subscription to *EVENT*. **Prizes:** $1,500 total plus publication. Judges reserve the right to award two or three prizes.

GRAYWOLF PRESS NONFICTION PRIZE
www.graywolfpress.org/resources/submission-and-contest-guidelines

For the best literary nonfiction book manuscript in progress by a U.S. resident not yet established in this genre. Literary nonfiction includes memoir, biography, and history.

Deadline: Submissions for the prize open every other year to allow for the longer lead time needed to develop and publish the winning manuscripts. **Entry fee:** none. **Prize:** $12,000 advance and publication of finished book.

GUIDEPOSTS WRITERS WORKSHOP CONTEST

www.guideposts.org/enter-the-guideposts-writers-workshop-contest

Contest is held in even years with a mid-June deadline. Submit an original, unpublished, true, first-person story (your own or ghostwritten for another person) in 2,000 words or fewer about an experience that changed your life. Show how faith made a difference. Twelve winners will attend an all-expenses-paid, weeklong writers workshop in New York to learn about inspirational storytelling and writing for *Guideposts* publications.

NEW LETTERS PRIZE FOR NONFICTION

www.newletters.org/writers-wanted/writing-contests

For unpublished essays. Length: 8,000 words maximum.

Deadline: Mid-May. **Entry fee:** $20. **Prize:** $1,500 and magazine subscription.

RICHARD J. MARGOLIS AWARD

award.margolis.com

Sponsored by Blue Mountain Center. Given annually to a promising young journalist or essayist whose work combines warmth, humor, wisdom, and concern with social justice. Submit at least two examples of published or unpublished work and a short biographical note, including a description of current and anticipated work. Length: 30 pages maximum.

Deadline: July 1. **Prize:** $5,000 plus a one-month residency at the Blue Mountain Center in Blue Mountain Lake, New York.

PLAYS, SCRIPTS, SCREENPLAYS

ACADEMY NICHOLL FELLOWSHIPS IN SCREENWRITING

www.oscars.org/nicholl/about

International contest open to any writer who has not optioned or sold a treatment, teleplay, or screenplay for more than $25,000. May submit up to three scripts.

Deadline: Submit between March 7 and May 2. **Entry fee:** $45-85, depending on submission date. **Prizes:** up to five $35,000 fellowships. Recipients will be expected to complete at least one original feature-film screenplay during the fellowship year.

AMERICAN ZOETROPE SCREENPLAY CONTEST

www.zoetrope.com/contests

To find and promote new and innovative voices in cinema. For screenplays and television pilots. No entrant may have earned more than

$5,000 as a screenwriter for theatrical films or television or for the sale of, or sale of an option to, any original story, treatment, screenplay, or teleplay. Prizes, fellowships, awards, and other contest winnings are not considered earnings and are excluded from this rule. Length: film scripts, 70-130 pages; one-hour television pilot scripts, 45-65 pages; half-hour television scripts, 22-34 pages.

Deadline: September 19. **Entry fee:** $35-$50, depending on submission date. **Prizes:** first place, $5,000. That winner and ten finalists will be considered for film option and development.

AUSTIN FILM FESTIVAL SCREENWRITERS COMPETITION

austinfilmfestival.com/submit

Offers a number of contest categories, including narrative feature, narrative short, documentary feature, documentary short for screenplays, screenplay, teleplay, and scripted digital competition.

Deadline: varies by type. **Entry fee:** varies by type and submission date. **Prizes:** $1,000- $5,000.

CHRONOS PRIZE FOR INSPIRING SCREENPLAYS BY ESTABLISHED FILMMAKERS

chronosprize.com/guidelines-criteria

Sponsored by Movieguide. Contest for established, professional writers with a religious message. For feature-length screenplays. Judges consider not only a script's entertainment value and craftsmanship, but also whether it is uplifting, inspirational, and spiritual, rather than merely humanitarian. Length: 87-130 pages; will accept scripts up to 150 pages (not counting the title page) for an additional $20.

Deadline: October. **Entry fees:** vary, depending on submission date.

KAIROS PRIZE FOR SPIRITUALLY UPLIFTING SCREENPLAYS

www.kairosprize.com

Sponsored by Movieguide. Unpublished, unproduced, unoptioned scripts suitable for a G or PG rating. Should refer implicitly and/or explicitly to biblical principles, values, and virtues and/or refer specifically to the Bible. Length: 87-130 pages; will accept scripts up to 150 pages (not counting the title page) for an additional $20.

Deadline: October 25. **Entry fee:** $50. **Prizes:** $15,000 for first-time screenwriters and $15,000 for professional screenwriters with a religious message.

MILDRED AND ALBERT PANOWSKI PLAYWRITING COMPETITION

www.nmu.edu/forestrobertstheatre/playwritingcompetition

Sponsored by Forest Roberts Theatre, Northern Michigan University. Unpublished, unproduced, full-length plays. Award to encourage and stimulate artistic growth among educational and professional playwrights. Provides students and faculty members the opportunity to mount and produce an original work on the university stage.

Deadline: Submit between June 1 and December 1. **Prize:** $2,000, a summer workshop, a fully mounted production, and transportation to Marquette, Michigan.

MOONDANCE INTERNATIONAL FILM FESTIVAL COMPETITION

www.moondancefilmfestival.com

Offers a variety of awards for films, screenplays, librettos, and features that raise awareness about social issues.

Deadline: May 30. **Entry fees:** $50–100. **Prize:** promotion to film companies for possible option.

SCRIPTAPALOOZA SCREENPLAY COMPETITION

www.scriptapalooza.com

Any screenplay from any genre considered; must be the original work of the author (multiple authorship acceptable). Shorts competition: screenplays fewer than 40 pages.

Deadline: May 1. **Entry fee:** varies by submission date. **Prizes:** first place, $10,000; each genre winner, $500 (action, adventure, comedy, drama, family, science fiction, thriller/ horror, historical). Plus access to more than 50 producers through Scriptapalooza's network.

SCRIPTAPALOOZA TV COMPETITION

www.scriptapaloozatv.com/competition

Scripts for television pilots, one-hour dramas, reality shows, and half-hour sitcoms. Length: pilots, 30-60 pages; one-hour program, 50-60 pages; reality show, one- to five-page treatment; half-hour sitcom, 25-35 pages.

Deadline: October 17. **Entry fee:** $45. **Prizes in each category:** first place, $500; second place, $200; third place, $100. Plus access to more than 50 producers through Scriptapalooza's network.

POETRY

49TH PARALLEL POETRY AWARD
bhreview.org/contest-submissions-guidelines

Sponsored by Western Washington University's *Bellingham Review*. Up to three poems in any style or on any subject.

Deadline: Submit between December 1 and March 15. **Entry fee:** $20; international entries, $30. **Prize:** $1,000 and publication.

ANHINGA-ROBERT DANA PRIZE FOR POETRY
www.anhingapress.org/anhinga-robert-dana-prize

Sponsored by Anhinga Press. For poets trying to publish a first or second book of poetry. Length: 48–80 pages.

Deadline: Submit between February 15 and May 30. **Entry fee:** $28. **Prize:** $2,000, a reading tour, and publication by Anhinga Press.

BALTIMORE REVIEW POETRY CONTEST
baltimorereview.submittable.com/submit

All styles and forms of poetry. Maximum of three entries.

Deadline: varies. **Entry fee:** $10. **Prizes:** $100-500 and publication.

BARBARA MANDIGO KELLY PEACE POETRY AWARDS
www.peacecontests.org

Sponsored by Nuclear Age Peace Foundation. Awards to encourage poets to explore and illuminate positive visions of peace and the human spirit. May submit up to three poems for one entry fee.

Deadline: July 1. **Entry fee:** adults, $15; youth ages 13-18, $5; none for ages 12 and under. **Prizes:** adult winner, $1,000; youth winner, $200; ages 12 and under, $200.

BLUE MOUNTAIN ARTS POETRY CARD CONTEST
www.sps.com/poetry

Biannual contest. Poems may be rhymed or unrhymed, although unrhymed is preferred. Poems also considered for greeting cards or anthologies. No limit to entries.

Deadlines: June 30 and December 31. **Entry fee:** none. **Prizes:** $300, $150, and $50.

BOSTON REVIEW ANNUAL POETRY CONTEST
www.bostonreview.net./contests

Submit up to five unpublished poems; no more than ten pages total. Submit manuscripts in duplicate with cover note.

Deadline: June 1. **Entry fee:** $20, includes a subscription to Boston Review. **Prize:** $1,500 plus publication.

CAVE CANEM POETRY PRIZE

cavecanempoets.org/prizes/cave-canem-poetry-prize

Sponsored by Cave Canem Foundation. Supports the work of black poets of African descent with excellent manuscripts and who have not found a publisher for their first book. Offered every other year. **Length:** 48-75 pages.

Deadline: varies. **Entry fee:** $15. **Prize:** $1,000 plus publication by a national press and fifteen copies of the book.

THE COMSTOCK WRITERS GROUP CHAPBOOK CONTEST

comstockreview.org/comstock-writers-group-chapbook

Submissions must be unpublished as a collection, but individual poems may have been published previously in journals. Length: 25-34 pages. One page equals 38 lines maximum, single-spaced, including spacing between lines. Poems may run longer than one page.

Deadline: Submit between August 1 and October 31. **Entry fee:** $30. **Prize:** $1,000 plus publication.

FLO GAULT STUDENT POETRY PRIZE

www.sarabandebooks.org/flo-gault

Sponsored by Sarabande Books. For full-time Kentucky undergraduate students. Submit up to three poems.

Deadline: October 30. **Prize:** $500 and publication.

HOLLIS SUMMERS POETRY PRIZE

www.ohioswallow.com/poetry_prize

Sponsored by Ohio University Press. For an unpublished collection of original poems, 60–95 pages. Open to both those who have not a published book-length collection and to those who have.

Deadline: November 15. **Entry fee:** $30. **Prize:** $1,000 plus publication in book form by Ohio University Press.

THE JAMES LAUGHLIN AWARD

www.poets.org/academy-american-poets/james-laughlin-award-guidelines

Sponsored by Academy of American Poets. To recognize a second full-length print book of original poetry, forthcoming in the next calendar year. Author must have published one book of poetry in a standard edition (48 pages or more); publication of chapbooks (less than 48 pages) does not disqualify. Length: 48-100 pages.

Prize: $5,000 plus publication. Copies of the winning book are purchased and distributed to approximately 1,000 members of the Academy of American Poets.

KATE TUFTS DISCOVERY AWARD
www.cgu.edu/tufts

Sponsored by Claremont Graduate University. Award presented annually for a first poetry volume published in the preceding year by a poet of genuine promise.
Deadline: June 30. **Prize:** $10,000.

KINGSLEY TUFTS POETRY AWARD
www.cgu.edu/pages/6422.asp

Sponsored by Claremont Graduate University. Presented annually for a published book of poetry by a midcareer poet to both honor the poet and provide the resources that allow artists to continue working toward the pinnacle of their craft.
Deadline: June 30. **Prize:** $100,000.

MURIEL CRAFT BAILEY MEMORIAL POETRY AWARD
www.comstockreview.org

Sponsored by *Comstock Review*. Unpublished poems up to 40 lines. No limit on number of submissions.
Deadline: Submit between April 1 and July 15. **Entry fee:** $5. **Prizes:** first place, $1,000; second place, $250; third place, $100; plus publication in *Comstock Review*.

NEW LETTERS PRIZE FOR POETRY
www.newletters.org/writers-wanted/writing-contests

A single poetry entry may contain up to six poems, and the poems need not be related.
Deadline: May 18. **Entry fee:** $20 first entry; $15 for every subsequent entry. If entering online, add a $5 service charge to entry fee. One-year subscription to *New Letters* included in price of first entry. **Prize:** $1,500 for best group of three to six poems.

PHILIP LEVINE PRIZE FOR POETRY
www.fresnostate.edu/artshum/english/levineprize

Sponsored by California State University Department of English. An annual book contest for original, previously unpublished, full-length poetry manuscripts. Length: 48-80 pages with no more than one poem per page.
Deadline: Submit between July 1 and September 30. **Entry fee:** $28. **Prize:** $2000.

POETRY SOCIETY OF VIRGINIA POETRY CONTESTS

poetrysocietyofvirginia.org/2016-psov-adult-poetry-contests

More than twenty-five categories for adults and students. Form and length limit of entries vary according to the contests. All entries must be unpublished, original, and not scheduled for publication before the winners of the competition are announced.

Deadline: Submit between November 1 and January 19. **Entry fee:** $4 per poem for nonmembers. **Prizes:** $100, $50, $30, 20, varying according to specific competition.

RICHARD PETERSON POETRY PRIZE

craborchardreview.siu.edu/pete1.html

Sponsored by *Crab Orchard Review*, Southern Illinois University–Carbondale Department of English. Unpublished poems by a United States citizen, permanent resident, or person who has DACA/TPS status. Length: five pages maximum. Limit three entries.

Deadline: Submit between February 21 and May 17 (may vary). **Entry fee:** $15. **Prizes:** first place, $2,000 and publication; finalists, $500 and publication.

SLIPSTREAM ANNUAL POETRY CHAPBOOK COMPETITION

www.slipstreampress.org/contest.html

Sponsored by Slipstream Press. Entries may be any style, format, or theme. Length: 40 pages maximum.

Deadline: December 1. **Entry fee:** $20. **Prize:** $1,000 plus 50 published copies of chapbook.

SOUL-MAKING KEATS LITERARY COMPETITION: JANICE FARRELL POETRY PRIZE

www.soulmakingcontest.us./poetry.html

Sponsored by National League of American Pen Women. Three poems per entry. One poem per page; one-page poems only. Free verse, blank verse, and prose poems.

Deadline: November 30. **Entry fee:** $5. **Prizes:** first place, $100; second place, $50; third place, $25.

SUMMERTIME BLUES POETRY CONTEST

www.thestorytellermagazine.com

Sponsored by *The Storyteller*. Poems may be rhyming or nonrhyming and should be about summer, although this topic isn't mandatory. Length: 40 lines maximum. Multiple entries accepted.

Deadline: postmarked by August 31. **Entry fee:** $5 per three poems. **Prizes:** first place, $25 plus publication; second place, $15; third place, $10.

TOI DERRICOTTE & CORNELIUS EADY CHAPBOOK PRIZE

cavecanempoets.org/prizes/toi-derricotte-cornelius-eady-chapbook-prize

Sponsored by Cave Canem Foundation. Dedicated to the discovery of exceptional chapbook-length manuscripts by black poets. Presented in collaboration with the O, Miami Poetry Festival.

Deadline: September 30. **Entry Fee:** $12. **Prize:** $500, publication, ten copies of the chapbook, and a feature reading.

TOM HOWARD/MARGARET REID POETRY CONTEST

winningwriters.com/our-contests/tom-howard-margaret-reid-poetry-contest

Sponsored by Winning Writers. Poetry in any style or genre. Published poetry accepted. Length: 250 lines maximum.

Deadline: Submit between April 15 and September 30. **Entry fee:** $10. **Prizes:** Tom Howard Prize, $1,500 for poem in any style or genre; Margaret Reid Prize, $1,500 for poem that rhymes or has a traditional style; $100 each for ten honorable mentions in any style.

UTMOST NOVICE CHRISTIAN POETRY CONTEST

www.utmostchristianwriters.com/poetry-contest/poetry-contest-rules.php

Sponsored by Utmost Christian Writers Foundation. Unpublished poems may be rhymed or free verse, up to 60 lines. Need not be religious in content. Maximum of five entries.

Deadline: February 28. **Entry fee:** $20. **Prizes:** $1,000, $500, $300, $200; ten honorable mentions, $100; best rhyming poem, $300; honorable mention rhyming poem, $200.

VIOLET REED HAAS PRIZE FOR POETRY

www.snakenationpress.org/submission-guidelines

Sponsored by Snake Nation Press. Length: 75-100 pages. Previously published eligible.

Deadline: August 31. **Entry fee:** $25. **Prize:** $1,000 plus publication.

WERGLE FLOMP HUMOR POETRY CONTEST

winningwriters.com/our-contests/wergle-flomp-humor-poetry-contest-free

Sponsored by Winning Writers. Submit one published or unpublished humor poem up to 250 lines.

Deadline: April 1. **Entry fee:** none. **Prizes:** first place, $1,000; second place, $250; ten honorable mentions, $100; plus the top twelve entries will be published online.

MULTIPLE GENRES

BLUE RIDGE CONFERENCE WRITING CONTEST

www.blueridgeconference.com/contest-info

Sponsors three book contests for fiction or nonfiction: Foundation Awards, Director's Choice, and The Selahs. Look for details about guidelines, deadlines, and entry fees on the website after January 1.

CHRISTIAN SMALL PUBLISHER BOOK OF THE YEAR

www.bookoftheyear.net/eligibility-guidelines

This award is designed to promote small publishers in the Christian marketplace, as well as to bring recognition to outstanding Christian books from small publishers. Only perfect-bound paperback or hardcover books available in the United States. Publishers and authors nominate titles for the award, and Christian readers vote to determine the winners.

Deadline: November 15. **Entry fee:** $45.

COLUMBIA JOURNAL CONTESTS

columbiajournal.org/submit/winter-contest

Fiction and nonfiction: 7,500 words maximum; poetry: five pages maximum.

Deadline: December 12. **Entry fee:** $15. **Prizes:** $500 in each category plus publication.

ERIC HOFFER BOOK AWARD

www.hofferaward.com

Eighteen categories for books from small, academic, and micro presses, including self-published, e-books, and older books. The prose category is for creative fiction and nonfiction fewer than 10,000 words.

Deadline: January 21. **Entry fee:** varies by category. **Grand prize:** $2,000; other prizes awarded in categories.

THE EUPLE RINEY MEMORIAL AWARD

www.thestorytellermagazine.com

Sponsored by *The Storyteller*. Open-genre contest but must be about family—good or bad. Can be fiction or nonfiction (indicate which). Length: 3,000 words maximum. No pornography, graphic anything, New Age, or children's stories will be accepted.

Deadline: June 30. **Entry fee:** $5. **Prizes:** first place, $50; second place, $25; third place, $15; honorable mention, $10. Plus an editor's choice award.

EVANGELICAL PRESS ASSOCIATION CONTEST

www.evangelicalpress.com/contest

Higher Goals awards in a variety of categories for periodical manuscripts published in the previous year. Although most submissions are made by publication staff members, associate EPA members may also submit their articles.

Deadline: early January. **Entry fee:** $50.

INSCRIBE CHRISTIAN WRITERS' FELLOWSHIP CONTEST

inscribe.org/contests

Sponsors contests for InScribe members: Fall Contest, Winter Contest, Word Challenge, FellowScript Contests, Barnabas Award, Janette Oke Award.

Deadlines, entry fees, and awards vary with each contest.

INSPIRATIONAL WRITERS ALIVE! OPEN WRITING COMPETITION

www.centralhoustoniwa.com/IWA_Brochure_Rev_01-2014.pdf

Categories: article, book proposal (fiction or nonfiction), devotional, drama, short story for young adults/adults, and short story for children/teens. Limit of two entries in each category. Members receive discounts on entry fees. Awards presented to winners at the Texas Christian Writers' Conference each fall.

Deadline: Submit between January 1 and May 15. **Entry fee:** $5–$15, depending on category and membership status. **Prizes:** first place, $30; second place, $20; third place, $15.

NARRATIVE MAGAZINE CONTESTS

www.narrativemagazine.com/submit-your-work

Biannual contests in a variety of categories, including short stories, essays, memoirs, poetry, and literary nonfiction. Entries must be previously unpublished. Length: varies by category.

Deadline: varies. **Entry fee:** varies. **Prizes:** vary by category.

NARRATIVE MAGAZINE 30 BELOW CONTEST

www.narrativemagazine.com/node/345528

For writers ages 18-30. Fiction, nonfiction, poetry (up to five poems), essays, memoirs. Length: 15,000 words maximum. Restrictions on previously published works.

Deadline: November 1. **Entry fee:** $22. **Prizes:** $1,500, $750, $300, plus ten finalists will receive $100 each.

NATIONAL WRITERS ASSOCIATION CONTESTS

www.nationalwriters.com/page/page/2734945.htm

Sponsors six contests: nonfiction, novel, young writers, poetry, short short, and David Raffelock Award for Publishing Excellence.

Deadline: varies by contest. **Entry fee:** varies by contest. **Prizes:** vary by contest.

NEW MILLENNIUM AWARDS

submit.newmillenniumwritings.org

Sponsored by New Millennium Writings. Fiction and nonfiction: 6,000 words maximum. Flash fiction (short-short story): 1,000 words maximum. Poetry: three poems to five pages total. No restrictions as to style or subject matter.

Deadline: November 30. **Entry fee:** $20, $45 for three entries, $72 for five entries. **Prizes:** $1,000 plus publication for each category.

OREGON CHRISTIAN WRITERS CASCADE AWARDS

oregonchristianwriters.org

Contests for novels; nonfiction books; memoir; young adult/middle grade fiction and nonfiction books; poetry; children's chapter and picture books; articles, columns, and blog posts; short stories/flash fiction; and devotionals. Separate divisions for published and unpublished authors.

Deadline: Submit between February 14 and March 31. **Entry fees:** $30-35 for members, $40-45 for nonmembers. Awards presented at the summer conference in Portland, Oregon.

SOUL-MAKING KEATS LITERARY COMPETITION

www.soulmakingcontest.us/home.html

Sponsored by National League of American Pen Women, Nob Hill, San Francisco Branch. Categories include flash fiction, short story, memoir vignette, humor, novel excerpt, intercultural essay, creative nonfiction, religious essay, young-adult poetry, and young-adult prose.

Deadline: November 30. **Entry fee:** $5. **Prizes in each category:** first place, $100; second place, $50; third place, $25.

WILLIAM FAULKNER–WILLIAM WISDOM CREATIVE WRITING COMPETITION

wordsandmusic.org/william-faulkner-wisdom-competition/competition-guidelines

Sponsored by The Pirate's Alley Faulkner Society, Inc. Seven categories: novel, novella, book-length narrative fiction, novel-in-progress, short story, essay, poetry, and short story by a high-school student. For previously unpublished work only.

Deadline: Submit between January 1 and May 15. **Entry fee:** varies by category. **Prizes:** $250-7,500, depending on category.

THE WORD GUILD CHRISTIAN WRITING AWARDS

thewordguild.com/contests

The Word Awards recognize the best work published in the previous year in 35 categories of writing, including novels, nonfiction books, articles, columns, poems, song lyrics, scripts, and screenplays. Fresh Ink Student Writers Contest for never-before-published student writers. In the Beginning for unpublished novice and emerging writers. The Grace Irwin Prize for Canadian writers who are Christians; recognizes the best book published in the previous year. The Leslie K. Tarr Award celebrates a major career contribution to Christian writing and publishing in Canada. The Partnership Award recognizes an individual or organization that has shown exceptional support and encouragement for Canadian writers and editors who are Christians.

Deadlines, entry fees and prizes vary according to the award and its guidelines.

WRITER'S DIGEST COMPETITIONS

www.writersdigest.com/writers-digest-competitions

Every other month, *Writer's Digest* presents a creative challenge for fun and prizes, providing a short, open-ended prompt for short-story submissions based on that prompt. Winner receives publication in *Writer's Digest*. Also sponsors annual contests for feature articles, short stories (multiple genres), poetry, personal essays, and self-published books (categories vary).

Deadlines and entry fees vary according to contest. **Prizes for annual contest:** first place, $1,000; second place, $500; and more places for each contest. **Grand prize:** $5,000.

THE WRITERS' UNION OF CANADA AWARDS & COMPETITIONS

www.writersunion.ca/content/awards

Short Prose Competition for Developing Writers: fiction or nonfiction by an author who has not yet published a book. Length: 2,500 words maximum. Danuta Gleed Literary Award for the best first collection of short fiction.

Deadlines: Short Prose, March 1; Danuta, January 31. **Entry fee:** $29. **Prizes:** Short Prose, $2,500; Danuta, $10,000 plus two finalist awards for $500 each.

WRITERS-EDITORS NETWORK ANNUAL INTERNATIONAL WRITING COMPETITION

www.writers-editors.com/Writers/Contests/Contest_Guidelines/contest_guidelines.htm

Nonfiction and fiction: 4,000 words maximum; children's literature (story, fiction-book chapter, poem, magazine article, or nonfiction-book chapter targeted to a specific age group): 4,000 words maximum. Poetry may be traditional or free verse.

Deadline: March 15. **Entry fees:** poetry, $5 for members, $10 for nonmembers; prose: $10 for members, $20 for nonmembers. **Prizes:** $150, $100, $75, plus one-year membership in Writers-Editors Network.

RESOURCES FOR CONTESTS

These websites are sources for announcements about other contests.

DAILY WRITING TIPS
www.dailywritingtips.com/25-writing-competitions

FREELANCE WRITING
www.freelancewriting.com/writingcontests.php

FUNDS FOR WRITERS
fundsforwriters.com/contests

NEW PAGES
www.newpages.com/classifieds/big-list-of-writing-contests

POETS & WRITERS
pw.org/grants

TETHERED BY LETTERS
tetheredbyletters.com/resources/contest-list

THE WRITE LIFE
thewritelife.com/27-free-writing-contests

THE WRITER
www.writermag.com/writing-resources/contests

DENOMINATIONAL PUBLISHERS

ANGLICAN
Anglican Journal

ASSEMBLIES OF GOD
Enrichment
God's Word for Today
Live
My Healthy Church
Take Five Plus

BAPTIST
B&H Publishing
The Brink
Common Call
Earthen Vessel
   Publishing
HomeLife
Judson Press
Mature Living
New Hope Publishers
On Mission
Point
Parenting Teens
ParentLife
Randall House
   Publications
The Secret Place
Triple J Publishing,
   LLC

BRETHREN
In Part

CATHOLIC
Acta Publications
America

American Catholic
   Press
*The Arlington Catholic
   Herald*
Catholic Book
   Publishing Corp.
Catholic Digest
Catholic New York
Catholic Sentinel
Catholic University of
   America Press
Columbia
Commonweal
Eureka Street
Franciscan Media
Image Books
Leaves
Liguorian
1Liturgical Press
Loyola Press
*Our Sunday Visitor
   Newsweekly*
Parish Liturgy
Pauline Books & Media
Paulist Press
Prairie Messenger
Resurrection Press
Scepter Publishers
St. Anthony Messenger
St. Catherine of Siena
   Press
St. Mary's Messenger
Tau-Publishing
U.S. Catholic

CHARISMATIC
See Pentecostal.

**CHRISTIAN CHURCH/
CHURCH OF CHRIST**
Christian Standard
College Press
   Publishing
CrossLink Publishing

CHURCH OF GOD
Bible Advocate
*The Church Herald &
   Holiness Banner*
The Gem
Gems of Truth
Now What?
Warner Press

EPISCOPAL
Forward Day by Day
Forward Movement
The Living Church

**EVANGELICAL FREE
CHURCH**
EFCA Today

**GRACE BRETHREN
CHURCHES**
BMH Books
GraceConnect

LUTHERAN
Canada Lutheran
The Canadian Lutheran
Concordia Academic
   Press

Concordia Publishing
House
Fortress Press
Langmarc Publishing
The Lutheran Digest
Lutheran Forum
The Lutheran Journal
Lutheran Witness
Northwestern
Publishing House
Sparkhouse Family
The Word in Season

MENNONITE
Canadian Mennonite
The Messenger
Purpose
Rejoice!

MESSIANIC
The Messianic Times

METHODIST
Abingdon Press
*Christian Living in the
Mature Years*
Good News (NY)
Light& Life Magazine
Methodist History
Pockets
The Upper Room
Weavings

NAZARENE
Beacon Hill Press
Holiness Today
Reflecting God

OPEN BIBLE STANDARD CHURCHES
*Message of the Open
Bible*

ORTHODOX
Ancient Faith
Publishing

PENTECOSTAL/ CHARISMATIC
Charisma
Empowered
Publications, Inc.
Harrison House
Publishers
Ministry Today
Pentecostal Messenger
The Vision
Whitaker House

PRESBYTERIAN
byFaith
Presbyterians Today
These Days
Westminster/John
Knox Press

QUAKER/FRIENDS
Friends Journal
Friends United Press

REFORMED
Christian Courier
Faith Alive Christian
Resources
P&R Publishing
Perspectives

SALVATION ARMY
Faith & Friends
New Frontier Chronicle
SAConnects
War Cry
Young Salvationist

SEVENTH-DAY ADVENTIST
Guide
Insight
*The Journal of Adventist
Education*
Ministry
Our Little Friend
Pacific Press
Primary Treasure
Vibrant Life

UNITED CHURCH OF CANADA
United Church Observer

WESLEYAN
Light from the Word
Wesleyan Publishing
House

GLOSSARY

Advance: Money a publisher pays to an author up front, against future royalties. The amount varies greatly from publisher to publisher and is often paid in two or three installments (on signing the contract, on delivery of the manuscript, and on publication).

All rights: An outright sale of your manuscript. The author has no further control over any subsidiary rights.

Anecdote: A short, poignant, real-life story, usually used to illustrate a single thought. It need not be humorous

Assignment: When an editor asks a writer to create a specific manuscript for an agreed-on price.

As-told-to story: A true story you write as a first-person account about someone else.

Audiobooks: Spoken-word books available on compact disc or in other digital audio formats (streaming via the Internet or mp3).

Backlist: A publisher's previously published books that are still in print a year or more after publication.

Bar code: Identification code and price on the back of a book read by a scanner at checkout counters.

Bible versions:
    AMP—Amplified Bible
    ASV—American Standard Version
    CEB—Common English Bible
    CEV—Contemporary English Version
    CSB—Christian Standard Bible
    ESV—English Standard Version
    GNB—Good News Bible

GWB—Gods Word Bible
HCSB—Holman Christian Standard Bible
ICB—International Children's Bible
KJV—King James Version
MSG—*The Message*
NAB—New American Bible
NASB—New American Standard Bible
NEB—New English Bible
NIrV—New International Reader's Version
NIV—New International Version
NJB—New Jerusalem Bible
NKJV—New King James Version
NLT—New Living Translation
NRSV—New Revised Standard Version
RSV—Revised Standard Version;
TLB—*The Living Bible*
TNIV—Today's New International Version

Bimonthly: Every two months.

Bio: Brief information about the author.

Biweekly: Every two weeks.

Bluelines: The last printer's proofs used to catch errors before a book or periodical is printed. (previously these were physical pages, now can refer to digital proofs in PDF format)

Book proposal: Submission of a book idea to an agent or editor. It usually includes a hook, summary and purpose of the book, target market, uniqueness of the book compared to similar ones in the marketplace, chapter-by-chapter summaries or plot synopsis, marketing and promotion information, your credentials, and delivery date, plus one to three sample chapters, including the first one.

Byline: Author's name printed below the title of a story, article, etc.

Camera-ready copy: The text and artwork for a book that are ready for the press.

Chapbook: A small book or pamphlet containing poetry, religious readings, etc.

Circulation: The number of copies sold or distributed of each issue of a periodical.

Clips: Copies of articles you have had published in newspapers or magazines.

Column: A regularly appearing feature, section, or department in a periodical with the same heading. It's written by the same person or a different freelancer each time.

Concept statement: A 50- to 150-word summary of your proposed book.

Contributing editor: A freelance writer who has a regular column or writes regularly for the periodical.

Contributor's copy: Copy of an issue of a periodical sent to an author whose work appears in it.

Copyright: Legal protection of an author's work. A manuscript is automatically copyrighted in your name when you produce it. You don't need to register it with the Copyright Office unless you are self-publishing a book or other publication.

Cover letter: A letter that accompanies some manuscript submissions. Usually it's needed only if you have to tell the editor something specific, to give your credentials for writing a manuscript of a technical nature, or to remind the editor that the manuscript was requested or expected. Often used as the introduction to a book proposal. Rarely used for an article submission—query letters are used instead.

Credits, list of: A listing of your previously published works.

Critique: An evaluation of a manuscript.

Defamation: A written or spoken injury to the reputation of a living person or organization. If what is said is true, it cannot be defamatory.

Derivative work: A work derived from another work, such as a condensation or abridgment. Contact the copyright owner for permission before doing the abridgment and be prepared to pay that owner a fee or royalty.

Devotional: A short manuscript based on a Scripture verse or passage that shares a personal spiritual discovery, inspires to worship, challenges to commitment or action, or encourages.

Editorial guidelines: See "Writers guidelines."

Electronic submission: The submission of a proposal or article to an editor by email.

Endorsements: Flattering comments about a book, usually printed on the back cover or in promotional material.

Essay: A short composition expressing the author's opinion on a specific subject.

Evangelical: A person who believes that one receives God's forgiveness for sins through Jesus Christ and believes the Bible is the authoritative word of God. This is a broad definition for a label with broad application.

Exegesis: Interpretation of a Scripture passage.

Feature article: In-depth coverage of a subject, usually focusing on a person, an event, a process, an organization, a movement, a trend, or an issue. It's written to explain, encourage, help, analyze, challenge, motivate, warn, or entertain, as well as to inform.

Filler: A short item used to "fill" a page of a periodical. It could be a timeless news item, joke, anecdote, light verse, short humor, puzzle, game, etc.

First rights: An editor buys the right to publish a manuscript that has never been published and to do so only once.

Foreign rights: Selling or giving permission to translate or reprint published material in another country.

Foreword: Opening remarks in a book to introduce the book and its author.

Freelance: Supplied by freelance writers.

Freelancer or freelance writer: A writer who is not on salary but sells his or her material to a number of different publishers.

Free verse: Poetry that flows without any set pattern.

Galley proof: A typeset copy of a book used to detect and correct errors before printing.

General market: Non-Christian market, sometimes called secular market.

Genre: Refers to a type or classification, as in fiction or poetry. For instance, westerns, romances, and mysteries are fiction genres.

Glossy: A photo with a shiny, rather than matte, finish. Also, a publication printed on such paper.

Go-ahead: When a publisher tells you to write or submit your article.

Haiku: A Japanese lyric poem with a fixed seventeen-syllable form.

Hard copy: A printed manuscript, as opposed to one sent via email.

Holiday/seasonal: A manuscript that has to do with a specific holiday or season. This material must reach the editor the stated number of months prior to the holiday or season.

Honorarium: A small flat fee, as opposed to paying a set amount per word.

Humor: The amusing or comical aspects of life that add warmth and color to an article or story.

Independent book publisher: A book publisher who charges authors to publish their books or buy a certain number of copies, as opposed to a royalty publisher who pays authors. Some independent publishers also pay a royalty. Sometimes called a subsidy, vanity, or custom publisher.

Interdenominational: Distributed to a number of different denominations.

Interview article: An article based on an interview with a person of interest to a specific readership.

ISBN: International Standard Book Number, an identification code needed for every version of a book.

Journal: A periodical presenting information in a particular area, often for an academic or educated audience.

Kill fee: A fee paid for a completed article done on assignment that is subsequently not published. The amount is usually 25–50% of the original payment.

Libel: To defame someone by an opinion or a misquote that puts his or her reputation in jeopardy.

Light verse: Simple, lighthearted poetry.

Little/Literary: Small-circulation periodicals whose focus is providing a forum for the literary writer, rather than on making money. Often they do not pay or pay in copies.

Mainstream fiction: Other than genre fiction, such as romance, mystery, or science fiction. Stories of people and their conflicts handled on a deeper level.

Mass market: Books intended for a wide, general market, produced in a smaller format, usually with smaller type and sold at a lower price. The expectation is that their sales will be higher.

Ms: Abbreviation for manuscript.

Mss: Abbreviation for more than one manuscript.

Multiple submissions: Submitting more than one manuscript at a time to the same publisher, usually reserved for poetry, greeting cards, or fillers, not articles. Also see "Simultaneous submissions."

NASR: Abbreviation for North American serial rights; permission for a periodical targeting readers in the US and Canada to publish a piece.

New-adult fiction: A developing fiction genre with protagonists ages 18-25. In the general market these novels often explore sexual themes considered too "adult" for the YA or Teen market. They tend to be marketed to the older teen reader.

Newsbreak: A newsworthy event or item sent to editors who might be interested in publishing it because it would be of interest to their readership.

Nondenominational: Not associated with a particular denomination.

Novella: A short novel, usually 20,000–35,000 words. The length varies from publisher to publisher.

On acceptance: Publisher pays a writer at the time the manuscript is accepted for publication.

On assignment: Writing a manuscript at the specific request of an editor.

On publication: Publisher pays a writer when his or her manuscript is published.

On speculation/spec: Writing something for an editor with the agreement that the editor will buy it only if he or she likes it.

Onetime rights: Selling the right to publish a manuscript one time to more than one periodical, primarily to nonoverlapping audiences.

Over the transom: Unsolicited manuscripts sent to a book editor. Comes from the old "transom" which was a window above the door in office buildings. Manuscripts could be pushed "over the transom" into the locked office.

Overrun: The extra copies of a book printed during the initial print run.

Pen name/pseudonym: A name other than your legal name used on a manuscript to protect your identity or that of people included or when you wish to remain anonymous. Put the pen name in the byline under the title and your real name with your contact information.

Periodical: A magazine, newsletter, or newspaper.

Permissions: Asking permission to use text or art from a copyrighted source.

Personal experience: An account based on a real-life experience.

Personality profile: A feature article that highlights a specific person's life or accomplishments.

Plagiarism: Stealing and using the ideas or writing of someone else as your own, either as is or rewriting slightly to make them sound like your own.

POD/Print-on-demand: A printing process where books are printed one at a time or in small amounts instead of in quantity. The production cost per book is higher, but no warehousing is necessary.

POV: Point-of-view. A term in fiction describing the perspective of the one telling the story. For example: First person vs. Third person.

Press kit: A compilation of promotional materials for a book or author, used to publicize a book.

Public domain: Work for which copyright protection has expired. Copyright laws vary from country to country; but in the US, works published before 1923 have entered the public domain.

Quarterly: Every three months.

Query letter: A letter sent to an editor about an article or book you propose to write and asking if he or she is interested in seeing it.

Reprint rights: Selling the right to reprint an article that has already been published. You must have sold only first or onetime rights originally and wait until it has been published the first time.

Response time: The number of weeks or months it takes an editor to get back to you about a query, proposal, or manuscript you sent.

Review copies: Books given to reviewers or buyers for chains.

Royalty: The percentage an author is paid by a publisher on the sale of each copy of a book.

SASE: Self-addressed, stamped envelope. Always send it with a hard-copy manuscript or query letter.

SASP: Self-addressed, stamped postcard. May be sent with a hard-copy manuscript to be returned by the editor to indicate it arrived safely.

Satire: Ridicule that aims at reform.

Second serial rights: See "Reprint rights."

Secular market: An outdated term for the non-Christian publishing market.

Semiannual: Issued twice a year.

Serial: Refers to publication in a periodical, such as first serial rights.

Sidebar: A short feature that accompanies an article and either elaborates on the human interest side of the story or gives additional information on the topic. It is often set apart by appearing within a box or border.

Simultaneous rights: Selling the rights to the same manuscript to several periodicals simultaneously. Be sure everyone is aware that you are doing so.

Simultaneous submissions: Sending the same manuscript to more than one editor at the same time. Usually this is done with nonoverlapping periodical markets, such as denominational publications or newspapers in different cities, or when you are writing on a timely subject. Most periodical editors don't accept simultaneous submissions, but they are the norm in the book market. Be sure to state in a cover letter that it is a simultaneous submission.

Slander: The verbal act of defamation.

Slanting: Writing an article to meet the needs of a particular market.

Slush pile: The stack of unsolicited manuscripts that arrive at an editor's desk or email inbox.

Staff-written material: Manuscripts written by the members of a magazine staff.

Subsidy publisher: See "Independent book publisher."

Subsidiary rights: All the rights, other than book rights, included in a book contract, such as translations, book clubs, and movies.

Synopsis: A brief summary of a work, ranging from one paragraph to several pages.

Tabloid: A newspaper-format publication about half the size of a regular newspaper.

Take-home paper: A small periodical given to Sunday school students, children through adults. These mini-magazines are published with the curriculum.

Think piece: A magazine article that has an intellectual, philosophical, or provocative approach to a subject.

Trade magazine: A magazine whose audience is in a particular business.

Traditional verse: One or more verses with an established pattern that is repeated throughout the poem.

Unsolicited manuscript: A manuscript an editor didn't specifically ask to see.

Vanity publisher: See "Independent book publisher."

Vignette: A short, descriptive literary sketch of a brief scene or incident.

Vita: An outline of one's personal history and experience.

Work-for-hire: A manuscript you create for an agreed payment and give the publisher full ownership and control of it. You must sign a contract for it to be legal.

Writers guidelines: Information provided by a publisher that gives specific guidance for writing for the publication or publishing house. If the information is not offered online, email or send an SASE with your request for printed guidelines.

INDEX

We Teach Writers

AUDIO COURSES • VIDEO COURSES • BOOKS
Taught by some of the industry's best teachers

The Christian Writers Market Guide is now **ONLINE!**

Keep the **most updated information** at your fingertips.